The Violent Pilgrimage

The Violent Pilgrimage

Christians, Muslims and Holy Conflicts, 850–1150

TIM RAYBORN

McFarland & Company, Inc., Publishers
Jefferson, North Carolina, and London

Excerpts in English translation from Bernard of Clairvaux's *De laude* in chapter three are taken from *In Praise of the New Knighthood* (Cistercian Fathers Series, 19B), translated by Conrad Greenia (© 1977, 2000 by Cistercian Publications, Kalamazoo, MI), and reprinted with permission.

LIBRARY OF CONGRESS CATALOGUING-IN-PUBLICATION DATA

Rayborn, Tim, 1968–
    The violent pilgrimage : Christians, Muslims and holy conflicts, 850–1150 / Tim Rayborn.
    p.   cm.
    Includes bibliographical references and index.

    ISBN 978-0-7864-6845-4
    softcover : acid free paper ∞

    1. Christianity and other religions—Islam. 2. Islam—Relations—Christianity. 3. Crusades—First, 1096–1099. I. Title.
BP172.R385 2013
261.2'709—dc23   2013004707

BRITISH LIBRARY CATALOGUING DATA ARE AVAILABLE

© 2013 Tim Rayborn. All rights reserved

No part of this book may be reproduced or transmitted in any form or by any means, electronic or mechanical, including photocopying or recording, or by any information storage and retrieval system, without permission in writing from the publisher.

Front cover: Crusaders embarking for the Holy Land (Photos.com/Thinkstock)

Manufactured in the United States of America

McFarland & Company, Inc., Publishers
  Box 611, Jefferson, North Carolina 28640
    www.mcfarlandpub.com

Table of Contents

Abbreviations vi
Preface 1
Introduction 3

1. Christians, Muslims and Conflicts Up to the First Crusade 15
2. The Founding of the Order of the Knights Templar 43
3. Bernard of Clairvaux's *In Praise of the New Knighthood* 58
4. The Cistercian Order in the Twelfth Century: Austerity,
    Crusading and Slavery 76
5. Peter the Venerable and Christian Writings in Islamic Spain 97
6. The End of the World: Apocalypticism and Antichrists 112
7. Dying for the Faith: Martyrdom in Medieval
    Christian Thought 129

Conclusion 151
Chapter Notes 159
Bibliography 203
Index 219

Abbreviations

CCCM

Corpus Christianorum Continuatio Mediaevalis. Turnhout, Belgium: Brepols, 1966–.

CCSL

Corpus Christianorum Series Latina. Turnhout: Brepols, Belgium: 1953–

MGH

Monumenta Germaniae Historica: Scriptores. 39 vols. to date. Hannover: Hahn, 1826–.

Sciptores rerum Germanicarum in usum scholarum. Hannover: Hahn, Berlin: Weidmann, 1871–.

Epistolae (in Quart). 8 vols. Berlin: Weidmann, 1887–1928, 1939, rep. 1985–95.

Epistolae Selectae. 5 vols. Berlin: Weidmann, 1916–26, 1952, rep. 1985–2004.

PL

Patrologia Cursus Completus, Series Latina. Ed. J.P. Migne. 222 vols. Paris: Garnier, 1844–64.

RHC

Recueil des Historiens des Croisades, Historiens Occidenteaux. 5 vols. Paris: Académie des Inscriptions et Belles-Lettres, 1841–1906.

RHGF

Recueil des Historiens des Gaules et de la France. Ed. Martin Bouquet, et al. 24 vols. Paris: Victor Palmé, 1738–1904.

Preface

This book is an updated revision of my doctoral thesis, completed at the University of Leeds, U.K., in 1999. Of course, during the years since much has changed, and as with many topics, scholars have produced numerous studies. Indeed, in conducting research, I was able to add more than 100 new bibliographic entries (including journal articles, books, and new primary sources), as well as something like 14,000 additional words.

The subject of this book is the development of Christian European attitudes about crusading and holy war, and changing views toward Islam, up until the mid-twelfth century, with a special emphasis on the turbulent period of the eleventh and twelfth centuries. It focuses on French monastic writings, since these were arguably the most influential in both recording and bringing about these changes, though crusade chronicles, as well as papal works, and various Spanish texts are also considered in some detail. This was a crucial time in the establishment of a new European identity, and the events and ideas discussed were essential to those changes.

Many who approach this subject for the first time are curious about its potential links to issues in the modern world, an understandable situation. This is a controversial subject, and by no means a settled one. It is far too easy to oversimplify and look for direct relations between events then and now where there may in fact be none, or where many other factors in the intervening nine centuries may also be involved. I have avoided trying to draw parallels, and therefore I have confined the discussion to medieval events only.

I had always intended to publish this study in book form eventually, but years of work in the early music field (as a performer and in other capacities) often prevented me from being able to devote sufficient time to any writing, much less to such a detailed work. I'm glad to have the opportunity now. On a personal level, I want to thank my dear Abby, for her patience and understanding when I spent long afternoons at the UC Berkeley Library, or sat late into the night at my computer, saying nothing for hours at a time, poring over the minutiae of chapter notes (among many other things) during the "big push" to revise it. And I would like to acknowledge Fanty the cat, without whose "help" this might have been finished a bit sooner.

Introduction

On the morning of July 15, 1099, something remarkable and terrible happened at the ancient city of Jerusalem. A ragged army of Christian soldiers, clergy, and hangers-on, who had made the long, treacherous, and even deadly trek from Western Europe, took the city from its Muslim rulers after a week-long siege. The culmination of a four-year effort, preached by Pope Urban II and known to history as the First Crusade, it must surely have seemed miraculous in the eyes of the victorious. To the inhabitants of Jerusalem, however, it was the beginning of an episode of shocking brutality and horror.

Raymond of Aguilers, an eyewitness chronicler of the crusade, describes how after retaking the city, the invaders killed every Muslim inhabitant they could find; to them this was considered a fit punishment for those who had committed blasphemy in the holy places for so long, and the crusaders, rejoicing in their killing, sang a new song to their Lord. So extensive was the carnage, that Raymond recorded walking knee-deep in corpses and blood in the Temple area.[1] This of course, was an exaggeration, and was a biblical reference used for literary and religious effect.[2] However, no mercy was shown to children, the aged, or the defenseless. In the name of Christ, mass murder was committed as a sign of divine retribution and of justice prevailing over evil. It was the first of many such horrid actions undertaken by both sides over the next two hundred years.

This book is not a history of the crusades, a chronicle of the crusaders' journeys, or a discussion of the military aspects of those campaigns. There are numerous fine crusade histories available for the interested reader, and new work continues to be done in the field at an astonishing rate. Many of these studies will be referenced in detail in the following chapters, particularly as sources for further information. Instead, the primary subjects of this book are the dramatic shift in thought in Christian attitudes toward war and violence, and the Church's perceptions of its rival faith, Islam, between roughly

850 and 1150, with a special emphasis on the mid-eleventh through the mid-twelfth centuries. This period witnessed great struggles between the Holy Roman Emperor and the papacy for political supremacy over Europe (previously tilted toward the emperor, but shifting to the papacy), the discovery of a common European identity after centuries of factional struggles and small wars, a surge in popular spirituality (including heretical movements dangerous to the Church's authority), and the resulting development of new monastic orders. There was a "renaissance" of learning, philosophy, and theological thinking, both in the monasteries and the new universities. Perhaps overshadowing all else, there was the momentous impact of the crusades. That fateful 1099 siege returned Jerusalem and the Holy Land to Christian hands for the first time in nearly four centuries, and more importantly, gave control of those territories for the first time to the Western Latin Church.

Those first crusaders endured several years of hardship and suffering on their journey, discovering that their quest would not be an easy one. Sickness, hunger, thirst, travels through hostile territories, and the deaths of many along the way had taken their toll. More died along the journey than lived to see its end. Nevertheless, it had long been a Christian tradition to suffer for the faith, and these armed pilgrims at the very least believed themselves to be doing just that. Who went to the Holy Land? Why did they go? What could possibly have made them decide to abandon everything for land that they had never seen, and knew nothing about?

Three recent studies have provided different approaches to the motivations of the lay crusaders and the methods used by the Church to encourage them to undertake such a dangerous journey; they show very well that many different factors were intertwined in a very complex set of ideals. William Purkis, in *Crusading Spirituality in the Holy Land and Iberia, c.1095–c.1187*, argues that the journey and the task were preached and popularized as a form of imitation of the life and sufferings of Christ, an irresistible idea in light of the growing phenomenon of popular spirituality. Susanna Throop makes the case for divine vengeance being a prime motivator for those armed pilgrims in *Crusading as an Act of Vengeance, 1095–1216*, where vengeance stood for justice, and righting the wrongs of a Jerusalem held captive by unbelievers. Finally, Jay Rubenstein, in his masterfully written *Armies of Heaven: The First Crusade and the Quest for Apocalypse*, makes a strong case for the pervasive influence of apocalyptic ideas in the crusaders' and Church's motivations; for many, the end of the world truly was at hand.[3] Each of these is highly recommended, and we will explore their ideas in more detail in the following chapters.

How does one make sense of chronicles, sermons, and numerous other writings, some of them over 900 years old? Historians use different methods of analyzing and interpreting the confusing mass of crusade information available, and as a result, have divided themselves over the years into adherents of four systems, sometimes taking more than one approach: the generalists, who hold that a "crusade" can refer to all forms of Christian holy war; the traditionalists, who maintain that the term should refer specifically to those expeditions which sought to liberate or defend Jerusalem and its holy sites; the popularists, who see crusading as an outgrowth of popular spiritual movements, and concerned with the end of time; and the pluralists, who emphasize the penitential aspects of crusading, and that it could be fought in many different forms.[4] Naturally, there is not a wall between these methods of interpretation, and many hold to more than one view at a time. It is not necessary for the general reader to delve deeply into these, unless so inclined, but it is a good reminder that interpretation of very old material is far from an exact science, history is frequently written by the winners, and our own biases and assumptions will always play a role in how we look at ideas and events from the distant past.

With this in mind, we can consider that those who lived to see Jerusalem fall back into Christian hands on that July day, after undergoing such an ordeal must have been overwhelmed by an experience of such spiritual exhilaration that it would be difficult for the modern reader to fathom its impact. The prophecies were fulfilled, the unbelievers driven out and slaughtered, and Christ reigned in the Holy City once again. Yet it was not to last. Within a half-century of what seemed to be God's ultimate victory, the city and region of Edessa (along the modern Turkish/Syrian border) fell from Christian control; a concerted Muslim counter-attack had begun, prompting a new crusade, even more monumental and expansive in its goals than the first.

Removed from those times and events, historians usually assume that the masses of lay people who undertook this arduous task held sincere beliefs about the righteousness of their cause. In their minds, to die for God in the manner of Christ in such an undertaking would surely be a death worthy of the martyrs of the early Church. Yet, as many chronicles indicate, along with this piety, there was savage brutality and cruelty. Several accounts exist of crusaders massacring Eastern Christians, sometime unable to tell them apart from Muslims, and not bothering to find out. There are stories of men, fierce barbarians in some accounts, killing and eating infants, or the bodies of enemies slain in battle, and doing so willingly, not just from desperate starvation, but also to instill fear in their enemies.[5] The slaughter of the inhabitants of Jerusalem at the climax of the Jerusalem siege is merely one of the more vivid and horrific early examples.

Nine hundred years later, it is difficult to understand the motivations of those who engaged in such violent and appalling activities. Were they overcome with battle rage and blood-lust? Perhaps after those long years, they sought only the booty of battle and were no longer concerned with religious issues. Yet why did the clergy who were present not object, and even seem to encourage their behaviors? Raymond, himself a chaplain, recounts the killings at Jerusalem with great joy and pride. What manner of theology could have been provided to support such actions?

Christianity was historically, a religion of peace, not of the sword. Early Christians had been forbidden to undertake military service in the Roman army. The model for this behavior had been drawn from Christ's own injunction to Peter to put away his sword at Christ's arrest and not to resist. Christ had thus "taken away" the Church's sword by this action, and Christians were expected to behave in a similar manner. Likewise, according to the Sermon on the Mount, they were to turn the other cheek against violence and not retaliate in kind. This view was held by Origen, for example, who in third-century Alexandria wrote that the battles of the Old Testament should be read allegorically.[6]

The philosophy of non-violence could never survive long in the real world of politics and armies, wars and territorial disputes, a world which had existed long before the advent of the Christian religion. With Emperor Constantine's declaration in the Edict of Milan in 313 declaring Christianity as a tolerated religion, and Christianity's triumph as the state religion of the empire in 380, it became apparent that certain Church teachings would have to adapt to the circumstances of the time. Some have argued that the Church lost its essence when it became allied to the state instead of opposed to it. Its place as the religion of the poor, the oppressed, and the outcast was often usurped to become the vehicle for the imperial ambitions of Roman Emperors, often despotic and tyrannical themselves. Later, after the empire fell and Germanic tribes rose to prominence, some sought conversion to Christianity, but had no intention of giving up their traditional warrior codes, so the Church had to be flexible on the issue.[7]

For better or worse, this was the faith bequeathed by Late Antiquity to the medieval period, and with it came numerous contradictions, unresolved dilemmas, and debates about how to retain the original Christian message and yet still be an effective force in a violent and uncertain world. What should the Church do with unbelievers? Clergy generally did not believe it to be in the nature of Christianity to force conversions, yet could Christians live side by side with such people? Was this not a failing of its principal missionary duty, or at the very least, to protect the faithful from dangerous ideas?

The Church fathers debated such issues intensely and attempted to establish their own sets of regulations. As we shall see, Augustine considered it acceptable to endorse forcing unbelievers into the faith for the sake of their own salvation, just as a loving parent might force a child to do something unpleasant, yet ultimately for the child's benefit. Likewise, it came to be believed that a war could be fought not only justly (provided the intention of those engaging in it was noble and pious, and not for personal gain or revenge), but also in a sanctified manner. Perhaps some Church fathers believed that this was the only method of compromise possible given the age and the circumstances; perhaps others were less concerned with ethics and more focused on allying themselves to power. Some later medieval writers were to argue that violence itself was a morally neutral act, that it was the intention of the perpetrator that was important.[8]

For those believers, it simply would not have occurred to them that their beliefs were false or in error in any way. They were the defenders of orthodoxy against heretics and pagans. The forces of evil seemed to be everywhere, and the Church could not afford to be complacent. The rise of Islam in the seventh century presented the Christians with a new dilemma, one which they never adequately solved. From the deserts of Arabia came an unexpected and frightening new political, military, and religious force, unlike anything that the Eastern Church had ever encountered. It swept away the older Persian Empire, significantly reduced the power of Byzantium, and effectively eliminated the power of the ancient North African Church in less than a century. Recent histories have tended to downplay the role of Islamic military aggression, but it is important to understand that many of these attacks were pre-emptive and unprovoked.[9] The First Crusade itself was as much as anything a response to a century or more of these aggressions.[10] Yet Muslims claimed to have the authentic religion of Abraham, and to revere the very same individuals and prophets that Jews and Christians had honored for centuries.

As groups of Eastern Christians such as the Armenians and Nestorians strove to understand Islam, some began to regard it as a heresy, one which had borrowed what it wished from Christianity and Judaism, and had invented new teachings and doctrines to suit its purposes. Polemical writings against Islam began to appear in the East in the eighth century, which were reasonably accurate in their portrayals of Islamic beliefs, often taking the form of dialogues between Christians and Muslims. Despite such animosities, many Christians (and Jews) lived under Islamic rule; some even prospered in centers of learning such as Baghdad (and later, Córdoba) flourishing with cultural and intellectual exchange.

Western Christians did not have such regular direct contacts, however, and for them, Islam was initially nothing more than a polytheistic religion of barbarians, akin to the Germanic tribes to the north. What little information was known to the Western Church was almost always inaccurate, a situation which largely remained until the twelfth century. Even in Spain, as we shall see, conflict between the two often arose as a result of these misunderstandings.

The prominence of Islam inevitably had to be addressed by the medieval Church. It came to believe that, like many trials of the day, Islam was an error which God had permitted, a test to the faithful that had to be defeated. The righteousness of the Christian cause could not be denied, and Christians had a duty to defend against this falsehood. The inspiring of popular religious enthusiasm in support of armed resistance against unbelievers was an approach that would remain a part of Church activity and policy throughout the Middle Ages, and was to have particularly wide-ranging implications during the Reform movement of the eleventh and early twelfth centuries.

An important area of study which cannot be treated in detail here is that of the relation between the theology of war and canon law (the ecclesiastical laws and regulations of the Catholic Church), particularly Gratian's *Decretum* (a kind of legal textbook), as this is an enormous topic in and of itself, deserving of a separate study.[11] A small number of references to the *Decretum* will suffice where needed. Twelfth-century theologians and canon lawyers often found increasingly different approaches to the subject of war. Two separate approaches (theological and canon law) concerning the consequences of war developed over time, especially after the year 1200. The theologians were more concerned with morality, especially in regards to the consequences of an action taken during a time of war versus the same action taken during a time of peace. Canon lawyers, on the other hand, focused on the issues of legal liability that were a result of damage suffered during military conflicts.[12]

Indeed, while Gratian's *Decretum* was completed around 1140, nearly fifty years after the First Crusade, it does not specifically address the crusades or the complications surrounding them.[13] However, drawing on Church tradition, the *Decretum* does make distinctions between acceptable and non-acceptable violence, especially in relation to war.[14]

A "just war" and a "holy war" were distinct entities. A holy war was always just, but a just war could be one fought for a rightful cause between two secular powers, such as in defense against aggression, as Gratian recorded,[15] or to avenge wrongs. Ecclesiastical approval of a war could classify it as "just,"[16] but not necessarily "holy." James Brundage notes: "A 'holy' war came to be designated as such if it were fought in defense of Christianity, and it thus entitled the participants to certain spiritual rewards for their efforts. In fact, it is these two features that define 'holy war' for writers and theologians throughout the twelfth century."[17] Just wars were bound by human laws. Holy war was not the work of mortal hands, but rather the will of God, enacted through those hands, and as such, things that were not normally permitted become acceptable, because God wished it.[18]

From this also developed the notion that killing in a holy conflict was not a sin, but rather a kind of blessing for the opponent.[19] Magister Rolandus, later Pope Alexander III, noted about 1150, in the aftermath of the disastrous Second Crusade, that the slaying of evil individuals in the cause of justice, "is actually to minister unto God."[20] Just and holy wars sat side-by-side throughout the twelfth century, and only became fully integrated over that 100-year period. Indeed, H.E.J. Cowdrey notes that during this time, there was no phrase such as *bellum sacrum*, or "holy war," whereas as *bellum justum* had been used since ancient times.[21]

There were guidelines, of course, so that the Church did not give its sanction to wholesale slaughter (events such as the Jerusalem massacre notwithstanding). Indeed, as we shall see in Chapter 1, it was partially out of a desire to eliminate factional and feudal violence and conflict within Europe that the crusading venture came to be. The Church decried and condemned the rampant violence that had plagued Europe over the previous centuries, where war-mongering knights battled each other endlessly for territory and booty. On the other hand, there was a general tolerance for violence that was committed in the name of the Christian religion. Such violence was justifiable, because it was for securing the peace, or protecting Christians or Church interests; such warfare was sanctioned by God.[22] Whereas a just war might impose limits on what punishments and suffering could be inflicted, "taking up arms for the realization of God's purpose tended to override all obstacles and do away with all limitations."[23]

Declarations from canon lawyers, appealing as they did to Church tradition, had a theological counterpart in biblical exegesis, which made use of scriptural references to support the crusade and the act of holy war. Indeed, theologians such as the famed abbot Bernard of Clairvaux (1090–1153) and various monastic chroniclers of the crusades were certainly not specialists in canon law, and yet developed their own complex ideas on the position of the Church and war. The Old Testament, in particular, was a prime source of such martial imagery. Medieval exegetes, especially those within monastic environments, did not distinguish the Jewish scriptures as a separate set of books. Throughout the Middle Ages, the Old and New Testaments were seen as a complete, continuing story, relaying the story of God's people, beginning with Israel and continuing into the rise of the Christian Church. The testaments were viewed as two separate, but related times, the time of the law (*tempus legis*) and the time of grace (*tempus gratiae*), each a different stage in the same salvific history. The Old Testament was interpreted by the New, but the New was better understood by the testament that preceded it.[24]

Thus, the age of grace brought about by Christ was a continuation of the law, and the military themes found in the Old Testament were logically employed in the justification of crusading. The notion of God intervening on the side of the righteous army can be found in several Old Testament accounts,[25] and became a favorite motif of crusade chroniclers, as we shall see. Writers, chroniclers, theologians, and scribes were well aware of these warfare passages, and used them as a kind of precedent in justifying the crusading effort, and to guarantee those who took the cross that they would have victory, just as the ancient Israelites had against their opponents, who were also the enemies of God.[26]

Several of the chroniclers of the First Crusade, writing in the early decades of the twelfth century, scattered Old Testament references about their works.[27] Books including *Job, Proverbs, Zechariah,* and *Isaiah* were referenced, containing prophecies which were believed to be literally fulfilled in the actions of the crusaders.[28] Diverse monastic writers such as Robert the Monk (from Rheims, *d.* 1122), Guibert of Nogent (a Benedictine, *ca.* 1055–1124), and Baldric of Bourgueil (an abbot then bishop, *ca.* 1050–1130) used different biblical passages from the prophets that seemed to them to be relevant, without any kind of agreed-upon means of selecting them.[29]

Essentially, these biblical justifications were a new undertaking without precedent. Before this time, Christianity had not taken the offensive on such a large scale, or in such a coordinated and successful manner. One can see how the magnanimous nature of the events of 1099 would have staggered the participants, and prompted comparisons with the great exploits of biblical heroes. Jonathan Riley-Smith summarizes:

> It was natural for them [the crusaders] to recall the exploits of the Israelites in the Old Testament and to compare them with their own. In their sufferings they were inspired by the patience of Job; in their march, their hardships and the blessings showered upon them they were like the Israelites journeying from Egypt to the Promised Land, [...] like the Maccabees they fought for Jerusalem, they faced martyrdom, and God's favour was revealed in miracles; only the crusade was even more miraculous than the enterprises of the Israelites and Maccabees, while the crusaders' sufferings were not surpassed by those of their ancient exemplars.[30]

Robert the Monk compared the retaking of Jerusalem with only two other events in history: the creation of the world and the redemption of the Cross.[31] Baldric of Bourgueil saw the crusaders being prefigured by the children of Israel, led out of Egypt to the Promised Land.[32] Guibert of Nogent proclaimed that though God had been glorified through the Jewish people, Christ also was thriving in the men of his time.[33] The use of the Bible in the context of addressing the contemporary concerns of the age will be discussed further in Chapter 3, for biblical references figure prominently in the justification for the Knights Templar, written by Bernard of Clairvaux. There were methods of exegesis favored by medieval monasticism, which were relevant for an abbot writing in defense of another monastic order.

Clearly, crusading and holy violence elicited strong responses from the theologians of the time, involving both Church tradition and biblical study. Many saw the phenomenon of armed pilgrimage as a true fulfillment of scriptural prophecy; a smaller number condemned the practice. This book will examine varied writings of some of the most prominent individuals of the ninth to the twelfth centuries, to gain a clearer understanding of Christian thought and its reactions to an unprecedented expression of faith. The writings of monks, and the theology that they developed, will be a chief area of focus, because it was from the monasteries that many of the strongest voices of support for crusading emanated. In addition to the pervasive influence of Bernard of Clairvaux and Peter the Venerable (Abbot of Cluny), several popes, such as Gregory VII and Eugenius III, came from monastic backgrounds and retained ties with their orders, as did important crusade chroniclers, such as Guibert of Nogent.

The seven chapters of this book discuss different aspects of the development of a theology of crusading, war, and violence, especially in the eleventh and twelfth centuries, and the Christian attitude toward Islam that both influenced and was a natural outgrowth of the new martial attitude of the Church. In fact, there were numerous different views, but the focus is primarily on French monastic treatises, papal correspondences, crusading chronicles of select French and German writers, and the writings of Christians living in and concerned with Spain, as these sources arguably had some of the greatest impact in both demonstrating and shaping the prevailing thought of the time. Where necessary, other writings, geographical locations, and eras will be brought into the discussion, to give a fuller picture of the development of a particular theme.

The first four chapters give a semi-chronological order of key events, from the roots of the Reform in the early eleventh century through to the near-contemporary development of the Knights Templar and the Cistercians, culminating in the failed Second Crusade and its aftermath in the early 1150s. The emphasis in these chapters is on French sources and events. Indeed, Muslims often viewed crusaders and Franks as synonymous (referring to them as the *franj*), and Christian chronicles, for example, refer often to the deeds and works of the Franks in the East.

Chapter 1 focuses on the events and thoughts that both led to and arose during the Reform movement of the eleventh and early twelfth centuries, with its implications for the idea of the holy war, and how Islam came to be viewed in this context. It also discusses the creation of the idea of the crusade as an armed pilgrimage, beginning with Pope Gregory VII in 1074, and earlier military expeditions that may have served as models for the crusade, preached in 1095 by Urban II.

Chapter 2 recounts the rise of the enigmatic Knights Templar, an improbable combination of monastic life with chivalric ideals. These "warrior monks" were strongly supported by Bernard of Clairvaux, and grew in popularity after a slow beginning. Initially created to protect Christian pilgrims to the Holy Land, they came under papal protection and expanded in power and prestige at a remarkable rate.

Chapter 3 is a detailed treatment of Bernard's justification for the Templars, *De laude novae miltiae*, written in the 1130s at the request of the order's head. It is an unusual document that presents Bernard's vision of a holy order fighting on behalf of Christ. There is no call for peace in its words, as the Templars are portrayed as fighting and killing with God's own authority, but he draws sharp and distinct lines between their activities and what he sees as the sinful and shameful practices of the secular knighthood.

Chapter 4 discusses the rise of the Cistercian Order. Born out of a desire to reform monastic practices, the Order soon became the most influential in Europe, fully involved in politics and the secular world which initially, it had been created to resist. Under the spiritual leadership of Bernard of Clairvaux, the Cistercians were key players in the religious and political drama of the twelfth century, supporting the Second Crusade with great enthusiasm.

Chapters 5 through 7 discuss other relevant areas in the developing theology of the time, particularly in Spain, where contact and conflict between Christianity and Islam extended back several centuries. These early confrontations had some effect on later ideas and approaches. Spain, with its *reconquista*, early examples of military orders with a resemblance to Islamic models, and use of Muslim slaves, often foreshadowed events in Northern Europe. Apocalyptic visions of Islam and cults of martyrs were known in the Iberian Peninsula, and parallels can be drawn between them and events both in the rest of Europe and in the Holy Land.

Chapter 5 takes into consideration what had the potential to be the most important theological event in Christian-Islamic relations of the period: the Spanish translation project of Peter the Venerable, Abbot of Cluny. In an effort to understand Islam so as to refute it properly, Peter commissioned the translation into Latin of important Islamic texts, including the Qur'an, while on a journey to Spain. This provided Western Christians with more accurate information about Islamic belief and practice. The chapter further discusses the relations between Jews, Christians, and Muslims in this frontier land, considering the works of the Sephardic Jewish convert to Christianity, Petrus Alfonsi, specifically his writings against Islam and their influence on European Christian thought. There is also a discussion of the status of Mozarabic Christians and their polemical writings, a matter of interest to Peter the Venerable.

Chapter 6 gives attention to the subject of apocalypticism in relation to Islam and the crusades. It was perhaps inevitable that Christians would come to view their enemy in these terms, and while a detailed theology would not be offered until the writings of Joachim of Fiore in the late twelfth century, there were numerous attempts to link the rise of Islam with the events described in the Books of Daniel and Revelation. This was done in an attempt to portray Muhammad as an agent of Antichrist, or indeed, an Antichrist himself. Such thoughts gave the crusades an added urgency and determination. Indeed, apocalyptic hopes may have occupied the minds of many, both preaching and taking part in the First Crusade.

Chapter 7 discusses the concept of Christian martyrdom in relation to fighting against enemies of Christianity and dying for the faith. Though not initially a canonical Church doctrine, there arose in the popular imagination a belief that to go on crusade and die at the hands of the Saracen was to die a martyr's death, worthy of the Classical Christian martyrs. A notable instance of voluntary martyrdom erupted in Córdoba in the 850s, and this is discussed in some detail, as it was the first true religious conflict between Christians and Muslims in the West, and embodied many of the ideals to be found in later Christian thinking.

This book is thus a survey of some of the most significant aspects of medieval Christian holy war and European perceptions of Islam up to and including the early years of the crusading phenomenon, and of available research in the field. It focuses less on actual history, and does not offer detailed discussions of any particular crusade, papacy, or movement involved with the crusades, but rather traces the development of a number of key themes relating to the theology and attitudes of the time.

These topics are of course too vast to be dealt with in a single work, and this is the principal reason that most studies of the subject focus on a narrower field. This book is a response to the need for a survey that is detailed enough to be a good introduction without becoming too diffuse. It also shows that many facets of the crusading venture overlapped and influenced one another. It can be used both as a reference and an introduction, and as a point of departure for further study. For language specialists and enthusiasts, and those who would like more details, the notes contain considerable numbers of primary text examples in Latin, including chronicles, letters, sermons, and treatises, so that those specialists can read the authors' views in their own words.[34]

There are many other topics which could have been included in this book, given the enormity of the subject and how deeply it impacted medieval life. The previously mentioned canon law is one example. The Knights Hospitaller (the Knights of St. John), contemporaries of the Templars, are certainly deserving of a detailed survey, but I have not included them, since I devote considerable attention to the Templars. The Hospitallers, as their name suggests, were originally founded to provide care for sick, injured, and poor pilgrims to the Holy Land, but also adopted a military aspect and distinguished themselves in battle against Islamic forces. Unlike the Templars, they survived suppression and dissolution, and still exist in various charitable organizations around the world today. Another important area is that of secular literature and poetry, most often written in vernacular languages, particularly Old French. These genres grew in popularity by leaps and bounds during the twelfth century, as courtly sophistication became more developed (under such figures as Eleanor of Aquitaine) and demand for secular verse increased. Lengthy *chansons de geste*, such as the *Song of Roland*, contained many harsh and distorted images of Muslims, as did a new genre, the crusade song. I have omitted a study of these works to focus on Church writings, rather than the secular, despite their obvious significance.

The actions and thoughts described herein are of great importance. Though we cannot always be sure what the laity and common people believed and made of the dramatic events taking place around them,[35] we can see how the Church and its thinkers saw their situation, and the ways in which they responded to their circumstances. There is, of course, always uncertainty in accepting at face value what writers from the past have set down. This is a natural state of affairs, for medieval concepts of history and recounting current events differed markedly from those of today. Propaganda and factional agendas played as much of a role in reporting the news then as now, even more so with such a strong overlay of religion and intense devotion. Personal biases and psychological issues are important, as well. However, we can see more clearly the actions taken as a result of these ideas and writings, and their often unfortunate consequences. The decisions and theological reasoning developed during this time exerted a tremendous impact on European thought during the remainder of the Middle Ages, and their ramifications would be felt for centuries.

1

Christians, Muslims and Conflicts Up to the First Crusade

How do ideas change? The shift can be abrupt or gradual; it can affect one individual or a nation. Sometimes, an old idea is merely re-stated and presented in a new way, adapted to fit a new time. Sometimes, it is deliberately distorted and given meanings it was never intended to have. Deeply-held convictions, such as religious beliefs, are no exception. A change in religious outlook may begin with one individual and spread, slowly or rapidly to a larger group. Indeed, this is how most religions are born. Those religious ideas themselves will inevitably change in response to world events and outside influences; they may die out if they fail to do so. Sometimes the changes are so drastic as to seem totally at odds with the original intentions of the early days of a belief. The medieval Christian embrace of the preaching of war against unbelievers as a penitential and sanctified act is one of the more remarkable examples of this shift.

Western attitudes toward Islam began to change dramatically during the second half of the eleventh century and into the beginning of the twelfth. Prior to this time, there had been less consideration of Christendom's rival, except at the frontiers where the two faiths met and interacted, particularly in Spain and Italy.[1] Such events as the Spanish Martyrs' Movement notwithstanding,[2] the primary resistance to Islam by the West was military rather than theological, and in these cases there was seldom any attempt to justify such actions with religious reasons.[3] Attempts at conversion and ideological debate were also minimal. It is even worth noting that the Carolingian kings had diplomatic relations with Islamic rulers in the East from the eighth century. Pippin the Short (d. 768) sent ambassadors to al-Mansur in 765, the Abbasid caliph in Baghdad, and received them in return. His son Charlemagne was well known for massacring the pagan Saxons who refused to convert to Christianity, and yet was famed for his good relations with the fifth Abbasid caliph, Harun ar-Rashid (of *Arabian Nights* fame),[4] who sent to Charlemagne, among many other fine gifts, and elephant named Abul-Abbas in 797. Charlemagne also discussed how to achieve peace with Moorish ambassadors from Spain, mindful of his grandfather's military victory.[5]

The common European name for Muslims used throughout the Middle Ages, "Saracen," had an ancient history. Originally used by Greco-Roman writers to describe the peoples who lived in Arabia, it came to be synonymous in the medieval mind with those of the Islamic faith, and to have negative connotations. Its first western appearance was in the seventh century in the Merovingian *Chronicle of Fredegar*, which refers to the Saracens as being descended from Ishmael, Abraham's son via his wife's maid Hagar; this is believed in Islamic tradition, as well, and shows that the *Chronicle* was taking some information from an accurate source. They are called both Agarenes (from Hagar), and Saracens.[6] Medieval Christians, however, believed that the term was evidence of how the Arabs lied about themselves, desiring to be seen as children of Sarah, rather than as children of a slave, Hagar. As a label, it stuck, because it signified that they were people of a lie, and lived in deceit.[7]

Initially, Islam was seen less as a unified religious threat to the West, and more as an impressive empire and potential military enemy. Even into the eleventh century, it was often ignored.[8] However, when lands in Spain and Southern Italy began to be recovered from Islamic control through Christian military victories by the middle of that century, the idea gradually formulated that it could be possible to make similar gains of territories lost to Christianity in the Holy Land.[9] This chapter will explore this development in some detail.

The concept coincided with the effects of the "Gregorian" Reform movement, a series of sweeping changes in Church structure and function which were to have repercussions for centuries. These reforms were officially begun under Pope Leo IX at the Council of Rheims in 1049, and ended during the papacy of Calixtus II at the First Lateran Council in 1123. The designation "Gregorian" derives from Pope Gregory VII (1073–85), its most enthusiastic supporter, and is now generally not used.[10] Three of the main issues involved were the introduction of the concept of a "papal monarchy," that is, Church unity through absolute adherence to the pope, even from the Holy Roman Emperor; the liberation of the Church from secular influence and control (a long-standing thorn in the side of Church officials); and the idea that the priesthood was separate from and superior to the laity in Christian society.[11] All of these, of course, delivered tremendous political advantages and power to the Church.

1. Christians, Muslims and Conflicts Up to the First Crusade 17

The third issue led to the concept of the nature of *Ecclesia*, that is, "the Church," being changed as well. It had first been developed by the Carolingians (eighth to tenth centuries) and was defined by the view that the emperor and the pope were the "supreme officials of two parallel hierarchies, one clerical and one lay."[12] The reformers altered this, assuming that *Ecclesia* would thereafter consist only of the clergy. The laity would have no leading role, but were still seen as a vital part of *Christianitas*, the Christian community. This was a clear sign of the developing new attitude; the Church and its officials wanted to remove themselves from the shackles of Imperial and secular power, while at the same time recognizing that theirs was in effect a symbiotic relationship. The Church needed the laity for many duties, even if it desired to assume more power over them.[13] From this, new ideas developed that would allow for the papacy to achieve the powers it sought and yet not alienate the people.

The crusading movement that ended the eleventh century was one such means of achieving this aim. In fact, the notion of an armed pilgrimage was the perfect solution to the pressing social and spiritual needs of the age. It allowed for the goal of papal preeminence to be realized, united the whole of Europe against a common foe (thus ending many internal conflicts), and helped the laity feel that they were a part of the sweeping changes occurring at the time. It was not, however, a flawless or trouble-free transition. These reforming attitudes sparked off fierce debates about papal authority, absolution of oaths to secular rulers, and clerical positions being obtained through simony, among other issues. Gregory VII, in particular, was heavily criticized by some, and strongly supported by others for his many proposed changes.

The movement was tightly bound up with monasticism and the resurgence of monastic ideals that had begun in the tenth century. The Reform sought to promote monastic values, particularly celibacy, and to impose them on all of the clergy.[14] At the same time, an identity crisis was developing in monastic communities. Many monasteries, most notably Cluny, had acquired vast amounts of wealth from generous benefactors, and in doing so had strayed away from their vows of poverty, a central feature of the monastic revival. New monastic movements began to arise, with the goal of returning to poverty and strict adherence to the Benedictine Rule.

It was from such a desire for reform that the Cistercian Order was created in the early twelfth century, its principal aim being to practice strict observance of the Rule. The Cistercians, under the spiritual leadership of Bernard of Clairvaux, were to have an enormous influence on papal policies in the twelfth century and beyond, especially in the area of crusading and the justification of violence by Christians, not only against non–Christians, but against other

Christians as well. Indeed, this was arguably the most important shift in Church teaching that the Reform brought. The Cistercians will be discussed in detail in chapter four.[15]

Another of the goals of the Reform movement went hand-in-hand with the concept of Christian unity within Europe. It sought to make friends of enemies in Europe by turning the attentions of warring factions to a common cause, namely the defense of the poor and oppressed, and of Christendom as a whole. Knights who had previously been engaged in factional and territorial disputes were now encouraged to set aside their differences and turn their swords against those who threatened Christians, first from within, and then more importantly, from without. Slowly, a theology of knighthood and war was developed and encouraged. For example, participation in the reconquest of Spain was justified on the grounds that it was in defense of Spanish Christians. However, the idea of the threat of Islam as a whole had not yet crystallized; the Moors were seen as a military and territorial threat rather than a spiritual one, a view that would soon change.

This new aggressive attitude necessarily posed a contradiction to traditional Christian thought. Indeed, well into the second half of the eleventh century, the Church viewed warfare (and the killing and maiming that came with it) as a severe sin, regardless of how legitimate it might be. It was a sin that required penance.[16] William the Conqueror's army, for instance, had to perform penance for the invasion of England in 1066, even though they had papal support.[17] Despite this, Christian writings about warfare had already begun to change in the first decades of the eleventh century. Among the most important of the writers who expressed a new outlook was the Benedictine monk from Cluny, Rodulfus Glaber (*ca.* 980—*ca.* 1046), whose *Historium Libri Quinque* provides fascinating insight into the thought-world of the early eleventh century.[18]

Glaber addresses the subject of war frequently, and more significantly, in the writing of Book I of his *Historium*, he becomes the first writer in Northern European history to discuss Islam.[19] Glaber presents the contradiction that becomes evident in the writings of the later eleventh and twelfth centuries: the support of armed conflict in the cause of righteousness, namely the defense of Christendom, and scorn for the petty wars and rivalries that abounded among the secular knights, nobility and royalty. It is the same contradiction that Bernard of Clairvaux would employ over a century later as his prime justification for the Knights Templar.

In Book IV, for example, Glaber writes approvingly of the Peace of God movement of his time, begun at the Synod of Charroux (*ca.* 989), with a view to protecting pilgrims and calling a cessation to warfare at certain times of the year, entitling the opening of the section, *De pace et habundantia anni millesimi a Passione Domini*.[20] In other sections, however, he gives tacit approval to the waging of war for the sake of restoring order.[21]

Glaber's discussion of Islam is of particular interest. Muslims are first mentioned in Book I, wherein he describes the capture of Mayol, abbot of Cluny (948–94) by the Saracens of La Garde-Freinet (near Saint-Tropez) in 971–2. In addition to the usual praises for Mayol's sanctity and restraint that one would expect, Glaber relates a remarkable incident that is all the more unusual for its likely accuracy:

> Another of the Saracens was smoothing down a piece of wood with a knife, when in his haste he placed his foot upon the man of God's book; it was the Bible which he always carried with him. When he saw this the saintly man groaned aloud, and certain of the less ferocious Saracens who had seen the incident reprimanded their companion, saying that great prophets should not be so scorned that he should tread their words under his feet. For the Saracens read the Hebrew prophets (or rather, those of the Christians), claiming that what they foretold concerning Jesus Christ, Lord of all, is now fulfilled in the person of Muhammad, one of their people. To support them in their error, they have in their possession a genealogy of their own, similar to that found in the Gospel of St Matthew, [...] But theirs says that "Ishmael beget Nebajoth," and continues with an erroneous fiction, which in deviating from the holy catholic account, strays equally from the truth.[22]

Glaber continues with an account of how the enraged Saracens cut off the foot of the transgressor, to teach him a lesson, and were thus inadvertently the agents of God's vengeance. This story, while containing an understandable Christian bias and perspective, is notable for its efforts to mention the veneration of the Judeo-Christian prophets by Muslims. The account must therefore certainly be true, since it is of little use as Christian propaganda. The brutality of the punishment was effective in relaying the Saracens' perceived savagery, but the religious context of the story shows Muslim belief to be much closer to that of Christianity than had been previously known by many. Glaber's is a remarkably different account from those provided by his contemporaries, Odilo or Syrus, who recount the event with invective and religious propaganda in mind.[23]

Glaber made the effort to relate other accurate and obscure facts concerning the Muslim world. For example, in his account of the destruction of the Holy Sepulcher by the mad Fatimid caliph, Al-Hakim bi-Amr Allah (996–1021),[24] whom he refers to as the *Ammirati Babilonis*, the Emir of Cairo, Glaber correctly notes that his mother was a Christian woman,[25] but incorrectly attributes the motivations that provoked the Caliph to a Jewish conspiracy. Glaber was also aware of the Aghlabid dynasty of Tunisia.[26] The probable source for this interest and the accuracy of his accounts came from his encounter with a group of Spanish monks whom he met while he was living at Cluny in the early 1030s, dispatched by King Sancho the Great of Navarre. These monks came to the monastery of Cluny in 1032. Indeed, Glaber mentions Spain frequently in his work, such as the defeat of a certain "Motget," most likely Mujahid ibn 'Abdullah, king of Denia, whose loss resulted in booty being donated to Cluny.[27]

Spain was to play a key role in the dissemination to Europe of knowledge about Islam, from the ninth to the twelfth centuries, as we shall see in chapter five. This knowledge, however, did not coincide with a desire to understand or tolerate the Muslim faith. Glaber, for example, felt that they must be fought and exterminated as enemies of the Roman Christian faith, and in this view he was no different from the later supporters of the crusade. He was also deeply anti-Jewish in tone, blaming the destruction of the Holy Sepulcher not on the Muslim caliph, but rather on a Jewish plot. According to Glaber, the Jews were the ones who prompted the caliph to persecute Eastern Christians. He said that they claimed that a large throng of Christian pilgrims were really an army coming to attack and take Jerusalem. Given the events of the First Crusade in the late eleventh century, this fiction proved to be astonishingly prophetic.[28]

Glaber was not interested in objective history,[29] and despite his even-handed account of the capture of Mayol, he wanted to promote views which were in support his Church. He was hostile to Islam, Judaism, and any foreign power or ideology which might threaten the Roman Catholic Church and Western Christendom. He equally disliked Byzantium (and by extension, Eastern Orthodoxy), which he blamed for bringing its woes upon itself.[30] In his description of Christian armies liberating Jerusalem, he unknowingly became a predictor of future events; in his account, the army was a lie fabricated by Jews, but it would soon become very real.

Bearing that in mind, there has been considerable debate about the extent to which Glaber's attitudes and writings "prepared" the latter part of his century for the idea of the crusade. Indeed, many theologians looked back to his writings and drew inspiration from the notion of war being acceptable in defense of the just, but not merely for its own sake. This seemed to be an adequate solution to the problem of how Christians should approach war, though it was not a new theology. St. Augustine had commented on the subject centuries before, which will be detailed in chapter three.

Glaber's ideas do not seem to be completely representative of the general outlook of Cluny, however. Cluny was still primarily focused on the next life, that is, on the salvation of the soul, and the retreat from the concerns of this world. It was not involved in developing theologies of war and the duty to fight infidels, though it certainly gave its support to various Spanish efforts.[31] It would be better to say that Glaber described several movements and attitudes of his time which later churchmen drew upon to justify their policies, rather than being the impetus for those policies himself. The critical link between war and pilgrimage had not yet been made in Glaber's time, though things were changing.

A close contemporary of Glaber's, was Adémar of Chabannes (*ca.* 989–1034), a monk associated with both St. Martial and Angoulême in central and south-west France. He was an early writer to connect Islam with heresy, believing like Glaber that Hakim's destruction of the Holy Sepulcher had been part of a Jewish-Muslim conspiracy to destroy Christendom, but adding that this was a prelude to the last days[32] (when in reality, it may have been due to his mental state, and a desire to "prove" his Muslim faith since his mother was a Christian). Adémar was aware of Islamic monotheism, but that made him spurn the faith all the more, because it rejected Trinitarian doctrine, and thus Church teaching.[33] While he was obsessed with this potent mixture of heresy and apocalypse, and all of the dangers they represented, Adémar was also implicated in a rather elaborate forgery. He embraced and embellished popular stories of how the historical Martial had been one of Christ's original apostles, forging a *Life* of the man, purportedly written by his successor. This may have been done in the hopes of increasing pilgrimage to St. Martial abbey, and the income it would bring. Eventually, his fraud was discovered, but he persisted, going so far as to invent a Church council proclaiming the truth of Martial's apostolic identity. Amazingly, he seems to have escaped from all of this with little punishment; the polemicist and the forger existed side-by-side.[34] He does stand as a remarkable early example of a Christian writer who understood Islam to be different than a pagan religion, but his concern was combating this heresy, not war or pilgrimage.

A few decades later, in 1053, Pope Leo IX made an unusual offer to German soldiers fighting under his command. If they would do battle against the Normans of southern Italy, he would grant them absolution for their sins.[35] This was not a pilgrimage, but the experiences of actual pilgrims journeying to the Holy Land were beginning to foreshadow later events.

Indeed, an important episode in the history of eleventh-century pilgrimage can be found in an incident in 1065 involving a bishop named Gunther of Bamberg, who was traveling with a very large group of German pilgrims to the Holy Land.[36] The group had faced harassment from the Turks at various points, at least according to the chronicler Lambert, of the abbey of Hersfeld near Thuringia, who wrote of the pilgrimage sometime after 1077. The affair shows an open hostility towards Muslims on the part of the pilgrims, and in this particular case, a willingness to depart from the normal pilgrim practice of non-violence. Despite its confrontational nature, it almost borders on the comic. There are different versions of events, of course, no doubt embellished like any good story. Lambert records a skirmish wherein the pilgrims were attacked by a group of Turkish marauders (probably Seljuks looking for a fight with the Egyptian Fatimids, testing their weaknesses, and such), and took refuge behind the walls of an old town near Rama in Palestine on Good Friday. For three days they held out against assault, and managed to take some prisoners, but they were low on supplies and were fast losing strength. They decided to buy their way out of it, and invited some of the Turkish soldiers in to discuss the matter, but the Turks had no intention of letting the pilgrims escape with their lives. Once inside, a skirmish broke out, and in the midst of it, an unusual event occurred:

> During the fighting, one of the Saracen leaders seized the piece of cloth which he wore around his head after the custom of his race, and made it into a lasso which he threw around Bishop Gunther's neck. The bishop was not prepared to put up with such a disgrace and gave his assailant a hefty blow in the face which sent him sprawling to the ground. As the man fell, the bishop shouted at him that he would pay him back for his impiety in having the audacity to raise his unclean, idolatrous hands against a priest of Christ.[37]

This unexpected action inspired the rest of the Christians, who immediately seized the attacker and bound him tightly, and then fell upon the others and did the same. They threatened to kill them if the Turkish forces did not retreat, which they were now obliged to do, following the intervention of a small Egyptian Fatimid army (the enemies of the besiegers), who set to fighting them. After this, the pilgrims were able to continue their journey to Jerusalem.[38]

This remarkable episode shows the readiness with which Christians were willing to use force to defend themselves, an action which by the strict Christian teaching contained in the Sermon on the Mount, was forbidden. Yet the monk Lambert extols them for their heroism, and at Jerusalem he records that they gave thanks to God for the victory and safe journey. There is no hint of repentance for the use of force here, or that their actions violated Christian teachings about non-violence. Furthermore, Lambert noted that Gunther "was a man of high moral and spiritual standing and well-endowed with worldly goods."[39]

This is an astonishing change of thought regarding the idea of pilgrimage. It was obvious that pilgrims anywhere, whether to Santiago, Rome, or Jerusalem, faced dangers from bandits, highwaymen, and other foes. The

Church had sought to minimize this when it declared times of peace within Europe, but obviously that would have no bearing on the lands in the East, or on the criminally-minded. Indeed, the need to protect pilgrims would be offered as the chief reason for the creation of the Knights Templar in the early twelfth century.

However, such an institution did not exist at this time, and there were no strict guidelines for the protection of pilgrims. The way to the holy city had become easier at the beginning of the eleventh century. With victories over pagans in Hungary, Stephen I had set himself up as that land's first Christian king, and had opened the way for Western Europeans to attempt the long and arduous journey; it was not necessarily easier, but it was at least somewhat safer. The fact that this had occurred at the time of the first millennium was not lost on those who undertook the pilgrimage.[40] Regardless of the hazards of travel, pilgrims were not expected to engage in armed resistance themselves, and this was especially true for the clergy. If this story is to be believed, Gunther's act of desperation, the response of anyone in a life-threatening situation, served to inspire his fellow pilgrims to an unexpected level of aggression and violence. Lambert records that they bound their captives so tightly that blood burst from their fingernails, and that they threatened them all with decapitation, swords being held over their heads.[41] If true, this episode shows how quickly those weakened by thirst, hunger, and fear can resort to violent acts in the name of self-preservation. Later aggressions were often preceded by just such a "miracle," which would rouse the sagging morale of a group of pilgrims or crusaders, and inspire them to use their remaining strength to inflict a terrible retribution on their assailants. The violence would then be justified as the will of God. It was a situation that was to be repeated time and time again over the long history of the crusades.

The spontaneous quality of the whole affair is not completely convincing. One can note with suspicion that the effect of Gunther's bravery was a bit too inspiring. Given how quickly the party of pilgrims was roused and carried out his orders for a counter-attack, it has the air of something planned in advance, and not just an act of faith in desperation.[42] Was this move conceived beforehand by the desperate bishop to look like a moment of divine inspiration, needing only the proper provocation from his captors? If so, it succeeded remarkably well. We cannot know for sure, but such a scenario makes sense in view of the dangerous circumstances. Despite claims of divine support, it may just have been a daring gamble that paid off.

Regardless of the truth, this little episode showed that relations between the two faiths were becoming increasingly hostile, the Fatimid rescue notwithstanding. Indeed, the pilgrims were not grateful to them, viewing it merely as Satan defeating Satan.[43] Christians were growing far less tolerant of Islam and the Islamic presence in the Holy Land. This may even have sprung from the Reform's new ideas about Christian unity. It is easy to see from such actions how an aggressive, military attitude toward Islam was developing.

The most dramatic changes in this attitude came during the papacy of Gregory VII. He made use of Christ's words, *compelle intrare*[44] ("compel them to enter," found in the Augustinian theology of just war and acceptable killing,[45] and developed later by Pope Gregory I)[46] to justify conversion to Christianity by force, if necessary, in order to secure the peace.[47] Gregory stated that the *militia Christi*, previously defined as the community of monks engaged in spiritual battle with the devil (and which would always take priority, regardless of changes), could also include the *militia secularis*, the knights who fought with weapons, a concept previously unthinkable.[48]

Nevertheless, prominent theologians such as the Italian Peter Damian (1007–72) rejected all war, allowing for no justification, regardless of the circumstances. Though an associate of Gregory VII, a Benedictine monk, a cardinal, and otherwise a supporter of the Reform, Damian denounced the use of force in relation to the conversion of non–Christians.[49]

If such opposition existed, what then was the official Church policy? It is important here to discuss briefly the issue of canon law and the precedents for just war as set forth by the early Church writers such as Augustine. One standard view on the Church's perceived change in policy was argued by Carl Erdmann in 1935, in his classic *Die Entstehung des Kreuzzugsgedankens*.[50] This work, though dated, is a key reference. Erdmann saw a fundamental shift in Church thought, one that involved the modifying of canon law to suit the new ideas being discussed. Essentially, Augustinian theology was reworked and interpreted in the eleventh century to suit the concept of the holy war against the infidel.

Decades later, however, this notion was challenged.[51] There were many objections, and various scholarly efforts have dispelled some popular notions about the changes that took place in theological thought in the eleventh century. Augustinian influence in the formulation of the crusading idea was not a given; in actuality, Augustine's doctrine of conversion denounced the use of violence and was thus in opposition to the attitude being developed by crusading advocates.[52] Nowhere in canonical literature is there mention of the Augustinian doctrine in support of crusading.[53] In fact, canon law collections remain curiously silent about the crusades until the thirteenth century, and say nothing about the usual components of the crusade.[54] So, there was a conflict between what the Church was beginning to preach, and what it held to in its own law books. Canon law still adhered to the older teachings regarding just war, and did not incorporate the newer ideas. And yet despite all of this, Augustinian concepts of just war certainly had a popular influence on crusading thought, even if the law did not specifically mention them.

Gilchrist argues that Augustine's original intentions regarding conversion tended to be followed and this had little, if anything, to do with the crusading movement. His doctrine allowed for the use of violence, but it was still grounded in a notion of love, something that we might find curious and contradictory today. Indeed, his writings were the most important of those studied on the subject of war during the time of the First Crusade, so naturally, his ideas would appear in later commentary. However, Augustine was primarily concerned with heresies and schisms, and applied his notion of loving violence to them. For him, keeping the Church unified was of prime importance, in a time when breakaway sects were common.[55]

The fact is that Gregory VII did employ the phrase *compelle intrare*, which was first commented on at length by Augustine, and reappeared many times throughout Christian history in different situations. Gregory was surely aware of the context within which Augustine had used the phrase, namely the forceful conversion of heretics (the Donatists in this case, who denied the validity of sacraments administered by priests who had renounced their faith under persecution, and later recanted and were reinstated). The fact that compulsion was to be undertaken with "love" for the misguided soul, and by avoiding violence if possible, did not prevent Gregory from using it. There was not only one method of interpretation of canonical texts. That the official interpretation of the phrase remained did not preclude other interpretations from being made, particularly in view of such radical ideas as an armed expedition to the East, one led by the pope. This was surely a concept never envisioned by Augustine, and while Gregory's plans were not the same as those of the crusade preached twenty years later, they did have an influence and effect on the theological thought of the 1090s. Thus, while Augustine could not be invoked as a direct advocate of a military expedition for the purpose of conversion (which in the reality of the crusades rarely occurred anyway), the spirit of the just war must surely have been in the minds of those who formulated the plans for the First Crusade. Put simply, some supported the new ideas and others opposed them.

In addition, one can question Gilchrist's argument, since it refers to the formative years of the crusading idea, specifically the latter part of the eleventh century, though he frequently brings in other accounts and writers from the first part of the twelfth century. Even if the focus is mainly on events prior to and including Clermont, it neglects to mention a point about Christian/Islamic relations, in the years before and after the First Crusade:

certain western Christians increasingly regarded Islam as a Christian heresy (or at least a mixture of heresy and paganism), as faint understandings about Muslim belief filtered into European circles. Indeed, as we have seen, this perception began well before the later 1090s, among a small group of learned theologians and writers, including Gregory VII. Alberto Ferreiro notes, "whereas in earlier Middle Ages heresiologists defined Islam as pagan, in the high Middle Ages the prevailing opinion emerged that it was instead a heresy [...] medieval writers were intent on demonstrating the heretical nature of Islamic doctrines and the perversity of Islamic morality."[56]

The perception of heresy as a grave danger in the Western Church seemed for many centuries to be of little concern following the demise of Arianism, a heretical movement from the fourth century which held that Christ had not always existed, but had been created by God. It had a wide-spread following, but died out by the seventh century. Later, Islam would be likened not only to Simon Magus' trickery (discussed below), but also to Arian beliefs, for its rejection of the divinity of Christ. Certainly religious texts between the fifth and tenth centuries have little to say on the matter, being more focused on disagreements of doctrine.[57] Glaber brought the issue to light again in the eleventh century, and from that time, it continued to grow, even coinciding with the Reform movement, and becoming an integral part of its objective to purify the Church.[58]

It is very interesting to note that Church concern about the spread of heresy among the common people seems to have taken on new force in the eleventh and twelfth centuries, but before that, it was less worrying, and this is not just due to a paucity of surviving sources. Indeed, in 1002, Burchard of Worms put together a collection of ecclesiastical law, the most comprehensive yet assembled to that date. He included no provisions for dealing with heresy, and did not even discuss how to address it in the popular sense; there is no mention of it even being a problem.[59] The reasons that concern about the spread of heretical ideas seem to become more prominent from this point onward are not completely clear.

Heresies in the eleventh century were often popular movements among the illiterate, who sought a life of complete simplicity, adhering to the Gospels without attaching importance to Church teachings or sacraments. Indeed, the sacraments were often denounced and considered unnecessary for true salvation. Other beliefs might include denial of the virgin birth of Christ, or his divinity, or the veneration of the cross.[60] In these more particular aspects, one sees how Christian perceptions of Islam began to focus on accusations of heresy as well, since certain Islamic tenets seemed to have much in common with the beliefs of heretical movements.[61]

Around the year 1100, a writer named Embrico of Mainz (about whom nothing is known) wrote the *Vita Mahumeti*, based on earlier Byzantine accounts. It is one of the earliest lives of Muhammad in Latin, and goes to great lengths to link Muhammad with the Antichrist, via the hated figure of Simon Magus, the arch-heretic of classical Christian lore. An apocryphal account (though widely believed) told that Simon Magus, after performing many false miracles with demonic help, challenged St. Peter and failed, falling to his death when the invisible demons carrying him (allowing him to falsely proclaim he could fly) were overcome by Peter's prayer. Embrico embellished the story to have "the Magus" act as a mentor to Muhammad, who fell under his spell and never recovered (the mingling of conflicting timelines was common feature of medieval writing). Indeed, the legend of Muhammad's night-time flight to Jerusalem was seen as proof of the diabolical, since flight was long associated with demonic help (and would later be invoked in the condemnation of witches' supposed aerial activities). Magus and Muhammad thus conspired to deceive the masses. By associating them, Embrico put Muhammad in the same company as all past heretics.[62] While both heretics and pagans were approached by missionaries, views about the two were different; heretics could be seen as having had the truth but having fallen into error, while pagans had never known the truth.

Gregory VII probably embodied an early example of this shifting attitude. He, along with abbot Hugh of Cluny, was known to be eager to convert the Muslim ruler of Saragossa, Ahmad al-Muqtadir (1046–81), and the Spanish Muslims of the region.[63] It seems that the word used for these attempts at conversion was "repentance,"[64] which certainly implies a falling away from the truth, in the manner of a heretic. There may also have been a fear that if al-Muqtadir were to accept Christianity, he might adopt the Mozarabic rite (a form of liturgy used by Spanish Christians, many under Muslim rule; their first language was often Arabic), rather than the Gregorian, and so there was a desire to persuade him into joining the latter.[65]

A remarkable letter from Gregory VII was addressed in 1076 to "Anzir," or An-Nasir ibn Alnas, the Hammadid ruler of Maghreb (Western North Africa) from 1062–88 or 89.[66] This conciliatory missive is among the earliest surviving missionary-style communications between a pope and a Muslim ruler.[67] It is a response to actions of friendship on the part of ibn Alnas, along with a promise to send papal messengers to his court. Gregory acknowledges that they both serve the same God:

> This affection we and you owe to each other in a more peculiar way than to people of other races because we worship and confess the same God though in diverse forms and daily praise and adore him as the creator and ruler of this

world. For, in the words of the Apostle, "He is our peace who hath made both one."

[...] For God knows our true regard for you [...] and how earnestly we pray both with our lips and with our heart that God himself, after the long journey of this life, may lead you into the bosom of the most holy patriarch Abraham.[68]

Regardless of the intention behind the letter, this is not the language that would be used to address a polytheistic pagan. Though knowledge of Islam was still limited at this time, there is nevertheless clear evidence in these statements that, at least in the immediate papal sphere of influence, the knowledge existed that Christians and Muslims worshipped the same deity, and that there was a desire to show Muslims their error. This exact sentiment would be reflected, at least in words, in the translation project of Peter the Venerable more than sixty years later.

Another notable letter from Gregory is his address "to all the faithful," dated 1084. This work is concerned about the threats to Christianity, from other nations, who do not let Christians practice freely. This could refer to the Turkish situation in the Holy Land, though he does not say so specifically. He specifically notes, however, that the rulers of these lands practice heresy, and seek to spread it.[69]

He then makes an important distinction. Having addressed the issue of heretics, he laments that the Christian faith has fallen, that the Church fathers are no longer honored, and are now a laughing-stock, not only to the devil, but also to Jews, Saracens, and pagans, who at least observe their own laws.[70] Jews and Muslims are classified as something different from pagans here, though he does not indicate that one group is better than another, but rather that none of their laws can save their souls.[71] Again, these are views that would be shared by Peter the Venerable, and the anti–Islamic polemicists of the thirteenth century.

Though the popular imagination continued to associate Islam with polytheism,[72] we have seen that some writers and theologians were aware that this was not the case. Indeed, Glaber's account proves that in at least some monastic circles in the early eleventh century, Muslim veneration of the Hebrew prophets and of Jesus was already known to be a fact. That some writers continued to distinguish between the heretics within Christendom and Muslims, whom they branded as pagans, does not detract from this.

In the 1140s, the abbot of Cluny, Peter the Venerable, made a detailed study of Islam, and implored Bernard of Clairvaux to write against the Muslims. His principal concern was that Islam was a heresy that was threatening the unity of the Church. In view of Peter's concerns, one cannot then suppose that Augustinian ideas simply had no influence on crusading thought, officially or otherwise. If Islam could be regarded as a Christian heresy, then the forced conversion doctrine could be applied to it as well. Whether Peter intended this has been the subject of much debate, and his views will be studied in detail in chapter five.

The arguments for and against the use of armed force in the conversion of non-believers, whether "heretics" or "pagans" might have remained forever in the realm of theological speculation, had not a momentous event occurred in 1071. In that year, Jerusalem was wrested from Arab control by the aggressive Turks, specifically by an adventurer named Atsiz ibn-Abaq, a vassal to the Seljuk Sultan Alp Arslan. They adhered to a more strict and orthodox form of Sunni Islam, and so the political climate of the Middle East took a drastic change. There were power struggles for several years after this incident; at one point the Egyptian Fatimids (members of the rival Shi'a sect) succeeded in retaking the city from Atsiz for a short time in 1075.[73] It would be wrong to focus on this incident as the major turning point in Christian relations with the East. Hostilities abounded previously (the incident with Bishop Gunther, for example). However, this Turkish invasion served as a new focal point for Christian indignation and retaliation.

The route for Christian pilgrims now became even more dangerous than before, owing to increased Turkish hostility towards the Christians. The previous Arab inhabitants of Jerusalem had often allowed Christian pilgrims to come and go without much hindrance (the destruction of the Holy Sepulcher notwithstanding), but the new Turkish rulers were not always so favorably inclined, though this may have been due as much to Christian perceptions and prejudices as to any real threat.[74] Nevertheless, with so many political and military power struggles between rival Muslim factions, there was bound to be danger to travelers. With the rising threat of Turkish power, Anatolia was now a very dangerous route for a pilgrim to traverse, but it was the only overland route by which they could realistically travel. Indeed, it could only be undertaken by armed escort, owing to the frequent hostile flare-ups in the area. Once in the Middle East proper, Syria was no better. Both regions were plagued with bandits and petty local lords who imposed high levies and tolls. Pilgrims that did manage to make it safely to the Holy Land and back returned with many a harsh tale about their miseries.[75]

With a major pilgrimage route believed to be in danger, a new form of *remissio peccatorum* began to take shape. Options for the remission of sin included becoming a monk, endowing a monastery, or going on a pilgrimage. The choice of a pilgrimage had traditionally involved the abandonment of all other activities until the pilgrimage was complete, for some a virtually impossible task. The notion of liberating Jerusalem from hostile Muslim hands presented what must have been seen as the perfect solution. It was an option particularly attractive to the knight. He had the opportunity to receive penance for his violent behavior through the exercising of his very reason for being, his martial skills.[76]

It would not be until the 1090s, however, that this connection was fully made, for while Gregory VII was an enthusiastic supporter of an armed venture to liberate the Holy Land from Turkish/Muslim control,[77] he does not seem to have conceived of the combination of a military campaign and a pilgrimage. Nevertheless, much of his correspondence addresses the issue of an armed expedition, and he implores his audiences to be receptive to his ideas. In his letter to "all Christians," dated March 1, 1074, he states:

> [...] we have learned that a people of the pagans have been pressing hard upon the Christian empire, have cruelly laid waste the country almost to the walls of Constantinople and slaughtered like sheep many thousand Christians.
> [...] Be it known, therefore, that we [...] are preparing in every possible way to carry aid to the Christian empire as soon as may be, with God's help. We adjure you [...] willingly to offer your powerful aid to your brethren in the name of Christ.[78]

Note here that he refers to the enemies as "pagans" when he would soon praise a Muslim ruler in North Africa for being devoted to the same God, but in a different manner. This was the start of a series of missives regarding his conviction to do something about the Turkish situation. Passing reference is made to the venture in a letter addressed to King Philip I of France concerning the church of Beauvais,[79] and at the conclusion of a letter to William, Count of Poitou and Duke of Aquitaine, concerning the annulment of his marriage to Hildegard, daughter of King Robert of Burgundy. He praises William for his willingness to offer military support for Gregory's venture, but then informs him that at that time, good news had arrived and the Christians had succeeded in driving the Turks back:

> Your assurance of readiness to act in the service of St. Peter was very welcome to us, but it has not seemed best to write you anything definite at present concerning an expedition, because the report is that the Christians beyond the seas have, by God's help, driven back the fierce assault of the pagans, and we are waiting for the counsel of divine Providence as to our future course.[80]

This temporary cessation did not last long, however, and by December, Gregory was once again making plans for a full-scale expedition to the east. He wrote to the Holy Roman Emperor, Henry IV, putting forth his plans in greater detail:

> Further, I call to your attention that the Christians beyond the seas, a great part of whom are being destroyed by the heathen with unheard-of slaughter and

1. Christians, Muslims and Conflicts Up to the First Crusade   31

> are daily being slain like so many sheep, have humbly sent to beg me to succor these our brethren in whatever ways I can, that the religion of Christ may not utterly perish in our time [...]
> I [...] have succeeded in arousing certain Christian men so that they are eager to risk their lives for their brethren in defense of the law of Christ and to show forth more clearly than the day the nobility of the sons of God. This summons has been readily accepted by Italians and northerners, by divine inspiration as I believe — nay as I can absolutely assure you — and already fifty thousand men are preparing, if they can have me for their leader and prelate, to take up arms against the enemies of God and push forward even to the sepulcher of the Lord under his supreme leadership.[81]

There follows a section wherein Gregory discusses the rift between the Eastern and the Western Churches, the recent *filioque* controversy in the Nicene Creed no doubt still in his mind. The two churches were clearly at odds, and Gregory appears here to be hinting at the chance to reclaim some of the East for the Catholic faith.[82] Indeed, his predecessor, Leo IX, had expressed a desire for a renewal of good ties between West and East, even if he preferred to refer to Rome and Constantinople as "mother" and "daughter" respectively, a designation of which the Greeks would hardly have approved.[83]

He wrote a letter to Countess Matilda of Tuscany on 16 December of 1074 with a similar theme:

> There are some whom I blush to tell, lest I should seem to be led by a mere fancy, how firmly my mind and heart are set upon crossing the sea in order that, by Christ's favor, I may bring help to the Christians who are being slaughtered by the heathen like cattle.
> [...] Now, I believe that many knights support us in such a task, also that our empress herself [Agnes of Poitou, widow of Henry III, mother of Henry IV] desires to come with us to distant parts and to bring you with her [...][84]

We can see that Gregory was the first to propose an armed religious expedition, and he actually offered to lead it himself. This was remarkable; the idea that a pope could command an army had until this time been unthinkable. Regardless, even with Gregory's plans to travel as far as Jerusalem, the idea of mixing a pilgrimage with war was probably not something that he envisioned. In fact, despite the reported 50,000 men waiting to make the journey (certainly an exaggeration), nothing came of these bold plans.

There are several reasons for this, most of which are due to the complex political situations involving the Normans and Byzantine claims to western lands. In 1074, Gregory had found himself embroiled in a battle of wills with the Norman Robert Guiscard, an adventurer-turned-noble, and Gregory had sought to raise forces against him, which would then proceed to the east in the quest to liberate it from Turkish control. This plan fell apart, and Gregory temporarily abandoned his hopes, though they were rekindled later in the year and into 1075, only to be dashed again, the second time mainly by a lack of interest.[85] His disappointment and disgust are evident in a letter written to Abbot Hugh of Cluny on 22 January 1075, wherein he decries the lack of faith in God, and that men seek only their own glory, while even the Italians proved themselves to be worse than the pagans and heretics, and the devil has his way.[86]

Within a year of his proclamations of armed expedition, Gregory was burdened with a problem much closer to home, the Investiture Contest, one of the principal side effects of the Reform movement, the great struggle between the Holy Roman Empire and the papacy. In short, the debate raged about whether the Holy Roman Emperor could appoint his own loyal bishops, and even influence the selection of popes. The emperor thought yes, the Church maintained that this duty was relegated to it alone by God. It would not be fully resolved (in the Church's favor) until 1122.[87]

Gregory's plans had been important, however. It was the first time that the notion of a Christian holy war to the East, with papal sanction, had been seriously considered. Further, although it was initially conceived to give support to Byzantium (an idea with mixed support at best), Gregory clearly entertained the idea of sending the mission all the way to Jerusalem, thus planting the seed of the idea of a war and pilgrimage combined together.[88] As for the effect this was about to have on Christian/Islamic relations, a pilgrimage with a military element would be the instigation of a new holy war.[89]

Gregory never abandoned the idea, however, and in the early 1080s, he summoned Anselm of Baggio, Bishop of Lucca, to Rome to write on the Church's right to wage war. In Book XIII of his collection of canonical texts (written at Gregory's request), he included many ideas which justified the use of violence when willed by God, stressing that it was the intention of the warrior that mattered, and that fighting could be just if engaged in with "goodwill."[90] Indeed, many of these statements would be found again in Bernard of Clairvaux's justification for the Knights Templar forty years later.[91] In another work, *De caritate*, Anselm went so far as to proclaim that the use of violence for holy ends could be seen as an act of charity.

Significantly, he was also a supporter of the idea of the Church itself having the authority to use force, without the need to rely on secular permission or enforcement.[92] Such thinking was very near that which was to be espoused by the supporters of the crusade.

The issue of Christian violence as an act of love and charity may seem very odd to the modern reader, but it formed a significant part of what was to become the theology of crusading, and it deserves to be discussed in more detail here. Actions taken to correct a wrong were legitimate in Christian teaching. St. Augustine had commented at length on the use of corrective force for a greater good. While he was not specifically referring to war, his comments were adapted to suit the situations of the eleventh and twelfth centuries. Further, since he also discussed the forced conversion of the Manichaeans in this context (a gnostic dualist faith that Augustine himself had been a member of, until his conversion in 387), it was only logical to transfer the same line of thinking to the Muslims. In his extended commentary on the Sermon on the Mount, he states:

> A punishment that is designed for the purpose of correction is not hereby forbidden; for that very punishment is an exercise of mercy, and is not incompatible with the firm resolve by which we are ready to suffer even further injuries from a man whose amendment we desire. But no one is fit for the task of inflicting such punishment unless — by the greatness of his love — he has overcome the hate by which those who seek to avenge themselves are usually enraged.[93]

In the twelfth century, Bernard of Clairvaux would echo these words in describing the virtues of the Knights Templar.[94] Essentially, the Christian soldier who divorced himself from hateful intent potentially had the moral authority to inflict punishment and commit violence for the greater good. Augustine continues with the view that the right to commit such acts must come from God:

> Nevertheless, noble and saintly men inflicted death as a punishment for many sins, although they knew well that no one ought to fear the death which separates soul and body. But they were acting in conformity with the sentiment of those who do fear it, so that the living would be struck with salutary fear. Those who were put to death did not suffer injury from death itself; rather, they were suffering injury from sin, and it might have become worse if they had continued to live. This authority was not exercised rashly by those to whom God had committed it.[95]

The influence that such a passage would have had in the formulation of the new martial ethic of the Church can clearly be seen.[96] Perhaps the most significant statement was to be found in Augustine's *City of God*, chapter 21:

> The same divine law which forbids the killing of a human being allows certain exceptions, as when God authorizes killing by a general law or when He gives explicit commission to an individual for a limited time. Since the agent of authority is but a sword in the hand, and is not responsible for the killing, it is in no way contrary to the commandment, "Thou shalt not kill," to wage war at God's bidding, or for the representatives of the State's authority to put criminals to death, according to law or the rule of rational justice.[97]

While such teachings had been a part of the Church since the time of the fathers, it took the innovations of the eleventh century to adapt them to the situations that Christians faced about the status of Jerusalem and the perceived threat of Islam. Islam, of course, did not exist in Augustine's time, but this was not an obstacle to the theologians seeking support for crusading.

An important French canonist who continued the thought of Anselm of Lucca was Ivo of Chartres (*ca.* 1040–1115), who in 1094, shortly before the Council of Clermont (wherein Urban II proclaimed the First Crusade), wrote his *Decretum* and *Panormia*. These works contained considerable speculation on the nature of Christian violence and justifiable war, and their relationship to love. In commenting on Augustine, he declared that a war fought by Christians was for the purpose of creating peace, and thus was an acceptable act;[98] it had as its aim a higher good. Those who would punish evil were not persecuting their foes, but in fact loving them,[99] and he distinguished, as Bernard of Clairvaux would, between war for its own sake and for a just cause.[100] Indeed, Christopher Tyerman notes that by his writings, "Augustine had moved the justification of violence from lawbooks to liturgies, from the secular to the religious. His lack of definition in merging holy and just war [...] produced a convenient conceptual plasticity that characterized subsequent Christian attitudes to war."[101]

The concept of Church-sanctioned, holy violence found its full flowering in the First Crusade, preached by Pope Urban II in 1095. In March of 1095, at the Council of Piacenza, ambassadors from the Byzantine Emperor Alexios I Komnenos arrived with an appeal for aid against continuing incursions by the Seljuk Turks. The emperor hoped for some military reinforcements, but what he received was beyond his imagination. Urban's response at the Council of Clermont in November of that year was to call for a full-scale armed assault on the East. He presented the crusade as a pilgrimage to worship at Jerusalem. However, it was an *armed* pilgrimage; remission of sins was gained *because* one was armed, which, for a pilgrim, had been forbidden. This was a groundbreaking move; there was no precedent for such an attitude, regardless of previous Church support for armed campaigns against Muslims in Spain. There, the Church had given its endorsement to the continuing efforts of the *reconquista*, even offering remission of sins for those who perished fighting Islam on Spain's soil.[102] The difference was that there was not yet the link with pilgrimage that characterized the whole of the crusading movement for the next 200 years and beyond. The reconquest of Spain was principally a military exercise, not an opportunity for pilgrimage.

Indeed, medieval writers referred to crusaders and pilgrims with exactly the same word, *peregrinus*.[103] As a result, it is not always clear whether the individual described in a given manuscript account is on crusade, or whether he is a traditional, non-armed pilgrim.

1. Christians, Muslims and Conflicts Up to the First Crusade   35

The reason for the novelty lay in its unique fusion, because, "its whole point seems to be rather that pilgrimage and war are fused together with the deliberate emphasis that remission of penance is not the automatic reward for waging this war, but that only he qualifies who '*pro sola devotione*, non pro honoris vel pecuniae adeptione, ad liberandam ecclesiam Dei Hierusalem profectus fuerit.' The moral discipline associated with pilgrimage is written into the qualification [...]."[104] In other words, devotion to the crusade as its own reward, and not to gain riches or honor, was the method by which salvation was attained. There is a clear distinction between war for its own sake and the necessity to complete the pilgrimage. The remission is gained for completing the pilgrimage; the fighting necessary to this end is not the means by which salvation is gained, but rather a useful tool. The intention must not be for personal glory, but rather only to glorify God and Christ.[105] Once again, this was a theme which was to be invoked by Bernard of Clairvaux in his support of the Knights Templar.

Therefore, the crusade was a new idea, and perhaps Urban felt the need to keep the concept out of the traditional boundaries of Church law. He was in uncharted territory with his proposals, and could have been unsure of how they would be received. It is not surprising therefore, that no attempt was made immediately to fit the idea of armed pilgrimage into existing Church statutes.[106] However, at about the same time, an encyclical was circulating, purporting to be from Pope Sergius IV (d. 1012), calling for the expulsion of the Muslims from Jerusalem for Caliph Hakim's crime of the Holy Sepulcher's destruction. The general consensus is that this document is a forgery, and was probably created for the purpose of giving Urban some historical precedent for his proposal.[107] It provides a prime example of how history was being manipulated to bring the new theology in line with existing beliefs.

Was the Holy Sepulcher the main goal? Erdmann put forth the argument that Pope Urban II's principal concern was aid to Byzantium and Alexios I, with the hope that such a venture would allow for the possibility of reuniting the Church (i.e., extending Latin rule in the East).[108] E. O. Blake has asked if Urban's intention was "not to convert the military venture into a pilgrimage, but merely to *divert* the benefits of pilgrimage to reward an act of war?"[109]

This is a possibility, and may have some truth, but it is also reliant on Erdmann's thesis of the crusade just being the logical extension of just war theology.[110] Erdmann adheres to the idea that the crusade was primarily about the practice of "legitimate" war, whereas later writers have argued that canon law was not invoked in crusading literature, and therefore the pilgrimage theme must be given more attention. Most likely, however, Urban held Jerusalem to be an important component of the expedition,[111] and probably the primary reason.[112] Baldric of Bourgueil recorded that Urban made use of Psalm 78:1–4 as part of his justification for the taking up of arms, since it proclaims that the heathen had defiled the holy places.[113] Indeed, with Jerusalem as the main goal, the whole idea could be more related to such areas as theology and apocalypticism, rather than simply just war.[114]

While the general assumption is that Alexios' letter was the principal spur to the crusade, Andrew Jotischky has recently suggested that pleas from the Jerusalem church may have played a role. Indeed, stories about the popular preacher Peter the Hermit (whom we shall meet presently) said that he was in possession of just such a plea, and that this was what gave rise to the whole crusade. This is an exaggeration, but contacts between Jerusalem and the West had been ongoing, and reports of turmoil and difficulties between Eastern Christians and various Muslim rulers (not just Hakim) had existed for centuries.[115]

Regardless of the ultimate aim, the idea became very popular. Part of the appeal of Urban's new proposition was because it was in the form of a sermon. Odd as this may sound, the growing popularity of sermons outside of the monastic community was certainly a factor in Urban's favor. Prior to the eleventh century, preaching was largely a monastic practice, and the focus of such sermons was on the patristic texts and scriptural exegesis. There was a good amount of theological contemplation, aimed at directing the minds of the monks toward heaven and spiritual concerns. Before the twelfth century, there was no real effort to bring such elevated spiritual ideas to the common people; indeed, it may have been only periodic. For example, the Council of Clovesho in 747 recommended preaching on Sundays, but did not require it as a part of the mass. In any case, it was assumed that the laity was not educated and intelligent enough to understand the complex ideas that monastic thinkers pondered. Instead, sermons were to concentrate on such topics as instruction in the faith, the meaning of the Creed, and how to be a good Christian.[116]

However, by the time of the Reform, there had appeared a new phenomenon, or at least a surge in popularity of an old one: the itinerant preacher. As the Reform movement took hold, there began to appear a large number of itinerant and lay preachers (particularly in France), who had no formal training or Church affiliation. These individuals most often called on the laity to adopt a life of poverty and humility, imitating Christ, and were wanderers who were often rough in appearance and hygiene, but their messages resonated with lay audiences far and wide. They had an immediate appeal, being commoners like those they preached to, far different from the distant, upper-class Church officials.

The chicken-and-egg question is, of course, whether they generated the popular spiritual movements, or were responding to them. This cannot be answered with certainty, but there is no doubt that their words were well-received by many. Such a situation could not help but pose serious challenges for those officials within the Church, especially as many of these preachers did not extoll the formal Church structures as the way to salvation. Given this popular yearning for spiritual meaning, Urban's Clermont sermon must have had tremendous power, being addressed not only to clergy, nobles, and knights, but to the common people, as well.[117]

The Clermont sermon was an inspired work, for it answered the spiritual needs of the laity by including them in its preaching. Here was a sermon from the pope himself, and one that spoke to all Christians, not just the privileged few. Urban must have been aware of the effect that his words would have; indeed, he meant to reach the people in just the way that he did. It may have even been a kind of official response to the popular preachers, one which gave the people hope in the same manner that the words of the wanderers did, but one with papal authority.[118]

There were unexpected and unfortunate events concerning one of those wanderers, Peter of Amiens, a priest known as the Hermit, who preached his own brand of the crusade. Peter was one of those "eccentric, unkempt" individuals, who exerted a strong charisma despite (or perhaps because of) his unwashed state, and he obtained many followers on his disastrous journey to the East in 1096. Whether or not he carried a plea for help from Jerusalem's patriarch,[119] his was the dark side of popular religious fervor. It led to some of his followers slaughtering groups of Jews living in the Rhineland, under the assumption that it was just as easy to kill the "enemies of God" near to home as to journey all the way to far-off Jerusalem. His vision of crusading differed dramatically from that of Urban's, "as unlike as reasonably clean water and a muddy pool covered with weeds."[120] Thousands followed Peter as far as Constantinople, where the Emperor Alexios, eager to be rid of them, arranged for their transport into Turkish territory. He told them to wait for him to send guards as an escort, but they set off, thus sealing their fate. Shortly afterward, they were massacred by the Turks.[121] Peter had escaped and returned to Constantinople with few followers left, but he remained a part of the crusade, and was given much credit for his later involvement by contemporary chroniclers.[122] We will meet Peter again in chapter six.

In spite of such a tragic and even embarrassing setback, preparations for the true crusade continued, and the idea spread very quickly throughout Europe. The notion of holy and just war gained popularity rapidly, and seemed to answer some great spiritual need of the common people, with its promise of liberation of the sacred sites, and remission of all sins.

Indeed, the idea of the crusaders engaged in the *imitatio Christi*, imitating the life of Christ, seems to have taken hold and been popular. William Purkis focuses on the imitation of Christ's life and passion as a major motivating force for those first crusaders. The idea of "taking the cross," that is, the sewing of a cloth cross onto one's clothing as a symbol of one's crusading vow, could be compared to the act of Christ shouldering his own cross on his final walk to Calvary: a heavy burden that led to an eternal reward.[123] This was seen as a living embodiment of Christ's admonition in Matthew 16:24 that all who would come after him must take up their crosses and follow him.[124] The crusaders were abandoning their homes and families, as Christ had commanded, to answer a higher calling. Upon reaching Jerusalem, they would literally be walking in the footsteps of Christ.[125] Those that did so and died in this holy endeavor could be seen as martyrs (we shall return to this topic in chapter seven). Even the ranks of the crusaders were seen in terms of the followers of Christ, with accounts that some contingents were numbered at 12 (the number of the apostles), that those who abandoned the crusade were akin to Judas, among other comparisons.[126]

The adversary that they would face was the quintessential enemy. Though the people knew little or nothing about Islam, Urban and his successors had succeeded in defining it as the greatest of all threats. Over time, the term Saracen would designate all of the enemies of Christendom, and their supposed practices would be assigned to all such enemies.[127] In a ridiculous example, a twelfth-century English monk mentioned that the pagan Saxons worshipped "maumets," a reference to Muhammad and the belief that Muslims worshipped him.[128] Islam was thus antithetical to Christianity; it was everything that Christians were not, or perhaps that they feared they might be. The excessive hatred and violence that could grow out of such a belief is obvious. Muslims were seen as a lost cause, inconvertible and fit only to be driven out or killed.[129]

The result of this change in attitude toward war was a completely new outlook for the Church, one which was to have dramatic repercussions for hundreds of years. By the end of the eleventh century, the idea of a Church-sanctioned holy war had fully taken shape, a new and important belief in Western history. It went far beyond Augustinian notions of what constituted a just war. War of a certain kind was now pleasing to God, whereas previously, it required penance, no matter how just its cause. Fighting in a war was not only permitted, it was divinely-sanctioned, and it earned the remittance of all sins, guaranteed by a papal proclamation.[130]

An important question that naturally arises from all of this activity is how sincere these various writers and theologians were in their beliefs. This is not always answerable, but it deserves some attention. As we have seen, there existed a curious double attitude toward Byzantium, which on the one hand condemned the Greeks for supposed treachery (a theme that would recur throughout the crusading period; indeed it was invoked by Peter the Venerable as a principal reason for the failure of the Second Crusade), and on the other considered it important to render assistance to the Byzantine army in repelling the Turks (though it must be pointed out that in no surviving account of Urban's Clermont sermon is Byzantium mentioned).[131] For the Church writers, perhaps it was a belief in the lesser of two evils, that it was better to have a schismatic Christian empire in the East than one controlled by the Turks. Or, the Byzantine appeal for help simply could have provided a timely and ideal opportunity to put the papacy's hopes and plans into action, with little regard for the safety of the Eastern Empire at all. It is clear that Alexios certainly did not anticipate the unruly mobs that descended on his lands a few years after his appeal.

Were these crusading sentiments merely shrewd political manipulations from a Church desperate to obtain complete power over the secular rulers of Europe? Sources cannot confirm this, and there were undoubtedly many (if not most) among the laity who felt a genuine sense of religious duty to engage in the perceived defense of Christendom. The possibility of undertaking a true *imitatio Christi* must have been irresistible to those who had no idea what was ahead of them. Still, human nature has shown throughout history that the prospect of attaining such total power must have held great appeal for those in charge. The Church, of course, did achieve a great victory through all of these new movements, both in the spiritual and political sense. The misery, brutality, and death wrought by the crusades and their earlier models in Spain had little impact on those in Europe who did not participate in the fighting, and the troubles experienced by the crusaders were completely overshadowed by the retaking of Jerusalem, which more than redressed the suffering. A more perfect example of divine reward for Christian humility, obedience and suffering could not have been envisioned.

Though Gregory VII offered to lead the first such expedition, his sincerity in this proposal will never be known. The rapidity with which the whole plan was dropped indicates either a lack of conviction or, just as likely, a preoccupation with events closer to home. Indeed, the Investiture Contest allowed the opportunity for the pope to exert the Church's worldly and spiritual authority without having to journey all the way to Jerusalem. The West probably was simply not yet ready for Gregory's call to arms. The knights and fighting men of Europe were not initially interested in Gregory's plan; in fact, it may have seemed quite odd to them. Long-standing conflicts and general mistrust among warring factions were enough to resist a call to fight under a papal banner in a *militia Christi*. In fact, the papacy could well have been seen by them as desiring the military expedition for its own ends, and so there was little appeal to a secular warrior, who had more to gain by waging war closer to his own home in Europe. So, unlike Urban's crusade of 1095, Gregory probably alienated secular knights to some extent, by adopting an approach that was too hierarchical. Gregory said that he wanted to command the army in his time, but Urban had a far better idea; letting the greatest of the French knights and nobility themselves lead the expedition. It was this strategy that ensured the strong popular response to Urban's call, where Gregory's had failed.[132] It is worth noting that before he became pope, Urban, as Odo of Lagery, was cardinal bishop of Ostia and was known as the *pedisequus* (valet) to Gregory VII, given their close friendship. So there can be no doubt that Gregory's ideas of holy war lived on in Urban.[133]

The crusaders themselves were certainly an enormously diverse group, and the reasons why so many took the cross and traveled such a perilous road to the east have been long questioned and debated.[134] In addition to the *imitatio Christi*, many felt other religious inspirations, while some may well have desired material gain. Urban was aware of this, and stressed that it was only those who undertook the burden without wanting honor or wealth would gain the full remission of sins.[135]

Susanna Throop has argued that a specific form of vengeance was also invoked as an encouragement to take the cross.[136] Drawing from Old Testament influences, it was known in the sources as *vindicta*, *ultio*, and *venjance*. This was not the petty vengeance of mortals (and thus forbidden to Christians), but rather the divine vengeance of righting wrongs, of punishing and committing violence with moral authority against those who had transgressed divine law. Indeed the First Crusade itself might be seen more as an exercise in punishment than an actual war.[137] While the Jews had killed Christ, a great affront to God, the Muslims were equally villainous, since they had willingly rejected Christ as God. They were the successors to the crime of deicide by their occupation of the holy places, and the crusaders saw it as a duty to take revenge on Islam for the perceived guilt of Judaism. Jews, heretics, and Saracens were equally enemies of God, and all were deserving of the same divine punishment.[138] God had been injured by the Muslims. Their rebellion against Christian law was likened to a kind of ongoing crucifixion. The Jews had crucified Christ once because of their lack of belief; the Muslims, by also not believing, did so every day.[139]

Looking at another possibility, Jay Rubenstein makes the case for apocalyptic hopes and fears playing a key role in the lives and motivations of the first crusaders. We will examine this in more detail in Chapter 6.

All of these can be put forward as being among the reasons for the success of the venture, and the ability to inspire thousands to take up arms.[140] Within that success, however, we must remember that there was a clearer line of demarcation between the duties of the clergy and the laity within *Ecclesia*, enhanced as a result of the increased gulf between the two groups, which the Reform created.

The absolute prohibition on monks joining the crusade, and the stipulation that other clergy needed to demonstrate justifiable reasons for doing so, are further examples of the difference between clerical and lay duties in this new vision of the Church. Indeed, Urban was faced with the problem of enthusiastic monks desiring to join the crusade, and had to expressly forbid it, reminding them that they had already devoted themselves to spiritual warfare. They were warned that they would face excommunication if they failed to heed his command.[141] Priests had never been permitted to shed blood, but they were, of course, expected to minister to soldiers and whole armies. The Church was defining its own role in crusading as something different from the laity. Penitential killing of the infidel was held to be meritorious for the secular man, who was by nature sinful and prone to violence and killing, but not for the priest or monk, who had sworn his life to peace and service to God.[142] And yet, certain chroniclers favorably compared the crusaders to monks, saying that they were more like monks than knights.[143]

Was this a means of allowing the masses of common people to perform the tasks that the Church desired, without it having to take undue risks itself? It is possible, though remember that in the structured organization brought about by the Reform, all classes of society were seen as having different duties to perform and different expressions of piety. By presenting a "secular" means of salvation, one that made use of both the imitation of Christ's sufferings and the use of "holy" violence, the laity would be active participants in the spreading of the Gospel in their own way. God's enemies could be defeated, and Catholic rule brought to the East (thus enhancing papal power and influence even further) without the pope having to exert great amounts of effort beyond preaching and encouraging feelings of support for the idea. The lay crusader was thus helping all of Christendom by undertaking the dangerous journey to the East, with the spiritual support of the clergy. The mere fact that the Reform sought to establish the Church as the supreme earthly authority and to elevate itself over the laity suggests that such measures of encouragement may have been employed, for both political and religious reasons. Helping the common people feel valued by encouraging their participation in the crusading venture was a most effective means of encouraging the spirit of cooperation in the formation of the new *Ecclesia*. Quite simply and obviously, the crusade would not have succeeded without lay support. How much of this was manipulative and how much sincere continues to be debated, though there may have in the end been little difference in motivation between the Church and lay society in general.[144]

It is clear from the correspondence and writings cited in this chapter that Christian writers of the eleventh century felt a genuine sense of outrage at Turkish and Muslim military activities directed against pilgrims, or at least catching them up in the "crossfire" of sectarian disputes. The situation in the East provided a coincidental and most effective means of helping the Church to secure power, and in their determination to counter the perceived Muslim threat, the papacy realized this. The solution to the problem of Islam could be found in the attitudes of the Reform movement itself, and was no doubt held by many to be God-given. The First Crusade was the result of this combination.

The papacy did not conceive of its ideas in a vacuum; it relied on the support of certain key institutions and thinkers to make the whole process of the new Christian war machine operate effectively. It was one matter to have the support of the laity, but that support had to be reinforced by many others within the Church itself. Perhaps somewhat surprisingly, it was in the monastic houses that this support often came with such strength. These shall be dealt with in detail in chapter four.

The Burgundian monasteries of Cîteaux and Cluny were to prove vital in maintaining support and engendering enthusiasm for future holy military ventures. The Cistercians, under Bernard of Clairvaux, were particularly important in this regard, for it was Bernard who so strongly advocated the Second Crusade, and who gave his support to the new Order of the Knights Templar of Jerusalem. This monastic order was created to deal with the Muslim presence and other dangers to pilgrims in the new Christian Kingdom of Jerusalem, as well as to defend the lands won by the Christian conquest. The Benedictine Cluniacs, while supporting the crusade, also played a role, for their abbot, Peter the Venerable, acquired a keen interest in Islam and its teachings. The next chapter surveys the creation of the Knights Templar, and how it achieved its rise to such prominence in the early twelfth century.

2

The Founding of the Order of the Knights Templar

> The Knights of the Temple, New Maccabees in this time of Grace, denying worldly desires and abandoning personal possessions, have taken up Christ's cross and followed Him. It is through them that God has freed the eastern church from the filth of the pagans and defeated the enemies of the Christian faith. They do not fear to lay down their lives for their brothers and protect pilgrims from the attacks of the pagans as they go on their journeys to and from the holy places.[1]
>
> — Pope Celestine II, *Milites Templi*, January, 1144

The Knights Templar have had a curious afterlife. Suppressed and destroyed in 1314 on what were almost certainly false charges, the mystique about the order has nevertheless continued over the centuries. Modern readers have no doubt heard their name in connection with an endless parade of conspiracy theories, secret societies, forbidden knowledge, and hidden treasures. Recent decades have seen a barrage of books and movies purporting to tell the "true" history of the order after its suppression: how it went underground, hid its fabulous wealth (which remains to be rediscovered), held on to ancient esoteric teachings from the time of King Solomon, and was the true source of Freemasonry, among many other stories. The fact is that despite assurances of all of this and more from various speculative authors, almost none of what they claim has any real evidence, or can be proven, and the evidence that they have put forward often requires tremendous leaps of faith and mental gymnastics to believe.[2]

We will steer clear of this mess of pseudo-scholarship, and focus instead on the order's earliest history, looking at the admittedly somewhat scant information about their founding and initial activities. Placing the Templars within their social, religious, and historical context shows just how innovative the concept of the military order was. We will examine the position of the order in the Latin Kingdom of Jerusalem, its relationship to various institutions of the time, and some of the theological justifications for its existence. This prepares the reader for a detailed study of Bernard's treatise in support of the knights in chapter three.

Attempting to construct an accurate picture of the Templars and their activities in the early years of their existence is a frustrating exercise for historians, partially because the Order's central archive, containing charters and documents about its Eastern activities from the time of its creation, was destroyed, probably by the Ottoman Turks during their invasion of Cyprus in 1571.[3]

Modern accounts note that the Templars had originally been founded to protect pilgrims from attacks by highwaymen and renegade Muslims in the new Christian kingdoms established after the First Crusade. According to the chronicler William of Tyre, the Order was founded in 1119/20.[4] Hugues de Payens and Godfrey of St. Omer, knights in Jerusalem, apparently conceived of the idea of forming a religious community whose purpose would be to ensure this protection. The king of Jerusalem, Baldwin II, gave them his sanction, as well as allowing them to quarter in the palace, near the site of the ancient Temple of Solomon, from which the Order drew its name. Curiously, an early seal for the Order shows on its reverse side the Dome of the Rock, the mosque which had been converted into a Christian church, and was known confusingly as the Temple of the Lord.[5] They ultimately became affiliated with the Augustinian canons regular of the Holy Sepulcher and lived a monastic, communal life.[6]

The notion of protecting religious pilgrims and travelers was not new, for in being unarmed and often in small groups, they had always been vulnerable to attack both in Europe and beyond, as we saw in chapter one. Indeed, the Church had in the past sought to exercise its power to correct this problem. At the Synod of Charroux (*ca.* 989), for example, laws were set forth that demanded the cessation of wars at various times of the year and the immunity of pilgrims from attack, with strong penalties for transgressors.[7] By 1059, Pope Nicholas II enacted the policy of making pilgrims' safety an obligation of the papacy.[8] Thus when Christian pilgrims to the Holy Land came under attack after the First Crusade, a familiar problem presented itself to Christendom.[9]

The idea, therefore, of a group of knights banding together to form an order dedicated to this protection would certainly have had appeal, and would seem the perfect answer to the needs of travelers to Jerusalem. This is the most viable explanation for the Templars' origin offered by most historians,[10] and there is undoubtedly truth in this proposition.[11]

Incidents of assaults were recorded by individuals who either experienced and survived them, or heard first-hand accounts, which were then disseminated to the larger population. The inhabitants of the Latin Kingdom were known to be fearful of attack until after the advent of the Templars. In *The New Knighthood*, Malcolm Barber stresses that "visitors to the kingdom were naturally deeply apprehensive."[12] He provides an account, that of a Russian abbot, Daniel, as a dramatic example of the peril of travelers, and the lack of water and provisions they often encountered, as well as the danger of robbery.[13] Whether or not most pilgrims knew the perils that lay ahead of them, it became obvious to those living in the new Latin kingdom that the issue had to be addressed.[14]

It is worth noting that a considerable amount of time passed between the capture of Jerusalem in 1099 and the formation of the Templars in 1118/19. If these attacks had been occurring since the end of the First Crusade, why did nearly twenty years pass before a definitive solution was reached? The most likely reason is that these attacks had a cumulative effect, and reached a point where they could no longer be tolerated.[15] The confidence in such a scheme, founded upon religious principles, would no doubt have been an additional factor in the Order's creation. Indeed, the fervor of the First Crusade had not yet diminished, and Edessa was still in Christian hands. For this short time, Christians were victorious and saw themselves as rightful masters of the most revered lands in the world. They had retaken the Holy Land, and it was their divinely-ordained task to keep it safe. It would have been a sacred duty to expel the remaining Muslims and to secure the lands around Jerusalem. Yet initially, it seems that virtually no one joined the new order.

Indeed, very few even took notice of it, save some generous and wealthy patrons. The historian Fulcher of Chartres, who was living and writing in Jerusalem in 1127, does not even mention the Templars, a testimony to their insignificance at that time. No contemporary writer or chronicler seems to have thought them worthy enough to mention their establishment, at least in none of the accounts that have survived. Only in the latter part of the twelfth century do we find such documents, in the writings of William, Archbishop of Tyre (d. *ca*. 1186), Walter Map, Archdeacon of Oxford (d. *ca*. 1208–10), and Michael the Syrian, Jacobite Patriarch of Antioch (d. 1199).[16] Given the tremendous impact that the Templars had exerted over affairs in the east by the end of the twelfth century, it is easy to understand why they were worthy of so much attention from later chroniclers. No one at the time of their creation could have foreseen what they would become.

William of Tyre lists the number of knights at only nine in 1128–9, a full ten years after the creation of the Order. Judith Upton-Ward considers this to be an underestimate,[17] but the total must have been quite small. Indeed, one finds that in many cases, medieval chroniclers have a tendency to overestimate when calculating numbers of people,[18] so William's numbering may be reasonable. It is certainly supported by the lack of attention the Templars received in their first decade of existence.[19] The problem of accuracy in narrating events far removed from their own times is evident in the fact that each of the three writers' works contain information not found in the other two.[20] Indeed, Malcolm Barber notes:

> [William's] view of the Templars is coloured by the development of an acute dislike for what he saw as their unfair manipulation and exploitation of their privileges in his own time. Michael the Syrian included details not found in William of Tyre, but is generally regarded as less reliable than William when describing matters outside his own experience and times, while Walter Map — the farthest removed from the events — is known as a man for whom a good story usually took precedence over historical inquiry.[21]

While we might find such medieval attitudes either amusing or frustrating, they present a central problem so common in many fields of medieval studies: lack of definite evidence for certain events, beliefs, and practices. The Templars, regrettably, are no exception, and so we have to rely on what survives to try to gain a clearer picture of their origins.[22] Their virtual anonymity raises questions about their founding and ultimate purpose as a religious institution. Barber points out that there is no evidence that either Godfrey or Hugues specifically took their vows for the purpose of protecting pilgrims, though this is most often assumed by historians.[23] If this protection was in fact the major consideration, then the idea may have originated with Baldwin II or Patriarch Warmund in response to a specific event which, perhaps not coincidentally, occurred in the same year as the Templar's founding.

At Easter of 1119, a group of pilgrims left Jerusalem for Jordan, and were ambushed near the castle of Cushet by Muslim raiders. According to Albert of Aachen, three hundred were killed and sixty captured.[24] These numbers, like many we have already encountered, are probably an exaggeration, but they must have been high enough for officials in Jerusalem to take notice. It is certainly possible that the Templars were founded in response to this act. A troop of armed knights was apparently sent out in response, but the attackers had already retreated to Ascalon and Tyre, and so could not be found.[25]

A general religious excitement and fervor was probably still present from the heady events of the First Crusade. Undoubtedly, some of the zeal had disappeared after twenty years, and many of the crusaders had returned to Europe, having fulfilled their vows (a decision that was ultimately to bring about the downfall of the Latin Kingdoms, due to a lack of population), but the residents of Jerusalem had not yet grown complacent. Indeed, their very presence in the Holy Land had encouraged a new wave of pilgrimages, which were at the root of the problem. There were too many pilgrims to protect them all adequately, yet rarely were there calls for reinforcements.[26] The size of the military order, which after ten years continued to have a limited membership, must surely have made attempts to patrol the Latin Kingdom quite difficult, much less protect large bands of pilgrims from even larger raiding parties. The Templars' presence in these early years was clearly not very effective, a state of affairs supported by the fact that they were all but ignored by their contemporaries. Their limited membership simply could not have been much use for pilgrim safety, either as an effective military force, or even in a symbolic sense, as defenders of the Temple.

However, if their numbers were too small, they would not have been able to receive papal support for their confirmation.[27] They were largely unknown in Europe, and it is possible that Fulcher did not mention them because he was also not aware of their existence.[28] Whether the order had nine or more members, it hardly could have served adequately the purpose for which it was created.

By the 1120s, it seems there was a general alarm among the residents of Jerusalem who increasingly feared for their safety.[29] The papacy and some Europeans had knowledge of the gravity of the situation. Religious leaders in the Latin Kingdom were aware of the dangers, and doubtless there were settlers who experienced attacks. There were occasional calls for help. Patriarch Warmund and Gerard, Prior of the Holy Sepulcher, wrote in January of 1120 to Diego Gelmirez, Archbishop of Compostella, begging him to send aid in the form of money, food, supplies, and soldiers. They declared that they were under attack by Saracens from such diverse places as Damascus, Ascalon, Tyre, and even Baghdad. Indeed, people could no longer leave Jerusalem without and armed escort.[30] Most of these attacks were probably by roving groups of Arab or Turkish bandits, rather than any organized resistance, much less one of any religious nature, though among Muslims, that idea was starting to take shape.

The citizens of Jerusalem may have been living in fear, but apparently they still took little or no notice of the new order. While the West knew of the troubles in the region, there were initially few responses, and only the occasional instance such as the communication noted above; these were the exception rather than the rule. Here is a probable resolution to the puzzle of the Templars' virtual anonymity in their first decade. The lack of military and civilian reinforcements, as attested in Warmund's and Gerard's letter, meant that there simply were not enough numbers arriving from the West to swell the ranks of the Templars, or even the secular militia, in the formative years of the new Christian Jerusalem. Since the majority of crusaders had returned to Europe, they left the small numbers who remained weak and often undefended.

Nevertheless, the Church certainly could not dissuade pilgrims from their journeys, which helped to keep peace in Europe, and brought economic advantages to the new settlements in the East. If stories of pilgrim massacres became commonplace in the West, the numbers of new pilgrims would have dropped dramatically. The credibility of the crusading enterprise and the new Christian settlements was at stake. While accounts of Saracen attacks were indeed recorded by chroniclers, their words were not as likely to reach the largely illiterate masses that were the actual pilgrims, and therefore would probably have been confined to the status of rumors. The countryside at the time had a mixture of religious faiths among its people.[31] It is even possible that Muslims were still a minority population during the First Crusade,[32] but bandits were a threat regardless. Therefore, a solution such as the Templars was probably inevitable. The novelty lay in the nature of the institution.

We can see the Templars and the concept behind their creation as a logical response to the nature of the threat, and it provides some clues to the solution for the conflicting ideals of the "crusading monk." This was viewed as God's work, a sacred trust. An ordinary militia designated to protect pilgrims would not have sufficed. Indeed, armed troops did accompany large groups of traders, officials, and religious representatives, yet the attacks continued.[33] The lack of attention paid to the order initially did not reflect on how important they were to become, or the fear that they would soon inspire in their Islamic opponents.

Despite many modern pseudo-historical claims to the contrary, the silence of the chronicles does not indicate that the Templars were a secretive society,[34] even though few outside of Jerusalem and apparently even in the city initially gave them much attention.[35] However, the order did finally attract the support of some very notable and influential patrons. The king and patriarch of Jerusalem both ensured that it had provisions for feeding and clothing its members. Important nobles joined, such as Fulk V, Count of Anjou (and later King of Jerusalem, also paternal grandfather to Henry II of England), who stayed at the Temple while on pilgrimage in 1120–22, and as a lay associate, granted them an allowance of thirty livres a year from his estates. Other nobles such as Hugh, Count of Champagne, also joined.[36] The order's credibility soared.[37]

The reasons for this surge in support could have been genuine religious devotion. The idea of such an order could have been a great inspiration to those who learned of it. Barber states that Hugues and Godfrey "took their vows because they were pious and Godfearing,"[38] though this is based on writings from the time, which may not relate their real motives. If they did not conceive of the order themselves, perhaps they simply believed in the ideals put forth by the king and patriarch.

One theory holds that the idea of the military order did not originate with any of these individuals, but rather can be traced back to the years 1099–1100. Some of the early writers seem to have confused the order's founding with the climax and aftermath of the First Crusade, which could indicate that there were other, smaller groups set up for similar purposes, comprised of ex-crusaders. Either these disbanded quickly, or were wiped out by their enemies.[39] There is not a substantial amount of evidence to support this claim, but it is an intriguing possibility. If such organizations existed, it could be that some or all of the principal figures in the Templars' creation took one as a model for their own order and gave it official sanction. The tradition of confraternities of secular knights was already known in Europe by the eleventh century. Such small bands would often swear allegiance to a church or monastery, and take an oath to defend it and pilgrims which might visit it.[40] Though interesting for the ideals they expressed, it is doubtful that most of these small brotherhoods had a direct influence on the Templars, with the possible exception of the Confraternity of Belchite, which we will examine in detail presently. Such organizations show that an additional novel idea was being formed about the function of the knighthood during the momentous events of the eleventh century.

Another much-debated theory identifies the model of the military orders, and specifically the Templars, with the "Islamic institution of the *ribāt*, which has been described as a fortified convent whose inmates combined a religious way of life with fighting against the enemies of Islam."[41] Some scholars believe that there is a definite connection.[42] Others, such as Alan Forey, however, argue that this was not likely the case, as there do not seem to have been *ribāts* along the borders of the crusader states in the early twelfth century. More recently, Jörg Feuchter has shown that the concept of the *ribāt* cannot be viewed in the same way as the Christian military orders.[43] The name had many applications, none of which applied to volunteer warriors of specifically religious inclination. Further, interest in *jihad* was only slowly being renewed at the time. Those who were soldiers within these organizations appear to have been secular men, who were only temporarily lodged in the *ribāt*, and had not devoted their entire lives to its service.[44] Forey concludes:

> There is no need to seek an Islamic model for the military order, and to have copied the ribat would in any case not have produced the fusion of the military and religious life that characterised the Christian orders. In fact, no Islamic influence on the Temple can be perceived at all without making ungrounded assumptions, and even then there would still be the obstacle that the Temple differed in its original function from the ribat. It is far easier to relate the military order to early twelfth-century Christian society in the West.[45]

A counter-argument states that this view relies only on the direct evidence, such as is found in chronicles, letters, or other writings, and that since no influence or cross-cultural connections between the concept of the *ribāt* and the military orders is attested to in contemporary writings, the assumption is that it must not have happened at all. The *ribāt* / military order hypothesis may be untenable, but even with a lack of evidence, it is possible that there were greater connections between Christian and Muslim groups through more indirect evidence, such as general cross-cultural connection. The possibility of Templar—Islamic associations is too intriguing and important to ignore or dismiss. It also shows the possibilities of a growing awareness within Christendom of the activities of its religious rival. Taking as an example the concerns of cultural anthropologists, one can see that provable examples of cultural borrowing are rare, as Elena Lourie argues: "What constitutes 'direct evidence' when discussing the problem of cultural borrowing? If not only the act of borrowing, but also the intention or awareness of borrowing, have to be documented in order to establish the fact of borrowing, then, except for the adoption of specific techniques and items of material culture as revealed in a borrowed vocabulary, very few cases of imitation between cultures would ever be proved; for rarely if ever can so exacting a requirement be met."[46]

There are examples which may indicate some indirect borrowing of certain ideas between the two institutions,[47] though these may well have occurred after the formation of Christian military orders. As always, the familiar warning reminds us that "correlation does not equal causation." Given this caveat, it is true that in addition to describing a military organization, the term *ribāt* was used to identify certain other pious organizations, such as hospices and places of prayer and contemplation.[48] This is reminiscent of Christian monastic orders, as well as the duties of the Knights Hospitaller. The strong counter-argument in favor of the military orders being a purely Christian creation rests on their relation to the outcomes of the eleventh-century reforms, and the subsequent benefits granted to crusaders, giving papal sanction to certain kinds of violence, a remarkable change in Church attitude, as we have seen.[49]

2. The Founding of the Order of the Knights Templar

Connected to this debate is an obscure institution founded in Spain in 1122, and thus contemporary with the Templars, the confraternity of Belchite. Perhaps significantly, the following year, the First Lateran Council declared that Spain was of equal value as a location for crusading.[50] The organization was established by Alfonso I of Aragon for the purposes of defending Spanish Christian frontiers and waging war against the Moors. Its key characteristic was that service in the confraternity was temporary, for perhaps a year, after which the individual received a remission for sins equal to having made a pilgrimage to Jerusalem. This in and of itself was astonishing, and was reconfirmed in by Alfonso VII of Castile in 1136. What is most important was that this was essentially a Christian version of the Islamic *ribāt*, which also granted spiritual benefit to temporary soldiers, who lived on frontiers and waged war against the enemies of Islam. One could certainly argue that the resemblance is too close to be a coincidence, and is evidence of some form of borrowing by the Christian forces in response to the continuing Muslim threat on the Spanish frontiers.[51]

The Belchite confraternity could have represented a kind of experiment with the adoption of these Islamic ideas. It must be noted, however, that the Islamic warriors had taken no religious vows and were essentially secular fighters. Further, the idea of temporary religious service was foreign to Christian practices. So, does this prove or disprove borrowing? The leap from this concept to a Christian monastic order is not as great as it may first seem. Indeed, the early Rule of the Templars had vague regulations for the status of temporary knights, who would join for a time as a penance, and then return to the secular world.[52] What was most important was that the members of the confraternity had ecclesiastical approval for their work.

Belchite disappeared about 1136, but it was already something of an anachronism. By that time, the Templars had grown into a much larger and formalized institution with full papal authority and monastic duties. Belchite had never been a true monastic order, because of its temporary service requirements, but in the end, it may have served an important function in helping to integrate two essentially incompatible ideas. Undoubtedly, there is far more to the creation of the Templars than simply following the Belchite model, and it does not seem that the confraternity was absorbed into the Templar structure, but its potential influence should not be dismissed entirely.

Regardless of the Templars' true origins, there is evidence that some members appear not to have joined for the godly reasons of Godfrey and Hugues. It seems that Hugh, Count of Champagne was largely motivated by marital difficulties; his wife, Elizabeth, presented him with a son, Eudes, in about 1117, but Hugh maintained that the boy could not be his, since he was sterile. Hugh had already gone to the east in 1114 and joined the Order of St. John in an attempt to escape from his wife then, though the canonist Ivo of Chartres, compelled him to return. Clearly, there were problems before the contested pregnancy. In 1125, he made another attempt, joining the Templars.[53] This time he was able to remain, probably because of the support he was able to enlist for the order, which shall be discussed presently. The likelihood of this story is strengthened by the fact that Bernard of Clairvaux wrote to him to congratulate him for joining the Order, though he expressed regret that Hugh had not chosen to join the Cistercians instead.[54] If Hugh desired to be away from his wife, the reason for his choosing to join the Templars becomes clearer: the Cistercians had no houses in the East. The Templars, by contrast, were at the time located only in Jerusalem. Thus Hugh enjoyed not only the benefit of being far away from her, but that he was entering a monastic order, and taking the appropriate vows. He had obviously tried this eleven years earlier and failed.[55] Still, even with his patronage, there are few records of Templar activities in the first ten years of their existence.

One reason may be the contradictory nature of the concept of the military order itself. The idea of killing in the name of Christ, as we have seen, had become acceptable under the Reform, and was particularly suitable when directed against Muslims and Northern pagans. The crusader was an armed pilgrim, a previously unthinkable concept. This idea gradually gained general acceptance in Europe, and killing as a remission for sins was seen as a valid demonstration of faith. Despite this, the life of the monk remained separate, an existence detached from the world where the wars fought were spiritual. As noted in chapter one, there were bans on monks joining crusades and they were forbidden to take up arms.[56] The very notion of fighting monks was a contradiction to this theology, despite some French stories from the ninth century that praised monks for battle skills against such opponents as the Vikings.[57]

In the early twelfth century, those who had conceived of the idea were undoubtedly faced with difficulties in reconciling this conflict (particularly if there was any influence, no matter how slight, from Islamic practice). Official papal recognition needed to be obtained if the new order was to have any hope of success. The Belchite confraternity, which was not truly monastic, had been a kind of experiment with a new Christian fighting force which did not last; some time was still needed for the full concept of the military order to take shape and be accepted.

This uncertainty may have been avoided through the use of a technicality in canon law, for while it forbade the clergy to fight, the individual members of the order of the Temple were not actually clerics. The general rule was that prohibitions applied to chaplains, who received tonsure. Lay brethren in monastic communities were simply those who were in the communities, trying to live a more religious life.[58] As such, they could fight when it was deemed necessary.

Despite their obscurity, the Templars had varying support from nobles and kings and occasional Church representatives for ten years, especially in the East, but no official sanction from the Church. This did not come until the Council of Troyes in 1129,[59] and it seems that much of this support came about through political maneuvers. It is likely that the initial request for support for the order by Bernard came from Hugh of Champagne.

Hugh was quite wealthy before joining the Templars and had given generously to many religious houses. He may well have donated the site of Clairvaux to Bernard,[60] so perhaps Bernard felt indebted to him for his generosity.[61] The support of a Church representative of the stature of Bernard would go a long way toward achieving that goal and allowing him to remain in the order; he was mindful that he had already been compelled once before to return to the secular life. In addition, there was almost certainly a connection between Hugh and Hugues; indeed Hugh may well have been attracted to the new Order by his association with Hugues after his attempt with the order of the Hospital failed.[62]

Before the Council, the concept of a military order had not been popularized, and the Templars probably were in danger of disappearing, owing to their lack of members.[63] This, along with Hugh of Champagne's prompting, was the probable impetus for Hugues to ask the greatest theologian of the day, Bernard of Clairvaux, to write a justification of the order, and bring it into the notice of the papacy. Upton-Ward notes that, "The count was therefore in a position to influence Bernard and he may have prompted a letter which purports to be from Baldwin II to Bernard [...] asking him to obtain approval of the Order from the pope. The rise of the Order is probably due to these influential friends, for otherwise the Templars may well not have been singled out from other small communities for recognition as a religious order with papal protection."[64]

A document of uncertain authorship records the status of the Templars at the time. It has been attributed to Hugh of St. Victor (a leading German theologian living in Paris), though it is more likely to be from Hugues de Payens.[65] It defends the position of the Templars, showing how they resist temptations and protect Christians from the infidel and evil, for the devil does not sleep.[66] Given the situation, the writer asserts that it is therefore not wrong to kill, because what the Templars hate are not men, but evil, and any booty seized from such battles is justly taken.[67] The language is very reminiscent of Bernard's justification, *De laude*, and it is likely that he had a copy in his possession when he wrote his treatise.[68] It also bears some resemblance to the Cistercian Isaac of Stella's words in his attack on the novelty of the military orders and their illicit taking of spoils of war, which we will examine in more detail in chapter four.

If the letter is indeed from Hugues, such assertions raise questions about the Templars' self-identity. The reasoning employed seems to be an attempt to convince those in positions of authority of the validity of the order's activities, as much as being purely a statement of religious conviction. It is as if the Templars had already come under criticism, or were in a desperate situation. Perhaps the knights were demoralized, and with the uncertainty of the concept of a military order lingering, this missive was probably an attempt to turn the tide of events in their favor.[69]

From the Council of Troyes, a Rule was drawn up for the order, based on the Benedictine and Cistercian models. Given that the order had been in existence for some ten years, it already had a fairly strict set of regulations. The original Rule was in Latin, though a French translation appeared sometime between 1136 and 1149.[70] This was because the knights themselves were not always educated in the manner of traditional monks, often having been warriors who desired to retire from secular life. As such, they needed a Rule in their own language, rather than Latin, which most brothers could not understand.

Once the Church legitimized the general concept of the military order, it gained a wider acceptance, and others began to appear. Indeed, within ten years of the Templars gaining recognition, the Hospitallers, "are recorded hiring mercenaries to protect pilgrims. The work was too much for one order alone."[71]

The Hospitallers, also known as the of Order St. John, would have had the same concerns regarding the protection of pilgrims in the early years of the twelfth century, and so they began their own transformation from a purely charitable organization of hospice and care for the sick, into one of equal martial skill to the Templars.[72] There was probably a good deal of uncertainty about the validity of creating military orders that could survive and grow, until it became clear that the Church would recognize and approve of them. Remember that Bernard initially showed reluctance to write a justification for the Templars, though he claimed that this was due to humility.[73] Clearly, the idea of holy killing did not always rest easily with Bernard's beliefs, though he championed the cause of the Second Crusade with great zeal. He also seems to have incorporated apocalypticism into his arguments in order to justify the violent measures which the concept of the military order demanded.[74]

Some of Bernard's contemporaries held different and even dissenting views about the Templars, the disapproving sermon of Isaac of Stella, for example, though many writings of the period are more favorable. Some writers, such as Orderic Vitalis, an English monk of St. Evroul in Normandy, stated that the Templars were worthy of admiration and faced becoming martyrs on a daily basis.[75] Richard of Poitou, a Cluniac monk also wrote approvingly in 1153, saying that the Templars were crucial in helping the Franks to maintain their hold on Jerusalem and the Holy Land.[76] One writer, Anselm, Bishop of Havelburg, managed to credit Pope Urban II with approving the Templars, a clever piece of invented history that linked them to the First Crusade, and thus emphasized its holy function.[77]

Several popes commented on the order at various times, as it continued its rapid growth. This chapter opened with the commentary of Celestine II, who wrote approvingly of the Templars in a papal bull 1144, stating that they imitated Christ by denying themselves and were the "new Maccabees," and suggesting that they deserved support and donations.[78] The papal charter for the Templars, given by Innocent II in 1139, made use of similar themes, likening the Templars to the Israelites, and invoking the virtues of love and charity among the brothers, in a manner akin to that of the non-hateful warrior extolled by Anselm and Ivo in the previous century.[79] The comparison between the Templars and the great warriors of the Old Testament finds a parallel, as we shall see, in Bernard's justification for the order, written only slightly earlier,[80] which sought to ground the new concept firmly in biblical tradition.

The origin of the Templars bears some resemblance to that of the Cistercians, as both were relatively obscure organizations founded on religious idealism in the wake of the effects of the Reform. They continued to view Bernard as the founder of the order throughout their existence.[81] This is not an entirely false view. It was Bernard who sought their approval from the pope, drew up their Rule, and wrote the justification, *De laude*. In a sense they were little or nothing before Bernard's efforts, and he made them into something far greater. Thus, he was in a very real way their founder.

Bernard's language and motivations bear resemblance to those during the initial call to the crusade in the late eleventh century: to bring order to Christendom by turning the attentions of the knights away from earthly pleasures to a higher cause, one that would ensure salvation and bring unity to the West. As we shall see in the next chapter, the Templars came to represent for him the perfect marriage of chivalry and piety, one to which all knights should aspire.

The knights were soon to stray from their avowed purpose of fighting the infidels, however, and it seems that from an early stage, they were becoming involved in secular conflicts and political disputes, which often wore the mask of religious motive.[82] Rivalries erupted in the 1130s between the Frankish, Armenian, and Greek inhabitants of Syria. A place called the Amanus March (north of Damascus) was still said by the Byzantine Empire to be its own territory. However, it came under the protection of the Templars, in a deliberate act of defiance of that claim. The message was clear: the Franks were counter-claiming this land for Latin Christendom, and would not suffer attacks from Muslims, Armenians, or Greeks without fierce retaliation.[83] Further, the Templars had the muscle to back up the threat, and were willing to use it.

The Templars were already at this early stage being used as a political fighting force as much as a religious one. To be sure, such conflicts were clothed in the rhetoric of religious ideals, but it seems that the Templars were quickly adopted as Frankish military elite; the interests of the Church were also the interests of the Franks. The distinction between politics and religion was often vague in frontier societies such as Spain and the Holy Land.[84] The papal position on this new belligerence against the Greeks was one of guarded support, as its own rivalry with the Eastern Church allowed it to sanction action against Byzantium at times.[85]

To conclude, the founding and existence of the Templars had become a far more complex affair than the simple notion of protecting Western pilgrims. While that motivation was certainly present, it was not the only issue. The Church needed to address the Muslim threat to pilgrims journeying to Jerusalem and other holy sites, but it was also becoming apparent that settlements themselves were in danger of attack, owing to a lack of reinforcements and low population. On a secular level, economic factors probably also contributed, with increasing worry about the effects of trade in the region. Most important was the issue of religion. Christendom could not afford to be weak (or equally importantly, appear to be weak), even helpless in preventing Muslim incursions.

The Christian West saw itself as righteous in victory. The success of the crusade was the culmination and reward for those shifts in theological teachings begun in the previous century. It surely must have offered proof to a newly-united Christendom that God had indeed willed the invasion of the Holy Land to conquer it in his name. The confidence of the papacy and the Church as a whole was in part strengthened by the existence of a strong Christian Kingdom of Jerusalem established with the blessing of God. Enemies of all kinds needed to be resisted, and resisted strongly.

As such, the inability of the city to control the surrounding areas, even near its own walls, by the early 1100s, was a serious development, and could

2. The Founding of the Order of the Knights Templar

have thrown the faith of untold numbers of potential pilgrims into doubt. The later theological justifications for both the fall of various kingdoms and regions, and the subsequent failures of the crusades to retake them show how serious an issue this was to the medieval Church.

The Templars were a response to this very real threat, but one with an uncertain future. While they remained in such small numbers, theirs was an impossible task; they needed the support and approval of official ecclesiastical bodies in order to survive, prosper, and undertake the tasks that they had set for themselves. At the same time, the very notion of a military order, with all its inherent contradictions, had not yet gained Church approval, though the non-monastic Belchite confraternity already had. Whether they were aware of events in Spain or not, the founders of the Templars would have known that they had not yet attained a similar designation, and so they were not able to be fully effective. It would take a Church representative of the stature of Bernard of Clairvaux to do what a king, a patriarch, and various French noblemen could not: gain papal acceptance for this new approach to dealing with the Muslim threat.

It is to his work, *De laude novae militiae* that we now turn. This landmark treatise was to have tremendous importance in succeeding centuries, leading to not only the necessary papal support the Templars needed, but also creating an accepted theology of combining the duties of monk and knight, that most difficult synthesis. An idea that had started in the previous century under Gregory VII as a means of creating a justifiable Christian army became, with Bernard's skills, something far more than Gregory had envisioned. Bernard was able to produce a convincing argument for the sanctity of killing done by monk-like representatives of the Church, and for the validity of violence in defense of the faith.

3

Bernard of Clairvaux's *In Praise of the New Knighthood*

His frame was emaciated from his self-inflicted depravations. His lack of concern for the meager and poor quality of the food he ate led to the development of a severe and painful stomach ailment, possibly an ulcer. His frailty hardly gave any hint of his true character, yet his eloquent words moved untold numbers of people, and his enthusiasm and vigor for his faith were boundless. It is a great irony that this physically weak man was to oversee the establishment of the Knights Templar, whose strength and ferocity in battle were to become legendary.

Bernard of Clairvaux's support for the Knights Templar is one of the most important aspects of the crusading movement in the first half of the twelfth century. It shows the extent to which the Reform had been successful in transforming the act of war from a sin requiring penance to an act of penance itself. The union of the armed knight and the cloistered, peaceful monk was masterfully achieved in the Templars, and Bernard, while slow in writing his defense of the Order, nevertheless committed himself to the enterprise wholeheartedly once he actually began it.[1]

Though Bernard, as much as any religious representative of his time, objected to the mingling of the sacred and the secular, he made an exception for the Order of the Temple. G.R. Evans has noted that, "Bernard saw [the Templar's duties] as an acting out in the external world of the spiritual warfare in every Christian soul. They were a living image of the battle between good and evil, virtue and vice in which he wanted every monk consciously engaged."[2]

It was probably at his request that the order was granted papal approval, for he drew up their Rule in 1128. As discussed in the previous chapter, his justification for the order, *De laude Novae Militiae ad Milites Templi* ("In

Praise of the New Knighthood"), was likely written at the request of Hugues, followed a few years later.[3] This work will be examined in more detail here. As we have seen, Bernard's support for the Templars arose in part from his good relationship with Hugh, Count of Champagne, a generous patron of religious houses, and perhaps the donor of the site for the abbey of Clairvaux. He eventually joined the Templars, after a series of marital troubles.[4]

Due to this unusual situation, we may wonder about the extent of Bernard's sincerity in writing the tract. Indeed, Bernard certainly took some time to write *De laude*, and admits this in his prologue, where he cites humility as his central reason, a common but not always insightful medieval disclaimer.[5] However, remember that Bernard was also rather slow to preach the Second Crusade, and seems only to have done so under papal pressure. Once he began his work, to be sure, he gave it his enthusiastic support, as he did with the Templars. The hesitancy in both cases, suggests a man with many duties spreading himself too thin. His often-mentioned poor health was a result of both his very austere lifestyle and of pushing himself too hard in his work; his already frail form was unable to cope.

Certainly, he would also have had reservations about killing, and did not support indiscriminate violence. Indeed, he cautioned that the Templar must be a monk first, a "spiritual warrior" who from time to time would be called to arms when necessary,[6] and he found it important to distinguish between the Templars and the secular knighthood. The former he designated as *militia*, the latter he punned as *malitia*. To him the Templars were the only knights of worth, as they upheld both chivalric ideals and maintained monastic vows. Their struggle against Saracen incursions was seen as the true embodiment of the Gregorian *milites Christi*. Bernard was quick to condemn what he saw as the young fops that knights had become, more concerned with the status of their clothing and hair than with the state of their souls. They spent their time hunting, engaging in war games at tournaments, and fighting each other over minor grievances. He had a hope that his new treatise would act as an enticement to these young men, drawing them away from their decadent and sinful lives and into a noble and holy cause.[7]

Bernard viewed the Order of the Temple and later, the act of crusading as an excellent means of attaining salvation, particularly for these noble boys, as well as for criminals and society's outcasts, all of those who appeared to him to have no hope otherwise. He was particularly pleased with the notion of winning over criminals and reprobates to the cause, as he states in *De laude*:

> [...] What could be more profitable and pleasant to behold than seeing such a multitude coming to reinforce the few? What, if not the twofold joy of seeing the conversion of these former impious rogues, sacrilegious thieves, murderers,

perjurers and adulterers? A twofold joy and a twofold benefit, as their countrymen are as glad to be rid of them as their new comrades are to receive them. Both sides have profited from this exchange, since the latter are strengthened and the former are now left in peace.[8]

In other words, he wanted to send Europe's dregs to the Holy Land, believing that the sacredness of that region and their mission would make new men of them. It was a win/win situation. However, this hopeful vision often failed to materialize. While it was true that the Templars attracted a specific and more dedicated form of follower, those who became crusaders were a different matter entirely, coming from all walks of twelfth-century life. Bernard didn't seem to understand that the murderers and thieves who went on crusade very often continued being murderers and thieves, both during and after their pilgrimages. They may have desired at the outset to do something about the precarious status of their souls, but this does not mean that they were always able to hold to that vow. Some probably never intended to do anything but seek plunder. The hoped-for conversion to a pious life could be a rather rare thing.[9]

Bernard, it seems, was over-optimistic in his assessment of the potential of this massive relocation effort. There was also concern that the Templars themselves at this early stage were not above indulging in certain secular activities while justifying them religiously. Peter Partner notes that:

> Hugues de Payns assured the Templars that they must not succumb to the temptation of thinking that they killed in a spirit of hate and fury, nor that they seized booty in a spirit of greed. For the Templars did not hate men, but men's wrongdoing; and when they seized booty from unbelievers they did so justly, because of the sins of the unbeliever and also because they had won the booty by their own labour, and "the labourer is worthy of his hire." The last may seem a naïve apology but it reflects the fact that much Templar time and energy was spent in plundering.[10]

So we find that Bernard's model knights could be as guilty of wanting and acquiring the spoils of war as any secular soldier, and furthermore, they seemed to spend a good deal of time making up excuses as to why this was acceptable.

Nevertheless, it was his desire for a different kind of warrior that allowed Bernard to confront the contradictions that existed between a religion theoretically dedicated to peace and the wars being waged in the Holy Land in the name of Christ. In assuming that becoming a soldier for Christianity would raise one from the lowest sinful position and elevate him to the ranks of the blessed, Bernard had found for himself a way of bringing together two essentially incompatible ideas.[11]

Something must be said here of Bernard's philosophical attachment to the Temple of Jerusalem, and his use of it in his writings. His imagery in connecting the earthly Temple with the spiritual one, and the individual "temple" of each Christian's soul has parallels in his writings in support of the Templars. This theological observation was drawn from the Pauline view of Christians as individual temples of the Holy Spirit.[12] He developed this theme in a collection of six sermons for feasts connected to church dedication.[13] Significantly, he likens the monastic community itself to a temple. Monks do not wield weapons (nor should they), but in their spiritual life, they defend the Temple. Their austere daily practices (prayer, humility, obedience) allow them to engage in this "warfare" against Satan and the forces of evil. The monastery is a place to be guarded against diabolic incursions, by monastic "soldiers." Their Temple of Jerusalem is one of the spirit, and is defended daily.[14]

The clear parallels between this monastic theology and his support for the Templars will be shown below. Much of the portion of *De laude* devoted to the Templars praises them for just these virtues. This is a new monastic community that fights not only on the spiritual level but, uniquely, on the physical level as well, and in doing so protects the earthly Temple, while defending the spiritual Temple with their faith.

Another connection that Bernard draws is between monks and angels. He stresses that the cloistered life prefigures heaven, and that the monks will take the place of the fallen angels.[15] The implications for the Templars are striking, effectively becoming fighting "angels" on earth, and show the degree to which such military thinking had penetrated into Church teaching by the early twelfth century.[16]

Note that while this type of thought developed from the Reform, Bernard's writings were not the only or first ones to discuss the issue of monks and the use of violence. A remarkable collection of miracles of St. Benedict was collected for over three centuries by the monks of Fleury Abbey in the Loire Valley.[17] These stories relate many miracles performed by Benedict on behalf of the faithful monks, and stress how his wrath and the wrath of God are brought down upon sinners and evil doers.[18] There are astonishing accounts of monastic violence contained within these stories, including an attack by Muslims on the abbey. One tale notes that the Saracens besiege the abbey, as well as the surrounding villages and manors. The monks flee, but regroup and prepare to go out to battle the invaders. Before engaging them, however, the monks invoke St. Benedict and make various charms and artifacts to carry with them to ensure victory.[19]

A more remarkable account can be found in a story of the seizure of the abbey by brigands. A group of outlaws is able to occupy the abbey by force, but the monks do not remain passive. The prior leads them in an armed resistance, again under the protection of St. Benedict. The description of the conflict contains all of the references one would expect in a scene of battle (arrows, fires, accounts of the dead and dying, even plunder). In the end the bandits flee, with thirty of their men having been killed in the fighting. The monks, by contrast, have lost only three, but these died only because their desire was for violence and fighting for its own sake, and thus they were punished.[20] Those who remained faithful and pure were unharmed.

This story bears a striking resemblance to the chronicles of the crusading campaigns in the East, with all of their violence and religious presuppositions, and the miraculous intervention of holy forces on behalf of the just, as well as the emphasis that the warrior must fight for God's glory, not his own. Though there is little evidence that these miracle accounts had any influence on the development of crusading theology, or of Bernard's own thought, nevertheless they are noteworthy for their casual acceptance of violence and the necessity for monks to resort to it in times of need. Jean Leclercq attributes this to a reaction to the violent times in which the monks lived, particularly in the centuries prior to the twelfth.[21]

Regardless of their commitment to peace, monks were at all times surrounded by violence. Indeed, soldiers and warriors often donated lands to and became patrons for monastic institutions. Abbeys were walled and locked against the outside world, as much for protection as seclusion; these enclaves of spiritual peace were also stone fortresses against some very real dangers. Monks themselves were not immune to aggressive tendencies, and numerous accounts exist of censures and punishments for violent acts committed within monastic communities.[22] This understanding of violence as a part of life certainly had an influence on the acceptance (by both the clergy and the laity) of the crusades and military orders as necessary and even desirable.[23]

Such an understanding allowed for the violent incidents recorded in the Benedict miracle stories, though the purpose of these was not to entertain, but to instruct. In the end, though violent acts are committed, goodness and justice always triumph. These stories, certainly embellished and fanciful, provided a kind of *exempla* for the proper conduct and way of thinking that their monastic audiences were expected to exhibit. Tales of military struggle represented the combat of the soul that monks engaged in daily; only faith in God and the saints ensured victory.

Such martial imagery appears in several of Bernard's other writings. These are worth noting, as they show the extent of his thinking outside of that specifically related to crusading and the Knights of the Temple. It is obvious that Bernard was steeped in military thought and imagery, being a soldier's son. William of Saint-Thierry records that Bernard's father, Tescelin le Sor, believed in the legitimacy of the military profession, and served God faithfully.[24]

Bernard continued to have contact with the military, and significantly, often sought soldiers as converts for the Cistercian Order.[25] William of Saint-Thierry records how on one occasion Bernard implored a group of soldiers to lay down their arms during Lent. When they refused, he offered beer to them which he had blessed. Having drunk this, the soldiers departed, but soon returned, eager to enter into the monastic life.[26]

Though the story is dubious, Bernard was known for his commitment to convincing military men to forsake their violent and secular ways and devote themselves to God. William records that such was Bernard's success in obtaining these recruits, that when he sought them at various castles and noble residences, wives and friends would try to hold back the eager young men, and mothers would hide their sons.[27] There is an element of humor in this account, but it nevertheless illustrates the abbot's appeal and charisma. This was no doubt due to Bernard's own deep commitment to the monastic way of life, and as with his preaching of the Second Crusade, his enthusiasm was infectious.

Bernard obviously had considerable experience with the world of the soldier, and this is reflected in *De laude*, wherein his criticisms of secular knights contain much accurate detail about their practices and pastimes. David Carlson notes that, "the Cistercian practice of adult recruitment meant that many monks, including Bernard himself, entered the monastery at Clairvaux, as they did other Cistercian monasteries, with some first-hand experience of chivalry and courtly love and often with literary experience of it as well."[28]

Indeed, Bernard was rumored to have possessed literary talents in the field of secular writing, and it is possible that he may have written some courtly verse at one time in his youth.[29] If this is true, such works have yet to be identified and attributed, if they even survive. This part of his youth would have certainly tainted Bernard's opinion of the knightly class following his conversion, for thereafter he never ceased to heap scorn on this secular way of life. If he had once written verses that extolled the knight's life, or even worse, love poems, they would have been a huge source of embarrassment to him!

In any case, Bernard set all of that behind him, but retained his admiration for things military, seeing the monk's life as one of spiritual warfare. In a letter to the Premonstratensians (a monastic order founded in 1120 near Laon in northern France), He referred to monks as "soldiers of peace," invoking *Ephesians* 6:12, with its warning of evil spiritual forces as the true enemies.[30]

His *Sententiae* have numerous references to weaponry and warfare, as metaphors for the spiritual struggle.[31] In one notable example, Bernard uses the metaphor of arrows (in groups of three) to "wound" the opponent before closing in to finish him off.[32] Another example contrasts the arms of virtue with the arms of evil.[33] At the beginning of his lengthy sermons on the *Song of Songs*, he again uses military images to describe the monastic life.[34]

Yet Bernard was also noted for his strong opposition to secular warfare, which features prominently in his justification of the Templars. In a letter to King Louis VII, for example, he condemns such wars as the devil's works, which only bring misery and suffering.[35] It is this curious contrast that makes his Templar treatise so unusual and worthy of examination.

It may seem odd that the same author who could condemn war for the misery it brings to the innocent could also endorse those same actions against the perceived enemies of Christendom. However, contemporary values and standards do not apply to an individual who would not have known or understood them. Bernard shows none of the same concern for the families of Muslims and other enemies of the faith save for a cautionary note in the treatise that the "pagans" should only be killed if necessary. We shall return to this comment presently.

De laude Novae Militiae is unusual in its content, since less than half of the work is specifically concerned with a defense and "praise" of the Templars. Only the first five chapters are devoted to the Templars and Bernard's justification. Chapters six to thirteen consist of descriptions in theological terms (and with much biblical referencing) of the various holy places which the Templars are given the honor of defending. However, the text only appears to be disjointed at first, for in naming beloved locations such as Bethlehem, Nazareth, and Calvary in a work devoted to praising the order, Bernard draws a strong link between the two, and strengthens their cause. The places named follow, in chronological order, the major areas associated with Christ in his lifetime, beginning with Bethlehem and ending with Calvary and the Holy Sepulcher. These are not ordered in any geographical order, but rather in the order in which Christ visited them in his lifetime. Thus, the Templars are given a model for their own lives, a form of the *imitatio Christi* which is unique for them, because they can walk not only on the spiritual path, but also the actual physical path of Christ. These chapters place a special emphasis on Christ's death, a central concern of the treatise as a whole, for the death of the secular knight was dangerous, but for the Templar it was salvation. For Bernard, the Templars alone were the true inheritors of the *imitatio Christi* of the First Crusade.[36]

All of this was necessary primarily because the Templars were a "new

3. Bernard of Clairvaux's In Praise of the New Knighthood 65

knighthood," and did not have a long tradition to support their existence, or indeed, a clear precedent for their type of function. Any justification would have to make links between the traditional holy places and the order to ensure its validity.[37]

In Bernard's portrayal, the Templars were depicted as inseparable from the lands that they defended, becoming a chosen order. A sense of the will of God was invoked, recalling the crusader's cry: "God wills it." Bernard is careful to make the association by ending his treatise with great confidence in the Templar cause, and stressing the universality of their mission, the defense of Jerusalem:

> [...] These delights of our world, this heavenly treasure and this heritage of all believers is now entrusted to your care, beloved brothers. It is confided to your bravery and prudence. [...] Ever say, "Not unto us, O Lord, not unto us give glory, but unto your own name," so that in all things he might be blessed who teaches your hands for war and your fingers for the fight.[38]

This quote from Psalm 113 became the official motto of the Templars, and summed up concisely the entirety of Bernard's justification: the Templars existed for the glory of God, not for their own glory. This theme will be discussed in more detail below.

Throughout the work there are extensive biblical references, employed by Bernard for the purpose of showing scriptural support for the new knighthood.[39] A full analysis of these would form a study in itself, but it is worth some attention here to discuss the role of monastic biblical exegesis during this period, so as to understand its importance in relation to the concerns of the time. Monastic authors wrote and commented prolifically on the Bible, both in its relation to spiritual matters and to the affairs of daily life.[40]

Two principal factors in monastic interpretation of scriptural texts include what Leclercq calls "biblical imagination,"[41] or the ability of the texts to evoke strong images in the minds of the readers, and "exegesis by reminiscence." This second technique, which he notes is somewhat akin to rabbinic practice, involved "explaining one verse by another verse in which the same word occurs,"[42] so that different passages took on new meanings in relation to one another. He describes: "As it was, thanks to the medieval mastication of the words, the Bible came to be learned 'by heart.' In this way, one can spontaneously supply a text or a word which corresponds to the situation described in each text, and which explains each separate word. One becomes a sort of living concordance, a living library [...]"[43]

Thus, monastic exegetes were able to draw upon a vast array of biblical texts to explain and supplement their commentaries on any given verse or situation described. These might seem baffling to those not schooled in this technique, but are logical within the confines of the tradition. Bernard's use of a large number of biblical quotations and allusions throughout his treatise becomes more understandable in view of this practice. As we saw in the introduction, the Old and New Testaments were viewed as inseparable documents of the history of the Church. The Templars are set by Bernard against the background of extensive biblical referencing, helping to show that they are indeed in keeping with the scriptural traditions of both testaments. They are a part of unfolding Church history, and are a new miracle from God, uniquely ordained to combat evil and do his will on earth.

What follows is a survey and summary of the first five chapters of *De laude*, those that are concerned with the Order and the justifications for its existence. The work begins by directly discussing the presence of the Templars in the Holy Land, and the significance of that occurrence:

> It seems that a New Knighthood has recently appeared on the earth, and precisely in that part of it which the Orient from on high visited in the flesh. As he then troubled the princes of darkness in the strength of his mighty hand, so there he now wipes out their followers, the children of disbelief, scattering them by the hands of his mighty ones. [...] This is, I say, a new kind of knighthood and one unknown to the ages gone by. It ceaselessly wages a twofold war both against the flesh and blood and against a spiritual army of evil in the heavens.[44]

Here Bernard begins with high praise for the order, and is eager to stress the revolutionary nature of its activities. He also makes quite clear his views of the enemy that they face. Bernard has been described as somewhat indifferent to the threat that Islam as a belief system posed to Christendom. Indeed, he declined Peter the Venerable's request to write a polemical attack on Islam, necessitating that Peter undertake the task himself.[45] Bernard was certainly more concerned with heresies closer to home. Nevertheless, this and other statements in *De laude* show that he did not take the matter lightly.[46] Bernard refers to the Templars' chief enemies, the Muslims, as "pagans" rather than heretics throughout. There could be a number of reasons for this, but most likely, Bernard is simply grouping together all of the enemies of Christians from the area. He is not concerned about the nature of Islam (as Peter would be), but rather about the growing threat from all sides that Christians in the Latin Holy Land faced, and how the Templars answer that threat. To his mind, Saracens, Greeks, and heathens are all worthy of scorn and must be resisted, so "pagan" is as good a derogatory term as any. The focus, after all, is on the New Knighthood, not their foes.

The remainder of the first chapter introduces the "two swords" doctrine (one physical and one spiritual, an important Bernardine concept), and the glory of the martyrdom which each Templar should seek. He describes the

3. *Bernard of Clairvaux's* In Praise of the New Knighthood   67

dual nature of the Templars' armor and weaponry, and again praises their novelty:

> [...] But when the one sees a man powerfully girding himself with both swords and nobly marking his belt, who would not consider it worthy of all wonder, the more so since it has been hitherto unknown? He is truly a fearless knight and secure on every side, for his soul is protected by armor and steel. He is thus doubly armed and need fear neither demons nor men. Not that he fears death — no, he desires it.[47]

The doctrine of the two swords was drawn from Luke 22:38, [...] *Domine, ecce duo gladii hic. At ille dixit eis: Satis est* ("The disciples said, 'See, Lord, here are two swords.' 'That is enough' he replied."). Bernard saw every aspect of the Templars' lives and mission in dual terms, for they were to be ever-mindful of their spiritual commitments, resorting to the sword and to battle when necessary. The theme of the two swords is taken up again in chapter three of the treatise, which we will examine below.

Bernard stresses that the Templar desires a holy death. He does not adequately explain this ideology, but rather seems merely to reinforce crusading ideology, again using biblical reference as a support:

> [...] and in every peril repeat, "Whether we live or whether we die, we are the Lord's." [Rom. 14:8]. What a glory to return in victory from such a battle! How blessed to die there as a martyr! [...] Life indeed is a fruitful thing and victory is glorious, but a holy death is more important than either. If they are blessed who die in the Lord, how much more are they who die for the Lord![48]

We shall return to the theme of martyrdom in chapter seven. Bernard is not advocating that the Templars adopt a suicidal desire, but rather advocates for their sacrifice. Indeed, John 15:13, "Greater love has no one than this, that he lay down his life for his friends," was frequently cited in Templar documents, including papal bulls and privileges. The Templars were living this ideal, as true imitators of Christ.[49] He also uses this imagery of self-sacrifice as a kind of segue to his scathing attack on the secular knighthood, which follows in chapter two. He concludes chapter one with a final justification for Christian violence, a theme to which he returns in chapter three. It is the attitude of the fighter which Bernard considers to be of the greatest importance:

> Indeed, danger or victory for a Christian depends on the dispositions of his heart and not on the fortunes of war. If he fights for a good reason, the issue of his fight can never be evil [...][50]

Chapter two does not concern the Templars directly, but rather contrasts the ways of the "old knighthood" with them. Bernard condemns these secular knights for their showy, extravagant nature, and asks of what use these articles and outer trappings are, when the knights are so sinful underneath:

> [...] You cover your horses with silk, and plume your armor with I know not what sort of rags; you paint your shields and your saddles; you adorn your bits and spurs with gold and silver and precious stones, and then in all this glory you rush to your ruin with fearful wrath and fearless folly. Are these the trappings of a warrior or are they not rather the trinkets of a woman? Do you think the swords of your foes will be turned back by your gold, spare your gold or be unable to pierce your silks?[51]

As noted, he was quite familiar with military and courtly practices, and clearly detested them. Here, he is derogatory and insulting, equating the marks of secular knighthood with ruin and emasculation. Bernard concludes this section by deriding the knights for their effeminate dress, and their decision to take up the life of the knight solely for material gain and earthly glory. These, he states are not good reasons:

> It certainly is not safe to kill or to be killed for such causes as these.[52]

Knights who die under such circumstances have lost not only their lives foolishly, but also the possibility of salvation for their souls. The remedy for this problem, he says, lies in the way of life adopted by the Templars, and it is with this in mind that he begins chapter three. The theme throughout this chapter is the justification of Christian violence, and its application to acceptable forms of war. As we have seen, this idea was not new, and was not invented by Bernard. There had existed for some time the notion that violence was a morally neutral act, even if it was to be shunned by Christians. It was the intention of the individual performing the act that was called into question. An example would be the amputation by a surgeon of a limb infected with gangrene, a violent act to be sure, and one which would involve immense pain and potentially hysterical resistance from the patient. The end result, however was to save that person's life, and therefore the act of violence was clearly justified.[53]

Bernard's great intellectual rival Peter Abelard (1079–1142), a renowned logician, philosopher, and scholastic lecturer in Paris, wrote in his *Ethics* about the problem of labeling acts morally good or evil, including a discussion of violence. While his views were not necessarily representative of the general theology of the time, they nevertheless merit some attention. David Luscombe summarizes:

> The point is made effectively in Abelard's discussion of the killing of one person by another. This too is a purely physical act, and as such it is one hundred percent morally neutral. The blade of a sword goes into a body and death fol-

3. Bernard of Clairvaux's In Praise of the New Knighthood 69

lows; what has happened is neither right nor wrong. What is right or wrong is the decision taken by the person wielding the sword. He may have swung the sword accidentally; he may have been acting under orders; he may have failed to understand properly what his orders really meant; he may have acted in self-defence; he may invincibly have mistaken his victim's identity; he may have surrendered to the desire to murder someone he loathes. What matters finally, at least in the sight of God, is why he did it, not what was done.[54]

Abelard further states that it goes beyond the physical act, to the mind. One can intend to kill and be thwarted, for example, yet the intention to sin was there. God will judge based on one's thoughts. Bernard also stresses this point: that the act of killing in the case of the Templars is for the glory of God.

Chapter three of *De laude* contains a detailed discussion on the nature of the Templars' unique duties. Here, Bernard has no hesitancy at all in proclaiming the righteousness of the use of violence. Bernard's is an angry God who delights in the death of his enemies at the hands of his faithful servants:[55]

> But the knights of Christ may safely fight the battles of their Lord, fearing neither sin if they smite the enemy, nor danger at their own death, since to inflict death or to die for Christ is no sin, but rather an abundant claim to glory. In the first case one gains for Christ, and in the second, one gains Christ himself. [...] The knight of Christ, I say, may strike with confidence and die yet more confidently, for he serves Christ when he strikes, and serves himself when he falls. Neither does he bear the sword in vain, for he is God's minister [Rom. 13:4], for the punishment of evildoers and for the praise of the good. If he kills an evildoer, he is not a mankiller, but, if I may so put it, a killer of evil. He is evidently the avenger of Christ towards evildoers.[56]

Bernard has here removed the taint of sin from the Templars and their duties; their actions are simply the will of God, and if they are carried out properly, they glorify him. Their swords can be the ministers of God's will. Killing in this case is not murder, but the killing of God's enemies.[57] Bernard displays a great confidence in his assertions, which vividly reveals his convictions about it all.

He then turns his attention to the enemies that the Templars must face, primarily the Muslims. He makes clear his intentions toward them and how the Templars should respond to their presence in the Holy Land:

> The Christian glories in the death of the pagan, because Christ is glorified; while the death of the Christian gives occasion for the King to show his liberality in the rewarding of his knight.[58]

However, he adds:

> I do not mean to say that the pagans are to be slaughtered when there is any other way to prevent them from harassing and persecuting the faithful [...][59]

This is immediately qualified once again to justify the Templars' position:

> [...] but only that it now seems better to destroy them than that the rod of sinners be lifted over the lot of the just, and the righteous perhaps put forth their hands unto iniquity.[60]

As a defense of the position that it is acceptable for the Christian to wield the sword, Bernard draws upon a reference in the *Gospel of Luke*, wherein John the Baptist tells the soldiers to be content with their wages[61]:

> What then? If it is never permissible for a Christian to strike with the sword, why did the Saviour's precursor bid the soldiers to be content with their pay, and not rather forbid them to follow this calling?[62]

Bernard employs a clever logic here, i.e., that something is permitted because it is not specifically prohibited,[63] and argues that the calling of the soldier is permitted to those so destined by God, and who more deservedly so than the Templars, who now protect the Holy City?[64] It was the best way he could imagine that an approval of holy war could be deduced from a religion that commanded its followers to turn the other cheek. Though violence against sinners could be neutral, it nevertheless only could be lawfully inflicted by the pious, such as the Templars.

He returns to the nature of the enemy, and revives his "two swords" model. He accuses them of thievery, and of attempting to claim the rightful heritage of Christianity as their own:

> They busy themselves to carry away the incalculable riches placed in Jerusalem by the Christian peoples, to profane the holy things and to possess the sanctuary of God as their heritage.[65]

This is followed by a brutal recommendation for the proper treatment of these "transgressors of divine law"[66]:

> Let both swords of the faithful fall upon the necks of the foe, in order to destroy every high thing exalting itself against the knowledge of God, which is the Christian faith [...][67]

Bernard is committed to the removal of Muslims by any means, and with these words seems not to have a preference for one method over another. He is just as willing to call for the killing of the enemy as to try to "attack" them with faith. They may be pierced with the sword of faith, or they may be killed with the sword of steel. This again shows his fervent adherence to the dual nature of the Templars, and he is very comfortable with their duties both as monks and soldiers.

The remainder of the chapter is devoted to Old Testament imagery,

3. Bernard of Clairvaux's In Praise of the New Knighthood

which he employs to show how the Templars are the actual fulfillment of biblical prophecy. He particularly makes use of the texts with exile themes:

> Here is the help sent to you from the Holy One! Through them is already fulfilled the ancient promise, "I will make you the pride of the ages, a joy from generation to generation. [...]" Do you not see how frequently these ancient witnesses foreshadowed the new knighthood? Truly, as we have heard, so we have now seen in the city the Lord of the armies.[68]

He adds that while all Christians should be encouraged by this literal fulfillment of the texts, nevertheless they should be mindful of the spiritual meanings as well, for the faithful should continue to live in hope for the future.[69] In addition, they should remember that while the earthly Jerusalem is a glory for all, it does not take the place of the heavenly Jerusalem:

> Furthermore, the temporal glory of the earthly city does not eclipse the glory of its heavenly counterpart, but rather prepares for it, at least so long as we remember that the one is the figure of the other, and that it is the heavenly one which is our mother.[70]

The first sections of chapter four are once again devoted to the contrast between the Templars and the secular knights for whom Bernard has such disdain. It is a theme with which he almost seems obsessed. He describes the lifestyle of the Temple knight and contrasts it sharply with the sinful life of the secular knight. Bernard includes a very brief summary of their Rule, and attempts to demonstrate how they carry out monastic duties with faith, obedience, and piety, unlike their secular counterparts.[71] In the second half, he returns to contrast with secular knights, this time to show how the Templars make use of his unique role to be unlike them:

> When the battle is at hand, they arm themselves interiorly with faith and exteriorly with steel rather than decorate themselves with gold, since their business is to strike fear in the enemy rather than to incite his cupidity.[72]

He then praises their fierceness and fearlessness in battle, for they seek not their own glory, but rather that of God (unlike their counterparts). They have set aside such desires and are focused solely upon the task at hand, relying on their faith in God to grant them victory, for victory comes from no other source:

> Once he finds himself in the thick of battle, this knight sets aside his previous gentleness, as if to say, "Do I not hate those who hate you, O Lord; am I not disgusted with your enemies?" These men at once fall violently upon the foe, regarding them as so many sheep. No matter how outnumbered they are, they never regard these as fierce barbarians or as awe-inspiring hordes. Nor do they presume on their own strength, but trust in the Lord of armies to grant them the

victory. [...] for victory in war is not dependent on a big army, and bravery is the gift of heaven.[73]

Note that he describes the Templar knight's normal state as one of "gentleness," just as that of any other monk would be. Indeed, he then ends the chapter by stressing that the union of monk and soldier is a miracle of God, the only one who could bring it about:

> Thus in a wondrous and unique manner they appear gentler than lambs, yet fiercer than lions. I do not know if it would be more appropriate to refer to them as monks or as soldiers, unless perhaps it would be better to recognize them as being both. Indeed, they lack neither monastic meekness nor military might. What can we say of this, except that this has been done by the Lord, and it is marvelous in our eyes. These are the picked troops of God, whom he has recruited from the ends of the earth; the valiant men of Israel chosen to guard well and faithfully that tomb which is the bed of the true Solomon, each man sword in hand, and superbly trained to war.[74]

The fifth and final chapter devoted to the Templars is also the first to describe the geography of the Holy Land itself, beginning with their quarters at the Temple in Jerusalem. This is an important link for Bernard, for he uses it not only to firmly place the Templars in their rightful home, but also as a means of justifying the order and its practices through a direct comparison with the anger of Jesus in ejecting the money lenders from the Temple:

> By all these signs our knights clearly show that they are animated by the same zeal for the house of God which of old passionately inflamed their leader himself when he armed his most holy hands, not indeed with a sword, but with a whip. Having fashioned this from some lengths of cord, he entered the temple and ejected the merchants [...] considering it most unfitting to defile this house of prayer by such traffic.[75]

It is because of this very act that the Templars are motivated to action, taking Christ as their model in purifying the Temple, not with whips, but with swords.[76] The presence of Muslims is far worse than the money-lenders:

> Moved therefore by their King's example, his devoted soldiers consider that it is even more shameful and infinitely more intolerable for a holy place to be polluted by pagans than to be crowded with merchants.[77]

Here is the strongest justification that Bernard could offer. The notion that the Templars are "cleansing" the Temple (as the crusaders have in Jerusalem and the Holy Land) in the manner of Christ is an argument that would be virtually irrefutable to the medieval mind. He succeeds in arguing that through their actions, the Templars are imitating Christ, which is what all of the faithful are to do in their own way (and as Urban urged the first crusaders to do).[78] Indeed, it is at this point that Bernard offers his solution

3. *Bernard of Clairvaux's* In Praise of the New Knighthood 73

to the problem of criminals and sinners, and how they may best be redeemed. Their countrymen are glad to be rid of them, the Holy Land welcomes them as new defenders, and they have an opportunity for redemption and salvation. Bernard's God worked in mysterious and miraculous ways.

The Templars were the ideal model for the crusaders, for in their holy lives they upheld the virtues to which all soldiers and common people who had taken the cross should aspire, and in so doing, they came closest to the perfection of the purely monastic life.[79] This optimistic vision shows his idealistic view of the best possible solution. Given his enthusiasm,[80] and keeping in mind earlier observations,[81] we can say that Bernard truly believed in the Templars' mission and cause, and was able to write with passion and conviction as a result.

The wondrous event that he hoped for, a mass conversion of sinners, was the ultimate act of divine retribution against those who had invaded and polluted the lands sacred to Christ:

> This is the revenge which Christ contrives against his enemies, to triumph powerfully and gloriously over them by their own means [i.e., sinners overcome by sinners] [...] Certainly the conversion of so many sinners and evildoers will now do as much good as their former misdeeds did harm.[82]

The remainder of this chapter is given over to the praises of Jerusalem itself, and sets the tone for the rest of the treatise, which proceeds to detail many of the sites sacred to Christians. These are now under the watchful eyes of the Templars, and Bernard uses numerous biblical references to reinforce the importance of their task.

These chapters are both fascinating and unsettling in their content and present modern readers with difficulties; a theology emerges that is unfamiliar, perhaps even offensive to some. In response, some scholars assert that one cannot employ this work alone to study Bernard's beliefs on these subjects as a whole. In his introduction to this translation, R.J. Zwi Werblowsky writes: "For it would be totally wrong to use this short treatise as a source book for St Bernard's 'theology of warfare.' Warfare is a grave problem to every conscience, and St Bernard's views on it would have to be pieced together from his utterances on the subject on many different occasions and in diverse contexts. St Bernard was first and foremost a man of peace and a maker of peace. Yet he certainly was no 'pacifist' since he firmly believed that in many cases war, with all its attendant violence and bloodshed, was the lesser evil."[83]

This is a good summary of the conflict which medieval theologians continually faced when dealing with war of any kind. One sometimes needed to choose the lesser of two evils in the hope of attaining a result that was pleasing to God. However, Werblowsky adds an additional statement concerning

Bernard's attitude toward "pagans" which is problematic: "Even so, St Bernard was much in advance of his times when he insisted that pagans were not to be killed except for the protection of Christians against actual physical or moral danger."[84] The interpretation of both dangers was immensely broad, and precluded little save premeditated murder, for any situation (indeed, the Muslims' very presence in and near the Holy Land) could be perceived as a "moral danger." Bernard's treatise is full of such instances (the cleansing of the "polluted" Temple, for example), and continually lauds the Templars for their efforts to drive the sinful from God's lands. The rejoicing of Christ at the death of his enemies is not the thought of a man well ahead of his time. In addition, Bernard's contemporary, Peter the Venerable, made similar assertions which seemed to express reservation about the killing of infidels in his treatises on Islam,[85] (but in reality masked other agendas, as we shall see in chapter five), and recall that, in the previous century, the Benedictine Peter Damian had rejected any notion of "holy war" in the conversion of non-Christians.[86] Bernard was not unique or new in making such statements, which in any case were not absolutes or pacifistic yearnings.

While we must indeed view Bernard's other writings for a fuller understanding of his theology in this area (and even bear in mind *De laude*, where his disdain for the secular knights who wage foolish wars is a recurring theme), there nevertheless emerges a concise picture of Bernard's general view on war. We have seen that Bernard was slow to write this work, and also to support the crusade. While he insisted that his own humble nature was the reason, his initial reluctance may have had more to do with his hesitancy to see the papacy become too involved in the affairs of the greater world.

Bernard was concerned with the growing legal and administrative duties of the papacy, which threatened to corrupt it with secular influence (ironically, his own monastic house would be afflicted with the same problem very quickly). The pope could not declare war; that was the domain of secular governments. He could only advise on the subject, and then determine the moral character of the dispute involved. Bernard argued that it was not the pope's place to take up arms or command armies, as Gregory VII had wished in the previous century.[87] He drew upon canon law and tradition to support his position.[88]

In conclusion, despite his reservation about the Church becoming overly involved in the act of war, Bernard clearly posits two types of warfare in *De laude*, one of which, that waged by the Templars and crusaders, is not only acceptable to the faith, but also pleasing to God. This idea is certainly a direct result of the reforming attitudes of the eleventh century, and therefore Bernard cannot be given sole credit for its development. However, it was his dynamic and charismatic personality which helped to disseminate the idea among not only his peers, but the people as well.

His theology of warfare is found in a compact version in *De laude*. Though still in an early form, it would take shape when preparations for the Second Crusade began more than a decade later. Regardless, the treatise presents an adequate, if incomplete, summary of his thoughts on this sensitive subject. While one must view his other writings as well, his *De laude* suffices as a summary of the main points of his theology of war. It shows that he was openly opposed to the trivial wars of the secular knighthood, and felt that to pursue such practices would lead only to the knights' downfall and the loss of salvation. The holy wars of the crusaders and new knighthood, however, stood in dramatic contrast, for they were struggles of the soul as well as those of the battlefield. The idea of the true "holy war" is apparent in these writings, with all of its consequences for the future.

However, there were some dissenting voices and opposing views, particularly that of Isaac, the abbot of Stella, who denounced the innovative idea of the military order. His views and those of others will be examined in the next chapter, which discusses the creation of the Cistercian Order, founded as a new monastic movement from the desire for reform, and its rapid rise to prominence in the early twelfth century.

4

The Cistercian Order in the Twelfth Century: Austerity, Crusading and Slavery

They wore white robes and sought out simplicity and austerity, rejecting the opulence of their contemporaries, and criticizing them harshly for it. In fact, they were critical of all aspects of life that fell short of the godly. Their early monasteries were far removed from civilization, emulating those first Christian desert hermits and ascetics in third-century Egypt, who withdrew from all contact with the secular world. In the wilderness, they sought to recreate the "pure" traditions of the early Church. For some of them, however, this isolation was not destined to last long.

The Cistercians were destined to exert a tremendous influence on the philosophical, theological, and political life of twelfth-century Europe, most notably through the actions and works of Bernard of Clairvaux. The order was instrumental in strengthening the positions won by the Church during the Reform, and in gathering support for the crusading enterprise and territorial aspirations of the Latin West in the Holy Land. The Cistercians were not as a rule interested in Islam specifically. However, their views (particularly Bernard's) about the crusades and the conversion or extermination of unbelievers nevertheless resulted in some type of relationship between the two being formed. Indeed, in at least one area, that of Muslim slaves held by Cistercian houses, the contact was direct. A brief summary of the events and ideas surrounding the creation of the order is necessary to place it in its proper context. This will be followed by an examination of some of the relevant writings and activities pertaining to the crusades and Islam.

The order which would become the Cistercians had its origins in the later eleventh century, as part of the monastic reforming spirit that went along with the Reform.[1] It had been universally accepted that cenobitic (communal) monasticism was the surest way to God and salvation, but that began to change in the second half of the eleventh century. In 1075, Robert de Champagne (later St. Robert) founded the monastery of Molesme in the diocese of Langres. He had been dissatisfied with the lax monastic practices of his day, and had been drawn to the hermit's life. This discontent was no doubt due in part to the controversies surrounding monastic dwellings in his age, and was dubbed the "crisis of cenobitism" by Germain Morin.[2] However, not all scholars and historians accept that the perceived corruption and decadence in the Benedictine order directly caused these popular religious movements, and a subsequent greater movement toward a hermit's life.[3] It is best to say that a contrast arose between the traditional Benedictine style of monasticism and the new austere movements, the former being outward-looking and concerned with the world, the latter being focused on an internal spirituality, and the need to save one's own soul before those of others.

One issue related to this difference of focus concerned the locations of monastic dwellings, which historically had been both rural and urban. In the eleventh century, the second of these two options gained favor, due to a number of factors. Among these were the growing involvement of the Benedictine monasteries with daily life and secular affairs, and perhaps more importantly, an increased need for security from raids and feudal battles.[4] Such skirmishes, as previously discussed, were most often carried out by the very knights that the Church eventually sought to redirect toward the more constructive purpose of crusading.

In addition, monastic settlements increasingly became popular locations for the common people for a variety of reasons, such as the establishment of markets and the need to manage nearby lands owned by a given monastery. Expanding monastic lands required more labor, which brought in tenants to work the fields. This led to settlements, which also attracted merchants, craftsmen and others to establish semi-permanent dwellings in the vicinity of the once-remote monasteries. Ultimately, monks had less labor to do in the fields, freeing up their time. In exchange for their work and commerce, the lay people came to expect protection from the abbot, and interaction between monks and outsiders became more common out of necessity. Portions of the Benedictine Rule were set aside in this new situation, something that reformers and critics bitterly opposed.[5]

With new monasteries being established near urban areas, there were far more opportunities for monks to become involved in the affairs of the secular world, foreshadowing monastic involvement in religious and political issues of the twelfth century. Indeed, all manner of commoners began to conduct business within monastic grounds, including women, a situation which many found intolerable. As monasteries acquired new wealth, some monks appeared to be more concerned with secular than spiritual issues, and to some, the original intent of the Rule seemed ever more distant and forgotten. It was in such an uncertain climate that Robert resolved to take action and attempt to return to the purity and strictness of the monastic life as envisioned by Benedict by creating a new settlement at Molesme.[6]

Ultimately, Robert himself became dissatisfied with the structure of his new community, and left in 1090 to again take up the life of a hermit. Though he was convinced to return, he left again in 1097, and petitioned Archbishop Hugh de Die of Lyon, the papal legate in France, for permission to found a new community, one dedicated to strict observance of the Rule. Hugh, an ardent supporter of the Reform, gave his blessing to the endeavor.

In 1098, Robert and twenty-one monks journeyed to Cîteaux, south of Dijon. The name derived from the Latin *Cistercium*, itself a derivative of the phrase *cis tercium lapidum miliarium*, a reference to its location on the old Roman road nearby, but it was initially known only as *Novum monasterium*. In 1099 Robert was called back yet again to Molesme, against his wishes, though he offered no protest, where he was to remain as abbot until his death in 1111.[7]

In Robert's absence, a new abbot, Alberic, was elected. During his abbacy, the monastery began to grow and take shape, for he succeeded in obtaining a bull of papal protection from Pope Paschal II, dated 19 October 1100, assuring both the abbey's security and the possibility of expansion. After Alberic's death on 26 January 1109, the monks chose the Englishman Stephen Harding, as his successor. Stephen's governance of the community was to be of the highest significance, as Louis Lekai explains, "he inherited only one of countless reform-abbeys of some notoriety; he left behind the first 'order' in monastic history, possessing a clearly formulated program, held together by a firm legal framework and in the process of an unprecedented expansion."[8]

It was Stephen who sought and obtained a new papal bull of support for the abbey and its many affiliated communities. It was also during Stephen's time as abbot that the young Bernard entered the order, in 1113. Pope Calixtus II issued the bull on 23 December 1119, commending the work of Stephen and his monks.[9] By this time, the order had drawn up a cohesive set of rules and regulations which all the houses were expected to follow. Thus, the Cistercian order was created, and was soon to have an enormous impact on many of the major papal decisions and policies.

St. Benedict's Rule was rigidly observed, and the order had additional documents that served as its constitution, containing the founding ideals and practices of Cîteaux, and aiming to ensure their continuation. Cistercian spiritual life initially returned to the purity and rigidity of the Rule, stripping monastic practices of several centuries of additions and reintroducing the tripartite monastic day of manual labor, liturgy, and personal prayer, but significantly, not encouraging study or artistic work. The Cistercian statutes prohibited the writing of books without the consent of the General Chapter, in an attempt to prevent the pursuit of scholastic fame outside of the cloister, which was seen as a distraction from monastic life, and a temptation to the sin of pride. Eventually, this prohibition was largely removed by the actions of Bernard and later, Ælred of Rievaulx in northern England.

The founders hoped and expected that such spiritual disciplines would be maintained in a cloister that deliberately set itself apart from worldly concerns and attachments, creating a self-sufficient monastic economy run with few or no links to secular feudalism. Initially, then, the Cistercians had no time for European politics, the crusades, or debating the issue of Christian relations with Islam. They only wanted to retreat from what they saw as a sinful world, and a return to early monastic ideals.

This strict asceticism arose from the fierce reforming spirit, but it was not to last long. Within forty years of the founding of their order, the Cistercians were incredibly rich, and completely immersed in the secular affairs and political issues of the age. Much of the order's early focus had been replaced by a more world-conscious outlook that allowed them to exercise considerable power.

One major reason for this rapid rise to prominence and influence was the charismatic and pious figure of Bernard of Clairvaux. Though he did not desire public acclaim and attention, his eloquent writings soon brought him the respect and admiration of both the clergy and rulers of Western Europe.[10] As we have seen, he was frequently called on to be a central figure in the major political disputes of the time, and his advice was widely sought and followed.

Bernard's various activities, combined with the tremendous personal energy and enthusiasm with which he engaged in them, transformed Clairvaux into a dynamic and forceful center. The Cistercians were stirred by his infectious energy and willingly cooperated with his work; the order and the man were frequently synonymous in the eyes of his contemporaries. The image of strength projected by Bernard through the order, despite his own poor health, attracted many pious and talented men desiring to enter the novitiate. This initially served to benefit Cistercian monasticism as a whole.

Ultimately, however, while large numbers of new monks did no immediate damage, the long-term consequence of this expansion was to push the order as envisaged by Stephen Harding and its founders in a completely different direction. Indeed, such rapid growth would probably not have taken place without the tireless efforts of Bernard.

The success and prestige of Bernard and his Cistercian contemporaries became affixed to the order of which they were a part. The resulting growth in the numbers of Cistercian monks and monastic houses led to a departure from the original spirit and letter of Cîteaux's self-imposed legislation. The Cistercians increasingly became drawn into public life and the affairs of the Church and state, the same institutions that those at Molesme had wanted to avoid. By the mid-twelfth century, the order had considerable influence within the Church. Clairvaux in effect housed Bernard's private "army" of reform (indeed, he probably did see this as a battle, fond as he was of military imagery), advocating and implementing the ideals of the Reform, especially during the papacy of one of their own, the Cistercian Eugenius III.[11]

All of this benefited Bernard, whose public standing continued to grow throughout the first half of the twelfth century. Lekai remarks on the reasons for his popularity, "the secret of his success was his moral superiority, his unselfish good will, and the magic of his personality. On the other hand, the fact that the whole European world obeyed the poor and humble Abbot of Clairvaux indicates an era when moral ideals still prevailed over brutal violence."[12]

This romanticizes the realities of the early twelfth century; the First Crusade, the central event which effectively birthed the new century, was a venture of brutality and butchery the likes of which had not been seen before. However much the church publicly did not approve of the murder of innocent civilians, the wholesale slaughter of the non–Christians in Jerusalem was, as we have seen, still spoken of with approval by the chroniclers and many others.[13] Whether officially sanctioned or not, some the new ideas were used to promote merciless violence against non–Christians. The modern reader can see the medieval contradiction which so freely juxtaposed Christian values such as peace, love, and forgiveness with the barbarity of such actions as the mass killing at the climax of the First Crusade, even when this kind of killing was supposed to be a last resort, when other methods of dealing with non–Christians had failed.[14]

Back in Europe, the Cistercians were not averse to using military imagery in their writings, evoking the popular theme of the monk as the spiritual warrior of Christ. These words evoked martial themes, and used them as an example of the soul's journey to God. Military virtues were equated with monastic ones. Indeed, for those men who entered the order from a former soldier's life (not uncommon for those seeking redemption from their old ways, and before the rise of the Templars, who gave some older warriors a new vocation in life), the Cistercians desired to re-direct that aggressive behavior and temperament into new spiritual battles, i.e., against temptation and worldliness. Indeed,

4. The Cistercian Order in the Twelfth Century 81

"the Cistercians' caritas was no gentle virtue but a monastic weapon with which a monk could slay thousands of his enemies by invoking it in all that he did."[15] Whatever contradictions to traditional Christian proclamations as a religion of peace we may find here, Bernard, as the de facto spokesman for the Cistercians, ultimately became the champion of these juxtaposed views in his support for the Knights Templar and the Second Crusade.

Having thoroughly examined the views of Bernard on the matter, we will now discuss the thoughts of some of his contemporaries in the order, for not all Cistercians were so favorably inclined toward the concept of the military orders. Indeed, a variety of other such warrior groups came into existence as a result of the success of the Templars, and some of the white monks were not pleased.

Isaac, the English-born Abbot of l'Etoile[16] (also known as Stella) near Poitiers from about 1147, was a good example of the disapproving opinion. In a sermon dedicated to warning his monks about the dangers of new ideas, he attacked an unnamed order which he asserted killed non–Christians, or forced conversions with weapons, and glorified their fallen as martyrs. It is not clear as to the identity of the order mentioned. The Templars are the most likely candidate of course, given their high profile, and also because of his references to the *nova militia*, which he called the *monstrum novum*.[17] This could be a play on words referencing the title of Bernard's justification. Isaac asserts that the order is licensed to despoil and religiously slaughter,[18] which seems a deliberate contrast to Bernard's insistence that the Templars do not kill out of hate, take pleasure in it, or force others into the faith at the point of the sword.[19] Isaac also refers to the order as the "order of the Fifth Gospel,"[20] with the damning implication that it did not follow the original four gospels, but was rather a law unto itself, apart from the Church, and by extension, God. He comes close to declaring the order to be heretical, yet takes the accusation no further. Isaac's words are harsh, and he argues that violence merely begets more violence:

> [...] a new and monstrous breed of military order emerged, whose rule — someone wittily described it as stemming from a fifth gospel — would force, with spears and clubs, unbelievers to embrace the Faith, while considering it right to despoil and devoutly kill those who do not have the name of Christian. And those of their order who are killed while at such pillaging they regard as martyrs for Christ. Surely it is obvious that these people give every excuse for antichristian cruelty to the champion of wickedness (Cf. 2 Th. 2:3). How could they put before such a one the gentleness and patience of Christ (2 Col. 10:1) and the pattern of his preaching? Why should the adversary not gladly do what he finds is done with a good conscience? Why should he not say, Do to the church as the church has done?[21]

Some have suggested that these passages may actually refer to the new military orders of Spain, since the Templars did not engage in forcible conversions.[22] This assumes that Isaac had a thorough knowledge of Templar activity, which is by no means certain. Given that Isaac was a Cistercian, he would probably have been aware of the Bernardine writings concerning the Templars, and would have had some knowledge of the structure and function of the order. This does not mean that his understanding of that function was completely clear. If he was dedicated to peace, as his sermon indicates, then it is possible that his charges derived as much from religious conviction and anger as from his learning.

In addition, the Order of Calatrava (the most likely Spanish candidate for his attack, if not the Templars) was not approved until the year 1164, only a few years before Isaac's death, and long after Bernard's.[23] Though the sermon is number forty-eight of a total of fifty four, this does not necessarily indicate a late date for its composition;[24] it is just as likely to have been composed at an earlier date. Indeed, given that the earlier part of the century witnessed more new ideas and innovations in the field of theology and war, the Templars are the more likely candidate for his criticisms, since they were the first true military order, and a completely original concept. Being the innovators of a new phenomenon, they represented exactly the type of potentially dangerous thinking that worried Isaac in this sermon. His use of a similar vocabulary to Bernard's supports this idea.

On the other hand, if Isaac did give this sermon late in life, it is also possible that he was attacking the military orders in general, by using a rhetoric which mimicked Bernard's own words, while at the same time drawing on the example of the newer Calatravan order to question the very practice of fighting monks. If he found the concept of a military order theologically unacceptable, then his attack would have been directed at the whole idea.[25] Perhaps he borrowed elements from more than one order to make his point, viewing the concept as a single movement, and a bad one, a poor idea that was spreading. Some have suggested that Isaac had a personal grudge against the Calatravan order,[26] but there is nothing linking Isaac to the Calatravan order in a personal way.[27]

So we return to the Templars as the targets of his invective. Given that at the time, it was not always necessary to gather facts about one's opponent in order to write against them (as true within the boundaries of Christendom as for perceptions of outsiders), we must consider seriously that Isaac's polemic was directed at the Templars. His choice of words is too close to Bernard's to be a coincidence, and would have far more relevance if it were roughly contemporary with Bernard's own writings. This idea is supported by the popularity of the Templars, and was enhanced by the relative newness of the concept of the fighting monk. Novelty, as we have seen, was the subject of Isaac's concern in this particular sermon. He was exhorting his listeners to continue to live with restraint and religious virtues, and not be seduced by things just because they were new. Further, "there had recently been some innovators in the field of theology and Isaac seems to refer to Abelard without naming him. There had also been innovations on a practical level, such as this 'new militia' which was really a 'new monstrosity'—that is, something unprecedented" [...]28

Given that Abelard and his dangerous philosophies are hinted at, and that he was a contemporary and adversary of Bernard, we have some further evidence that the new militia probably refers to the Templars. The "monstrosity" could be either the military order, or novelty itself, or even both. Yet he did not condemn the military orders completely. He merely questioned their motives and warned that there was a great danger of good deeds becoming evil, as most evil in the world originated from things that were intended to be good, but were allowed to be corrupted. Ironically, he could not have chosen a better description of the crusading movement itself.

Despite this huge difference of opinion from Bernard's teachings and what was by then a well-accepted theology among the Cistercians (namely, endorsement of the military orders), Isaac was an enthusiastic supporter of Bernard in other areas of theological teaching and was one of the strongest proponents for his canonization, even referring to him as a "saint" during his lifetime.29 Where they disagreed, it was not usually in a way that promoted conflict. Their contrasting natures were present in the realm of the physical as well, as Hugh McCaffrey amusingly notes:

> Given that both had a sense of humor, the Laurel and Hardy scene William of Saint Thierry provides when depicting shy and haggard Bernard and his sleek and handsome Cistercian companion going to William of Champeaux's headquarters for Bernard's priestly ordination offers, perhaps, some idea of the contrast in physique between the delicate and emaciated abbot of Clairvaux and the doughty, energetic abbot of Stella.30

They also differed greatly in their attitudes toward the treatment of monks, Bernard adopting the maternal outlook that graced so much of his theology, and encouraging this treatment of monks in the Cistercian order. His Marian devotion extended to the daily lives of the brothers in his care, oddly referring to them as women.31 Isaac, on the other hand, stressed strict discipline, rigid adherence to the Benedictine Rule, and advocated that the monks effectively "crucify" their physical forms, to be one with Christ.32 Indeed, Isaac believed that if the abbot of any given group of monks was not harsh enough with them, then it was their duty to be harsh on themselves.[33]

Isaac's views of the larger phenomenon of crusading are unknown, but would likely reflect the attitude in his sermon: that the knights were not to be wholly condemned. For him, crusading was probably another of those activities which had a noble purpose but could be corrupted and tainted with sin all too easily.[34] Likewise, he never wrote of Islam or its perceived threat to Christianity, but it is clear that he did not favor forced conversions. Indeed, this seems to have been the central issue which stirred him to include his denunciation of the military orders in his sermon in the first place. His writings display none of the military imagery found in Bernard's texts, imagery that was central to Bernard's teachings about the battle of the spirit and the battle against the enemies of the church.

As Bernard became the spokesman-by-consensus for the Cistercians, his theology was effectively theirs as well. His particular teachings on the issues of holy war, crusading, and the military orders essentially had Cistercian approval.[35] The protests of Isaac notwithstanding, it seems that in general the Cistercian order favored the policies pursued by the papacy in the Holy Land, as well as the complicated theological justifications that went with them.

In 1146, Bernard was charged by Pope Eugenius with the task of preaching the Second Crusade, a task which, as we have noted, he was initially unwilling to undertake. There are several reasons for this, including the obvious one that there were strict controls on who within the Church was allowed to preach to the masses. This was originally intended as a means of assuring the dissemination of orthodox teaching to the lay congregations, and preventing the spread of heresy. Only the diocesan bishop or the pope had the right to confer preaching privileges to the lower-ranking clergy. Bernard, therefore, required such papal approval before his mission could begin, and he always noted in his correspondence that he acted as a papal legate in such matters.[36] A summary of Bernard's crusading preaching can be found in his *Epistola* 363, which was addressed to the Franks living in the East. It stresses the need to defend the Christian holy sites from the unbelievers, which in turn glorifies God, and brings about redemption to the faithful.[37] In a revival of the theme of divine vengeance, he also called on them to take revenge in God's name for the affront that the Muslims had caused, recalling how 50 years earlier, the previous armed pilgrims had done the same.[38]

The Cistercian Eugenius saw the new crusade as an extension of the work begun by Urban II 50 years earlier. His bull, *Quantum predecessores*, may have been the first official papal proclamation of a crusade,[39] and it carried on the ideas of his predecessor. Urban had spoken of using the crusade as a means of remitting those punishments set down by the church, actions requiring penance. Eugenius, taking very seriously his role as the true successor to St. Peter, included the idea that God himself had set down the crusade as a means of granting absolution from punishments, independent of anything that the church might offer.[40] This was not the first time that absolution from divine punishment had been discussed,[41] and Purkis notes that, "it is obvious that he did not wish to be thought of as an innovator."[42] Further, there seems to have been little or no stress, from either Eugenius or Bernard, on the concept of crusaders engaging in the *imitatio Christi*, as there had been during the First Crusade.[43] For Bernard, crusader vows were temporary. After they had fulfilled them, they would return home to their families and worldly lives, and as such their commitments were not on par with the life-long vows of monks or Templars, who had renounced the secular world forever. Indeed, since the Templars had appeared, they had taken on the role of imitators of Christ, in Bernard's view. It was noble to seek the earthly Jerusalem, of course, but far greater were those who sought the spiritual Holy City, one reason Bernard so vehemently opposed monks joining the crusade; they would be taking a step backward.[44]

Nevertheless, Eugenius' bull was an important statement, which helped to give an identity and purpose to the crusade, an all-out military offensive that was fought on numerous fronts, from Spain to North Africa, from the Baltic to the Holy Land. This time, the crusades were not led just by noblemen (as had been then case in the first), but by kings; the task was elevated to a whole new level. The enormity of it and the passionate preaching by Bernard must have assured many that Christendom was pre-destined to win this holy war and triumph once and for all over the infidels, pagans, and forces of evil. After all, they had done so a half-century before. The excitement engendered must have been immense. Perhaps many again saw the coming of the apocalypse, for surely the armies of God were gathering as foretold.[45]

Eugenius was insistent that the crusade be undertaken out of genuine religious motivation, not "as a convenient method of avoiding inconvenient obligations at home."[46] Like Urban before him, he held that only the truly penitential should undertake this task. The stressing of religious motivation further helped to enforce the belief for many that the venture was being guided by God.

Undoubtedly, similar feelings had been aroused by the First Crusade, but the political climate of the 1140s was different from that of the 1090s. Christianity had established itself in the East and controlled Jerusalem, but now it seemed that God had allowed the forces of evil to retake the city and county of Edessa as a test of faith. Edessa fell in 1144 (on Christmas Eve, to be exact) to Imad al-Din Zangi, ruler of Aleppo and Mosul, and the shock of that loss reverberated throughout Europe. This was the first major loss of Christian territory in nearly 50 years. In the minds of some it was undoubtedly the long-awaited prelude to the final victory over Satan. This development and its effects are of great importance in twelfth-century history and thought.

By 1147, the papacy was firmly committed to the idea of the new crusade, with King Louis VII of France and Conrad III of Germany the most notable rulers to take the cross. It was planned not only for the Holy Land, but as a vast military assault on unbelievers at several frontier borders of Christendom, including Iberia and the Baltics. Wars which had previously been secular conflicts could now come under this banner, if they were fought by Christians against non–Christians.[47] Papal bulls were issued declaring the forgiveness of sins for undertaking the effort in any of these campaigns. Further, as Constable notes, "in the crusading bulls of Eugene III the concept of the papal crusading indulgence was developed in its classic form, and around it there began to crystallize an institutional concept of temporal privileges and military regulations that exerted its influence on Christian thought throughout the Middle Ages."[48]

Enthusiasm and expectations were running high. With a Cistercian pope and the order's greatest spokesman extolling the virtues of the venture, the Cistercians were clearly lending it their support. The excitement of 1099 must have been rekindled for many. Unfortunately for them all, these hopes were dashed with the failure of the crusade in the East in the summer of 1148. It did not just fail, it failed disastrously, a complete and total loss for the Christian forces, after they were defeated and forced to withdraw from an ill-conceived effort to retake Damascus. Economic troubles and short-sighted, overconfident leadership were two major factors. Only in the west did the crusade see any success, with the recapture of Lisbon from the Moors in October, 1147.[49]

With modern eyes, we can see that the inability to accept such a catastrophe and all of the crises of faith that this would have evoked, led to rationalizations about the crusaders' collective sinfulness, and divine wrath at their unworthiness for such a task. It had not been the fault of those who called for and preached the crusade, of course, but rather the fault was with those who undertook the fighting, pretending to be pure in heart when God knew otherwise. Regardless of who deserved the blame, it created a climate where there was hesitancy about taking the cross for future endeavors, and one monk named Peter of Troyes even questioned whether Christians should be fighting and killing at all.[50]

Nevertheless, there was also an immediate reaction in the form of a plea that a new and stronger crusade must be mounted that would correct the errors of the previous venture and remain true to its holy intentions. Needless to say, Bernard threw himself wholeheartedly into this, seeing it as a means of personal vindication as much as of spiritual renewal. It did not do well for the most prominent figure in Christendom to be viewed as a failure, a subject of mockery, or even as one deceived by the devil.

On 7 May, 1150, an assembly was called at Chartres to discuss the options concerning a new military campaign to the east. Brenda Bolton notes:

> Present were King Louis VII of France, one of the military leaders just returned from the Holy Land, and a great collection of senior churchmen, most notably Suger, abbot of St. Denis, and Bernard of Clairvaux. The Cistercian pope, Eugenius III, although not present in person, appears to have dominated the proceedings with his letter, *Immensumpietatis opus*, dated April 25, 1150 and circulated to the whole assembly. Eugenius, aware of all the difficulties, counseled extreme caution and stressed that nothing should be done without the tacit support of the king of France.[51]

At that time, the Cistercians were in some turmoil, and were dealing with internal affairs. The rapid growth of the order over its first fifty years had caused serious organizational problems. Its virtual unrestricted growth had led to open worries about corruption, and straying from its ideals. Indeed, in 1150, a major quarrel with the Premonstratensians erupted over the issue of expansion, and the encroachment of the larger Cistercian order into the realm of the latter, which felt threatened in terms of its own ability to expand.[52] We should not be surprised that those of such a high-minded spiritual inclination could argue over territorial disputes; it is human nature to protect what one has.

The Cistercians now desired that all new houses conform more closely to the order's original intentions, and may have even altered some of their earliest documents to make them simpler, and more effective in stressing this demand.[53] This nobly-intended action helped the Cistercians consolidate and centralize their powers and affairs.

It was against this backdrop that questions regarding another crusade were raised, and it seems that the Cistercians overall were not interested in the idea, being more preoccupied with their own concerns. This marks a significant change from their previous position. While the order did not oppose a new crusade as such, it did, as seen by the pope's statement, recommend caution. Having been stung badly by the failures of 1148, they were not so eager to risk a second humiliation.

Bernard, however, was much more enthusiastic, to the chagrin of his brethren at Clairvaux. During his time in preaching the Second Crusade, he had been beseeched by his fellow monks to return to the abbey, where they felt lost without him. Now that the crusade was over and he had returned, the monks were at peace. Talk of a new crusade, however, aroused their fears once again, but Bernard would not be deterred.[54] He eagerly attended the assembly. Indeed, he was actually chosen to lead the new crusade, but he literally begged the pope not to allow this, because he was both weak in body and unskilled in the arts of war. Further, it was against his monastic vows and duties. He wanted the pope to be the leader, but Eugenius was equally unhappy with suggestion.[55]

Despite his enthusiasm for the expedition, Bernard was not at all pleased with how things were developing, and probably had not even anticipated it.[56] In response, he wrote with great passion to Eugenius:

> Do you then, the friend of the Bridegroom, prove yourself a friend in need. If you love Christ as you should, with all your heart, with all your soul, and with all your strength; if you love him with that threefold love about which your predecessor was questioned, then you will make no reservations, you will leave nothing undone while his bride is in such great danger, but rather you will devote to her all your strength, all your zeal, all your care, and all your power. [...] I expect you must have heard by now how the assembly at Chartres, by a most surprising decision, chose me as the leader and chief of the expedition. You may be quite sure that this never was and is not now by my advice or wish, and that it is altogether beyond my powers, as I gauge them, to do such a thing. Who am I to arrange armies in battle order, to lead forth armed men? I could think of nothing more remote from my calling, even supposing I had the necessary strength and skill [...] All I beg is that with the love you owe me especially, you will not allow me to be the victim of men's caprice.[57]

This plea was as much for putting himself at peace, as it was for the idea of launching a new attack on the Holy Land. Bernard had been deeply distraught at the failure of the Second Crusade. It had been for him as much a personal failure as one for Christendom. His reputation was damaged, and he probably experienced a great spiritual crisis; we might call it depression. However, he didn't point fingers. At a sermon given in Chartres, "he explained the disaster as a combined result of the sins of man and the judgement of the Lord, rather than identifying particular individuals, or groups, as responsible,"[58] a wise move if he would need to approach some of those same individuals about taking the cross again. Still, he probably blamed himself in part, and with talk of a new crusade, saw a chance to redeem himself not only in the eyes of God, but also in the eyes of all the Christians he must have felt that he had let down. Some had come to Bernard's defense, but he still insisted on taking responsibility, his faith in God unshakable even in the face of disaster.[59]

4. The Cistercian Order in the Twelfth Century   89

Astonishingly, some writers went so far as to condemn the entire failed venture as the work of the devil, and its advocates as false, an attitude which can be found in the anonymous German *Annales Herbipolenses*:

> Thereupon, certain pseudo-prophets were in power, sons of Belial, heads of Anti-Christ, who by stupid words misled the Christians and by empty preaching induced all sorts of men to go against the Saracens for the freeing of Jerusalem.[60]

Such a damning condemnation is striking for its implications. To imply diabolical connections to the crusade, and that the two most prominent figures in Christendom were false prophets was a bold move indeed, obviously the best reason for its anonymity. Nevertheless, the work is very spiritual in content, and contains much accurate information about the crusaders and their experiences.[61] Critics of crusading would always be a minority throughout the Middle Ages, but their surviving words show that not everyone was enamored with the newer, more aggressive approach to spreading the gospel.

Regardless of the reasons for the outcome of the crusade (diabolical or just ineptness and hubris), initial talks went ahead to plan another expedition to the East, as noted. A significant absence from the assembly at Chartres to discuss the matter was the important and influential Peter the Venerable, Abbot of Cluny, who had been implored by Abbot Suger and Bernard among others to be present at this most important of meetings.[62] Peter's lack of attendance has led some to conclude that he did not support the idea of a new crusade, or even the idea of crusading in general,[63] but this notion is misinformed. Peter's response to their request adequately sums up his position and makes clear his opinion of the new venture:

> I am sorry and grieve more than I can say not to be present at the Council of Chartres where the lord king will proclaim your wisdom and that of others. Believe me, dear friend, believe what I say. I really am unable to come and because I cannot, I am sad. Who would not grieve to miss such a meeting, where the only person to gain thereby — by a new crusade — is none other than Christ Jesus![64]

Prior to receiving the invitation to this assembly, Peter had already summoned a meeting of the Cluniacs for the very same day as the proposed assembly. He was unable to neglect the abbey's duties, and was forced to remain at Cluny. Nevertheless, his words clearly indicate his support for the proposed crusade.[65] He even made an offer to attend a future meeting, if one were held, and to give his support for the venture as far as he was able.[66]

Ultimately, this new crusade was never to come about, because there was considerable papal hesitancy concerning it. Other contributing factors included a general blow to the morale of Europe following the disaster of the

Second Crusade, very real issues such as a lack of sufficient funds, armies, and volunteers to fill their ranks, and a general disillusionment (though only a temporary one) with the idea of crusading.[67] Above all of this, there is no doubt that a major contributing factor was the political concerns of the papacy and various rulers of Europe. The crusade had caused considerable secular political upheaval (as they always did) in its failed aftermath, with allies becoming enemies and vice versa. There were always those who set aside differences temporarily while crusading together, but these quarrels could come surging back afterward, especially in the event of a failed expedition. Pope Eugenius wisely saw that trying to organize a new vast military push so quickly could damage both the papacy and various secular rulers. He was being realistic in contrast to the idealism of various churchmen.[68]

For believers, the church's credibility had been seriously undermined, first by Zangi's unfathomable victory over the Christians at Edessa, and second, and more importantly, by the failure of the Christian West to retake the territories it had lost. The first situation could be justified by claiming that it was a test of faith, just as God had allowed ancient Israel to be invaded and overwhelmed by the Babylonians for the unfaithfulness of its people, and indeed, for the Jews to be scattered from their homeland after failing to recognize Jesus as their Messiah.

The failure of the crusade, however, was less easily explained away, though as noted above, Bernard used similar arguments to support his position. In such theological justification, it is always easier to rationalize and invoke divine goodness if one is on the winning side. These arguments were naturally as much for his own peace of mind as for that of his followers. One senses that Bernard really did believe much of his rhetoric, and that the crusade's failure came as a considerable blow to him.

Rather than a new crusade taking place, other means of supporting the Eastern territories were employed. Suger of St. Denis, for example, offered the idea of sending money and reinforcements to the East via the Templars, a kind of "mini-crusade" that would help strengthen the existing defenses, and be at least a show of help. He died before his plans could be fully implemented, however.[69]

It is clear that the Cistercians were not immediately prepared to endorse another armed pilgrimage, and so Bernard was left relatively alone in his desire for vindication. They would again become supporters of the concept of crusading as the twelfth century progressed, culminating in the Third Crusade of Richard the Lionheart in 1189; it took the loss of Jerusalem to Saladin in 1187 to ignite the West's eagerness for another full crusade. The Cistercians remained committed to the idea of evangelizing and converting unbelievers,

4. The Cistercian Order in the Twelfth Century 91

if possible, though they never rejected the alternative of killing, if such action became necessary. A distant and exotic belief like Islam was not a central concern to an order already having to cope with its own internal problems.

Curiously, one area where the Cistercians did have direct contact with Muslims was that of slavery. It is an issue which seemed to contradict the commitment to conversion or a return to faith, so enshrined by the order,[70] and would surely have had an influence on Cistercian attitudes toward Islam and the crusading effort in general. Initially, lay brothers had been introduced into the order, to help prevent either the choir monks from compromising their spiritual duties, or having to accept external sources of labor, and by extension, their inevitable ties to the feudal economics of rents, services, and revenues (a growing problem, as we have seen). In practice, however, within a few decades, the Cistercians were accepting both tenants to manage their vast land acquisitions, and holding slaves, both Muslim and Christian, to carry out the day-to-day tasks of ever-growing monastic houses.[71] The Cistercians of Spain particularly seem to have had some involvement with the trade of Muslim slaves. Benjamin Kedar discusses the issue:

> Since [...] baptism entailed a limitation on the economic exploitation of a Muslim slave and, in some regions, paved the way for the slave's liberation, some Christian masters strove to prevent the conversion of their Muslim slaves. Surprisingly enough, the earliest piece of evidence about such endeavors relates to monastic masters. A clause in the Cistercian statutes of 1152 states that "the ancient rule about the Saracens should be observed, namely, that they should not be bought or prohibited from being baptized." Evidently the Cistercians, who founded their first Spanish houses in the 1130s, must have faced the problem before 1152 [...] Since the clause recurs in the statutes of 1157, 1175, and 1215, the question undoubtedly remained acute.[72]

This brings up several interesting points, most notably concerning the issue of slavery in monastic institutions itself. Even Pope Urban had declared in 1088 that Moors who had come under Christian rule in Spain should be convinced to convert by example.[73] The fact that religious houses were engaged in such practices might seem surprising, but slavery had been justified by biblical means for centuries, and had been common in early medieval Europe.[74]

The Church's position on slavery throughout its history had been one of conflicting positions. The church fathers had permitted slavery, drawing on Pauline writings,[75] but it was understood that the slave was not to be mistreated, and that the master must not regard himself as superior to the slave, for in fact, all were slaves to God.[76] Augustine wrote that slaves should willingly fulfill their role as a Christian duty, and that they should not seek manumission.[77] Indeed, in 340, the Council of Gangra in Asia Minor declared that to use religion to encourage a slave to leave service was anathema. This was in response to a heretical Manichean teaching.[78] Isidore of Seville noted rather astonishingly in the seventh century that slavery was the result of divine providence, and that those who were not fit to be free, God "more mercifully inflicted with slavery."[79] Also beginning in the seventh century, slavery began to be imposed as an ecclesiastical penalty by local Church councils, if they felt that the crime warranted such a punishment.[80] These attitudes persisted into the medieval period. Indeed, in the twelfth century, Guibert of Nogent recorded that Radulphus, Archbishop of Rheims, denounced manumission, quoting the statutes of the Council of Gangra.[81]

Monastic institutions had specific guidelines concerning the admission of slaves seeking to become monks into their orders. The early thirteenth-century lawyer, Azo of Bologna, summarized the long-standing rules:

> If any unknown man enter a monastery, he is not to receive the habit for three years, and if within that time his master appears and proves that he is his slave, or adscriptius, or colonus, and that he has fled to the monastery to escape his work, or because he had committed some theft or other crime, he is to be restored to his master, on an oath that he will not punish him. But if after three years he has received the habit, no claim is to be entertained.[82]

It may seem surprising that a system of monastic slavery could develop, given that the monk was supposed to have relinquished all possessions. However, the distinction was that monks could not own *personal* property; slaves were held in common by the monastery, and so were not viewed in the same manner. In relation to Muslims in particular there is a curious choice of wording. The Cistercian proclamation of 1152 does not expressly forbid the practice of Muslim slave-ownership, it merely discourages it. The fact that the proclamation ultimately was reissued so many times is a testament to its ineffectiveness. Similar content often surrounded Christian writings about the Jews.[83] It is possible that the vague reference here was intentional, born from a combination of a lack of sympathy for the Muslim slave in question, plus very real economic issues for the slave owner, whether he be of the church or a secular individual.[84] A mass conversion of Muslim slaves in, say, a Spanish Cistercian monastery might have brought about economic ruin if the house were then compelled to free them.[85] This way, the order could attempt to address the problem, without being bound to carry out the command.

Initially, it is probable that the Cistercians simply were adopting an institutionalized practice that had been in existence, particularly in Spain, for centuries. Slavery had been prominent in Iberia since Roman times and before, and it existed throughout the Islamic world. The gradual shifting of power from an Islamic Spain to a Christian one during the medieval centuries resulted in a shift in the demographic of the slaves. In the earlier Middle Ages, the

4. The Cistercian Order in the Twelfth Century

slave trade had been to southern Iberia, when both Christians and pagans had been sold to slave traders in Spain and North Africa, to be shipped on to the greater Islamic world in the East. By the twelfth century and beyond, that route had shifted somewhat to the north, and Spanish Muslims were being sold to northern Spain and southern France and Italy.[86]

Practically speaking, slavery derived from economic necessities, rather than ideological conflicts, though enslavement for having the "wrong" religion was certainly a major justification. Indeed, a common convention of slaving in Spain was that the slaves were of a different religion from their captors. Often slavery was justified by religious differences.[87] Jews, Christians, and Muslims all had various regulations forbidding or at least discouraging the enslavement of co-religionists.[88] Therefore, pagans from northern Europe were most desirable as slaves ("slave" and "Slav" are related etymologically), thus avoiding any complications. All three religions could and did freely trade pagan slaves among themselves with clear consciences.[89]

Baptism was apparently the preliminary step in the gaining of freedom by a Christian-held slave.[90] That some Cistercians in practice discouraged it goes against one of the principles that the order stood for: the support for efforts to convert pagans and heretics. This is a serious contradiction, and a sign of some of the failings that the order was so optimistically founded to correct. Given that the practice may date from as early as the 1130s in both Spain and possibly southern France, it seems that the Cistercians were, at least in this area, afflicted with worldly practices almost from their inception. As soon as the order began to grow, the taint of secular affairs and concerns crept in almost immediately.

Maybe this was simply unavoidable, for virtually no medieval religious institution founded on ideals such as purification and simplicity was able to remain true to that state for long. Indeed, the fact that the Cistercians were so preoccupied with their own affairs in the early 1150s and would not lend their support to another crusade shows that they were well aware of the serious problems in their expanding institution. It fell to the idealists such as Bernard and Peter once again to continue the fight against the enemies of Christendom in the form of rhetoric and invective.

It is notable that one of the early forms of contact between the Cistercians and Muslims was slavery, an issue with which the Cistercians had not at their founding desired to be involved. This could easily have affected the order's attitude toward Islam, and brings up an important question. How could the Cistercians on the one hand be concerned with conversion (even if the crusades were not, other than in the sense that Saracens should only be killed if there is no other choice, and they refuse to convert), and at the same time discourage conversion for Muslim slaves which they owned or who were living in Christian lands? The conflict between religious ideals and economic realities was never really resolved, and shows the extent to which the order had to adapt its early intent to the real world in order to survive.

The Cistercians were not alone in this contradictory practice. The Templars also owned Muslim slaves, and in Spain, had Muslim tenants. There is evidence that the Templars were reluctant to accept conversions as a first step to freedom.[91] Indeed, if these tenants converted to Christianity, they could be penalized by having their lands seized; such tenants paid higher rents than Christians, and were obliged to engage in certain labors that Christians were not.[92] Slaves who wanted to convert were viewed with suspicion, and often prevented from converting (even though conversion had never been a Templar goal). Obviously the first objection would be that said slaves were merely undergoing a false baptism in order to gain their freedom. They could easily then just disappear and go on practicing their old faith. Economics also played a significant role, as slaves provided important unpaid work, could be sold for profit, and could even be used in bargaining to exchange for Christian prisoners, though this last option was more common in Spain than in the Middle East.[93]

Indeed, the monetary aspects of slave-ownership were simply part of the necessities of the time. As we have seen, the desire for religious differences between master and slave was long-standing, and the Cistercians, in particular would probably have complied with it. With the increasing amount of territory coming under Christian control as a result of the *reconquista*, the supply of slaves from a new source would also have increased: Muslims from Spain rather than pagans from northern Europe. In purely economic terms, it would have been far more feasible for monasteries to buy slaves locally than to have them imported from the North.

The Cistercians were engaged actively in establishing new monastic settlements in areas of Spain recently reconquered from the Moors, which strengthens this argument. The wealthiest and greatest of these houses was the Royal Monastery of Santa Mariá de Poblet in Catalonia. It was founded in 1150, shortly after the surrounding lands had been retaken. Like other monasteries in Spain, it engaged in the slave trade and owned Moorish slaves, apparently both Muslim and Christian.[94] This house was deliberately established on the frontier between Christian and Muslim lands. At first this seems a dangerous idea. Indeed, not only was there the danger of retributive Muslim attack, it was contrary to the pervading practice of new monastic settlements becoming more urban. Being a Cistercian house helps to explain the choice of location (remembering that by this time, the order was trying to return to its original intentions), though it also had many practical reasons, and one said to be because of a miracle.

In 1148, Count Ramón Berenguer was besieging the Moorish settlement of Ciurana and witnessed the presence of three lights, to which he attributed his victory in taking the stronghold. As a result, he invited the Cistercians of Fontfroide (located in southern France) to move to his lands and establish a new monastery. In 1150, a small group of thirteen monks came, and founded a daughter house at the site of the miracle. Ramón granted them significant land (2,800 acres), and offered other practical support. The audacious act of founding a monastery in this dangerous area was one of several strategies he was using to consolidate the land for Christendom and, in effect, change its character from Islamic to Christian.[95]

The monastery grew rapidly and became essential in funding future campaigns against the Moors, particularly attacks by rebels in Islamic territories. It also contributed significantly to the settlement of the lands by Christians, through cultivation and irrigation which attracted lay workers and other settlers. In addition, it is significant that Templar houses in nearby areas were also seeking land acquisitions in the same territory.[96] Their military nature and avowed purpose of combating non-believers sent a strong message to the conquered Moors. This seizure of land was a means of establishing legitimacy as well as securing the territory for the new Christian settlers.

Thus, Poblet was a remote settlement in the classic Cistercian sense that quickly became a kind of urban one, which had been its benefactor's intention from the beginning. Here, we see the irony of the Cistercians, a would-be reclusive order accepting the establishment of a nearby secular and commercial settlement from the very outset of the foundation of a new daughter house. Further, this house was intended to help fund military campaigns against the Moors, rather than exclusively to pursue conversion, and it engaged in the practice of owning and selling Muslim slaves, even when those slaves accepted Christian baptism. The holding of such slaves may have had an impact on the local Muslim populations as well. It was surely symbolic of their status as a conquered people, and it provided the monasteries with a free labor force to help in the cultivation of the land. This in turn encouraged more Christian settlers, and so the whole area grew.

Since these activities were present from the creation of the house at Poblet, and were basically designed into it, it is easy to understand the great turmoil that the Cistercian order faced in the 1150s, and why talk of a new crusade could not be the most pressing concern. Numerous problems and vexing questions such as the situation at Poblet existed, and there must have been many who objected to this direction for the order. Such practices raised many theological questions, which undoubtedly were hotly debated. It seems that effectual solutions were not easy to define or enforce. The continued issuing of the Cistercian statute regarding Muslim slavery and conversion is an example of the limits to which the order could be effective in imposing a unified standard on its numerous daughter houses.

To sum up, the Cistercian order was a very complex and contradictory organization almost from its inception. They rejected what they saw as the administrative complexity and liturgical pomposity of traditional Benedictine houses such as Cluny, attempting instead to simplify the monastic life, but this was a nearly hopeless task right from the outset. Through the figure of Bernard, the Cistercians were swept up into the middle of twelfth-century politics and the major religious struggles, indeed the greatest issues facing the Church at that time. Perhaps they had no choice but to comply with the prevailing thoughts of the age, yet they were often willing participants, seeking to disseminate their particular interpretations of the venerable Benedictine Rule to the widest possible audience during the unsettled environment of the first half of the twelfth century.

The issue of Muslim slaves and the situation with Poblet underscore the significance of Spain as a center for conflict between the two faiths, perhaps even more so than the East, because of its proximity to the rest of Europe. Despite the geographical closeness of the Islamic world to Christendom in the Iberian Peninsula, there remained considerable ignorance in northern Europe regarding Islamic belief and practice. The task of seeking an understanding of Islam that was not merely rumor, folk tradition, speculation, and outright falsehoods fell to Bernard's contemporary and friend Peter the Venerable, Abbot of Cluny. His extended translation project to gain a more accurate understanding of Islam, including the first translation of the Qur'an into a European language, was an astonishing undertaking, in view of the prevailing attitudes in Christian Europe, though it was not nearly as successful as he hoped, nor was it a breakthrough to new understanding between the two faiths.

The next chapter will consider Peter's efforts in Spain, the frontier and meeting place of these two civilizations, as well as the status of Mozarabic Christians still living under Muslim rule, who as we shall see, were probably connected to Peter's work. It will also briefly examine the work of Petrus Alfonsi, the enigmatic Sephardic Jewish convert to Christianity who wrote on Islam in at least a somewhat accurate manner, and brought his ideas and theology to northern Europe.

5

Peter the Venerable and Christian Writings in Islamic Spain

By the time of the First Crusade, Cluny was the largest, wealthiest, and grandest of the monastic houses of Europe. This had brought considerable criticism from reformers, as we have seen, but did not diminish the importance of the Cluniacs in life, religion, and politics. As abbot from 1122 until his death in 1156, Peter the Venerable wielded considerable power and influence. He is also an important figure in the study of Christian perceptions of Islam in the first half of the twelfth century. It was through his efforts that the West was brought somewhat reliable information about its enemy, including a translation of the Qur'an, though it was not Peter's intention to foster understanding or peaceful relations between the two faiths.[1] His agenda was in line with the religious attitudes and goals of the time, but he devised a different method to achieve those ends.

Cluny had a history of some involvement with Islam, such as with Glaber's writings, and Cluniac monks were supportive of reconquest efforts in Spain. In one vivid example, King Alfonso IV recaptured Toledo from the Moors in 1085. He promised the Muslim inhabitants of the city that they could continue to use the main mosque for worship, as a gesture of goodwill, and in his desire to rule all the people. However, when the king was absent, his wife, with the help and support of a Cluniac monk named Bernard de Sédirac, and reinforced by Christian soldiers, entered the mosque and proceeded to convert it to a church.[2] This belligerent attitude would be reflected in Peter's work and approach.

As we have seen, Bernard of Clairvaux had no desire to write against Islamic doctrines. It was Bernard's contemporary Peter, who developed an interest in (or rather, a great fear of) Islam and who had encouraged Bernard to write such a refutation; he was alarmed that it was so wide-spread and yet no one had taken up the call to properly refute it. Peter saw this as a religious duty, on par with similar work by the ancient Christians. By the time that Edessa fell, and talk of a new crusade began, Peter was already engaged in an ambitious project to study Islam with a view to refuting its teachings and beliefs as heretical, an undertaking that R.W. Southern calls "a landmark in Islamic studies."[3] As a result of this work, the first reasonably accurate translation of the Qur'an into Latin, made by the Englishman Robert of Ketton, became available to Western theologians, as well as several other works, previously only to be found in Arabic, though they were destined to have very little impact in the long term. This chapter will explore in detail the translation project and Peter's anti–Islamic writings, as they were an important development against the backdrop of the events we have looked at so far.[4]

Pierre Maurice de Montboissier was elected abbot of Cluny in 1122 at the age of 28 (not particularly young by medieval standards), three years after the official establishment of the Cistercian Order.[5] Indeed, Cluny itself had been founded in 910 as a center for monastic reform,[6] but there was a strong belief in Peter's time, both from within and without, that the order itself was now in need of its own reforms. A heated debate took place between the Cistercians and the Cluniacs, led by Bernard and Peter respectively.[7] It occurred mainly between the years 1123 and 1125, though it continued to be spoken of for a considerable time afterward. The chief difference concerned the proper observance of the Benedictine Rule, which the Cistercians believed that the Cluniacs were abusing. Though at times the two abbots were on opposing sides of the arguments, nevertheless they held one another in high esteem and became good friends. Indeed, Peter was supportive of many of the suggested reforms, and strove to enact them, often against the wishes of Cluny's numerous daughter houses. As late as 1143, he wrote to Bernard that he desired peace between the two orders.[8]

Various scholars have argued that Peter had an indirect, though significant, effect on Bernard's outlook, which at the time of the debate, was extremely introspective and world-denying. Peter faced Bernard's harsh and even at times satirical criticisms with dignity. His even-handed response apparently impressed Bernard greatly, and, as Adriaan Bredero notes, the "experience opened his heart again to the world."[9] This may or may not be true, but was probably not the whole reason. The fact that it was shortly after this conflict that Bernard began to write his justification for the Knights Templar is not necessarily evidence of a new world outlook. We have seen that Bernard was motivated to write *De laude* for political as much as theological reasons. If anything would demand a return to the world it would be this,

5. Peter the Venerable and Christian Writings in Islamic Spain

not Peter's respectful response to his criticisms. If Bernard had been so impressed with Peter's conduct, why not write the refutation of Islam at Peter's request? Bernard may indeed have respected Peter's dignified behavior, but this was not likely the main reason for his entry into the worldly affairs of the Church.

Peter probably conceived of the idea of studying Islam by providing translations of key texts when he journeyed to Spain in 1142, at the invitation of Alfonso VII (King of Galicia, and then of León and Castile from 1126[10]), who ceded a Castilian Abbey, San Pedro de Cardeña, to Cluny, and an annual stipend for the monastery first granted by his grandfather, Alfonso VI.[11] Alfonso VII needed Cluniac support for his candidate in the politically important election to the arch-bishopric of Compostela. The gifts given to Cluny were given in return for that support. Whether or not Peter intended to make or actually made a pilgrimage to Santiago de Compostela is uncertain. He does not say so in his writings about his time there.[12]

However, another more intriguing and convincing explanation for his decision to study Islam lies in the writings of a remarkable individual named Petrus Alfonsi. Alfonsi was a Sephardic Jewish convert to Christianity, whose life was contemporary with the First Crusade. The exact dates of his birth and death are unknown, as are the reasons for his abandonment of Judaism and adoption of the Christian faith.[13] At some time before 1116, Alfonsi emigrated to England, where he taught, and may have acted as a physician to Henry I.[14] At some point after 1120, he journeyed to France.

Alfonsi's life offers a unique perspective on the issue of Jewish-Christian-Islamic relations in medieval Spain. He was educated in al-Andalus, with knowledge of both Hebrew and Arabic. As such, he associated extensively with Muslims, and came to know their religion and way of life, being particularly interested in Arabic astronomy. By the early twelfth century, he was in Aragon, for he records that he was baptized in 1106 in Huesca, the capital city. It was at this time that he took the name Petrus, his birth name being Moses.[15]

Between 1108 and 1110, Alfonsi produced his *Dialogi contra Iudaeos*,[16] a lengthy polemic which attacked not only Judaism, but in chapter five, Islam as well. This was a work of major importance to Northern European theologians, for it was the first to present the basic tenets of Islam to Christians in an accurate manner from one who had first-hand experience with the Moors, and indeed, could have chosen to convert to Islam rather than to Christianity. Whilst it is a rational and essentially correct description, it does not attempt to be a sympathetic portrayal of the Muslim faith. Alfonsi's intent throughout is to show the inferiority of both Judaism and Islam, for he asserts that both contradict rationality.[17]

His knowledge of Arabic served him well here, for he was familiar with such works as the *Risālah* (*Apology*) of al-Kindi (discussed later in this chapter), as well as the Qur'an (though it is from al-Kindi that Alfonsi draws all of his Qur'anic quotes).[18] He was not an expert in languages, however, and modern scholars do not always regard him as a great medieval thinker. His knowledge was adequate, and in some areas, such as astronomy, superior to that of scholars in Northern Europe, but he certainly did not possess the genius of Abelard or Bernard.

Throughout the *Dialogi*, the style, as the title suggests, is in the form a dialogue between two individuals. However, these two are really one and the same, as Alfonsi has cleverly portrayed them as Moses and Petrus; in other words, it is a debate between his former Jewish and new Christian self. The dialogue of chapter five begins with Moses questioning why Petrus chose Christianity, when he had for so long been in the company of Muslims. Moses gives a detailed summary of Islamic beliefs, including its monotheism, belief in the Prophethood of Muhammad, the fast of Ramadan, the Hajj, its disdain for alcohol, its ritual acts of purification before entering a mosque, and so on.[19] This list of attributes and tenets was the first occasion that such information was offered systematically to Latin Christians. Considering that many, if not most Christians who were aware of Islam at all believed that Muslims were polytheistic pagans who worshipped Muhammad, this was indeed a major change.

Petrus responds to Moses' discourse by effectively congratulating him on his knowledge and accuracy. He then proceeds to list the many reasons why he feels Islam to be mistaken in its beliefs. Although his description up to this point has been truthful, his polemic is not kind, and begins to show signs of error.[20] This is particularly true of his analysis of the religious practices surrounding Mecca, and their origins, and is likely due to a long tradition within medieval Sephardic Jewish commentary on the status of the "Ishmaelites" (i.e., the Arabs, who trace their lineage to Abraham via his son Ishmael, rather than by Isaac, as the Jews do),[21] and the origins of Islamic beliefs. The general tone of this polemic is that while it concedes that Islam is a monotheistic religion and considers itself of the same tradition as that of Judaism and Christianity, it nevertheless retains many pagan practices to which the pre-Islamic Arabs adhered.[22] Most of these concern activities at Mecca, and in particular, the Ka'ba, which was a prime target of both Jewish and Christian polemicists throughout the Middle Ages. Alfonsi, the self-styled astronomer and astrologer, is keen to identify the black stone in the Meccan mosque as an idol of Mercury, confusingly arguing that though Muslims now worship Allah, they are still engaging, if ignorantly, in a pagan practice devoted to Saturn.[23] As to its origins, Alfonsi establishes a pagan heritage for the Ka'ba, in an effort to show how it contradicts the Qur'an and Islamic beliefs. Whereas the Qur'an states that it was founded by Abraham and Ishmael, Alfonsi puts forth that it was rather a center for idol-worship from the beginning, created by the disgraced sons of Lot. Alfonsi may have invented this idea, or he may have taken it from a now-lost source, because it doesn't appear elsewhere.[24]

Alfonsi also perpetuates a Jewish belief at the time that idols remain in the Ka'ba, and are still worshipped, again ignorantly, by Muslims who consider their practices monotheistic. Curiously, he does not mention the daughters of Allah or the Satanic Verses,[25] though he erroneously states that the Hajj is an annual duty for Muslims, drawing connections with a supposed pre–Islamic cult of Venus.[26] He accuses Muhammad of many of the things which would become stock subjects for anti–Islamic invective throughout the Middle Ages. Alfonsi scholar John Tolan summarizes:

> For Alfonsi, Muhammad is a greedy, disrespectful cheat who poses as a prophet. He learned the tenets of Judaism and Christianity from heretics of both religions. [...] Islam was designed to appeal to Arabs, a greedy, lustful, essentially pagan people. [...] Ritual ablutions are useless, Peter continues; Muslims confuse corporeal cleanliness with spiritual cleanliness. [...] Muhammad promised his followers carnal pleasures in paradise. Peter declares that this contradicts reason; this is Alfonsi's only invocation of reason in his anti–Islamic dialogue. Since the soul and the four elements that made up the body will be separated from each other, pleasures of the body will be impossible in the next life [...][27]

What Alfonsi presented to the Christian world was a strange mixture of accuracy and fallacy. The *Dialogi* was a valuable source of information made available for the first time to the Latin west, but it was heavily tainted with his own prejudices and a strong tradition of Jewish commentary and polemic.[28]

Alfonsi's own background helped significantly to lend authority to his arguments, not only against Islam, but also against his own former religion. The *Dialogi* became the most widely-circulated and read polemic against Judaism, not only in the twelfth century, but in succeeding centuries.[29] Indeed, seventy-nine copies of it are extant in various manuscripts,[30] a testimony to its importance. Alfonsi was apparently regarded as a respected authority, and in effect, living proof to Christian minds of the superiority of Christianity. Two copies of these manuscripts concern us here, for they suggest connections to not only Peter the Venerable, but also Bernard of Clairvaux.

We do not know how much of Alfonsi's work was known to either Peter or Bernard, but we can deduce that Bernard was probably familiar with some of it, and Peter most certainly was. A copy of the work was contained in a manuscript at Cîteaux from the 1140s,[31] which also contains thirteenth-century additions.³² Another copy contains not only Alfonsi's work, but Peter the Venerable's own harsh attack on the Jews, *Adversus Iudeorum*.³³ Though space precludes a detailed treatment of this work, it is important to note that it was composed by Peter in 1143, while still in Spain. His work borrows heavily from Alfonsi, featuring long passages which are included verbatim.³⁴ It also foreshadows his writing against the Saracens, in that he blames the Jews and their deceptive tales for inspiring Muhammad, and even claims that they recognized Ibn Tumart (*ca.* 1080–1128/30), the Moroccan Berber founder of the puritanical Almohads (who would conquer southern Spain in the twelfth century), as a prophet.³⁵

We can conclude that there is a good possibility that Peter's decision to study and refute Islam was drawn from his familiarity with the *Dialogi*. Whether he first discovered the text in Spain, or had read it previously in France is not known. It certainly was influential in his much more ambitious project regarding Saracen beliefs.³⁶

In order to accomplish his objective, Peter needed skilled translators to render Islamic texts into Latin, so that they could be studied. Several cities in Spain were known for their scholarly works, and for the remarkable intellectual and cultural exchanges between Jews, Christians, and Muslims which persisted despite the *reconquista* and Church teachings. The translators that Peter met were working in Toledo, mostly on scientific and mathematical texts in Arabic, but he convinced them to turn their attentions to religious matters. Peter did not learn Arabic himself, but rather, trusted in the competence of these individuals. The city was known for the Toledo School of Translators, which under the direction of its archbishop, Raymond, was actively involved in translating classical Arabic, Greek, and Hebrew texts into Latin.³⁷

The two principal figures in this group were Herman of Dalmatia (d. 1154) and the Englishman Robert of Ketton (fl. 1141–1157), archdeacon of Pamplona, the latter earning the distinction of translating the Qur'an.³⁸ Another of the translators was Peter of Toledo, about whom virtually nothing is known. This is remarkable, because he seems to have been the one who planned the entire project for Peter the Venerable, and was also the annotator. This would have placed him at the head of the translation group, and yet it seems that nothing else is known about him.³⁹

A very intriguing possibility, however, is that "Peter of Toledo" may have been Petrus Alfonsi,⁴⁰ given the extensive knowledge of Islam found in the annotations of the Latin Qur'an.⁴¹ If so, this would also explain the prevalence of Alfonsi's words in Peter's anti-Jewish polemic, and in his writings against Islam. A fourth translator to work on the project was Peter of Poitiers, a monk of Cluny, who assisted Peter of Toledo in the translation of the *Risālah of Al-*

Kindi. He was the *notarius*, or secretary of Peter the Venerable. The last of the individuals involved was a mysterious figure known only as Muhammad, who served to verify the context and meanings of Arabic words, and presumably, Islamic doctrine as well. If he was a Muslim (and probably one of some learning), his work would have been a violation of Islamic law, which forbade the presentation of the Qur'an to non-believers or the translating of it into another language. His name is conspicuously absent from the final edition, in the *Epistola de translatione sua*. This may or may not have significance. Perhaps Muhammad was a Christian, or a potential convert. If so, the secrecy would make more sense, as apostasy would bring a death sentence under Islamic law. He would have been put in danger by being publically named. Or it is possible that Peter wanted his name removed, so as not to cause scandal and upset to his monastic readers.[42] It does seem unlikely that a Muslim would volunteer to be involved in such a project, for while the translations are accurate in parts, they still contain a strong Christian bias, one of which a Muslim certainly would not approve.[43]

The resulting collection, known as the *Collectio toledana*, and also the *Corpus toledanum*,[44] consisted of the Qur'an (called the *Lex Sarracenorum*), the *Epistola Saraceni et Rescriptum Christiani* (the *Risālah of Al-Kindi*), the *Fabulae Saracenorum*, the *Liber Generationis Mahumet*, and the *Doctrina Mahumet*.[45]

The *Risālah of Al-Kindi* was a famous work in Spain, indeed the best-known Christian apology in Arabic. I contains two "letters," the first of which claims to be by a Muslim related to Caliph Al-Ma'mun (813–33). The second is a reply to that letter, allegedly written by a Christian in service to the same caliph.[46] The two individuals, Al-Hashimi and Al-Kindi, spell out the tenets of their respective beliefs, with the Muslim going first. Strikingly, Al-Kindi's reply is six times longer, which clearly shows Christian authorship.[47] This was exactly the kind of material that Peter was seeking, for it would help him in creating his own writings.

The *Fabulae Saracenorum*, "'is a typical potpourri of Islamic traditions."[48] It is a collection of Islamic legends and traditions commonly found in the Muslim world that is rather haphazardly put together, and the original source document has not been identified.[49] The subtitle, *Chronica mendosa et ridicula Saracenorum*, shows the attitude of its translator, Robert of Ketton.

The *Liber Generationis Mahumet* is another collection of "a great many Judeo-Islamic legends about creation and the lives of the patriarchs and prophets."[50] It traces the genealogy of Muhammad from Adam, and includes many miracle stories surrounding the Prophet's birth, which have Judeo-Christian parallels. Herman of Dalmatia translated this work, and also produced the *Doctrina Mahumet*, dialogues between Muhammad and four Jews who have come to question him about their law.[51]

The Latin version of the Qur'an also comes under Christian attack. Though the translation itself was reasonably accurate, it suffered the same fate that most translations from Arabic do: the loss of a great deal of the poetry and meaning. Given the great differences between the Semitic and Indo-European languages, this is not surprising. It did, however, give additional fuel to the fire for the Christian ideological assault. The annotator of Robert's edition displays this attitude quite clearly, though it is obvious from the remarks that he had knowledge of Arabic. He fiercely attacks apparent repetitions and contradictions in the work.[52] At the same time, he shows a very detailed knowledge of Islamic belief, such as the Muslim claim that Islam was a perfection and correction given to Muhammad because the other Peoples of the Book had strayed from their own laws.[53] It seems that some of these annotations were taken directly from Qur'anic commentaries. Thomas Burman notes that, "this indicates that the Annotator had such a Qur'anic *tafsir* open next to him as he annotated Robert's translation of the Qur'an. [...] he has frequently followed the model of the Qur'anic commentaries, explaining ambiguous terms and listing the various theories regarding the occasion of revelation for certain verses; thus he has effectively made his annotations into a polemical Christian *tafsir* on the first Latin version of the Qur'an."[54]

With these in hand, Peter felt that he had sufficient material to allow for a refutation of Islamic beliefs to be written. Though he regarded Islam as a Christian heresy, he also did not hesitate to call it a pagan belief, and seemed to go back and forth about which it was,[55] because like heretics, Muslims accepted some Christian truths, but like pagans, he felt that they were also tainted by great impiety.[56] Even after reading these translations, he admitted to having no proper knowledge about Islamic customs and daily life, and he did not care.[57] For him, it was sufficient that Islam was the enemy of Christendom, given its partial acceptance of Judeo-Christian tradition, and because of its reverence for Christ and Mary, but its refusal to acknowledge Jesus as the Son of God, seeing him rather as a great prophet. In this latter belief Peter likened Islam to Arianism, and saw Muhammad as the transitional figure between Arius and the coming Antichrist.[58] In fact, he said that Muslims had rejected more of Christian teachings than any other heretics had in the past, including baptism, the mass, and the sacraments.[59] As a result, Peter felt that the laws and doctrine of Muhammad were not just made up by a clever man, ridiculous though they seemed to him. They could, in fact have only come from Satan, and were part of a deliberate plan to deceive as many as possible and turn them away from God and true religion in the approach to the end of the world.⁶⁰ He did seem to feel some pity that so large a portion of humanity had been so deceived,⁶¹ but still considered Islam to be a kind of repository of all errors.⁶²

Peter feared that these beliefs might infiltrate the Church and lead the weak-willed astray, a central reason to begin with for his undertaking the project.⁶³ Thus, he wrote to Bernard, urging him to join in the campaign to refute Muslim beliefs, since no one had yet done so. What better time could there be, with talk of a new crusade beginning? A perfect opportunity presented itself to Peter, in offering the greatest theologian of the age a chance to refute the heresy that Peter had committed himself to denouncing. In his *Epistola* to Bernard, he described the Spanish translation project, and then implored Bernard to write a polemic against Islam. He described it as a Christian duty, especially of one so learned and venerated as the Abbot of Clairvaux.⁶⁴

He shows his concern for the effects of Islam upon the "weak" in his argument that if the refutation could not serve to convert Muslims, it would at least provide strength to those whose faith was in danger of faltering and perhaps being led astray,⁶⁵ most likely his actual reason for taking up the project at all.⁶⁶

Despite this passionate plea, Bernard did not accept his request. It is possible that relations were not good between the two at the time. Their friendship had been strained, owing to the continuing issues of criticism of Cluny by Bernard and the Cistercians, as well as issues around elected church officials, the problem of Peter Abelard, and other such day-to-day problems.⁶⁷ Further, Bernard was far more committed at the time to Christians in Europe, and combating heresies nearer to home kept him from writing against Islam. The closest he would come was to preach the crusade and support the Templars.⁶⁸ While these were certainly not insignificant actions, they attacked Islam in a secondary manner, rather than directly through the kind of theological polemic that Peter had wanted.

Indeed, at that time, Bernard was particularly concerned with the preaching of Peter of Bruys, who argued that priests and sacraments were not necessary for true salvation. Though Peter of Bruys was killed by an angry crowd around 1131, his followers, the Petrobrusians, lingered for some time after. Bernard and Peter the Venerable joined in fighting this heresy,⁶⁹ but Bernard also extended his efforts to several others.⁷⁰ Again, Bernard evoked the military image of the battle for souls between the Church and her opponents, specifically renegade Christians. For Bernard, these individuals and movements posed the greatest threat. The presence of Islam in the Holy Land, while a cause for Christian concern and indignation, could be countered effectively with crusading and the Templars. Further, Bernard held to the view that once brought under Christian rule, it would be acceptable to await the eventual conversion of Muslims, a policy akin to the treatment of Jews in Christian lands.[71] Their error was to be held up as an example to all, and it would be made right in the end. Unlike Peter, he did not perceive the Islamic threat to the Church from within. In addition, Bernard's temperament was probably not suited to the task. His spiritual life was centered around mysticism, and the extensive rationalism and book-study needed to write such a refutation was not his preferred way. He may have even viewed the whole thing as a futile effort that would accomplish very little, and in the end convince no one, least of all Muslim audiences.[72] Thus, the task fell to Peter, who unwillingly agreed to undertake the project.[73]

Peter's *Liber contra sectam haeresim Saracenorum* was the result of the project, a treatise which sought to refute various Muslim doctrines.[74] In addition, he composed the *Summa totius haeresis Saracenorum*, a summary of Islamic beliefs which has the distinction of being reasonably accurate in content, certainly far more so than any other document at the time,[75] possibly including Petrus Alfonsi's. The actual audience for which Peter intended these works is the subject of continuing debate. Did he have hopes of it reaching Muslim readers? In the *Prologus* to the *Liber*, he expresses the wish that his words might be translated into Arabic.[76]

There is his well-known opening address, which seems deliberately created in order to gain a favorable hearing from an Islamic audience, stressing that his attack was with words, not arms, and in love, rather than hate.[77] Peter tells his audience that he loves them, and in loving them, invites them to salvation. On the basis of such statements, some scholars have concluded that Peter was far more favorably disposed to Islam than his peers, and genuinely sought conversion rather than subjugation. Indeed, the translation project itself could be seen as evidence for this. James Kritzeck has argued for this position.[78] He admits, however, that his evidence is "thin,"[79] and that while conversion was possible, it was not usually the primary goal. However, he fails to provide more than circumstantial evidence that Peter was any more in favor of conversions than his contemporaries.

There is some evidence that Peter considered conversion a worthwhile effort,[80] but remember that most medieval theologians held that the outcome of the crusades should be either to kill or to convert the enemy (with emphasis generally upon the former), so there is nothing particularly unusual about Peter's position. Evidence contrary to Kritzeck's arguments is more convincing, as shown by Virginia Berry[81] and others.[82]

More recently, Benjamin Kedar has pointed out that reading Peter's loving words at face value takes them out of their context, and completely ignores his support for both the Second Crusade, and for the proposed military action following the failure of the crusade to wreak vengeance on the Greeks for their supposed treachery to the crusaders.[83] In a letter to Roger, King of Sicily, Peter urges him to take up this action. Virginia Berry translates:

> And there is something else which *far more* kindles our hearts and the hearts of nearly all of our Gauls to love and seek peace between you, namely that most wicked, unheard of, and lamentable treachery done by the Greeks and their wicked king to our pilgrims, i.e., the army of the living God. For to speak according to what I see in my mind, if it be necessary, as far as can befit a monk I would not refuse to die if the justice of God would deign to avenge the death of such great and such noble men, nay rather of almost all Gaul and Germany, which was destroyed by trickery.[84]

There was a strong anti–Greek attitude among many in the Latin Church, who viewed them as false Christians, in a sense almost as bad as the heretical Muslims themselves. Peter was one of many, including Suger of St. Denis and Bernard of Clairvaux, who actively encouraged a new military assault against Byzantium.[85] Such an action could hardly be admirable from a religion devoted to the notion of turning the other cheek, and Peter's support for it further undermines the theory that he held a conciliatory attitude toward Islam. If he would not extend love to his fellow Christians, then it is doubtful that he had any love for heretics, namely Muslims.[86] Kedar comments on Peter's capacity for love toward Muslims:

> And while Peter's words on love have sometimes been likened to Francis of Assisi's approach less than a century later, they may also be considered in conjunction with a gloss-ordinary on Gratian's *Decreta*, also from Francis' day. Commenting on the injunction by Julianus Pomerius that we should love our neighbors because they share with us the same nature (an idea very close to Peter's explanation of the reasons for his love for the Saracens), the glossator wryly remarks [...] "the Jews and the Saracens are our neighbors and ought to be loved by us as we love ourselves; nevertheless, all works of love ought to be employed according to each man's condition." Evidently, the glow of such a love was not always bright.[87]

Peter was indeed supportive of the violence involved in crusading, when it was necessary.[88] Statements to the contrary are rare in his works, and are typical of the mixed messages in such matters found in much medieval crusading theology. He did not comment on the relationship, if any, between his words of peace and love on the one hand, and his support of violence and extermination on the other. Several of his letters to various individuals clearly show his advocacy of armed resistance to the Saracens.[89] He was also a supporter of the Templars and their activities.[90]

Peter's remarkably conciliatory opening statement bears a strong resemblance to the literary style found in the *Risālah of Al-Kindi*. So it is likely that Peter was deliberately using this style in his address, one with which he presumed an Arabic-speaking audience would be familiar, as a kind of literary device.[91] Indeed, the general tone of Peter's works resemble that of al-Kindi, just as Petrus Alfonsi had borrowed heavily from it in his own work.

As such, Peter probably did intend to have the work translated into Arabic. Whether such a translation would have been used for Muslims seems unlikely. It is significant that throughout the work, for example, there are no expositions of Christian doctrines, as would be expected in a tract devoted to conversion. Peter "invites them to salvation" but gives no clues as to how this might be achieved by the potential convert. This makes no sense, and renders the work useless as a missionary tool. Curiously, there is also no attack on the Five Pillars of Islam, the duties incumbent on all Muslims, unlike Alfonsi, who devoted attention to each of them.[92] He held that even if it were translated into the "strange language" of Arabic, it would only help those whom God wished to save.[93]

Therefore, it seems that the work was intended to be used to strengthen the faith of Spanish Christians, whose first language was Arabic. He may have seen his work as being especially relevant to Spanish clergy who were faced with the prospect of members of their congregations being lost to heresy, or who had already converted to Islam. Living on the frontier between the two faiths, they would have been ideal candidates for the conversion to Islam that Peter feared. Whether or not this was intended for Spain, or for anywhere where the two came into contact, Peter did hold that the work should be used as a weapon in the defense against the incursions of ideological Islam. Further, he hoped that it would dispel any notions that some Christians living in those frontier areas might have had about the Muslims they encountered regularly, namely that they might have good qualities, genuinely pious beliefs, or even worse, some share of divine truth.[94] This supports the idea that he borrowed the style of the friendly and loving introduction from al-Kindi's work, with which many Arabic-speaking Spanish Christians would have been familiar. Mastnak observes, "the real addressee of Christian polemicists was the insecure Christian self. The potential enemy was not so much without as within. The Muslim was used — or abused — so that the Christian could talk to himself."[95]

Peter was not alone among French theologians in taking an interest in the affairs of the Spanish peoples. Hugh of St. Victor, in his *Epistola ad Johannem Hispalensem Archiepiscopum*, expresses a desire for efforts to undertake missionary work, which would naturally be to Spanish Muslims.[96] He stresses the salvation of Christianity, which only it can provide, for what true life is there without it?⁹⁷ Those who deny Christ (as the Muslims presumably do) do not have him, and are therefore damned.⁹⁸ There is evidence that such missionary work was not always undertaken with great zeal in those times, even in areas regained from Islamic control, and this may have been due to a desire to keep the respective communities separate, and shield Christians from possible lingering Islamic influence.⁹⁹

Peter's journey to Spain could well have alerted him to the perceived dangers faced by Christians there, prompting the mention of the "weak" in his letter to Bernard.¹⁰⁰ It is not known if he was aware of the works of Alvarus and Eulogius, though his reaction to Christians, Muslims, and Jews living in such close proximity might have been as alarmed, if not as intense, as that of the Córdoban martyrs three centuries earlier, whom we shall meet in chapters six and seven.

In fact, the Mozarabs were keenly aware of their position in relation to their Muslim rulers, and produced a number of important polemical works written against Islam in the twelfth and thirteenth centuries.¹⁰¹ These works show a considerable knowledge of the Qur'an and *hadith*, and frequently use quotes from both sources to show the inherent defectiveness of Islam. They clearly draw from the Eastern Christian polemical tradition, and have the expected characteristic of condemning the Qur'an as a non-revelation, a collection of misquotes, and a mass of confusing repetitions. Yet when it suits Christian argument or supports a Christian claim, the Qur'an naturally has authority.

What is unique about the Mozarabic writings against Islam is that they also clearly draw upon contemporary Latin theology from France, in particular the works of Abelard and Hugh of St. Victor concerning the nature of the Trinity.¹⁰² Abelard, for example, developed in his *Theologia "summi boni"* a theology of a central divine attribute to each of the members of the Trinity: *potentia* (power) for the Father, *sapientia* (wisdom) for the Son, and *benignitas* (benevolence) for the Holy Spirit. Though condemned by some, this theology was taken over by many of the great thinkers of the twelfth and thirteenth centuries, including Hugh of St. Victor, and later, both Bonaventure and Aquinas.

Soon after Abelard elucidated this belief, his followers altered or substituted certain terms, replacing *sapientia* with *scientia* (knowledge), and *benignitas* with *voluntas* (will, or good will). The three attributes, *potentia-scientia-voluntas*, have an exact correspondence in contemporary Mozarabic literature on the Trinity, appearing in Arabic as *qudrah-'ilm-iradah*.¹⁰³ This terminology is found in the *Tathlīth al-waḥdānīyah*, which may have been written by Alfonsi, and does not appear prior to Abelard's time.

It is obvious that this new Christian theological concept must have found its way to Muslim-controlled Spain relatively rapidly, and was taken up by the Mozarabs in their own writings against Islam. If Peter the Venerable was concerned for the "weak" Spanish Christians, his fears were probably unfounded. The Mozarabs had sufficient means to dispute and combat their rival faith. In any event, Peter's polemic was never translated into Arabic, so whatever his plans for it in this area, they remained unrealized.

Peter's contribution to the field of early Islamic studies seems at first to be quite significant, yet it did not mark the beginning of a new discipline of cross-cultural religious study in the West. It seems to have reached very few, and his *Liber contra sectam haeresim Saracenorum* only survives in two manuscripts.[104]

As we have seen, his purpose had been to understand the enemy of Christendom in order to challenge and disprove its beliefs. This was certainly a novel idea to an extent, but it was not intended to create understanding and coexistence between the two faiths by means of friendly theological debate. In its own way the refutation probably contributed to the continuation of crusading policies and enmity towards Islam, and its learned approach did little to dispel the popular untruths that continued to be disseminated throughout European society, partially because it perpetuated many untruths. As Mastnak insightfully observes, "since the hostile image of the Muslim world was not based on knowledge about the Muslims, it was unaffected by increases in knowledge."[105] In addition, the work did not encourage a great revolution in thought among the educated of the twelfth century.

So, the translation project was largely a failure, if we assume that its agenda was to create such a revolution in thought. Peter probably accepted this, for he was a relatively conservative theologian, who was in accord with the religious teachings and political institutions of his time. The fact that he readily agreed with many of the criticisms directed at his own monastic institution by the zealous new Cistercian Order is proof enough of this. It was not in the best interest of the church or the supporters of the crusades to foster new understanding between Christianity and Islam, for there could be no tolerance; it was incompatible both with what the Church saw as its mission in the East, and with its new identity as the self-styled supreme authority on earth. Since Peter was not especially interested in the conversion of Muslims, he instead sought a greater understanding of Islam for the sole purpose of discrediting it, which in the end could only help the Church's cause.

In conclusion, the works of Peter the Venerable and his predecessor, Petrus Alfonsi, had potentially opened new doors of understanding to Christendom. They were, however, quickly shut once more, for the only effect of

5. Peter the Venerable and Christian Writings in Islamic Spain 111

the transmission of this more accurate and new information was to inspire greater hatred and intolerance. The attitudes which had been taking shape for the previous century before Peter's project ensured that an understanding and toleration of Islam was not a Christian objective.

Indeed, as the focus on the Holy Land intensified with the First and Second Crusades and the rise of the military orders, the polemic against Islam increased and was more deeply incorporated into Christian theology. This was particularly apparent in the theology of the end time and apocalyptic beliefs. Though it had been the subject of such accusations in previous centuries, Islam now presented to Christendom more discernibly the perfect source for clear signs of the end of the world. It seemed in the vivid, fiery, and imaginative theories of theologians and exegetes that ancient apocalyptic prophecies were being fulfilled in their own time by the turmoil that continued to unfold in the East.

6

The End of the World: Apocalypticism and Antichrists

Thoughts, fears, and hopes about the end of all things loomed large in the medieval Christian mind. The apocalypse was the end of history and the fulfillment of the divine plan. Though for more than a thousand years, the faithful had been advised and even warned that it was not for them to know the time and the place, its inevitability was stressed constantly. At all times, everyone should be ready, and should see to it that their souls were not in danger. In defiance of this stern warning, of course, many did attempt to calculate the precise date of the end (a practice that continues in the modern world). As time passed, vivid literary descriptions and artistic depictions of these cataclysmic events developed, becoming more and more detailed, until reaching a state of appalling realism during the Renaissance.

Broadly defined, the apocalypse was seen as the fulfillment of God's plan, set in motion since the time of the Incarnation. Various omens and natural calamities would accompany its approach, but the true sign would be the arrival of the Antichrist, persecution and suffering, and then the second coming of Christ. Before his arrival, confusingly, there would be many lesser "antichrists" who prepared the way: heretics, schismatics, pagans, etc. Though Antichrist is only mentioned briefly in the Epistles of John, the Book of Revelation provided the raw material for other creative interpretations; its bizarre and confusing imagery (which was influenced by the Old Testament Book of Daniel) was readily adapted and shaped with successive generations. The rise of the Antichrist and his heralds, the trials and tribulations of the earth, the final battle between Satan and Heaven… all of these and more the people expected and feared, even if they were not always immediately on their minds. Indeed, around the year 954, the Cluniac monk Adso of Montier-en-Der (*ca.* 910–92) compiled a work on the Antichrist, entitled *De ortu et tempore Antichristi*, which brought together much of the thought about this terrifying figure, though Adso was not concerned about him appearing anytime soon.[1] We will return to this work later in the chapter. There is a general difference between eschatological belief, which is a belief in the eventual realization of the divine plan for history, and apocalyptic belief, which says that realization is immanent. Everyone from clergy to kings to commoners debated this in the Middle Ages, with no definitive solution.[2]

Nevertheless, a state of low-level apocalyptic paranoia was a fact of life in medieval Christendom, and as such, it could also be easily used during theological disputes and for political gain. For example, it was not uncommon for those who debated and argued to call one another "antichrists." Bernard had done so to Abelard. It seems that this was more a form of insult and verbal abuse, rather than a declaration of anything truly diabolical.[3] However, it could certainly be applied in a much more literal sense, so it is not surprising that Islam and Muslim military expansion would come to be viewed within this framework, though interestingly, it did not happen as quickly as we might expect. Still, the very act of taking up arms to resist and fight unbelievers was, as we have seen, a way of enacting the will of God, and any actions which did this were necessarily moving God's plan forward to his end of the world. Thus, in one sense, crusading had an apocalyptic thread woven into it from the start.

While its presence was pervasive, apocalypticism was not always a popular or even approved method or spreading the Christian message. Lone, itinerant preachers, the type that multiplied during the Reform, were prone to uttering things which were unacceptable and even heretical. Indeed, apocalyptic visions and preaching could all too often be opposed to the Church and its teachings, dismissing aspects of worship, the sacraments, or even the entire institution itself. There were many attempted "reformations" before Martin Luther, and images of the end of the world often fueled their fire.

This chapter discusses some of the most important references to apocalyptic thought in relation to Islam up through the period of the Second Crusade. One notable twelfth-century figure is absent. Joachim of Fiore (*ca.* 1135–1202) regrettably will not be studied here, because the period of his activities is later than the time frame of this book. Though he was born in 1135, he was a child during the Second Crusade and the other events that so preoccupied Bernard and his colleagues. Joachim's detailed apocalyptic writings relate to the political and religious turmoil of the end of the twelfth century, and naturally focus on the Third Crusade and the conflict between Richard the Lionheart and Saladin. Joachim, the Calabrian abbot and prophet, was a principal writer and commentator on apocalyptic themes during the Middle Ages, and one of the first to deliver a systematic treatment of Islam as the prophesied enemy of Christianity in the last days. He envisioned Muhammad as representing the fourth head of the Beast of the Book of Revelation, and Saladin as being the sixth.[4]

In the thirteenth century, his works were taken up on numerous occasions, often without church approval, and used in all manner of political and religious conflicts. Perhaps the most extreme of these had nothing to do with Islam at all, being the conflict between the secular masters of the University of Paris and the Mendicant Orders (the Franciscans and Dominicans), the latter being accused of being precursors to Antichrist and the beginning of the end of the world as foretold by Joachim.[5] It is unfortunate to neglect such a fascinating figure. However, there are many instances of similar thought in earlier writings, and this subject was one of great concern, even if no definitive theology was put forth.

Apocalyptic thought had been an important element of Christian belief from its earliest days. As mentioned, the church rather curiously maintained an anti-apocalyptic stance in many cases, dating back to its first centuries. St. Augustine of Hippo had steadfastly opposed literal interpretations of apocalyptic texts, preferring instead to meditate upon their symbolic meanings. This had been the position of many of the early Church fathers, most notably Augustine and Jerome. Indeed, for many early Christian writers, trying to read apocalyptic meanings into texts was an outdated practice; they believed it was too similar to the literal way in which they thought the Jews continued to read their scriptures. The Revelation of St. John, for example, was not viewed as some sort of prophecy of terrible events to come at the end of the world, but rather an allegorical statement about the ongoing trials of Christians and the eternal battle between good and evil at that time (an interesting fact that is unknown or ignored by many today). If any had the thought to try to calculate when these events would occur, they were negated by the statement in Acts 1:7, "It is not for you to know the times or the dates."[6]

Augustine supported this position, but regardless of his caution, he was in some ways responsible for the future development of apocalyptic thought in the West, developing such ideas as the theory of the ages of the world (with each age lasting approximately 1,000 years). He did employ the Pauline concept of the age of grace with a view of larger patterns of history, and his theories prefigured later medieval thought. It is interesting that later medieval writers cited church fathers such as Augustine and Jerome more frequently as authorities on apocalyptic matters than genuine early apocalyptic writers such as Irenaeus and Commodien, and that these Church fathers were used to endorse views that they had not actually supported.[7]

Naturally, a full history of the development of apocalypticism in Western

Christianity cannot be entered into here.[8] This chapter will focus mainly on the development of apocalyptic thought during the Reform period, in relation to Islam and the justifications for crusading. The intensity in the texts of this period lies mainly in the accounts written immediately after the First Crusade (i.e., the first decade of the 1100s). With the fall of Edessa three decades later, a new sense of urgency appears in the Second Crusade preaching.

Interestingly, some assert that apocalyptic fears seem not to have been a central issue in the eleventh century,[9] or rather they were not of greater concern than usual, and that compared to the fervor of the next few centuries, the writings from then are quite tame by comparison. This argument is based on assumptions about the lack of new material in the genre appearing at that time, and perhaps that the year 1000 had come and gone without a hitch. This does not prove that such thoughts were far from people's minds, however, merely that there was not a great movement of new ideas in the area. One could perhaps assert that the old beliefs and fears were strong enough to sustain the anticipation of the end time without the necessity of novel ideas. In the eleventh century, the West had yet to encounter Islam on a large scale, and therefore recognizable signs of the end were relatively sparse.

It is, of course, impossible to gauge the importance of such events in the minds of those Europeans without attempting to enter into a psychological study of the effects that these expectations would have had on them. However, regardless of the presence of apocalyptic beliefs throughout the eleventh century, it does seem that the often-assumed wide-spread fears regarding the year 1000 have been over-stated by some historians.[10]

With the passage of the millennium, apocalyptic writings seemed to lessen (regardless of popular sentiment), or at least nothing new was brought forth. However, with the two most dynamic events of the century, the Reform and the First Crusade radically changing the history of the West, a renewed interest in apocalyptic thought surged in Christian eschatology.[11] What began with Urban's sermon, sparked an attempt at European unity, and strengthened the consolidation of power for the Church, ending with the retaking of Jerusalem from Islamic control, an event of absolutely enormous significance for Christian eschatology. This opened the gates to a whole new wave of apocalyptic thinking. Indeed, it was widely believed that one of the key events that must happen before Antichrist would appear was the retaking of Jerusalem, and that precondition had suddenly and violently come true.[12]

The capture of the Holy City heralded the beginning of a new era for the church, one in which it was now able to show its supremacy quickly and forcefully. The success of the crusade was a vindication for the policies that the church had been pursuing for the previous quarter of a century, but it could not afford to rest for too long. With Jerusalem again in Christian hands there was talk of the ancient prophecies beginning to be fulfilled. Guibert of Nogent, writing in the early twelfth century, records:

> You ought to consider with deep deliberation whether, as a result of your pains, with God acting through you, it should happen that the mother church of all churches begins to bloom again with the Christian religion. You ought also consider whether perhaps he may not wish other parts of the East restored to the faith against the approaching times of the Antichrist. For it is clear that Antichrist will not wage war against the Jews and pagans [i.e., Muslims in this context], but, according to the etymology of his name, he will attack Christians. If he finds no Christians there (as today there are scarcely any), there will be no one to oppose him or whom he may legally overcome. [...] If then you are forward in waging holy war, just as you once received the seed of the knowledge of God from Jerusalem, so now you will return a repayment of borrowed grace there, so that the Catholic name will be propagated, that name which is opposed to the perfidy of Antichrist and his followers.[13]

This language is typical of post-crusade commentary on the subject. There is a clear conviction that the end is approaching, and that the Christians would do well to be prepared for it. It was necessary to purify the Holy City of all outside influences, hence the brutality of the slaughter of all non–Christian inhabitants. The joy at this massacre becomes more understandable if we see it from an apocalyptic point of view. Interestingly, in an account of Tancred's (a Norman leader of the First Crusade) capture of Jerusalem on 15 July, 1099, it was noted that an "idol" allegedly found in the Al-Aqsa mosque was an image of Muhammad, one of the Antichrists.[14] This was therefore an idol to Antichrist, and further proof (if any were needed) of the sinfulness of the Muslims.[15] Given the Islamic prohibition on the making of images, such an item (perhaps an old piece of Roman statuary) would not likely have been found in a Muslim's possession, least of all in a mosque.

In looking at the First Crusade, did new apocalyptic theology develop after the retaking of Jerusalem, or rather was it used as a prelude or a justification to take the cross? How much these beliefs may have motivated the population to action has been debated, though the ideas were circulating.[16] Bernard McGinn has argued that the liberation of Jerusalem may have been largely a political affair focused on the concerns of the papacy and the Church in exercising their newly-gained powers.[17] This is a certainly a valid point, and it supports the discussion in chapter one, that the clergy understood the importance of the image that the Church needed to present of itself in the years following the First Crusade, and indeed, throughout the Investiture Contest. The religious and political concerns and ideas that brought about the First Crusade continued long after its success. As we have seen, a major point in these policies was the need provide reassurance of God's continuing support of Christian efforts in the Holy Land.

Some have posited that the crusade, being a popular religious movement, did not come about as a result of apocalyptic fears and hopes, but rather, served to revive those ideas in the decades following the capture of Jerusalem.[18] This may be true to a certain extent, given that there was certainly a renewed interest in eschatological themes following the crusade, yet it would be wrong to dismiss the notion that such ideas already existed among the populace during the events leading up to the crusade. The dream of liberating Jerusalem could not help but stimulate such thoughts.[19] Research suggests that there was already an expectation of a coming end, a few decades before Urban's Clermont speech.[20] Indeed, "a turning point was, perhaps, the great pilgrimage [which included Gunther of Bamberg, whom we have already discussed], which set out from Germany for Jerusalem in 1064/65 because Easter Day 1065 coincided with the feast of the Annunciation. This coincidence was believed to be especially meaningful, and might bring with it the second coming of Christ, the Parousia; the pilgrims wanted to be in Jerusalem when this came to pass."[21]

If news of this circulated far enough, it could certainly have at least been in the backs of the minds of some of the First Crusade's participants, even if the Second Coming had failed to materialize in 1065. It shows that there was a popular expectation. After all, Clermont was held in 1095, 30 years later, so perhaps that was significant? Or perhaps it would occur in 1098, 33 years later, the same as Christ when he died? Medieval minds constantly turned over such things, as people in every age seek certainty and reassurance. It is fine to tell people not to expect something (such as the admonition from Acts that knowledge of Christ's return is not known to any but God). It is quite another to expect them merely to abide by this and ignore something so tantalizing and frightening. Of course, one cannot argue, on the basis of this longing, that apocalyptic expectations were a major impetus for the popular fervor for the First Crusade; there is not enough evidence. However, it could well have been one of many means of generating and encouraging mass support for the venture. Therefore, though the motivations for the crusade may well have had political origins, as McGinn argues, one aspect of those political concerns could certainly have been the use of apocalypticism to stir the popular imagination.

Jay Rubenstein has recently argued that apocalyptic expectations did indeed play a key role throughout the First Crusade,[22] noting that the chronicles written after the event are replete with apocalyptic imagery, not due to the failure of such an event, but because of its being fulfilled.[23] In *Armies of*

Heaven, he vividly recounts the entire journey to Jerusalem and its aftermath. At the very outset, Peter the Hermit was there. Riding a mule and eating no meat (though he was happy to take fish and wine),[24] he stoked the fires of popular religious imagination and added his own brand of fiery preaching to the movement. It was said that he had been to the Holy Sepulcher, and been instructed by Christ himself to take a plea for help back to Western Europe. Whereas Guibert of Nogent viewed him with scorn, Albert of Aachen noted he possessed a charter from the Patriarch of Jerusalem, but it morphed into something entirely more significant: it had come from heaven itself. This charter implored all Christians to retake Jerusalem for the time was at hand.[25] This was obviously fanciful and the result of a good story being embellished with each new telling, but it shows the power of effective preaching to inspire and inflame those who heard it. Peter would remain with the crusade throughout its entirety, and despite the massacre of his followers by the Turks (detailed in chapter one), he would be both a source of inspiration and a thorn in the side to various key crusade leaders, a constant reminder of apocalyptic fervor in the ranks. Indeed, his undisciplined followers (the survivors of whom joined other crusading armies) would have been more receptive to his apocalyptic style than the professional soldiers and knights, and they made things difficult for the more trained crusaders. However, at one point before the city of Antioch fell, he decided that perhaps he had been mistaken about it all, and attempted to flee from the crusade with a companion, William the Carpenter. Tancred, one of the crusade's leaders, had them hunted down, captured, and brought back. While Peter was not punished (and William deserted again, permanently, a few days later), his reputation was certainly damaged, but some undoubtedly remained loyal.[26] Charismatic leaders can always find a select group who will follow them, no matter how foolish or disappointing they turn out to be.

It wasn't just apocalyptic thoughts which infested the minds of these crusaders. Some held to the idea of millenarianism, which drew on ideas in the Book of Revelation that there would be a time of a thousand-year peace on earth, before Satan was released and the final battle began. This brand of apocalyptic thought lent itself especially well to predictions and speculations about just when it would occur, which explains why official Church teaching was so opposed to it, going back to the time of Augustine. With the goal of capturing Jerusalem, and many nobles openly expressing interest in assuming the leadership role once the city was taken, it is easy to see why speculation was rife about if this was the beginning of those thousand years.[27]

Official proclamations for the crusade were less emphatic about apocalyptic themes, of course. Indeed, Urban never made use of the Antichrist in his preaching,[28] though Guibert provided plenty of apocalyptic references in his account of the Clermont speech. Further, Guibert had Urban note that according to Daniel 7:24, Antichrist would kill three kings (from Egypt, Ethiopia, and Africa), and this obviously could not happen until those lands were once again under Christian rule,[29] a perfect reason to begin by recapturing Jerusalem.

Whatever the chroniclers might say (and they certainly disagreed with one another), the Church could not deny the efficacy of Peter's techniques, even if it sought to keep them under control. And while the princes may have had their own motivations for taking the cross (some not always so godly), the people certainly had a multitude of reasons, some of which we have already discussed. As preaching of the crusade spread, stories of ominous and miraculous signs began to circulate, as well: comets and blood-colored clouds in the sky, visions of celestial warriors on horseback, a baby born with the ability to talk, another born with four arms and four legs, the list goes on. Others claimed that they had been branded by God with the sign of a cross (though even then, some recognized these as fakes and self-mutilations).[30] No one required that these stories be verified, of course, for they were not miracles needing qualification. It was enough that someone had seen and reported them, and told their friends, who told their friends, and so on. The urban legend was alive and well in that time.

Up until the end of the First Crusade, apocalyptic hopes continued to play a part, with the taking of the city being seen as a fulfillment of prophecy. The orgy of slaughter that followed was one outcome of that. The question, however, was what happened next? To accept a crown and become King of Jerusalem might open the doors for the Antichrist's return, a move not to be taken lightly. The role fell to a crusader named Godfrey of Bouillon (*ca.* 1060–1100), a Frankish knight and Duke of Lower Lorraine. He refused the title of king, however, believing that belonged to God alone. While some had hopes that his ascension to power and the humility he showed would mark the beginning of the reign of peace, it was not to be. Despite military successes, he died only a year after the taking of Jerusalem, and his brother Baldwin assumed the leadership, officially taking the title of King of Jerusalem, and establishing a more secular kingship. For the time being, the apocalypse may have been forestalled.[31]

Battles against the Muslims continued, of course, as they still comprised the majority of the population in surrounding lands. As we have seen, Islam was viewed as the polar opposite of Christianity. As such, to battle against it was a form of recreating history; it represented the eternal struggle between good and evil. With each conflict, all of the old battles from the Old Testament and elsewhere were replayed, and indeed, those ancient battles pointed to the ones now being fought by the crusaders, and proclaimed that the end of history approached.

Could the emotionally-charged theology of the end time have been used in a manipulative manner by the recently-empowered Church, if not before the crusade, then after? It is certainly possible. On the other hand, there were undoubtedly numerous individuals and Church representatives who felt a genuine sense of the approaching end, a mixture of fear and excitement. Indeed, as we have seen, such feelings may have been a significant contributing factor to the almost inexplicable event of thousands of people abandoning their everyday lives to journey to Jerusalem on the armed pilgrimage in the first place.[32] Still, many are also recorded as making provisions for their families and properties, hardly the actions of those who expected the end of the world.[33] We must consider that the Church was able to use this fervor to its advantage, and that this, like the later portrayals of the Holy Land in chronicles, helped to enhance Church status. In an apocalyptic sense, the strength it gained would certainly signal a change of events which was potentially of cosmic importance.

Some scholars have argued against any earlier use of apocalyptic imagery on the basis of expectations regarding the Last World Emperor. Given the conflict between Church and Empire, and the Investiture Contest, it seems that apocalyptic themes would have been unwelcome by Gregory VII.[34] However, this only considers the branch of apocalypticism associated with the Sibylline oracles,[35] a collection of Greek prophetic exameters that over time became a curious blend classical pagan, Jewish, Christian, and Gnostic beliefs, written and compiled up until about the fifth century C.E., adapted by both Jews and Christians. They were influential and important well into the Middle Ages, but by no means the only version of the end time known to medieval theologians (Bernard himself was to make use of them in his support of the Second Crusade, a topic which will be discussed presently). It follows logically that a prophecy which emphasized an emperor uniting the world would be unpopular with a Church which had sought to wrest imperial power into its own hands. However, given the fact that Sibylline prophecy was never officially sanctioned by the Church, it cannot be viewed as the only method of interpreting the events of those times. In fact, it seems logical that an alternative eschatology would be presented, one in which the Jerusalem journey would not be made by an emperor, but rather by the humble masses (or the pope himself, as Gregory had hoped).[36]

Was one aspect of preaching the First Crusade an attempt to de-emphasize the Sibylline vision of the end of the world in favor of one more acceptable to the papacy trying to consolidate its power? We cannot be sure, but it does provide an explanation for the enthusiasm with which the crusade was preached. If the people's attention could be turned away from prophecies which supported an emperor in favor of a new eschatology emphasizing the Church's leadership, so much the better.

We will turn our attention away from this interesting topic, and focus on the relation of Christian apocalyptic to Islam. As we have seen, prior to the eleventh century, Western Christian writings about Islam were generally only periodic and usually contained little of substance. The subject of apocalypticism is rare, with a few notable exceptions, one of the more remarkable of which is the Spanish Martyrs' Movement of ninth-century Córdoba, which will also be discussed in greater detail in chapter seven.

This whole unusual affair, which took place in the decade of the 850s, was an extreme example of hostility between the two faiths in Spain, where relations, if not always good, were nevertheless usually less strained. Its chief champions were Eulogius, titular Bishop of Seville (who successfully achieved his own desired martyrdom in 859), and the layman Paul Alvarus, both of whom actively encouraged fanatical Christians to become martyrs for the faith by deliberately blaspheming Islam and denouncing the Prophet Muhammad in the Muslim-controlled city. The authorities, aware of the strategy behind their actions, tried to avoid executions and thus inciting other would-be martyrs, but the persistence of the Christians eventually left them feeling that they had no choice, the penalty for such actions being death. Eulogius and Alvarus wrote their apologies for the martyrs to "construct an unambiguously derogatory image of Islam, not only to justify the radical actions of the martyrs, but to embarrass those Cordoban Christians who felt at ease working within the framework of Arabo-Islamic society."[37]

Alvarus' writings in particular are replete with apocalyptic imagery concerning Islam, perhaps the first major example of such a phenomenon in the West. In his *Indiculus luminosis*, he makes extensive use of the book of Daniel, chapter seven.[38] A splendid example of the complex and convoluted exegetical method that he employed may be found in his interpretation of Daniel 7:25, which states in part: "He will defy the Most High and oppress the holy people of the Most High. He will try to change their sacred festivals and laws, and they will be placed under his control for a time, times, and half a time."[39] Alvarus seized upon the latter portion of this verse as conclusive proof for his warnings. He took all of this to mean that Islam would reign for three and a half ages of seventy years each, 245 years in total. He wrote this in 854, and calculated that the Muslim era had begun in the early seventh century (whether he knew the exact date is doubted; he may have thought it to be a bit earlier than it was, i.e., in 622). As such, he reasoned that the end of the world must arrive very soon. R.W. Southern further notes, amusingly, "By a curious coincidence — since everything conspires to support a hypothesis we desire to believe — the Emir of Cordova Abd ar-Rahman II died in 852 and he was succeeded by Mahomet I, 'the man of damnation of our time.'"[40]

And so "Muhammad" had returned to reign over them. This seemed to be absolute confirmation of the Spanish Christians' fears. For Alvarus, Islam conformed perfectly to the prophecies of Daniel, and he wrote at length on the subject in the *Indiculus*.[41] An important distinction must be made here. For Alvarus, Muhammad was not *the* Antichrist, but rather *an* Antichrist, one of many who prepared the way for the true enemy; he drew on the writings of Jerome in formulating his opinion. The Prophet of Islam and his followers prefigured the great sufferings Christians would endure in the true apocalypse, but Alvarus was more concerned with showing how their culture was completely against all that Christianity stood for, and therefore that it must be rejected, lest Christianity lose itself.[42]

These writings hearkened back to Byzantine polemic in their content, though it would be wrong to say that there was a direct connection. The Spanish martyrs were in possession of a life of Muhammad modeled on Byzantine sources, which related the popular fallacy that the Prophet had died in the year 666.[43] Generally, however, the writings of the Greeks in the first centuries of Islam had little or no immediate influence upon the West, but often became popular in the later Middle Ages. One good example of this is the writing of Pseudo-Methodius (mid-seventh century, wrongly attributed to Bishop Methodius, who died *ca.* 300), one of the first Byzantine polemicists to produce an apocalyptic interpretation of the rise of Islam.[44] It gained a supreme popularity in the West and was translated into numerous languages.[45]

The idea of apocalypticism in relation to Islam was to lie dormant for several centuries after the Martyrs' Movement. The major apocalyptic writer living between the time of the movement and the crusades was Adso, whom we have already met. His chief contribution to the literature was a detailed description and interpretation of the figure of Antichrist in his *Libellus de Antichristo*.[46] Yet here he is also a traditionalist, stressing that Antichrist would arise from the Jews, particularly from the tribe of Dan.[47] He was not concerned with Islam, concentrating instead on anti–Judaic polemic. Adso's work is unique in that it presents, for the first time, a comprehensive life of Antichrist, in many ways similar to the *vitae* of the saints. The life is essentially a parody, a grotesque imitation of the life of Christ, but also draws upon Sibylline themes such as the Last Emperor. The work was to have considerable influence. It foreshadowed later developments in apocalyptic traditions by organizing for the first time the various sets of beliefs about Antichrist and his deeds. Later writers on the topic took this very seriously, and the *Libellus* clarified for them the role of Antichrist. This work even influenced how this great enemy was portrayed in literature and art.[48]

In Europe, the Church was still in the process of vigorously continuing its reforms, which were not to reach a conclusion until the Concordat of Worms in 1122, when the conflict between the papacy and the Holy Roman Emperor was settled, the final agreement coming the following year at the First Lateran Council. As noted, this new order of power in Europe called for a rethinking of the traditional apocalyptic themes, particularly those of the Sibylline prophecies, which had for so long stressed the importance of the Emperor. If the "holiness" of the empire was being called into question, it placed new emphasis on the role that the papacy might play in the last days. It was, of course, unthinkable to suggest that popes were in error.

During this period, more writers and theologians began to speculate on this major turn of events, and its implications for apocalyptic and eschatological thought. Some, such as Rupert of Deutz (*ca.* 1070–1129), Otto of Freising (*ca.* 1110–58), and Gerhoh of Reichersberg (1093–1169) focused their writings on the clash between empire and papacy, which continued throughout the twelfth century despite the agreements of 1122–3 (nobles and royals would never cease quarreling with popes over the centuries). They managed to see these events in apocalyptic terms and reinterpret the old signs accordingly.[49]

Other writers, particularly Peter the Venerable and Bernard of Clairvaux, turned their attention to the East. For Peter the clearest sign of the approaching end was to be found in what he saw as the great heresy of Islam, which to him was the only heresy that had not yet been properly refuted. Here we will explore his linking of Islam and Muhammad to Antichrist and the end of the world.

Peter discusses the nature of Muhammad in vivid and certain terms in his *Summa Totius Hæresis Saracenorum*. Kritzeck provides a translation:

> The highest purpose of this heresy is to have Christ the Lord believed to be neither God nor the Son of God, but (though a great man and one beloved of God) simply a man — a wise man and the greatest prophet. Indeed, that which was once conceived by the device of the devil, first propagated through Arius, then advanced by that Satan, namely Mohammed, will be fulfilled completely, according to the diabolical plan, through the Antichrist. [...] This most wicked Mohammed seems to have been appropriately provided and prepared by the devil as the mean between these two [Arius and Antichrist], so that he became both a supplement, to a certain extent, to Arius, and the greatest sustenance for the Antichrist, who will allege even worse things before the minds of unbelievers.[50]

This damning condemnation clearly reveals Peter's beliefs. As discussed in chapter five, it was a matter of great importance to him that this heretical belief be refuted and stopped. He was familiar with the Islamic version of eschatology, and included an accurate summary of many of the beliefs contained within it in his *Summa*.[51] He outlines, for example, the Islamic belief in Antichrist (*al-Masih ad-Dajjal*, "the false messiah," not mentioned in the Qur'an), that Christ would slay Antichrist with the *gladio suae uirtutis*, convert the Jews, and teach the Christians the error of their ways, followed by his own death and resurrection and intercession (though not actual judgement) on the behalf of the Christians. These last two points in particular conflicted with Christian belief, which held that Christ was the judge, and intercession was useless after the end of time. In response to these views, Peter wrote yet more condemnatory words:

> For thus the very wretched and wicked Mohammed has taught them who, by denying all the mysteries of the Christian religion whereby particularly men are saved, has condemned almost a third of the human race by some unknown judgement of God and by unheard-of, raving mad tales, to the devil and eternal death.[52]

It is worth noting that Peter, like many theologians after him, offers no explanation as to why God would allow this third of humanity to be so seduced, and thus condemned because of their ignorance. His sole response to this vexing and uncomfortable question is found at the close of the *Summa*:

> As to why it was permitted him [i.e., for Muhammad to spread the heresy of Islam], He alone knows to whom no one can say, "Why did you act this way?" and who has also said that "of the many called, few are chosen." [Matt. 22:14] On that account I choose rather to tremble than dispute.[53]

Peter is content with the idea that the "few" mentioned in Matthew are the (presumably European) Christians, and that all others must be excluded. Why this heresy continues to spread is known only to God, and is not for mortals to question. It is the duty of all Christians, however, to prevent it and any heresy from growing further, if they can.

In his refutation of Islam, the *Liber Contra Sectam Sive Hæresim Saracenorum*, Peter challenges the Muslims to consider whether or not they might also have been deceived by the devil, for often in the past the Church itself had faced such difficulties, and many had been led astray, including the Jews who will believe Antichrist to be the messiah.[54] How can Muslims be so sure that their prophet is who they say he is?

Peter was quite clearly convinced that the presence of Islam in the world signaled the beginning of the end of history. In his writings we see the first sustained attack with apocalyptic themes on Islam in the West since the time of Alvarus and Eulogius. Indeed, the writings of these self-styled martyrs were available in Spain during Peter's time. It is possible that Peter's use of the link between Muhammad, Arius, and Antichrist may have been influenced by the link proposed by these ninth-century militant Christians.[55]

Peter's work, however, is far more significant, given his position as the abbot of the greatest monastery in Christendom, whereas the writings of the Spanish martyrs had much less impact; they wrote at the center of the Western Islamic world, but a city that was unknown or largely ignored by the rest of Europe. It is true that Peter's polemics did not inspire a great interest in Islamic studies or a new genre of specifically anti–Islamic apocalypticism, but they did provide a model for future apocalyptic writings that would last for several centuries.

Bernard was, of course, less concerned with the activities of Islam as a heresy or a threatening force to Christianity. His use of apocalyptic imagery is more sparing, and in relation to Islam came primarily from his activities in the preaching of the Second Crusade. However, Bernard's other writings do contain same references to Antichrist and the apocalyptic genre in general.[56] He used the example of Antichrist, and the rhetoric that came with it, in his arguments with others, such as the Antipope Analectus II (so-called because a dispute arose over how he was elected; Bernard was not in favor of him, but rather another pope who had taken the name Innocent II), and as he had against Abelard. Further, "Bernard proposed a four-age division of the church's history. In most texts this is tied to an exegesis of the four temptations described in Psalm 90:5–6, but in one *Sententia* the four ages are symbolized by the four horses of the Revelation chapter six. The saint's increasing pessimism after the failure of the Second Crusade may have moved him to more openly apocalyptic views toward the end of his life."[57]

Indeed, Bernard's justification for the Templars contains no mention of Antichrist or apocalyptic themes. It may or may not be significant that it was written when he was younger, and likely more idealistic. Perhaps the idea of linking the two did not strike him as important or necessary at the time that he wrote his defense. Only when he began preaching in support of the Second Crusade as an older man did apocalyptic themes surrounding Christian involvement in the East manifest in his thoughts. Whereas the church may have sought to avoid the Sibylline prophecies, he returned again to them, especially where they concerned the Last World Emperor. One particular prophecy stressed that he would Christianize the remaining heathens and symbolically restore kingship to Christ in Jerusalem. Importantly, the emperor's name would begin with the letter "C."[58] There was indeed one man who fit this description perfectly: Conrad III of Germany. His initial reluctance to take the cross prompted a concerted effort on Bernard's part to convince him that it was his religious duty. Maybe Bernard was seeing in him the fulfillment of predictions of the end, or maybe it was just a convenient device. Some have argued that Bernard may have been testing himself as much as the emperor. Bernard essentially bullied Conrad about it until he gave in, and he may have been trying to test the waters, so to speak, to see if there really was any validity to the prophecy. If Conrad accepted, then maybe there was something to it after all....[59]

It is indeed interesting that a theologian of Bernard's standing would adopt views that were essentially outside of official Church teaching, even though it is true that eschatological thought had a certain fluidity to it. That he did so shows the enduring popularity of the belief, and the nature of the times in which he lived. The sudden shock of the loss of Edessa obviously called for drastic action, even to the point of adopting views not necessarily popular with or endorsed by the reformed Church. It was also an opportunity to seize on the old beliefs and make them again relevant to the age. The emperor could indeed lead an army to destroy the infidels as prophesied, but it would be under the banner of a Church-sponsored crusade wherein the emperor received the same blessings and absolutions as the common people. Thus, the prophecy could be fulfilled, but not at the expense of Church power and prestige.

A case can be made that it was the urgency of the situation, along with this intense need on Bernard's part to test and justify the ancient prophecies that allowed him to sanction fully the crusade and its violent means to desirable ends. If these were the last times, extreme measures were necessary, including, as Hans-Dietrich Kahl states, "the monstrosity of teaching radical extirpation at the point of a sword as a form of missionary work."[60] This is a rather dramatic view, and doesn't address the fact that Bernard had already justified the Christian use of violence two decades earlier in his justification for the Templars (even if not for missionary work). Given that Bernard did not indulge in apocalyptic language when defending the New Knighthood, we may perhaps conclude that the Templars were justified more for political reasons, and the crusade was preached from a genuine religious conviction. It is just as likely, however, that we see in his later writings, an older and wiser Bernard, whose youthful enthusiasm for the Templars and their mission had given way to a sense of Christian duty for a more wide-spread campaign to protect the Holy Land.

Bernard stopped short of asserting that the Antichrist was already alive in the world, as some of his contemporaries speculated.[61] Indeed, his strongest words on the appearance of the Antichrist are in the preface to his *Vita sancti*

Malachiae, a life of a reforming Irish saint, written after 1148 and the failure of the Second Crusade.[62] Did disappointment and disillusionment have an influence on this?

We can see the importance of both Peter and Bernard in shaping European attitudes toward Islam and the East, and in applying apocalyptic thought to Western perceptions. The monasteries played a significant role in the development of both public opinion and church doctrine in these areas, perhaps the central role. Remember that these monastic writings were not limited to the cloister as instructions for the spiritual battle of every monk. Cluny was the greatest and richest of all the Western monasteries, and Peter was its head. Bernard was the most influential Christian in Europe apart from the pope, and thus he wielded almost as much power, at least in the area of popular persuasion and molding of public opinion. Indeed, in the latter he was certainly more influential than the pope, the primary reason that he was chosen to preach the crusade. The disillusionment following the crusade's failure and the blame which many placed on Bernard are both testimony to the influence that he had, and to the people's willingness to believe in his preaching and trust him.

These two men thus held a very high position and considerable power between them. Their pronouncements on any given topic would be taken very seriously by not only the people but by those within the Church. Both took established beliefs and traditions, and reshaped them according to the realities of the early and mid-twelfth century. To proclaim, as Peter had, that Muhammad was the middle figure between Arius and Antichrist was not only to draw on Church tradition, but in a sense, to create a new tradition as well, one applicable to the times and events that he witnessed occurring around him. When Bernard took inspiration from the Sibylline prophecies to justify his crusading sermons, he was also reaching back deep into Christian (and even pre–Christian) tradition, but he made use of them in a different world, one where the power of the Holy Roman Emperor had been challenged by the Church and significantly diminished. This called for a new approach to and a new interpretation of the old legends, which Bernard successfully provided.

Apocalyptic writings and fears flourished in the latter twelfth century, and for most of the thirteenth and fourteenth centuries as well. A significant part of these beliefs concerned Christianity's relationship to its rival, as well as new heretical movements. The developments in thought about Islam that took place at this time were having a lasting influence on the medieval Christian vision of the end of the world. The opposites so exhorted by the Church to differentiate Christianity from Islam: East and West, orthodoxy and heresy,

Christian and Saracen, a religion of lusts and a religion of temperance; all of these fit well into a larger scheme of apocalyptic contrasts: heaven and hell, God and Satan, good and evil.[63] However, regardless of expectations, the appeals to history and biblical prophecy, the end did not come. Those that hoped for it were disappointed, and those that feared it died never knowing that it failed time and again. Rubenstein notes, "Apocalypses and history are, from any perspective, uncomfortable bedfellows. History is the study of what happened, and the Apocalypse, by definition, hasn't happened. At least not yet. When it does, there will be no more history."[64]

As many Christians during these times were preparing for the end, some also sought to achieve the glory won by their predecessors in the centuries of the early church, the great prize of martyrdom. Christianity had never been short of enemies by whose hands a true believer could be martyred. However, with the legalization of the faith in the fourth century and the eventual disappearance of the persecuting society in which it had been nurtured, the true martyr's death became less common. When Western Europe was plunged into chaos following the disintegration of the Roman Empire, the invading barbarian tribes killed indiscriminately, though lawlessness gave way to new kingdoms. In the relative stability of the Carolingian period which followed, Christians were able to establish a kind of unity and faced less danger as a result of their beliefs. The Viking raids, for example, were not based on religious differences, and the new Christian kingdoms that emerged were becoming aggressive and persecutory themselves.

However, with the advent of Islam, a new opportunity presented itself to those who sought to follow in the footsteps of the saints. At first, such resistance to Islam in the hope of martyrdom was rare, except in isolated areas, such as ninth-century Córdoba. By the time of the First Crusade, however, a theology of martyrdom was developing in conjunction with that of holy armed resistance, and the concept of what a Christian martyr actually was began to take on new meanings that would have been unthinkable in the time of the early church. It is to this development that we now turn our attention.

7

Dying for the Faith: Martyrdom in Medieval Christian Thought

Martyrdom had always played an important role in defining the theology of the Church and the conduct of its followers. From the earliest days of the Roman persecutions, martyrs for the faith had been held up as exemplary Christians, sharing fully in the passion of Christ through their sufferings. This position was problematic, however, for while such a death was something to be praised, there came with it the real danger of encouraging a voluntary martyrdom akin to suicide, something which was condemned in Church teaching. This grey area has been crossed many times throughout the history of Christianity, particularly in the early and medieval periods. Among the more dramatic examples was the Córdoban Martyrs' Movement, which we will examine in detail, as it represents the first significant theological conflict between Christianity and Islam in the West. Though partially forgotten in the centuries immediately following it, its aggressive and martial attitudes were revived in the twelfth and thirteenth centuries, as we have seen, and there were instances of it being remembered in monastic communities.

During the period of the first two crusades, the question of martyrdom in relation to the armed pilgrimage became increasingly important. It would be wrong to state that the concept played a central role in the shaping of crusade ideology, at least initially. Indeed, it does not seem to have been considered in the same light as the penitential action of crusading. Officially at least, there was little or no relationship between the action of crusading and the possibility of achieving martyrdom as a result of dying on crusade. Remember, however, that in practice, the actions of the church and its followers did not always conform strictly to official teachings, and there were many variants in belief, particularly among the crusaders themselves. Bernard of Clairvaux, as we have seen, encouraged martyrdom when speaking of the Templars.[1]

The word "martyr" seems to have been used liberally by many writers to describe the fallen of the crusades. Initially, the idea was that those who engaged in the war against Muslims were undertaking God's work. Doing so was a way to ensure salvation, but if one were killed in battle (or otherwise), it would not necessarily constitute martyrdom, in the classic sense of what that entailed for suffering Christians. Those writers who talked about crusaders and pilgrims being "martyred" most often were appealing to emotion as much as anything, and not to any official designation granted by the church.[2] Indeed, Housley notes that "crusaders themselves regarded their dead comrades as martyrs, while the Church exercised much greater caution on the matter."[3] Further, despite these references, charters produced by the dead men's heirs do not refer to them as such.[4]

Sentiment and popular literature indeed played a role in the propagation of the myth of the heroic slain crusader,[5] but a number of religious writers did use the term in the early twelfth century, and by the time of Bernard's preaching, the idea had gained much more acceptance. H.E.J. Cowdrey has shown that while the idea of martyrdom did not necessarily play a central role in the shaping of the theology of the First Crusade and Urban's vision of it, nevertheless there were a small number of references to the idea from monastic and clerical sources which prepared later thinkers and theologians to be more receptive to the concept.[6] Indeed, he attributes the growth of the military orders at least in part to this idea,[7] and there is certainly some evidence for this.[8]

These references deserve further study. However, a more detailed treatment of the Martyrs' Movement in the ninth century is necessary at this point, as a background. It was a landmark event in the history of Christian relations with Islam, foreshadowing the conflicts of ideology that would erupt in the eleventh and twelfth centuries. Indeed, the similarities with later crusading episodes were often striking, more so given that the whole movement was imbued with a sense of military activity and themes, and several of the martyrs appear to have been ex-soldiers, eager to wage a kind of religious war against Islam by their activities.

Before proceeding, it is worth noting that the Islamic belief in martyrdom merits a special study of its own, and regrettably falls outside the boundaries of this work. It is as complex a phenomenon as Christian martyrdom, and space therefore does not permit its treatment here. There is no conclusive evidence for the influence of one religion's concept of martyrdom on the other, despite the close contact between the two in several of the examples and incidents listed below. The philosophies behind dying for one's faith were separate concepts in the two religions, and they appear to have developed independently. Certainly, early Islamic concepts may have been drawn from Christian accounts, but in the instances given here, they are not related.

And so on to the Martyrs' Movement.[9] As we saw in the previous chapter, this antagonistic episode was the first real religious conflict of any importance between Christianity and Islam in the West. It displayed many of the characteristics that would later be found in the Christian attitude toward Islam that developed before and after the First Crusade. It is further relevant to this discussion in that it arose among the monastic community of Córdoba, just as two and a half centuries later, the greatest critics of Islam and the advocates of a kind of crusade martyrdom also came largely from the monasteries.

Though not as well remembered outside of Spain, this event would have been known in certain Northern monastic communities, and quite possibly, as we have seen, by Peter the Venerable's translators. Given the close contact between Cluny and its affiliated Spanish houses, it is reasonable to assume that some form of this story circulated, particularly in the twelfth century, as interest in Islam was increasing. We have already noted that Peter may have been aware of it.[10] Norman Daniel has stated that while the story did not exert direct influence on the later literary styles and polemics of the high Middle Ages, nevertheless, the writings of Eulogius, the Movement's principal champion, did find their way into other Spanish writings, and from there into Northern Europe, very possibly with Peter's collection of translations of Islamic texts.[11] Eulogius' fabrications about Muhammad, which he drew from a life of Muhammad originating in the East, also appear in later writings and western biographies of the Prophet.[12]

Cutler has shown a number of instances wherein the writings of Eulogius and knowledge of the events appear to have surfaced in later writings. The names of some of the executed Christians were to appear in the late ninth-century *Martyrology of Usuard*.[13] This work, he notes, "must have been widely read in later times, especially when, during the Crusades, Christian interest in relics and martyrdom (in battle) at the hands of the Muslims reached its peak."[14]

The Mozarabic martyrology, known as the *Liber Ordinum*, dates from the tenth century and records the events of the Martyrs' Movement.[15] Later writers, such as Hugh of Fleury (early twelfth century) and Petrus Alfonsi show signs of having read Eulogius' work.[16]

It seems that Eulogius' writings became standard in Christian discourses about Islam circulating in Spain. This may at first appear puzzling, given that accurate information was readily available from close contact with the Muslims themselves, but as we have seen throughout this study, such understanding was often lacking. The popular and traditional falsehoods about Islam were commonly perpetuated by Christians, even in the very midst of their spiritual rivals. In ninth-century Spain, this was the result of a long-established and increasing hostility among certain small groups of Christians brought about by a feeling that the "native" Christian culture had been supplanted by the Muslim invaders. Norman Daniel notes that, "in the form of the odium theologicum many kinds of discontent were concentrated, the hatred of the unprivileged for the privileged, of the once-privileged for their successors, of a minority for their surroundings, of one cultural tradition for another, of the users of one language for another."[17]

The stimulus for this resentment is somewhat difficult to explain. Overt oppression and forced conversion were not generally features of Muslim rule in medieval Spain; indeed, some wide-spread tolerance seems to have been exhibited at various times throughout the seven centuries of Islamic presence on the Iberian Peninsula, though not always, of course. The Berber Almohads, who began their rise to power in 1120 and took hold of Iberia by the mid twelfth-century, just as many of the events described in this book were unfolding, were often quite harsh in their treatment of Jews and Christians. Powerful and religiously conservative, they were a force to be reckoned with for over a century. At other times, Spanish Christians still faced some of the usual Islamic restrictions regarding the construction and repair of churches and general freedoms of religious expression. However, it does not appear that they, unlike their eastern counterparts, were restricted in terms of dress or the ringing of church bells, for example.[18]

Perhaps because of this openness, hostilities among the exceptionally (indeed, overly) pious among the Christians were aroused. The general freedoms allowed by the Muslims for their Christian and Jewish subjects led to greater contact and social interaction among the three faiths. Those zealous Christians seeking to remain pure and untainted by perceived heresies and apostasies saw their cultural uniqueness being threatened with absorption into the dominant Islamic society, for them an alarming notion. The use of language provides a good illustration of this fear. With Arabic being the *lingua franca* of Muslim Spain, Latin fell increasingly into disuse both as a literary and liturgical language. Christian services were often celebrated in Arabic, the first language of the majority of the congregation.

On a larger scale, regardless of the freedoms allowed to Christians (as well as Jews), they were still viewed as a minority despite their actual numbers, and were as a result accorded a form of second-class status ("brought low" in the Qur'anic command[19]), in what they felt was their own country. Further, the Muslims were not only regarded as invaders, but also as heretics at best and pagans at worst. As a result, a small but determined number of Christians began to see their situation as a test of faith from God. In Córdoba, this fanaticism was to have violent and deadly consequences.

It was in this volatile religious climate that the Martyrs' Movement was able to occur. Yet initially, it seems to have been incited almost accidentally. It began in the year 850 with an unwilling participant, a monk named Perfectus, possibly a Latinized version of a common Arabic name, al-Kamil. This is also the case with a later martyr referred to as Servus Dei, very likely a Latin translation of the Arabic name Abdallah. That these Christians would have Arabic names further shows the extent of Islamic influence.

Apparently, Perfectus was one day approached in a market by a group of Muslims (probably with mischievous and provocative intent) and asked to assert the Christian views of Christ and Muhammad. Wary of being led into a trap, Perfectus expounded Christian doctrine, but withheld any commentary on the Prophet. However, they continued to press him, and he ultimately responded with a vociferous attack on Muhammad, citing biblical references to false prophets. The initial reaction was one of surprising moderation. Although speaking against Muhammad was a crime under Muslim law, it seems that Perfectus' tormentors realized that they had deliberately pushed him too far. As a result, they let him go. That should have been the end of the whole affair.

However, the next time Perfectus came to the market, the same group again derided him, accusing him of a crime in voicing his blasphemous views. This exchange resulted in the market crowd rising up, capturing him, and bringing him before a judge. There he denied his words, but was nevertheless imprisoned, owing to the number of witnesses against him. As a result, he began to protest his situation by further proclaiming his Christian faith, and attacking Islam. He was executed publicly at *Eid al-Fitr*, at the end of Ramadan.[20]

This, followed by the public humiliation and beating of a merchant named John for swearing by the Prophet's name,[21] caused a small group, which initially consisted of ascetic zealots, to come forth seeking voluntary martyrdom. The first of these, about a year after Perfectus' execution, was Ishaq (Isaac), a government secretary who had renounced his position to adopt an ascetic monastic life, and from there to go willingly to his death. Given his erratic behavior, as described in Christian sources, it is possible that he was insane, for he was prone to fits and ecstatic visions, likening himself to God. Indeed, when questioned by the *qadis*, the judges who ruled in accordance with Islamic law, he was pronounced drunk and sentenced to imprisonment. Ishaq, however, insisted upon his execution, which was eventually carried out.[22]

This voluntary martyrdom was, regrettably, to prove infectious. Several other members of Ishaq's order followed his example. They attempted to draw a parallel between his "sacrifice" and the attempted sacrifice of Isaac by Abraham. At first, the martyrdoms were confined to the monastic and priestly orders, but later, others began to come forward with their own suicidal pronouncements about Muhammad and Islam. They included soldiers, government officials, and former Muslims who had secretly converted to Christianity, an action itself punishable by death.[23]

As noted in the previous chapter, Eulogius was a supporter of these outbursts, and was ultimately a martyr himself in 859. Indeed, it was his death which brought about an end to the whole movement, for he had been a prime instigator, and without his abrasive polemics to incite fellow radical Christians, the movement lost much of its fervor. Paulus Alvarus, the learned laymen, friend of Eulogius, and co-conspirator, failed to achieve his goal of being martyred.

Both enthusiastically supported the movement, and wrote tracts defending the actions of the would-be martyrs. Eulogius produced his *Memorialis Sanctorum* in three parts, a chronicle of the martyrs (indeed, a kind of martyrology) in 851 and 853, as well as a sequel in 857, the *Apologeticus Martyrum*. Alvarus produced his *Indiculus Luminosis* in 852 and 854, as a general defense of their actions, which in addition to its apocalyptic warnings, evoked the image of St. John the Baptist as a model for those who stood up to ungodly authority and willingly sacrificed their lives for God.[24] Alvarus was particularly concerned with the loss of Latin culture, which he believed had flourished in the days of Visigothic Spain and had been suppressed by Islamic rule.

The writings are, as a result, flowery and eloquent, though occasionally overly dense and stilted. They are clearly attempts to idealize a hypothetical Latin Christian past, by copying older forms in order to create a kind of Renaissance of new Latin Christian culture, so long denied to them by the presence of Islam. They wrote in a style that was "as a result highly mannered, and they drew an almost absurdly archaic vocabulary from the writings of Isidore, notably the *Etymologiae*, that allowed them for instance to refer to the regnal years of the amirs as 'consulships' and to call young men 'ephebes.'"[25]

Despite these pleas for a return to a former Latin glory (whether real or imagined), it seems that adherents of the mainstream Spanish Church were not impressed. Indeed the majority of Christians who were even aware of the movement opposed it. It was condemned, at least in word, by Bishop Reccafred of Seville at a Córdoban Church council in 852, at the request of the emir Abd ar-Rahman II 822–52.[26] As a result, Eulogius was imprisoned by the bishop, being accused of deliberately trying to stir up dissent and encourage voluntary martyrdom, which was forbidden (it had been condemned at the fourth-century council of Elvira near Granada).[27] It was this action which provoked both Eulogius and Alvarus to write their defenses.

However, it is possible that Reccafred was a collaborator with the Muslim rulers, in effect a puppet who sought his own advancement by keeping in their favor. He had imprisoned several bishops for crimes of questionable validity (always in favor of prevailing Islamic law), and was apparently resented by some of the Christian clergy.[28] In general, however, it does appear that the martyrs' extreme actions were not approved of by the Church. It is worth noting that, in response to Eulogius' polemic, he was asked how these dead could be considered legitimate martyrs, when they were executed by those who both worshipped God and had a law of their own. This statement shows just how integrated the two societies had become by then,[29] a fact that must have infuriated Eulogius beyond measure. The fact that the movement came to such a quick end with his death is evidence for this integration. Further, the events in Córdoba did not inspire similar actions in other areas.

The movement took on the qualities of mass hysteria, with nearly fifty people going to their deaths before it subsided, having been caught up in the emotions and even perverse excitement that it engendered. Daniel has posited an intriguing link between the attitudes of the movement and the language of Eulogius and Alvarus with militarism:

> With this classical sentiment went also a frustrated feeling for military imagery [note the similarity between this and the writings of Bernard] [...] Images of war as well as of the gymnasium persist in both writers [...] It is crucial that these people were many of them frustrated soldiers [including Alvarus himself] and to remember that their martyrdom was their best or only means of aggression. Psychologists who see asceticism as a death-wish and suicide as an aggression must see in this movement the epitome of their theories.[30]

The works of both are the main Latin chronicles of the events of the 850s, and are obviously very much in favor of the extreme Christian position, rendering a truly objective view of the affair more difficult to obtain. It is interesting to note, however, that in their writings, they do note the Muslim reluctance to carry out these death sentences for blasphemy (though this may have been influenced again by classical motifs, see below). If true, this resistance was no doubt due to the fact that the Islamic officials were well aware of what was happening and had no desire to create a martyrs' cult.

Indeed, Alvarus records that at Eulogius' trial, brought about by his harboring an Arab girl who had converted to Christianity, he was offered the chance to convert to Islam in name only, and thereafter he would be free to practice Christianity without fear of persecution.³¹ This was an amazing gesture on the part of the officials, in the light of the extent of Eulogius' involvement in inciting others to go to their deaths. He rejected the offer, however, and he was finally executed after further insulting Islam and the Prophet to ensure that he received a death sentence.

At first, it would seem that since this episode is mentioned amid the Christian polemic suggests that it is a true story, for Alvarus would have had nothing to gain by inventing a story which showed the enemies of Christianity in a favorable or tolerant light. However, there are problems with the accuracy of these accounts of the martyrdoms, stemming from the excessive emulation of the supposed glorious Latin past. The accounts recall very similarly various descriptions of early Christians going to their deaths at the hands of pagan Romans. Therefore we cannot be sure what is factual and what is embellished for the sake of recalling that longed-for golden age of Latin Spanish Christianity. Perhaps some martyrs did deliberately imitate those who had gone before them, perhaps not. Further, as Roger Collins notes, "the blandishments and apparent worldly wisdom of the Muslim *qadis* and officials are identical in tone to many of the arguments put into the mouths of Pagan Roman judges and governors in the earlier passions."³²

Regardless of whether we are reading truth, fiction, or a blend of both, the theme of persecution and martyrdom fed into the use of apocalyptic ideas and imagery, especially in the *Indiculus* of Alvarus. In it, he takes great care in his exegesis of the apocalyptic elements of several biblical passages to draw parallels between the warnings therein and the dangers he saw in the advent of Islam. Eulogius and Alvarus were most significant in being the first Western writers to relate Muhammad to Antichrist, and by extension, to the arch heretic Arius.³³ Their Christian successors in the twelfth and thirteenth centuries would write similarly, invoking much of the same imagery. Alvarus' use of Daniel 7:24–5, represented what to him was a clear sign of the dangers confronting Christians, for Muhammad had indeed arisen (*consurget*) and his empire had triumphed over the Byzantine, Gothic, and Frankish kings (*tres reges*). Further, he sought to exchange the Christian Law with the Qur'an and to "alter the times" (*mutare tempora, et leges*) with the new calendar dating from the *Hijra*.³⁴ Those who would die a martyr's death were doing so at just the right time.

If such exegetical work seems strained, remember that Alvarus, like Eulogius, was a passionate Christian, who desired to identify and stand against the unholy presence that he perceived. As noted, Southern astutely and correctly remarks, "[...] everything conspires to support a hypothesis we desire to believe,"[35] and the Córdoban martyrs intensely desired to believe. In a strictly analytical sense, Alvarus makes more logical connections based on his knowledge than some of the polemicists of later periods were to do.

Though the Christian sources do not indicate it, it seems that Alvarus, unlike Eulogius, was not destined to become a martyr himself, a fact which troubled him. He also had a desire to become a monk, which never materialized.[36] Alvarus apparently deeply wanted to take on the monastic life, but because he had once been married, this was not an option at that time. This disturbed him, for he felt that marriage was a sign of weakness on his part; he was filled with self-loathing. Modern psychologists might see in this an attempt to project that loathing onto an "other," in this case the Muslim rulers of Córdoba.

So, the movement came to an end with the death of Eulogius in 859, most likely due to the lack at that point of potential martyrs to carry on; a suicide cult can only continue for so long. It is also probable that his death caused a demoralized feeling among the remaining but dwindling numbers of adherents to the cause. No further works, save Alvarus' life of Eulogius appeared in connection with the movement, and there was no attempt to revive it at a later date. Undoubtedly, intense resentment remained among small groups of Christians, but the rash actions of the Córdoban martyrs were not repeated.

We may see in this episode some similarities between Eulogius, the charismatic religious leader, and modern cult leaders, who so incite their followers that they are willing to do anything for that leader, including sacrifice their lives. As soon as the leader is gone, the group disintegrates, deprived of its focus, but not necessarily of its purpose. The individual is thus more important than what he sets out to do. Although removed from modern sensibilities by over 1,000 years, much about this movement can be related to the cult phenomenon, wherein a small group sets itself against the prevailing society as superior, provoking violent confrontation to achieve its ends. Eulogius and Alvarus would surely make for a fascinating psychological study.

The way was opened for this aggressive philosophy to be rekindled at a later date, however, as news of the events was brought out of Spain and into France. In the year 858, two monks, Odilard and Usuard of the monastery of St. Germain-des-Prés, brought with them from Spain relics of three of the victims of the movement, Aurelius, Nathalia, and George. They also brought a passion of these three, probably written by Eulogius himself and prepared specifically for the monks, as it differs slightly from the extant Spanish version.[37] It contains special information to those readers who had no knowledge of Islam:

> The Saracens think that only those who leave their sect and turn to the Christian faith, and those who utter blasphemies against their Legislator, deserve death.[38]

This is as unambiguous as can be, and was directed to those farther north who did not live under Muslim law, and indeed, may have had no knowledge of them. It found its way into France and had a long life, because a version of it survives in seven manuscripts, mostly from monasteries in or near Paris, from the ninth to the fourteenth centuries.[39]

That this story was preserved in a number of monastic manuscripts suggests that it may have had an influence on the development of later Christian thought. Peter the Venerable and his monks may have been aware of the work, prompting further interest in the plight of Spanish Christians. There is also some evidence that this warning about Islamic executions may have even prevented some early missionary activity.[40]

It was only later, during the assertion of a unified Christian identity in the eleventh century that the confidence necessary for such actions would be gained, especially when Christianity effectively went on the attack with the First Crusade, and stories of martyrdom began to circulate. This was a sign of a new self-confidence which the church of earlier centuries could never have displayed. It was not strong enough politically and Europe was too divided. It is possible that had the Martyrs' Movement begun in the eleventh or twelfth centuries, it would have met with more church approval, and perhaps even the promise of military aid. This lack of unity and power did not prevent certain popes from extolling the virtues of dying while fighting for the faith, however.

Curiously, at the exact time that the Movement was gaining momentum, Pope Leo IV (847–55) issued in 853 an appeal to the Frankish army for aid to fight against Saracen marauders who had attacked Rome in 846 and desecrated the Church of St. Peter. Apparently, they were still operating in the same area when the appeal was made. The letter reminded the Franks of earlier victories against this enemy, and significantly, offered the promise of heavenly reward for anyone killed in battle against them. This is a most important provision, for it shows what is perhaps the earliest identification of salvation with the meritorious act of fighting against the Muslims. It goes so far as to promise eternal life in heaven for such an act, in effect identifying it not only with martyrdom, but also holy war.[41] The pope for the first time made the link between fighting against unbelievers in the defense of the Christian faith with salvation for doing so. This type of warfare was meritorious, even holy.[42]

This idea was restated in 878 by Pope John VIII (872–82). The pope was answering the question of a group of bishops who had asked if those who died in defense of the faith (as well as their own governments, interestingly) were forgiven their sins. John replied that these fallen warriors would indeed gain salvation and eternal life, and he granted a general absolution to those who died.[43] It is worth noting that John detested the Saracens, seeing them as being hated by God, highly dangerous to Christians everywhere, and spreading like locusts. He hated that some Christian rulers in his time had made alliances with various Muslim rulers, and he attacked the idea without reservation, saying that they violated divine law; indeed to make and keep the peace with such an evil was sinful and forbidden.[44] However, in both cases the conditions of indulgence, as featured in the later crusading proclamations, are not to be found, namely the remission of punishments for sins. These statements are merely general words of praise and offer assurance of heavenly reward, but they are clear that to wage war on infidels is holy work, and brings great benefit to the warriors who engage in it, provided they happen to be killed as a result.[45] Those that survived, then, were not granted the remission for sins that the crusaders would be given; in other words, the marriage of holy war and pilgrimage is not to be found in these statements. What is contained here is the concept of eternal reward for the fallen, and therefore this clearly identifies death in battle with martyrdom.

These passages and the contemporary events in Spain show an early conception in the minds of some Christians of how martyrdom had changed and was still changing since the first centuries of Christianity. The Church had gone from being a persecuted institution to the central spiritual authority in Western Europe. Hence, the doctrine of martyrdom necessarily had to evolve. The focus naturally shifted outward, to lands where the perceived enemies of Christianity still resided. This coincided with the gradual awakening of a European Christian identity following the so-called Dark Ages, and continued into the time of the reforms and Renaissance of the eleventh and twelfth centuries. The first hints of a rekindling of the spirit of martyrdom can be seen in these examples.

In one isolated incident in the tenth century, a Frank whose name was Vulfra, came to Córdoba in 931, and yearning for martyrdom, succeeded in arousing the anger of the Muslims, and was put to death.[46] His executors would likely have been familiar with the Martyrs' Movement, and certainly would have had no desire to have a repeat of that affair. However, luck was on their side, and the dreadful events of the 850s were not revived. No one knows why he came to Spain, specifically Córdoba, to achieve that martyrdom. Perhaps he had read or heard of Eulogius' account of the three martyrs and sought for himself a similar fate. He may have had access to one of the monastic copies of Eulogius' work and resolved to end his life in the same dramatic manner.

The next signs of revived interest in martyrdom came in the eleventh century, during the height of the Reform. Prior to this, there was allegedly one other significant statement. At the time of the First Crusade, the papal encyclical purporting to have originated with Pope Sergius IV was promoted as proof of earlier papal approval of military action against infidels, and it contained a reference to those dying in such a cause being granted salvation. However, as we have seen, this work is in all likelihood a forgery, circulated at the time as propaganda.[47] Later on, Gregory VII naturally had his own opinions regarding the deaths of those fighting against Islam. To him it was certainly a deed of righteousness and merit that deserved salvation. His own grand plan to lead an eastern expedition against the Turks fit well into this idea. Gregory held strong views on martyrdom in general.[48] As successor to St. Peter, he saw it as a papal duty to follow in those footsteps, if necessary, setting the same example that Peter had, and he also expected this of his clergy, as well as of kings and princes.[49] If the supreme power on earth was an institution founded by a martyr, then he expected no less devotion from all of those under him, religious and secular alike.

This view extended to military campaigns. A document of particular interest, though it is not a French monastic source, is the *Carmen in victoriam Pisanorum*, which recounts the Mahdia campaign of 1087. This was a seaborne military expedition consisting of Pisan and Genoese troops that launched an attack against the town of Mahdia and its suburb Zawila in what is today Tunisia.[50] This pre-emptive strike was allegedly in retaliation for Muslim raids in Italy, and it was given full papal support, as well as the support of Matilda, Countess of Tuscany,[51] whose correspondence with Gregory VII we have already examined.[52] In short, this was not merely another military expedition, but had certain unique characteristics about it that have led many to see in it a foreshadowing of the crusade eight years later. This adventure was not exactly a prelude to the crusade, but it did share some important similarities. The most significant of these was that the Pisans and Genoese were wearing purses, the pilgrim's badge, into battle.[53] The chief difference was that these pilgrim insignias were worn for a pilgrimage already completed by the soldiers in Rome, rather than that the participants were setting out on a new one.[54] So, they did not see their venture as a pilgrimage, and there is no evidence that they took any form of vow before undertaking it, or that they would receive spiritual benefit from it, though their deaths would have been lauded as holy and martyr-like. We cannot call it a proto-crusade, but the papacy did give its sanction to the effort, and the presence of pilgrimage paraphernalia indicates that the idea of pilgrims bearing arms was acceptable (even one already completed). There was an air of holiness about the entire thing that was remembered afterward.

Indeed, in the 1090s, Urban II may have looked back to this event, among many other things, for his inspiration, for, "as a scion of a French aristocratic family and a former grand prior of Cluny, he already had a deep insight into the forces which were impelling western chivalry to such an enterprise as the Crusade, and he was able to mobilize them for it."[55]

Religious significance was certainly attached to the venture, and importantly, the theme of martyrdom is invoked in the *Carmen* for the death of the Pisan *vicecomes*, Hugh. He is praised for his valor, and it is noted that his death was for Christ.[56] Thus, a deliberate act of violence is linked with being favorable to Christ, something that would have been almost unheard of only a few decades before. The letters of Leo and John only deal with defensive actions against non–Christians, and the deaths that may have resulted. Here, however, we see praise for an unprovoked attack, endorsed as a "defensive" measure to ensure future safety, just as the crusades would be presented, and the fallen are praised as martyrs.

The *Carmen* is also important as a rare example of a pre-crusade source to mention the name of Muhammad, and to condemn him for his denial of the trinity, likening him to Arius.[57] As his followers, the Muslims receive no better treatment.[58]

The overall message of the chronicle is clear: The Muslims and Muhammad are the agents of Antichrist. It is right to initiate fighting against them, indeed, it is the will of God, and anyone slain in such a conflict wins the death of a martyr and the promise of eternal life. With this philosophy already in place, and endorsed by the papacy, it was a relatively easy step to bring in the final element, that of pilgrimage, which would make the concept of the First Crusade complete.

Penny Cole has shown some interesting relations in medieval exegetical thought made between the idea of warring for the faith and the accounts of battle in the books of Maccabees,[59] described as "the first religious war in the history of mankind."[60] The exegete Hrabanus Maurus (d. 856), for example, saw the whole affair between Mattathias and Antiochus as prefiguring the roles of Christ and Antichrist, and he attempted to imbue each episode in the conflict with a parallel Christian interpretation. Antiochus was portrayed as an Antichrist, who polluted and defiled the Temple. Muhammad and Islam would later be viewed in the exact same terms.[61]

Thus, it is possible to see through these events the growth of a renewed interest in martyrdom prior to the crusades. Cowdrey has argued convincingly that the idea of martyrdom itself was not necessarily influential in the initial formation of the crusading vision. However, once success had been achieved in 1099, and histories of the crusade began to be written, the concept of crusading martyrs began to feature in theological and monastic works. The writings of Guibert of Nogent, Albert of Aix, and Robert the Monk all contain allusions to this concept and it would be developed over the next few decades by Raymond of Aguilers, Baldric of Bourgueil, Pope Calixtus II, and most importantly, by Bernard of Clairvaux. Against the background of Christianity's triumph in the Holy Land, the rise of the Templars (the most significant example of the ideal of the crusading martyr), and the Islamic retaliations culminating in the Second Crusade, Christian martyrdom took on new meaning and significance. We will explore this growth further.

Martyrdom as an aspect of crusading always remained in one sense a popular notion, that is, it increasingly captured the imaginations of the people, particularly the laity who were on crusade. Remember that officially, the death of a crusader was not a true martyrdom, though the church did not seek to discourage chroniclers and preachers from portraying it in such a manner. Martyrdom was a part of the popular sentiment, increasingly used by theologians to extol the virtue of fallen crusaders. This representation was certainly good for promoting the idealism of the crusade, and it served a useful and even inspiring purpose. That the concept of aggressive martyrdom could achieve a wide-spread appeal following the First Crusade is indicative of how much had changed in Christian thought in such a short period of time, even if it was technically outside of official Church teachings.

The idea of aggressively pursuing the martyr's fate was obviously not new in Christian thought, and could have helped to provide a precedent for the popular ideas of the crusaders and chroniclers. Stories of saints in Classical times who willingly went to their deaths, and provoked and mocked their persecutors were well known and circulated throughout the medieval period.[62] The difference between them and the crusaders was that the crusaders were armed, and sought out the deaths of their "persecutors," ironically producing martyrs in the eyes of Islam as well.

The writers named above invoked the vision of martyrdom to praise those who had fallen on the journey to the Holy Land, or those who were killed in battle. These writings may or may not have been very persuasive at first,[63] the question remains open. They might have given some stimulus for lay people in deciding to take the cross, but these comments were not the result of a swelling of popular enthusiasm that sent thousands of crusaders off to the Holy Land seeking voluntary martyrdom at the request of the papacy. Rather, the writings influenced later thought, and they did indeed prepare the way for later teachings, culminating in the provocative actions of the Franciscans and the ideas of Ramon Llull in the thirteenth century, both of whom displayed ideas and actions strikingly familiar to the attitudes that had motivated Eulogius, Alvarus, and the Córdoban martyrs four centuries earlier.[64] In each instance, direct ideological confrontation with Islam led to the deaths of the Christians who initiated it, and they went to those deaths willingly, even joyfully.

The sentiment is found in chronicles of the First Crusade itself, for example in the writings of Guibert of Nogent, Albert of Aix, and Robert of Rheims,[65] as well as in the anonymous *Gesta Francorum*. Though the references are brief, this does not necessarily imply that martyrdom was not an important concept. Rather it may suggest the opposite: that it was already commonly accepted and therefore no great attention needed to be given to it.[66] It is best to say that in these writings, clerics were both reflecting on and encouraging the idea of martyrdom on crusade by extolling the deeds and virtues of the crusaders. Certainly, popular sentiment (particularly among the literate who could read the chronicles) and clerical opinion influenced one another on this matter, and a popular notion of crusading martyrdom developed without specific church teachings or the issuance of papal encyclicals.

Guibert of Nogent attached a particular importance to the idea of the crusading martyr. He was the abbot of Nogent-sous-Coucy from 1104, and began his account of the First Crusade sometime before 1108, largely a restatement of the *Gesta Francorum*.[67] Of all the early historians of the crusade, he seemed most attracted to the idea of its fallen participants being deserving of the status of martyrs. In fact, Guibert "saw martyrdom as a discipline, a glory, and a reward; it was the *main incentive* [my emphasis] to the Crusade."[68] This is most important. Guibert would not simply have conceived of such an idea on his own. He was well-read and aware of current theological thought, though he was not himself a participant in the Crusade. In his account of Urban's speech at Clermont, he has the pope extolling the virtues of fighting for the faith, equating death in such a battle with martyrdom:

> Until now you have fought unjust wars: you have often savagely brandished your spears at each other in mutual carnage only out of greed and pride, for which you deserve eternal destruction and the certain ruin of damnation! Now we are proposing that you should fight wars which will contain the glorious reward of martyrdom, in which you can gain the title of present and eternal glory.[69]

One particularly poignant account records the death of a friend of Guibert's, a young knight named Matthew. They had been childhood friends, as Matthew's family "had held a fief in Guibert's family lordship."[70] Guibert portrayed him as almost saintly in all things. He had been in the ill-fated army of Peter the Hermit, and had been captured by the Turks in Asia Minor. When he refused to renounce his faith, he was beheaded.[71]

One can only speculate on the emotional motivation for the writing of this passage. Surely the violent death of a childhood friend would have caused him much grief, a notion which is borne out by the fact that he devoted a whole section of Book Four to this story. Guibert used it as a didactic passage. Matthew's example "demonstrated how a layman could achieve salvation in his own way."[72] Perhaps this was the greatest honor he could accord to his friend, to hold him up as an example to all.

The fact that other writers also allude to martyrdom (though not as glowingly or importantly) is evidence that the idea was spreading among not only the laity, but the clergy as well. Robert of Rheims, known also as Robert the Monk, a monk of Marmoutier-lez-Tours, implies that the entire expedition was a form of martyrdom.[73] He writes as if he were present at Urban's speech, which, if true, would provide a valuable first-hand account. He records about the crusade, and the status of Jerusalem, which requires the support of the Franks, because God has granted them military superiority. The journey will be for the remission of their sins, and the "unfading glory of the kingdom of heaven."[74]

The implication is that crusading brings a heavenly reward, even if martyrdom is not specifically mentioned. We must be careful, of course, not to rely too heavily on his narrative, which was probably written in the first decade of the twelfth century. Thus, it came well after the actual event, which would certainly have affected the tone of his writing. The pope and audience in his version may well have been given a greater confidence than they possessed, since the outcome was already known to the author. Looking back, he would have been able to word Urban's speech in a way that success was a foregone conclusion. God had pre-ordained their victory, through his new chosen people, the French. The crusade became elevated to a divine intervention on par with the creation and incarnation, and it fulfilled biblical prophecies.[75] This literary display of religious confidence is understandable when one is creating history with full knowledge of a situation that the participants could not envisage, namely, their victory in 1099. It may be that many present at Clermont felt this way, but they did not have the advantage of Robert's hindsight. It would be most interesting, for example, to know what his thoughts at the time were, and how they might have changed over time.

Baldric of Bourgueil, prior and abbot of Saint-Pierre-de Bourgueil from 1089 to 1107, and thereafter archbishop of Dol in Brittany, was another to have attended the sermon at Clermont. About 1108, he provided his own account of events, contained in his *Historia Jerosolimitana*.[76] At one point, he has Urban II declare:

> It ought to be a beautiful ideal for you to die for Christ in that city where Christ died for you, but if it should happen that you should die here, you may be sure that it will be as if you had died on the way, provided, that is, Christ finds you in his company of knights.[77]

Here, he is importantly equating death along the way with martyrdom, provided the crusader is of right mind and faithful. The place of death is not so important as how one dies, should God allow it to happen. The knight who drowns in a shipwreck en route will be saved if his heart was pure and godly, while the one who fights for his own gain and vanity will not, even if he is struck down by a Saracen's sword. Again, we must consider that this document was produced about thirteen years after the events described, with the benefit of hindsight. How much can be attributed with certainty to Urban II and how much was motivated by the later sentiments inspired by the victorious Christian forces cannot be known.

Another writer, Albert of Aix also considered the crusade itself a kind of martyrdom.[78] His remarks are often made more in passing, though they still assume that martyrdom is a given fact of the crusading mission.[79]

It may be significant that all of these writers were monks who did not participate in the crusade and never set foot in the Holy Land. However, we have seen that the notion already existed of the crusading army being effectively a giant "monastery in motion," owing to the vows and expected conduct of its participants. Cloistered monks could therefore write with a feeling of kinship that allowed them to make their theological pronouncements.

Riley-Smith has distinguished three types of crusading martyrs from the various accounts: The first consisted of those who had died of disease or at any time while on the crusade. This was not apparently a universally-accepted notion initially, but became more so over time, especially in the decade following victory in Jerusalem. In the second category were the laymen and priests who had suffered the "traditional" martyrdom, the passive death. It could include knights as well, as this martyrdom was usually in connection with those captured by Muslims who refused conversion to Islam and chose death instead. The third category includes the type discussed here: those who died while actively engaged in combat against the Muslims, initially a small category until the idea gained wider acceptance.[80] The only definition of martyrdom that was completely accepted at first was the traditional one. The other two categories were adopted as success was achieved in the East and people began to have confirmation that this venture truly was a mission sanctioned by God.

Three accounts regarding this are worth mentioning, for they brought the issue into the metaphysical realm, and were circulated as positive proof of the hand of God directing the crusaders' actions. They extended the honor of martyrdom to those who had died passively, as well as those who had died fighting. They were stories of spiritual visitations by the dead, who offered some confirmation of the martyrdom of fallen pilgrims. Bishop Adhémar of Le Puy, a papal legate, died of Typhoid on 1 August 1098,[81] and was reported to have appeared to four different individuals following his death. The central issue of these appearances was to confirm the validity of the Holy Lance,[82] a relic (the spear which pierced Christ's side) said to have been found buried in the Church of St. Peter in Antioch by the direction of a young pilgrim named Peter Bartholomew. Even before Christians took the city by siege in June 1098, Peter had been having dreams and visions of St. Andrew, who told him where to find the Holy Lance, the spear that according to tradition, the Roman soldier Longinus had used to pierce Christ's side at the crucifixion. After the taking of the city, a spear was found where Peter had said it would be, though trickery was suspected at the time, and ever since.[83]

The second account records a vision beheld by Anselm of Ribemont the night before he was killed in February 1099. He was visited by the ghost of a knight named Enguerrand of St. Pol, who informed him that he would shortly be joining the ranks of the glorious martyrs who had died for Christ on crusade.[84] These ghostly visitations confirmed the validity of a disputed relic, and more importantly that those who died in the campaign, even if not in battle, would be ushered into paradise like the martyrs of old times.[85]

The final account is that of a fallen warrior, Galdemar Carpenel, the army's standard-bearer, who was killed in a battle with the Fatmids in 1101, well after the victory at Jerusalem. He was mourned by many, and buried with high honors. Archbishop Hugh of Lyon, recalled how Galdemar's spirit came to him in a dream, sitting atop a white horse, holding a banner and a spear, but looking away, When Hugh inquired as to why he was doing this, he replied that he was "threatening Babylon."[86] A martyr in life, he continued his work in death.

Returning to Peter Bartholomew, he was destined for a grim fate, however. His visions continued, and as he became more consumed with them, he ultimately called for the purging of the armies, in other words, killing off the sinful among the ranks, so that only the truly faithful remained. Naturally, the armies and their leaders balked at this, and Peter offered to undergo a trial by fire to prove his story. Two large bonfires were built and lit, a foot apart, and he walked through them. He failed, being badly burned, and died days later.[87] His few remaining followers undoubtedly considered him a martyr.

Even if crusading martyrdom did not immediately gain acceptance and was not the result of official theological teachings, it nevertheless denotes an important philosophy that would be taken up in later decades and future crusades. Spurred on by their enthusiasm for the monumental events occurring in the Holy Land, the various monastic chroniclers were eager to show how God had always been the guiding hand in the expedition from the very beginning, and that the rewards for those faithful enough to see it through to the end were salvation and paradise. Accounts of the siege of Antioch recorded that those who fell were ushered into heaven as martyrs. In one particularly vivid example, a warrior named Hugh the Insane (a remarkable name, whether given in life or posthumously!) died in a tower, fighting a multitude of Turks. His body was riddled with arrows, and knowing that he was dying, he leapt into a throng of Turkish fighters below, using his body as a weapon to take down as many as he could. As Rubenstein notes, this was "one of the first instances in history of suicide, martyrdom, and murder combined in a single gesture."[88] Writers about these events had succeeded in formulating a concept which would be central to the new idea of the Military Orders, and in particular to Bernard's crusading theology.

In *De laude*, as we have seen, he states the many virtues of his favored knights and how they differ from the sinful and unscrupulous secular knighthood. Among these is not just their lack of fear of death, but their *desire* for martyrdom, because this is the greatest of all honors bestowed by God. He frequently alludes to the blessings of martyrdom in the first five chapters of the tract, stating for example, in chapter one, "[...] but death in battle is more precious as it is the more glorious."[89]

This attitude, to the modern mind, comes close to an endorsement of suicide, considered in Christian thought to be one of the greatest of all sins. It might appear that an idea which once brought condemnation was now being given the Church's blessing. The medieval mind would not have seen the two as the same, however. The act of suicide seeks to take away the life God has given, an action of vanity and pride, whereas martyrdom is the act of dying for God, the supreme act of Christian service and humility. Indeed, Bernard's words are no less fervent and provocative than the attitude of the Spanish martyrs. Yet here a similar idea, with all the same military imagery, is given sanction by the greatest figure in Western Christendom in the early twelfth century. Other writers of the time expressed similar sentiments.

One finds, for example, in Odo of Deuil's account of the Second Crusade, the *De Profectione Ludovici VII in orientem*, an acceptance of the concept of death on crusade as being the will of God. He states, almost in passing in Book One, "But because mortal wisdom and prudence do not exist against

God, they who were destined to die chose the route through Greece."⁹⁰ What is important here is the route in question, and the crusaders are secondary to that point. Note that he writes that they are destined to die.

Overall, Odo says relatively little of the crusaders dying the martyr's death, possibly due to the embarrassing nature of the outcome of the crusade, though one could proclaim spiritual victories even in the face of such humiliating military defeat. His account breaks off at the point when Louis VII reached Antioch in 1148. At this stage the crusading armies were severely weakened from previous toils, and the ultimate failure of the crusade was due to the earlier losses.⁹¹ Perhaps there was already a feeling of pessimism among the crusaders. In any event, it can hardly have been the best setting to proclaim the ideal of martyrdom, since failure in such ventures was usually attributed to the displeasure of God.

He does at one point, however, ascribe that most glorious of fates to the fallen in a skirmish with the Turks near Laodicea (in south-western Turkey) that went disastrously wrong for the crusaders. He speaks of a group of knights being shot with arrows, which allowed their retainers and servants to escape. Odo sees in this a grand metaphor for the sacrifice of Christ:

> For lords to die so that their servants might live would have been an incident calling for lamentation, had not the Lord of all given an example thereof. The flowers of France withered before they could bear fruit in Damascus. In saying this I am overcome by tears, and I groan from the bottom of my heart. Concerning this tragedy, however, the sober mind can comfort with the solace that this and earlier examples of their valour will live on in the world and that their death, whereby their errors were swept away through fervent faith, has won the martyr's crown.⁹²

To sum up, this turn in church policy and theology can be explained in several ways. Primarily, it is an example of the profound change in attitudes in Christian thought over the period of three centuries regarding relations with Islam and the acceptable methods of dealing with it. In addition, the agenda and goals of the Church had changed drastically, as a result of its new political and temporal power. In the ninth century, with much of Europe still emerging from the so-called Dark Ages,⁹³ survival was the central issue, not a unified Christendom (despite Charlemagne's efforts), or an assault upon the Islamic peoples. The idea of regaining Jerusalem would probably have not occurred to anyone, save a handful of religious idealists and military enthusiasts. Islam was the dominant political, religious, and intellectual power of the known world, yet the majority of Western Europeans probably never even knew of its existence.

Bernard employed the same method of justification for his theory that had been used by Alvarus and Eulogius: scriptural exegesis. *De laude* is filled with biblical references, and Bernard liberally quotes from scripture.[94] The difference is that in Bernard's case, he was successful. Alvarus, a layman, and Eulogius, a provincial clergyman, had much less chance of seeing their ideas spread widely beyond the confines of Córdoba, not only because of the different political and religious climate of the ninth century, but also because of their remoteness.

Bernard, by contrast, was working and writing at the beginning of the twelfth-century Renaissance, and had the audience of kings, emperors, and popes. The conditions were right for him. He was able to present the concept of martyrdom at the hands of the Muslims as the special reserve of a small but committed monastic army, dedicated to fighting and dying for Christ. We have seen that many monastic chroniclers lauded those who had fallen in the First Crusade as martyrs, though this was more a popular notion, rather than one of official sanction. Bernard's knights, by contrast, were given papal approval for their actions and way of life, ultimately becoming answerable only to the pope himself.

They were held up as the ideal combatants in the war with Islam. Whether officially stated or not, martyrdom could become a worthwhile goal of all who would go on crusade. The Templars were the models to be emulated. Indeed, we have already seen how John 15:13 was invoked as a key text for the conduct of the Templar knights. The notion that they would willingly lay down their lives for their brothers was central to the ideology of the order.[95] As the Templars grew rapidly in size and status, this idea would no doubt have spread.

Curiously, Bernard said little about the status of martyrdom in the actual preaching of the Second Crusade. He did not seem to use it as a means of encouraging the masses to take the cross. Perhaps this was deliberate; it was one thing to proclaim the glories of retaking the holy places for Christ, but another to announce to thousands that they were in all likelihood going to their deaths. While Urban may have used such an approach in 1095 (if later chroniclers are to be believed), the mood of this crusade was different; the triumphant Christian settlements had suddenly been put in a defensive position, and the main theme would have been one of strengthening them and enacting divine revenge, not marching off to a glorious martyr's fate. This more somber tone meant that Bernard preferred the encouragement of assured victory for the Christian forces. Nevertheless, there were doubtless many that were inspired by the martyr ideal, as witnessed by Odo's remarks even when the crusade was falling apart. Modern readers might observe that the church had succeeded in transforming an action that was essentially a sin (the seeking of one's own death) into the highest form of service to Christ. To the medieval mind, however, there was a great distinction between selfish suicide and the humble act of dying for God, and it had a long and glorious history.

There are numerous examples of this throughout the second half of the twelfth century, and particularly in the thirteenth, a discussion of which lies outside the boundaries of this chapter. We have seen here how this idea was first condemned (or at least discouraged) and then slowly evolved into an acceptable theology to fit the needs of the military ventures of Christendom. It was probably inevitable that some form of exalted voluntary martyrdom would come into being to address the real problem of what happened to the fallen soldiers of Christ. This was an issue not specifically treated in scripture,[96] but one for which the theologians and exegetes were capable of constructing a solution, through the use of biblical interpretation.

An ancient Christian ideal, to die for the faith, was effectively incorporated into the Christian military machine, and helped to inspire countless thousands to take the cross and the perilous road to the Holy Land, safe in the knowledge that whether they lived or died, paradise was theirs as a reward for their commitment. Once again, we can see how the dramatic changes wrought by the reforms of the eleventh century shaped papal policies and Christian thought. It was these varied changes and their consequences which would continue to influence Christian methods of confronting and dealing with Islam for many centuries to come.

Conclusion

This book has discussed the remarkable complexity of how the medieval Church came to support and sanction war, in the process asserting its authority, both spiritual and political. The ideological rivalry between Christianity and Islam, and the great appeal that both faiths held for their respective adherents meant that conflicts between them were inevitable. Such conflicts, as we have seen, often manifested themselves in the form of unrestrained violence and brutality, wrapped in a cloak of religious piety and devotion, and justified by the Christian West through extensive theological argument, Church traditions, and biblical parallels, particularly those found in the Old Testament. Islam used similar methods, a topic worthy of its own extensive study.

The energy, vigor, and even novelty with which theologians and monastic writers devoted themselves to justifying and explaining the concept of holy violence and war and its proper applications, showed the ability of the Christian Church to adapt ancient teachings to the political needs of the time. Perhaps some readers would view such new theologies as being audacious. However, these monks, bishops, and popes were not trying to shock, but rather to incorporate very different new concepts into a body of accepted tradition, concepts which at times appeared completely opposed to that tradition. The use of classical Christian *exempla* and *auctores* to strengthen their positions was essential, and the writings of Augustine, Gregory I, and several others were employed to this end.

We have examined many of the elements that were a part of the growth of religious support for holy war and Christian hostility to Islam. The new, aggressive, political Church that emerged in the late eleventh century may seem a glaring contradiction to the peaceful ideals of the Sermon on the Mount, or Christ's commandment for Peter to put away his sword. One must be wary, of course, of judging on the basis of modern standards, or as the result of events which occurred long after those discussed here and which could not have been envisioned at the time. If it appears that some elements of the Reform and the new martial attitude of the Church contradicted the core of the Christian message, it also must be remembered that this was a message which had already been transformed under centuries of allegiance to the Roman Empires of the East and West. A tradition of adaptability had already been established.

Those such as Peter Damian and perhaps Isaac of Stella, who opposed Christian militarism were a minority compared with those like Gregory VII, who sought to advance papal power and influence; Urban II, who first sent the crusading armies on the march to the East; and Bernard of Clairvaux, who was filled with a deep religious conviction for the cause of both the Templars and the Second Crusade. Ultimately, their goals proved to be only partially attainable. The loss of Edessa and the failure of the Second Crusade were the first in a long succession of bitter disappointments and setbacks for the Christian West which continued until the end of the thirteenth century and beyond.

The great question, that many have attempted to answer in a variety of ways, is why such theologies developed at all. As we have seen, a very complex series of events, cultural conditions, religious movements, and ideological shifts all contributed to the creation of the new Christian militarism in the eleventh and twelfth centuries. A new European identity, the loss of Jerusalem to the Turks, the rise of the papacy as a political power, the Reform, and popular religious movements, were very different and new concepts, but there is no one definitive answer to the question. Numerous theories have been put forth, both in this study and in the works cited herein. It is more appropriate to look for the answers in each of the individual elements, and to note their impact on one another, which then allows for a clearer picture of the whole to be seen. That is the intention of this book. Each of the subjects treated here both influenced and was influenced by the unfolding events of the time.

As we have seen, the Reform, born from a desire to purify the Church and consolidate papal power, brought numerous changes in theological thought and actions, and in traditional views of the relation between the Church and the State. Along with this there seems to have been a surge in spiritual longing and feeling. Popular religious movements were one notable result, with both new monastic orders sanctioned by the church and heretical ideologies becoming more prominent. With the papacy able to assume greater power, Western Europe was given the opportunity to end its internal strife, unite against a common Muslim enemy, and to work for a common goal, the liberation of Jerusalem and the Holy Land.

The military power now wielded by the Church found its most symbolic expression in the Templars, and their great advocate, Bernard. The Knights of the Temple were a remarkable innovation that may have borrowed from other models, as well as incorporating the essence of the new martial theology of the time. Bernard's justification placed them firmly within a biblical and Church tradition, and their power and prestige grew at an astonishing rate once they were granted papal sanction.

At the same time, the Cistercian Order was also growing rapidly and influencing the theology of the age considerably, most often through Bernard, its unofficial spokesman. His prominence had not only guaranteed success for the Templars, but also for his own monastic order. Ultimately, one of its own monks became Pope Eugenius III, who preached the failed Second Crusade. Though seeking initially to escape the world, the Cistercians had become even more embroiled in it than the Benedictines they had criticized, accumulating vast wealth and even being actively involved in the slave operations of the Iberian Peninsula.

In Iberia, a region of long-term contact between Christianity and Islam, there had for many centuries been a mixture of peaceful co-existence and open hostility between the two faiths, which swung back and forth like a pendulum depending on political and religious whims. From the Martyr's Movement in the mid ninth century to the polemics of Petrus Alfonsi, there was a much greater awareness of Islam than in Northern Europe. Peter the Venerable's project to study Islam was a major undertaking, and brought new information to Europe that had previously only been known in a small circle of monasteries and theological specialists.

This project, however, only served to further hostilities, when it was known at all. As Christianity learned more about its religious counterpart, it developed new means of ideological attack to stand alongside the physical confrontation of the battlefield, and give such conflicts added impetus. Drawing on ancient Byzantine polemical writings, and the condemnations of the ninth-century Córdoban Christians, theologians and chroniclers began to formulate new apocalyptic visions of Islam that seemed to correspond well with earlier prophecies of the End Time. The liberation of Jerusalem was seen as further evidence of this, and as Christian soldiers marched off to the East to die for their faith, they began to be accorded the status of martyrs, though initially only in the enthusiastic accounts of crusade chronicles. Nevertheless, the concept of absolution of sins and waging a war as penance could not help but contribute to this idea. The Templars were seen by Bernard as exemplary models of the new Christian martyr, bravely fighting and dying for God to protect the Christian presence.

One begins to see how each of these many strands weaves together, at times overlapping and influencing one another. We have observed how these different aspects of the crusading movement were formulated and ultimately contributed to one another's growth and prominence. These distinct areas shaped or were shaped by the others. The Templars would not have survived without Bernard, who would not have had the prominence he did had not the Cistercians grown so rapidly and effectively altered their initial spiritual mission of retreat. That even this was the result of earlier aspects of the Reform and popular religious fervor shows how intertwined all of these events were.

Had Bernard written a refutation of Islam instead of Peter the Venerable, it might have had a different impact on Christian-Muslim relations, given Bernard's prominence and his reputation as an outspoken supporter of holy military conflict. Had Peter not employed an apocalypticism in relation to Islam (possibly drawn from the models written during the time of the Martyr's Movement), there may have been a different emphasis in some European writings.

What we can say is that each of these ideologies, movements, religious orders, and theologies, while developing in their own ways, relied to a great extent on other events and thoughts taking place around them. None developed completely independently, or could have been realized in the manner that they were without the influence and presence of other factors.

Each of these topics had a profound impact on Christian-Islamic relations and on Christian concepts of acceptable and holy violence. This period represented the most dramatic shift in Christian teaching and ideology since its legalization by the Roman Empire in the fourth century. A series of factors, a chain of events, and the logical progression of certain theological ideas from Antiquity all coincided to bring about the fundamental shift in Church teaching, effectively rendering the propagation of the Christian message by the sword a valid and sanctified act.

However, it would be incorrect to single out Christianity as the sole precursor of such activities. It must be remembered that Islam originally had gained many of these territories through its own military conquests centuries earlier. Drawing from a *hadith*, or saying of the Prophet, Islamic tradition held to the notion of the greater *jihad* of the internal struggle, which is superior to the lesser *jihad* of the external struggle in defense of the faith. However, from the earliest days of Islam, armed conflict had played an important role in establishing the religion's legitimacy. In subsequent centuries, such "defensive" battles for the faith involved much foreign conquest far from the land of Muhammad's birth. Unprovoked attacks on Christian lands and communities were common in Islam's early centuries, and certainly helped explain its rapid advancement in the seventh and eighth centuries.

Nevertheless, by the eleventh century, Islam itself was torn apart by rivalries, and conflicts between Sunnis and Shi'ites, Arabs and Turks. Islam had no central political unity, and as a result, had lost some of its ability to engage in organized military campaigns against Christians in either the East or West. The Christian forces were seen as the aggressors and invaders, disrupting a way of life that had existed for centuries, though what peace existed had been established by military conquests of their own, it must be noted. Ironically, it was the Frankish invasions in the form of the crusades that allowed for a unified Islam to re-emerge. Ultimately, the Mamelukes, under al-Ashraf Khalil, defeated the Christian forces at Acre, expelling them from the Holy Land forever in 1291, thus bringing an end to what Nur ad-Din had begun a century and a half earlier. This event also contributed to the suppression of the Templars in the early fourteenth century, for after such a loss, they were an order without a land to defend. The ruthlessness with which the Mameluke armies executed this military victory, involving total destruction of Christian property and no prisoners taken, mirrored the actions taken by the West toward Islam in decades past, and some of the Islamic practices of its early centuries. Crusading would continue, but its focus would shift to countering the growing power of the Ottomans, who would supplant the Seljuks in the fourteenth century.

Back in the West, a kind of mob mentality regarding the crusades sometimes settled over Europe, and whilst this was strongest in the first fifty years of crusading, it only gradually declined over the succeeding centuries. Anti-Jewish pogroms and the sack of Constantinople in the "crusade" of 1204 are two of the most graphic examples of this, but there were many others. The Church, in attempting to unify Europe, had unwittingly released something terrible, merely channeling a collective aggression away from its own borders and toward other lands and peoples.

As we have seen, Muslim resistance to the Frankish invasion began almost immediately, giving rise to the Knights Templar, and to a series of smaller Christian military expeditions that took place between the major ventures now labeled as "crusades." These victories for Islam had not come suddenly, but were the result of a gradual building up of resistance and strength. Under Saladin in the late twelfth century, the *jihad* was fully revived, partially inspired by the Muslim success during the Second Crusade. That success itself had been the result of the humiliation of the loss of Jerusalem and many other cities to the Franks. The very act of taking Jerusalem in 1099 thus opened the way for the eventual Christian defeat.

It is an easy matter for a modern study, with the benefit of hindsight, to discuss the inevitable losses of Eastern lands by the Christian forces, or even the futility of the crusading enterprise. To exert such tremendous effort, as well as intellectual and theological speculation, exegesis, and argument for an undertaking that ultimately failed completely could easily be seen as one of the great wastes in human history. When the input of time, energy, financial expense, and costs in lives on both sides are added to this, the tragedy of crusading becomes even more apparent.

Of course, this ultimate outcome could never have been known to the participants in these events, and each failure was simply viewed as a further test of faith sent by God as a punishment for the sinfulness of the crusaders and their supporters. From a medieval spiritual viewpoint, this explanation was the only acceptable answer for Christians trying to understand how God could have failed them. The fact that talk of crusading continued well into the Renaissance and beyond, when the Ottomans were a much closer and more real military threat to Europe, showed that, in many minds, the idea remained perfectly valid, and it was only human failings which had prevented it from becoming a reality in the past.

The mingling within Christianity and Islam of love, charity, and peace with an acceptance of violence, killing, intolerance, and war, must stand as one of the most significant commixtures of ideologies in the history of religion. The ramifications of this striking theology would be evident throughout the rest of the Middle Ages, and many argue that the effects are still being felt in the Middle East today. Indeed, the fierceness and mercilessness with which the Christians were expelled from Syria and Palestine at the end of the thirteenth century is evidence that the Islamic leaders of these lands ultimately hated the West with the same intensity that it hated them. This statement does require some qualification. The crusading movement only affected those Islamic communities situated around the Mediterranean; for others, it was not a real concern. While there is certainly some truth in the idea of the West engendering enmity for itself, and this being one reason why the West has continued to misunderstand and mistrust the Islamic world for the past nine hundred years, it must again be remembered that Islamic forces had struck first centuries earlier, wiping out Christian nations that had existed for hundreds of years. Those losses were not forgotten.

The medieval writers and theologians discussed here, of course, could not know of future events. They saw themselves as guardians of the true faith against the forces of evil, and as such, drastic measures were necessary to combat them. Many, particularly by the thirteenth century, fully expected the immanent end of the world, fired by the terrifying predictions of Joachim of

Fiore and the popularity of Catharism. Others merely sought the conversion, or more often, destruction of the unbelievers, so that the Christian religion might reign throughout the world. At the time their actions certainly seemed to be pleasing to God.

Ultimately, the theology of crusading, as developed in monastic environments, was a logical extension of the events and thoughts of the time, and perhaps it was unavoidable. A newly-unified civilization seeking both an outlet for its aggression and a way of satisfying its spiritual needs could not have asked for a more all-encompassing solution. That monks and monastic institutions were among the most prolific and vocal supporters of crusading in its first half-century is something of a sobering notion when considering Christianity's identity as a religion of peace. However, as we have seen, the conflicting ideologies of war and peace had to be reconciled in a manner appropriate to the times, and this is precisely what theologians set about doing. That theological justifications, polemics, and biblical referencing with regard to crusading continued for nearly three centuries is a testimony to how difficult and complex medieval writers and clerics found the subject, and how careful their reasoning and ideas had to be formulated. This was especially true during times of defeat, when the faith of those who believed earnestly in the crusades was strained to the breaking point.

To the monks of the time, on the other hand, their position was seen as one of great logic and simplicity, even as divinely inspired. Their role as spiritual warriors had long been established; they were at war spiritually with satanic forces on a daily basis. God, in his infinite mercy and wisdom, had offered the opportunity for the laity to take part in the same struggle, but on the physical plane; the crusading armies were truly viewed as mobile monasteries. It must have seemed a miracle that such a mission now became so obvious. Who better than the monastic orders to offer guidance and instruction to the laity on how to conduct themselves? And who else but monks could produce the appropriate learned theological commentaries needed to enact the divine plan? Ultimately, it was that sense of the miraculous and of divine intervention that inspired Latin Christendom in the wake of the Reform to attempt the impossible, assured of victory against the enemy because "God wills it."

Chapter Notes

Introduction

1. Raymond of Aguilers, *Historia Francorum*, RHC 3, 231–310, Cap XX, 300D-E: "Justo nimirum judicio, ut locus idem eorum sanguinem exciperet, quorum blasphemias in Deum tam longo tempore pertulerat. Repleta itaque cadaveribus et sanguine civitate, confugerunt aliquanti ad turrem David, et poposcerunt a comite Raimundo securitatis dexteram, et dederunt ei arcem. Capta autem urbe operae pretium videre devotionem peregrinorum ante Sepulcrum Domini, quomodo plaudebant, exsultantes et cantantes canticum novum Domino."

2. This appears to be based on Revelation 14:20: "et exivit sanguis de lacu usque ad frenos equorum [...]" "and blood came out of the winepress, even unto the horse bridles," See Benjamin Kedar, "The Jerusalem Massacre of July 1099 in the Western Historiography of the Crusades," *Crusades* 3 (2004): 65.

3. William J. Purkis, *Crusading Spirituality in the Holy Land and Iberia, c.1095–c.1187* (Woodbridge: Boydell, 2008), especially the first three chapters, 12–119; Susanna A. Throop, *Crusading as an Act of Vengeance, 1095–1216* (Aldershot: Ashgate, 2011); Jay Rubenstein, *Armies of Heaven: The First Crusade and the Quest for Apocalypse* (New York: Basic Books, 2011).

4. Norman Housely gives a detailed discussion of the merits and weaknesses of all four methods in *Contesting the Crusades* (Malden, MA, and Oxford: Blackwell, 2006), 213. See also Purkis, *Crusading Spirituality in the Holy Land*, 4–5.

5. For a discussion of cannibalism during the crusades, see L. A. M. Sumberg, "The 'Tafurs' and the First Crusade," *Mediaeval Studies* 21 (1959): 224–46. Rubenstein discusses the use of cannibalism (or at least a faked version) to inspire fear in *Crusading Spirituality*, 151–152, and 240–41. See also 85–86, and 107–08, where he discusses Frankish psychological warfare and terror tactics. Helen Nicholson takes a broader view of the phenomenon in her Crusade Q&A, accessed September 17, 2112, http://freespace.virgin.net/nigel.nicholson/SSCLE/Crusade Faqs/f-babies.html.

6. Christopher Tyerman, *God's War: A New History of the Crusades* (Cambridge, MA: Harvard University Press, 2006), 32.

7. Ibid., 35–36.

8. Peter Abelard, for example, as we will see in Chapter 3.

9. An excellent account of early and later Islamic campaigns can be found in Paul Fregosi, *Jihad* (New York: Prometheus Books, 1998), which makes extensive use of Arabic accounts to show that early Islam was militarized and aggressive, and used its religious zeal to forcefully spread the faith.

10. For a short review of this, see Paul F. Crawford, "Four Myths about the Crusades," *The Intercollegiate Review* 46:1 (2011): 14–16, and Fregosi, *Jihad*.

11. See H.E.J. Cowdrey, "Christianity and the Morality of Warfare During the First Century of Crusading," *The Experience of Crusading, Volume 1: Western Approaches* (Cambridge: Cambridge University Press, 2003), specifically at 186–88, for a discussion of how Gratian wove the concept of just war into canon law in the mid-twelfth century.

12. James Brundage, "The Hierarchy of Violence in Twelfth- and Thirteenth-Century Canonists," *The International History Review*, 17 (1995): 676.

13. Ibid., 673–74.

14. See also note 8 above. This distinction will also be discussed in Chapter 3, in an examination of Abelard's writings on the subject of violent acts as morally neutral.

15. Gratian, *Decretum, Corpus Iuris Canonici*, ed. by A. Frieberg, 2 vols. (Leipzig: Tauchnitz, 1929), I, Causa 23, Quest. 3, Cap. V, 897: "Fortitudo, que bello tuetur a barbaris patriam, uel domi defendit infirmos, uel a latronibus socios, plena iustitia est."

16. Ibid. Tthis is discussed in detail in Quest. 2, Cap. I–III, 894–951.

17. Brundage, "Hierarchy," 677. He gives a good schematic diagram that classifies violence as it was understood at this time, in Appendix I, 682. Initially, violence is divided between public and private. Public then becomes sacred or profane, just or secular war, and so on, to holy war. Private is either individual or collective, which can also be sacred or profane, criminal or not, defensive or feudal. See also 680 for these distinctions.

18. Tomaž Mastnak, *Crusading Peace: Christendom, the Muslim World, and Western Political Order* (Berkeley: University of California Press, 2002) 60–63 gives a good summary and discusses some aspects of this in the early Church. See also H.E.J. Cowdrey, "Christianity and the Morality of Warfare," 176.

19. This will be discussed more in Chapters 1 and 3.

20. Brundage, "Hierarchy," 679, quoting from the *Summa magistri Rolandi*, ed. by Friedrich Thaner (Innsbruck: Wagner'schen Universitæts-Buchhandlung, 1874), Cap. 23, Quest. 5, 93: "Causa vero correctionis et iustitiae malos interficere Deo vere est ministrare."

21. Cowdrey, "Christianity and the morality of warfare," 176. See also 187–88 for a discussion of the process of integrating the two concepts of war over that time.

22. Jonathan Riley-Smith, *The First Crusaders, 1095–1131* (Cambridge: Cambridge University Press, 1997), 42.

23. Mastnak, *Crusading Peace*, 62.

24. Jean Leclercq, *The Love of Learning and the Desire for God: A Study of Monastic Culture* (New York: Fordham University Press, 1961), 80–81.

25. A few instances will suffice here. See, for example, the siege of Jerusalem, as recorded in Jeremiah 6, wherein God speaks of destroying Zion, (v.2): "[4] Speciosae et delicatae assimilavi filiam Sion." Further in Jer. 6:4–5, where there is a call to prepare for battle: "Sanctificate super eam bellum; Consurgite, et ascendamus in meridie: Vae nobis, quia declinavit dies, Quia longiores factae sunt umbrae vesperi! [5] Surgite, et ascendamus in nocte, Et dissipemus domus eius." II Chronicles 13:12, states, that if an army has God's support, an enemy cannot hope to succeed against it: "Ergo in exercitu nostro dux Deus est, et sacerdotes eius, qui clangunt tubis, et resonant contra vos: filii Israel nolite pugnare contra Dominum Deum patrum vestrorum, quia non vobis expedit." *Biblia Sacra Juxta Vulgatam Clementiam*, ed. Alberto Colunga and Laurentio Turrado, 7th ed. (Madrid: Biblioteca de Autores Cristianos, 1985).

26. Brundage, "Hierarchy," 672.

27. Riley-Smith provides a fine summary of some of the more obvious examples in *The First Crusade and the Idea of Crusading* (London: Athlone Press, 1986), 140–48.

28. Ibid., 142. See, for example, Robert the Monk, *Historia Iherosolimitana*, RHC 3, 717–882, Cap. XXVI, 882C-D: "Hæc et multa alia invenimus in propheticis libris quæ congruunt huic liberationi factæ ætatibus nostris."

29. Riley-Smith, *First Crusade*, 142.

30. Ibid., 91–92.

31. Robert the Monk, *Historia, Prologus*, 723B: "Sed post creationem mundi quid mirabilius factum est præter salutiferæ crucis mysterium, quam quod modernis temporibus actum est in hoc itinere nostrorum Iherosolimitanorum?"

32. Baldric of Bourgueil, *Historia Jerosolimitana*, RHC 4, 1–112, *Liber primus*, 14E: "Filii Israel ab Ægyptiis educti, qui, Rubro Mari transito, vos præfiguraverunt, terram illam armis suis, Jesu duce, sibi vindicaverunt."

33. Guibert of Nogent, *Gesta Dei per Francos*, RHC 4, 113–264, *Liber primus*, 123F: "Si Deum in Judaico populo magnificatum audivimus, Jesum Christum, sicut heri apud antiquos, ita et hodie apud modernos, esse et valere certis experimentis agnovimus."

34. A major source for these is the vast *Patrologia Latina* collection, published by Jacques-Paul Migne between 1844 and 1855. Though it is clearly dated and contains errors, it is still often the only source for some writers' texts in modern editions. The website at: http://pld.chadwyck.co.uk/ contains more recent annotations and notes concerning textual errors. Later works, such as the ongoing *Monumenta Germaniae Historica* (abbreviuated as MGH) also feature as an important source for this book.

35. For a general discussion of the laity and its responses and attitudes to crusading, see Riley-Smith, *First Crusaders*.

Chapter 1

1. On this lack of attention, see Kenneth Baxter Wolf, "The Earliest Spanish Christian Views of Islam," *Church History* 55 (1986): 281–82, and 291. For a good general introduction to evolving Christian attitudes, see Michael Frassetto and David R. Blanks, eds. *Western Views of Islam in Medieval and Early Modern Europe: Perception of Other*. New York: St. Martin's Press, 1999.

2. This event is discussed in detail in Chapters 6 and 7.

3. For example, one of the first Spanish references to Muhammad, in the *Chronica Byzantia-Arabica* from 714, refers to his followers worshipping him and proclaiming him a prophet of God: "Quem hactenus tanto honore et reuerentia colunt, ut Dei apostolum et prophetam eum in omnibus sacramentis suis esse scriptusque adfirment." *Corpus scriptorum muzarabicorum*, 2 vols, ed. Juan Gil (Madrid: Instituto "Antonio de Nebrija," 1973), 1: 9.

4. Mastnak, *Crusading Peace*, 67–68.

5. Ibid., 96.
6. Ibid., 97.
7. Jay Rubenstein, *Armies of Heaven*, 120–21.
8. Mastnak, *Crusading Peace*, 114, which discusses how other enemies were seen as more threatening by various ruling powers, even initially by Gregory VII.
9. Purkis, in *Crusading Spirituality in the Holy Land and Iberia*, argues that these cannot be considered true "proto-crusades," when he says at 121 that "there is very little evidence that their exploits were regarded as being religious in cause or penitential in character." See also Marcus Bull, *Knightly Piety and the Lay Response to the First Crusade* (Oxford: Clarendon Press, 1993), 70–114.
10. This term is now considered anachronistic, given that Gregory VII was only one of many individuals involved in the reforms that spanned the eleventh and twelfth centuries. For background studies on the life of Gregory VII, see H.E.J. Cowdrey, *Pope Gregory VII, 1073–1085* (Oxford: Oxford University Press, 1998), and H.E.J. Cowdrey, *The Register of Pope Gregory VII, 1073–1085: An English Translation* (New York: Oxford University Press, 2002).
11. Karl F. Morrison, "The Gregorian Reform," in *Christian Spirituality: Origins to the Twelfth Century*, ed. Bernard McGinn, John Myendorf, and Jean Leclercq (London: SCM, 1989), 177.
12. Yael Katzir, "The Second Crusade and the Redefinition of Ecclesia, Christianitas, and Papal Coercive Power," in *The Second Crusade and the Cistercians*, ed. Michael Gervers (New York: St. Martin's Press, 1992), 4.
13. Gregory VII set down a memorandum in 1075, included in the letters of the papal register for that year, known as the *Dictatus papae*, in which he set out what he felt the privileges of the reformed papacy should be. I. S. Robinson discusses them briefly in *The Papacy 1073–1198: Continuity and Innovation* (Cambridge: Cambridge University Press, 1990), where he notes that many of the declarations did not have the backing of canon law, and were merely statements or chapter headings concerning the authority that Gregory desired for the papacy, 404. A fine summary of these in English is given in Joseph H. Lynch, *The Medieval Church, a Brief History* (London and New York: Longman, 1992), 146–48, drawing from Gregory VII, *Das Register Gregors VII*, II, Ep. 55, MGH, *Epistolae selectae*, ed. Erich Caspar (Berlin: Weidmannshe Buchhandlung, 1920–23, 1920), 201–8.
14. Morrison, "Gregorian Reform," 188.
15. As we will see, the Cistercians themselves quickly fell into the traps that they sought to avoid, i.e., acquisition of wealth, corruption, and bureaucracy. Most medieval religious institutions founded on the ideals of poverty, humility, and adherence to strict rules found themselves in trouble at one time or another. The Franciscans and Dominicans would be prime examples of this same problem from the 13th century onward.
16. H.E.J. Cowdrey, "The Genesis of the Crusades," in *Popes, Monks, and Crusaders*, by the same author (London: Hambledon Press, 1984), 17.
17. For a discussion of Anselm of Lucca's correspondence with William the Conqueror, as well as Norman penance in the aftermath of Hastings, see Cowdrey, "Christianity and the Morality of Warfare during the First Century of Crusading," in *The Experience of Crusading, Volume 1: Western Approaches*, ed. Marcus Bull and Norman Housley (Cambridge: Cambridge University Press, 2003), 180–81.
18. John France, a leading Glaber scholar, provides a fine summary of the setting in which the histories were written in "War and Christendom in the thought of Rodulfus Glaber," *Studia Monastica* 30 (1988): 105–11. He is also the editor and translator of *Rodulfi Glabri—Historium Libri Quinque* (Oxford: Clarendon Press, 1989), the complete edition of the histories. Both works provide good biographical material, placing Glaber in the context of his time.
19. France, "War and Christendom," 111, drawing from Southern, *Western Views of Islam in the Middle Ages* (Cambridge, MA: Harvard University Press, 1962), 28.
20. France, *Historium*, 194.
21. France, "War and Christendom," 111–12, provides many good examples.
22. France, *Historium*, 21–23. The Latin text reads: "Alius quoque Saracenorum eorundem, cultro deplanans ligni astulam, posuit incunctanter pedem super uiri Dei codicem, bibliotecam uidelicet quam ex more secum semper ferre consueuerat. Dumque uir sanctus intuens ingemuisset aliqui minus feroces ex ipsis perspicientes suum increpuerunt comparem, dicentes non debere magnos prophetas sic pro nichilo duci ut illorum dicta pedi substerneret. Siquidem Sarraceni Hebreorum, quin potius Christianorum, prophetas legunt, dicentes etiam completum iam esse in quodam suorum, quem illi Mahomed nuncupant, quicquid de uniuersorum Domino Christo sacri uates predixerunt. Sed ad errorum illorum comprobandum etiam ipsorum genealogiam penes se habent, ad similitudinem uidelicet Euangelii Mathei [...] Illorum inquiens 'Hismahel genuit Nabaiot,' ac deinceps usque in erroneum illorum descendens figmentum, quod scilicet tantum est a ueritate alienum quantum a sacra et catholica auctoritate extraneum." 20, 22.
23. Odilo, *Vita Maioli*, PL 142, 960C-2B, is particularly vicious, referring to the Saracens as "rabid wolves" and noting how they have caused immense harm and destruction: "Sarracenorum improvisus adventus, Christianorum afflictio, monasteriorum et urbium destructio, ipsius beati Maioli capitio, redemptio, et liberatio, et ejusdem

ferocissimæ gentis a Christianorum finibus, Christo auxiliante, dejectio. Quod vel quale est illud præsagium memorabile? Præcessit enim crudelissimam infestationem Sarracenorum rabies inaudita luporum in illis maxime partibus, in quibus post transitum maris totus Sarracenorum efferbuit impetus. Diximus pro modulo qualiter liberata est fidelium multitudo a Sarracenorum persecutione, dicamus proposse quo ordine liberata est patria a luporum infestatione." (960C). Syrus, in the *Vita Maioli*, PL 137, 763D–68D, is no kinder: "Feroces itaque barbari peracto scelere ad suas latebras dum redirent cum captivorum multitudine, beatum Maiolum cernunt a longe solum sedentem in lapide." (765B). There follows a detailed account of the captivity. See also Scott G. Bruce, "An Abbot Between Two Cultures: Maiolus of Cluny Considers the Muslims of La Garde-Freinet," *Early Medieval Europe* 15, no. 4 (2007): 426–440.

24. A brief summary of al-Hakim's reported atrocities and destructions can be found in Andrew Jotischky, "The Christians of Jerusalem, the Holy Sepulchre and the Origins of the First Crusade," *Crusades* 7 (2008): 44–45. The religious communities of the Druze trace their origins, or at least their legitimacy, to the followers of Al-Hakim. Originally an outgrowth of the Shia sect known as Ismailism, they adhere to a synthesis of Islamic, Neoplatonic, and Gnostic practices, and as such are not considered by Muslims to be a sect of Islam in the same manner as the modern Shi'ites, for example. Some Druze consider themselves to be Muslims, others do not.

25. France, *Historium*, 3, vii, 25, 136–37.

26. Ibid., 1, v, 17, 32–33. By 909, well before Glaber's time, the Aghlabids had been overthrown by the Fatimids, so it is rather curious that he mentions them at all, but this may simply reflect the slow pace at which some news traveled in those times.

27. Ibid., iv. Glaber describes the meeting in 3, iii, 12, 114–15.

28. France, "War," 113. The account in France, *Historium*, 3, vii, 24, 134–5, reads: [...] "they [letters from the Jews to the Caliph] alleged that if he did not quickly destroy the venerable Church of the Christians, then they would soon occupy his whole realm, depriving him of all his power." [...] "et quoniam nisi clerius domum Christianorum uenerabilem subuerteret, sciret se in proximum Christianis regnum illius occupantibus omni penitus dignitare carere." Hakim believed himself to be God incarnate (Riley-Smith, *First Crusaders*, 25), and ultimately turned against Muslims as well. Given the Caliph's mental condition, he may well have initiated the destruction himself, without any external promptings.

29. It would be inaccurate, of course, to assume that historical chronicles of the time were meant to be employed in the manner of modern historical accounts and research; circumstances and ideologies were completely different. The concept of "objective" history was unknown. See France, "The Destruction of Jerusalem and the First Crusade," *Journal of Ecclesiastical History* 47 (1996): 11: "The early eleventh century was an age of poor communications. [...] News of an important event might well be unevenly disseminated. The number of people writing anything resembling history at this time was very small."

30. He records in 1, iv, 16, for example: "Because the power of the government rested upon tyranny rather than upon gentle mildness or hereditary right, it was proper that stubborn rulers and their subjects should suffer the blows of repeated invasions." "Et quoniam magis contingebat tyrannide imperari quam uel liberali pietate uel originali propagine, idcirco par erat talium contumaciam cum sibi subditis crebris infestationum plagis atterere." France, *Historium*, 30–31. The anti-Greek sentiment among Western theologians intensified following the controversies of the mid-eleventh century, and continued right through twelfth century, culminating in the tragic sack of Constantinople in 1204. This was an ironic development, as it was theoretically in aid of Byzantium that the crusades were originally mounted, and this attack is probably what set the Byzantine Empire into its long period of decline, ending in 1453 with the taking of Constantinople by the Ottoman Mehmet the Conqueror. The Orthodox and Catholic branches of Christianity coexisted uneasily for more than 150 years before breaking into conflict at the beginning of the thirteenth century.

31. Ibid., 116–17.

32. Michael Frassetto, "The Image of the Saracen as Heretic in the Sermons of Ademar of Chabannes," in *Western Views of Islam in Medieval and Early Modern Europe: Perception of Other*, ed. David R. Blanks and Michael Frassetto. New York: St. Martin's Press, 1999, 86–85.

33. Ibid., 87–88, taking from note 32, at 95: "Iudei autem et Sarraceni qui dicunt non se credere sanctam trinitatem sed in unum Deum ideo nullum Deum credunt quia in sanctam trinitatem non credunt. Et magis ipsum verum Deum blasphemant et ad iracundiam provocant quia tollunt ab eo trinitatem."

34. For a discussion, see James Grier, "Hoax, History, and Hagiography in Adémar de Chabannes' Texts for the Divine Office," in *Representing History, 900–1300: Art, Music, History*, ed. Robert A. Maxwell (University Park: Pennsylvania State University Press, 2010), 67–72.

35. Tyerman, *God's War*, 46.

36. This incident is given a detailed treatment in Einar Joranson's classic essay, "The Great German Pilgrimage of 1064–1065," in *The Crusades and Other Historical Essays*, ed. Louis J. Paetow (New York: F.S. Crofts, 1928), 3–43. Though dated, the article makes some valid points, for ex-

ample: "Close study reveals that the character of the pilgrimage has usually been misunderstood; it raises grave doubt as to the validity of the recent dictum that 'but for the coming of the Seljuqs popular indignation in Europe would have slumbered and the crusades might never have taken place'" [quoting H.M.J. Loewe, in *Cambridge Medieval History*, ed. H.M. Gwatkin and J.P. Whitney, vol. 4 (Cambridge: University Press, 1923) 316], 3–4. According to Joranson, the number of pilgrims was more than 7,000, at 3, 12. For a recent discussion of Gunther's life, pilgrimage, and death, see David Jacoby, "Bishop Gunther of Bamberg, Byzantium and Christian Pilgrimage to the Holy Land in the Eleventh Century," in *Zwischen Polis, Provinz Und Peripherie: Beitrage Zur Byzantinischen Geschichte Und Kultur*, ed. Lars M. Hoffmann. (Wiesbaden: Harrassowitz, 2005), 267–285.

37. Elizabeth Hallam, ed., *Chronicles of the Crusades* (New York: Weidenfeld and Nicolson, 1989), 35–36. Lambertus Hersfeldensis, *Annales*, PL 146, 1084A: "Nec moratus, linteum, quo caput more gentis obvolverat, expediens, facto vinculo, in collum episcopi injecit. Episcopus, ut erat vir liberalis verecundiæ et maturæ admodum gravitatis, ignominiam non ferens tanto nisi pugnum ei dedit in faciem, ut uno ictu consternatum ad pavimentum usque præcipitem daret, vociferans insuper, prius eum pœnas pro impietate daturum, quod impuras manus in sacerdotem Christi profanus et idololatra mittere præsumpsisset." An alternate account appears in the Annals of the Monk of Neider-Altaich, who described the same incident, but added that Gunther pressed his foot down on the Arab's neck and urged his fellow pilgrims to action. Relayed by Joranson at 33. *Annales Altahenses maiores*, 1065, MGH Scriptores rerum Germanicum, ed. E.L.B. von Oefele (Hannover: Hahn 1891), 69: "[...] collumque eius pede suo pressit: 'Eia,' inquiens, 'mei, insurgite, omnesque istos comprehensos vinculis fortiter constringite, telisque suorum, qui nos impugnant, nudos opponite.' Nec mora, simul cum dicto factum est, quod iussit."

38. Joranson gives a detailed account in "German Pilgrimage," 35–37. For another summary with some different details, see Rubenstein, *Armies of Heaven*, 9–12. I have slightly combined the two accounts here.

39. Hallam, *Chronicles*, 36. [...] Lamberti, PL 146, 1086B: "Guntherus Baben bergensis episcopus, heu! immatura morte præventus, prosperæ ac lætæ reversionis lugubrem omnibus exitum fecit. Decessit autem 10 kalendas Augusti, ætate integra ad perfruendum hoc seculo maxime matura, vir præter morum gloriam et animæ divicias corporis quoque bonis adprime ornatus."

40. Rubenstein, *Armies of Heaven*, 4.

41. Hallam, *Chronicles*, 36. Lamberti, 1084A "[...] ut sanguis plerisque rupta cute per ungues proflueret. [...] apposito super capita eorum spiculatore, qui districtum in manibus gladium tenens, clamitabat per interpretem, nisi ab obpugnatione quiescerent, non armis se adversum eos sed principum capitibus dimicaturos."

42. Joranson, "German Pilgrimage," 33.

43. Rubenstein, *Armies of Heaven*, 11.

44. Cowdrey, "Genesis of the Crusades," 17. The phrase itself derives from the parable of the invitation to supper in Luke 14: 15–24, wherein the master of the house orders his servant to go into the street and make the poor and lowest enter into his home to eat after all those whom he had invited had declined to attend. Luke 14: 23–4 states: "Et ait dominus servo: Exi in vias, et sepes, et *compelle intrare*, ut impleatur domus mea. Dico autem vobis quod nemo virorum illorum qui vocati sunt, gustabit coenam meam." *Biblia Vulgata* (Madrid: Biblioteca de Auctores Cristianos, 1985), p. 1029. Medieval exegetes thus saw the house of the master as representative of the House of the Church, into which those outside of it could be made to enter. It was a simple matter to transfer this explanation and belief to the policy of forced conversion and later, into crusading. This was probably not the original intent of the passage, but it shows how said exegetes could make use of creative interpretations for specific purposes.

45. The phrase receives a detailed treatment in Augustine's letter to Donatus, *Ep.* 173, 10, PL 33, 757, where he employs the metaphor mentioned in the note above: "Vide nunc quemadmodum de his qui prius venerunt, dictum est, *Introduc huc*; non dictum est *compelle*: ita significaba sunt Ecclesiæ primordia ad hoc crescentis, ut essent vires etiam compellendi. Proinde, quia oportebat ejus jam viribus et magnitudine roborata etiam compelli homines ad convivium salutis æternæ, posteaquam dictum est, *Factum est quod jussisti, et adhuc est locus*; *Exi*, inquit, *in vias et sepes, et compelle intrare*. Quapropter si ambularetis quieti extra hoc convivium salutis æternæ et sanctæ unitatis Ecclesiæ, tanquam in viis vos inveniremus; nunc vero quia per mulas mala et sæva que in nostros committitis, tanquam spinis et asperitate pleni estis, vos tanquam in sepibus invenimus, et intrare compellimus. Qui compellitur, quo non vult cogitur; sed cum intraverit, jam volens pascitur. Cohibe itaque tam iniquum et impacatum animum, ut in vera Ecclesia Christi invenias salutare cinvivium." Augustine clearly believes that those outside of the Church, i.e. heretics, can be forced to enter it, whether they wish to or not, for the good of their souls. He also presents a justification for killing under certain circumstances, including war, in *De Civitate Dei*, I, 21, where he states: "Sed his exceptis, quos Deus occidi iubet sive data lege sive ad personam pro tempore expressa iussione, non autem ipse occidit, qui ministerium debet iubenti, sicut adminiculum gladius utenti; et ideo nequaquam contra contra hoc praeceptum fe-

cerunt, quo dictum est: *Non occides*, qui Deo auctore bella gesserunt aut personam gerentes publicae potestatis secundum eius leges, hoc est iustissimae rationis imperium, sceleratos morte punierunt; [...]." See also his *Quaestiones in Heptateuchum*, 6.10, CCCM 33, pp. 318–19, where further justification can be found.

46. Gregory comments on the phrase in his *Homilia* XXXVI, on Luke 14:16–24, PL 76, 1270C-D: "Cum de vicis et plateis ad cœnam quosdam Dominus invitat, illum videlicet populum designat qui tenere legem sub urbana conversatione noverat; cum vero convivas suos colligi ex viis et sepibus præcipit, nimirum agrestem populum colligere, id est gentilem, quærit, de cujus significatione per Psalmistam dicitur: *Tunc exsultabunt omnia ligna silvarum ante faciem Domini quoniam venit* (*Psal.* XCV, 13). Ligna enim silvæ gentes vocatæ sunt, quia in infidelitate sua tortæ et infructuosæ semper fuerunt. Qui ergo ex illo agresti usu conversi sunt, ad cœnam dominicam quasi ex sepibus venerunt." Gregory held very strong views about conversion, and the suffering that one must endure to receive the grace of God. He advocated that all seek out that suffering and endure it willingly. An excellent summary of his views on the subject may be found in Carole Straw, *Gregory the Great, Perfection and Imperfection* (Berkeley, California: University of California Press, 1988), 194–212. At the heart of Gregory's concept of conversion is fear, even terror, as Straw notes, "The sinner recognizes that God has the power to destroy him utterly, and he begins to fear for the ultimate safety of his soul," 211. Further, "In Gregory's program of reform, fear serves as the first stage and the very foundation of change, for often only fear of God's judgement repels the Christian from worldly involvement [...]," 213. It is easy to see from such a theology how the notion developed of "compelling" others to enter the Church for their own safety.

47. Cowdrey, "Genesis of the Crusades," 18. For some interesting commentary on the phrase by Bernard of Clairvaux, see his *De Consideratione*, PL 182, 440, and *Sermones de Diversis*, Sermo XCIX, PL 183, 726.

48. Cowdrey, "Genesis of the Crusades," 20. See also his "Pope Gregory VII and the Bearing of Arms," *Montjoie: Studies in Crusade History in Honor of Hans Eberhard Mayer*, ed. by Benjamin Kedar, Jonathan Riley-Smith, and Rudolf Hiestand (Aldershot: Variorum, 1997), 21–36.

49. He states, for example, in his *Epistolae, Liber* VIII, 9: "Si ergo pro fide, qua univeralis vivit Ecclesia, nusquam ferrea corripi arma conceditur, quomodo pro terrenis ac transitoriis Ecclesiæ facultatibus loricatæ acies in gladios debacchantur? Porro, sancti viri cum prævalent, hæreticos idolorumque cultores nequaquam perimunt; sed potius ab eis pro fide catholica perimi non refugiunt. Quomodo ergo pro rerum vilium detrimento fidelis fidelem gladiis impetat, quem secum utique redemptum Christi sanguine non ignorant?" PL 144, 316A. Peter also remarks disapprovingly upon a smith making weapons in *Opusculum* 43, Cap. 3, PL 145, 681–82.

50. Erdman, *Die Entstehung des Kreuzzugsgedankens* (Stuttgart: Kohlhammer, 1935), trans. Baldwin and Goffart as *The Origin of the Idea of the Crusade* (Princeton and Guildford: Princeton University Press, 1977).

51. John Gilchrist, "The Erdmann Thesis and Canon Law, 1083–1141," in *Crusade and Settlement*, ed. Peter W. Edbury (Cardiff: University Press, 1985), 37–45.

52. Ibid., 41. A similar argument can be found in Jonathan Riley-Smith, "Crusading as an Act of Love," *History*, lxv (1980), 185 and 189.

53. Gilchrist, "Erdman Thesis," 39. The sole reference to the *compelle intrare* phrase by Gratian, for example, is merely a restatement of the Augustinian view, with no attempt to modify it. Gratian, *Decretum, Pars Secunda, Causa* 23, *Quæst* IV, Cap. 38, I, 917–19, also in PL 187, 1198C.

54. Gilchrist, "Erdmann Thesis," 41. See also James Brundage, "Holy War and the Medieval Lawyers," in *Holy War*, ed. T.P. Murphy (Columbus: Ohio State University Press, 1976), 122. He also notes at 102–03, that Augustine never formulated a clear idea or doctrine of holy war, in the sense of it sanctifying the warrior and conferring spiritual reward. See Cowdrey, "Christianity and the Morality of Warfare," 186–88, for Gratian's work on the just war.

55. Gilchrist, "Erdmann Thesis," 41.

56. Alberto Ferreiro, "Simon Magus, Nicolas of Antioch, and Muhammad." *Church History* 72: 1 (2003): 53.

57. R. I. Moore, *The Formation of a Persecuting Society* (Oxford: Blackwell, 1987), 13. For a specific discussion of popular heresy during the period of the Reform, see also Moore, "Heresy, Repression, and Social Change in the Age of Gregorian Reform," in *Christendom and its Discontents*, ed. Scott L. Waugh and Peter D. Diehl (Cambridge: University Press, 1996), 19–46.

58. Moore, "Heresy," a summary of eleventh-century events is given at 13–19.

59. Ibid., 23–4.

60. Ibid., 17.

61. Allan Cutler is inclined to believe that Islam may already have been viewed as a heresy during those early centuries, in his review article, "Peter the Venerable and Islam," *Journal of the American Oriental Society*, 86 (1966): 187. He discusses various reasons for the lack of Christian response, mostly centering on the preoccupation with converting pagans in the Germanic north. Certainly some viewed Islam as a heresy, but not all.

62. Ferreiro, "Simon Magus," 56–62. See also John Tolan, "Anti-Hagiography: Embrico of

Mainz's *Vita Mahumeti*," *Journal of Medieval History* 22 (1996): 25–41.

63. Cutler, "Peter the Venerable," 186. A longer article about the missionary efforts to Muslim Spain in the eleventh century, also by Cutler, is "Who was the 'Monk of France' and when did he Write?" *Al-Andalus* 28 (1963): 249–69.

64. Ibid., 260.

65. Ibid., 264–5.

66. Cutler, "Peter the Venerable," 193.

67. Cutler, "Monk of France," 267, though he does not consider it a true missionary letter in the manner of later thirteenth-century papal communications.

68. Ephraim Emerton, ed. and trans., *The Correspondence of Gregory VII* (New York: Columbia University Press, 1932), 94–5, from *Das Register Gregors* VII, MGH *Epistolae Selectae* 2. Ed. by Erich Caspar. III, 21, 288: "Hanc utique caritatem nos et vos specialius nobis quam ceteris gentibus debemus, qui unum Deum, licet diverso modo, credimus et confitemur, qui eum creatorem seculorum et gubernatorem huius mundi cotidie laudamus et veneramur. Nam sicut apostolus dicit: 'Ipse est pax nostra, qui fecit utraque unum.' [...] Scit enim Deus, [...] ut ipse Deus in sinum beatitudinis sanctissimi patriarche Abrahe post longa huius vite spatia te perducat, corde et ore rogamus."

69. H.E.J. Cowdrey, ed. and trans., *The Epistolae Vagantes of Pope Gregory VII* (Oxford:Clarendon Press, 1972), Ep. 54, at 128–30: "Principes enim gentium et principes sacerdotum cum magna multitudine conuenerunt in unum aduersus Christum, omnipotentis Dei filium, et aduersus apostolum eius Petrum, ut christianam religionem extinguerent et hereticam prauitatem propagarent." He further states at 130 that Christians must resist being dominated by them: "Non enim pati debemus ut filii sanctae ecclesiae hereticis, adulteris, et inuasoribus quasi patribus subiciantur atque ab eis uelut adulterina infamia notentur."

70. Ibid., 130–32: "[...] immutato antiquo colore, ceidit non solum in diaboli uerum etiam in Iudeorum Sarracenorum atque paganorum derisionem. Illi enim leges suas [...] prout credunt obseruant."

71. Ibid., 132: "[...] licet hoc tempore ad nullam animarum salutem utiles [...]"

72. See Lucy-Anne Hunt, "'Excommunicata Generatione': Christian Imagery of Mission and Conversion of the Muslim Other between the First Crusade and the Early Fourteenth Century," *Al-Masaq*, 8 (1995): 80–1, for additional commentary and notes on Christian ignorance of Islam at the time of the First Crusade, including beliefs in a pantheon of Islamic gods, and the notion of Islam as the opposite in all things to Christianity. This latter belief would be a central feature of Christian-Islamic relations throughout the Middle Ages.

73. Steven Runciman, *A History of the Crusades, Volume I: The First Crusade* (Cambridge: University Press, 1951), 75–76.

74. Ibid., 76. Runciman notes, for example, that a period of stability came into being under the governorship of Ortoq, a lieutenant of the Seljuk Prince Tutush, who had ordered Atsiz murdered in 1079. During this time, Christians do not seem to have been treated overly harshly, at least in an official capacity. Christian pilgrims were, as the Muslims had recognized, good for the economy, but there were always dangers beyond their control, such as bandit attacks.

75. Ibid., 79.

76. Cowdrey, "Genesis," 21–3.

77. Cowdrey, *Epistolae*, 10–11, *f.*, where he states, "Gregory's plans for an expedition to defend Byzantium from Turkish attacks began to take shape early in 1074."

78. Emerton, *Correspondence*, 25. PL 148, 329B: "[...] cognovimus gentem paganorum contra Christianum fortiter invaluisse imperium,et miseranda crudelitate jam fere usque ad muros Constantinopolitanæ civitatis omnia devastasse et tyrannica violentia occupasse, et multa millia Christianorum quasi pecudes occidisse.

"Scitote igitur nos, [...] omnibus modis id agere atque parare ut adjutorium Christiano imperio quam citius, Deo juvante, faciamus. Unde vos [...] et vestra virtus pro Christi nomine non invitam fatigationem ad ferenda fratribus auxilia subeat."

79. Emerton, *Correspondence*, 32–33.

80. Ibid., 39, Book II, 3. PL 148, 361C-D: "Quod autem ad servitium sancti Petri promptam vos habere voluntatem mandastis, gratanter accepimus, sed determinate vobis de expiditione scribere ad præsens non satis discretum fore prævidimus; quoniam rumor est in transmarinis partibus Christianos, miserante Deo, paganorum longe propulsasse ferocitatem, et nos de reliquo quid acturi simus adhuc divinæ Providentiæ consilium exspectamus."

The pope shortly after sought William's help in bringing Philip I under control, who was engaged in ventures of pillage and plunder, including churches. Gregory implored William to exert influence on Philip, and to inform him that he risked excommunication (Emerton, *Correspondence*, 50–51, Book II, 18). Ironically, William's son, William IX (1071–1127) was destined to fall out with the Church, being excommunicated twice before being reconciled shortly before his death. He is also the first identifiable troubadour, and shows a mastery of poetic style and verse in the usage of the Langue d'Oc (Occitan, a Romance language related to modern Catalan). He also probably supported the call to military action, though most doubt that his intentions were particularly pious. In fact, he adopted many Arabic practices, including acquiring his own harem of young Saracen women. He was the classic medieval warrior, exactly the type of lustful, war-monger (although a poetically and musically gifted one) that the Church sought to turn to its advantage in advocating the First Crusade. William took the cross in 1100, and returned to Europe in 1102, his military expedition a dismal failure. Considering the prevalence of such ruffians among the nobility, it is rather astonishing that the Church was able to convince them to do anything at all.

81. Emerton, *Correspondence*, Book II, 31, 56–58. PL 148, 385-7 (386 A-B): "[...] quia Christiani, ex partibus ultra marinis, quorum maxima pars a paganis inaudita clade destruitur, et more pecudum quotidie occiditur, gensque Christiana ad nihilum redigitur, ad me humiliter miserunt, nimia compulsi miseria implorantes ut modis quibus possem eisdem fratribus nostris succurrerem, ne Christiana religio nostris temporibus, quod absit, omnino deperiret."

"Ego [...] procuravi Christianos quosque ad hoc provocare, ad hoc impellere, ut appetant, defendo legem Christi, animam suam pro fratribus ponere et nobilitatem filiorum Dei luce clarius ostentare. Quam admonitionem Italici et ultramontani, Deo inspirante, ut reor, imo etiam omnio affirmo libenter acceperunt, et jam ultra quinquaginta millia ad hoc se præparant, ut si me possunt in expeditione pro duce ac pontifice habere, armata manu contra inimicos Dei volunt insurgere, et usque ad sepulcrum Domini, ipso ducente, pervenire."

82. Emerton, *Correspondence*, 58. *Filioque* is Latin for "and from the Son," a portion of the Nicene Creed which declares that the Holy Spirit proceeds from both Father and Son. It is not present in the Eastern Orthodox Creed, and this was the subject of controversy and harsh words between the two in the mid-eleventh century.

83. Cowdrey, "The Reform Papacy and Origin of the Crusades," in *Le concile de Clermont de 1095 et l'appel à la Croisade*, Rome: École fraînçaise de Rome, 1997), 66–67.

84. Cowdrey, *Epistolae*, 11–13, also with Latin text, 10–12: "Quanta sit mihi meditatio quantumque desiderium mare transeundi, ut christianis qui more pecudum a paganis occiduntur Christo fauente ualeam succurrere, erubesco quibusdam dicere ne uidear aliqua duci leuitate.

"[...] Credo enim multos milites in tali labore nobis fauere, ipsam etiam nostram imperatricem nobiscum ad illas partes uelle uenire teque secum ducere, [...]"

85. There are many different accounts of the exploits of Guiscard and the conflict between him and Gregory VII, and a full historical discussion falls outside of the boundaries of this book. A good summary, which considers the affair in relation to Gregory's aspirations to eastern military glory can be found in Cowdrey, "Pope Gregory VII's 'Crusading' Plans of 1074," in *Outremer:* *Studies in the History of the Crusading Kingdom of Jerusalem Presented to Joshua Prawer*, ed. Benjamin Kedar, H.E. Mayer, and R.C. Smail (Jerusalem: Yad Izhak Ben-Zvi Institute, 1982), 30–37.

86. "Circumvallat enim me dolor immanis et tristitia universalis, quia orientalis ecclesia instinctu diaboli a catholica fide deficit et per sua membra ipse antiquus hostis christianos passim occidit, ut, quos caput spiritualiter interfecit, eius membra carnaliter puniant, ne quandoque divina gratia resipiscant.

"Iterum cum mentis intuitu partes occidentis sive meridiei aut septemtrionis video, vix legales episcopos introitu et vita, qui christianum populum Christi amore et non seculari ambitione regnat, invenio. Et inter omnes seculares principes, qui preponant Dei honorem suo et iustitiam lucro, non cognosco. Eos autem, inter quos habito, Romanos videlicet Longobardos et Normannos, sicut sepe illis dico, Iudeis et paganis quodammodo peiores esse redarguo." MGH, *Epistolae Selectae 2, Gregorri VII Registrum Lib. I-IV*, ed. Erich Caspar, 189.

87. For a discussion of the resolution, see Stanley A. Chowdrow, "Ecclesiastical Politics and the Ending of the Investiture Contest: The Papal Election of 1119 and the Negotiations of Mouzon," *Speculum* 46 (1971): 613–40.

88. James Brundage, *Medieval Canon Law and the Crusader* (Madison, Milwaukee and London: University of Wisconsin Press, 1969), 27.

89. Cowdrey, "Genesis of the Crusades," 26.

90. Anselm of Lucca, *Collectio Canonica*, Lib. XIII, PL 149, 533A-34B. Some examples include:
 "1. Quod Moyses nihil crudele fecit quando præcepto Domini quosdam trucidavit.
 2. De vindicta non odio sed amore facienda.
 3. Quod bella cum benevolentia sunt agenda.
 4. Quod militantes etiam possint esse justi; et quod hostem deprimere necessitas non voluntas debet.
 5. Quod pugnaturo orandum est. [...]
 18. Quod qui potest perturbare perversos et non facit, eorum impietati consentit.
 19. Quando mali sint tolerendi, vel quando deserendi."

Other passages show a more peace-embracing philosophy, and reinforce that humanity is not to judge:
 "10. Ut temperetur vindicta.
 12. Ut mali non occidantur, sed corrigendi.
 17. Ut non nobis imputentur si quid mali acciderit."

Jean Leclercq interprets this mixture as a sign of enlightened restraint on Anselm's part, recognizing as he did the need to use force when necessary, but cautioning against violence for its own sake, "Saint Bernard's Attitude toward War," in *Studies in Medival Cistercian History*, ed. by John R. Sommerfeldt (Kalmazoo, MI: Cistercian Publications, 1976), 9. He writes similarly of Bernard of Clairvaux. Leclercq was a Cistercian himself, and so his work, while invaluable, must be read with some caution for its understandable biases.

91. See Chapter 3. It is possible that Bernard had familiarity with the writings of Anselm and his attempted synthesis of the use of violence and pious intentions, as some of Anselm's work was incorporated into the later writings of Ivo of Chartres and Gratian. See Jean Leclercq, "Saint Bernard's Attitude," at 10, *f.* 27. For an opposing view of the importance of Anselm in influencing thoughts on *militia Christi*, see France, "Destruction," 1.

92. Leclercq, "Saint Bernard's Attitude," p. 8.

93. Augustine, *Commentary on the Sermon on the Mount*, trans. Denis J. Kavanagh OSA, Fathers of the Church, vol. 11 (Washington DC: Catholic University of America Press / Consortium Books, 1951, rep. 1977), 89. *De sermone Domini* I, ed. by Almut Mutzenbecher, CCSL 35, (Turnholt: Brepols, 1967), 20, 63, at 72: "Neque hic ea uindicta prohibetur quae ad correctionem ualet. Etiam ipsa enim pertinet ad misericordiam, nec impedit illud propositum quo quisque paratus est ab eo quem correctum esse uult plura perferre. Sed huic uindictae referendae non est idoneus nisi qui odium, quo solent flagrare qui se uindicare desiderant, dilectionis magnitudine superauerit."

94. See, Chapter 3.

95. Augustine, *Sermon*, 90. *Sermone*, 20, 64, at 73: "Magni autem et sancti uiri, qui iam optime scirent mortem istam, quae animam dissoluit a corpore, non esse formidandam, secundum eorum tamen animum qui illam timerent nonnulla peccata morte puniuerunt, quo et uiuentibus utilis metus incuteretur, et illis qui morte puniebantur non ipsa mors noceret sed peccatum, quod augeri posset si uiuerent. Non temere illi iudicabant, quibus tale iudicium donauerat deus."

96. See Jonathan Riley-Smith, "Crusading as an Act of Love," *History*, LXV (1980): 185–87, for a further reference, and a discussion of those aspects of Augustine's thought that were not utilized by the apologists for the crusade.

97. Augustine, *City of God*, Books I-VII, trans. Demetrius B. Zenna S.J., and Gerard Walsh S.J., Fathers of the Church (Washington D.C.: Catholic University Press / Consortium Books, 1951, reprinted 1977), vol. 6, I, ch. 21, 53. *De Civitate Dei*, PL 41, 39A: "Quasdam vero exceptiones eadem ipsa divina fecit auctoritas, ut non liceat, hominem occidi. Sed his exceptis, quos Deus occidi jubet, sive data lege, sive ad personam pro tempore expressa jussione: non autem ipse occidit, qui ministerium debet jubenti, sicut adminiculum gladius utenti: et ideo nequaquam contra hoc præceptum fecerunt, quo dictum est, Non occides, qui Deo auctore bella gesserunt, aut personam gerentes publicæ potestatis secundum ejus leges, hoc est justissimæ rationis imperium, sceleratos morte punierunt."

98. Ivo of Chartres, *Decretum*, PL 161, X, cap. 105, 724B: "Apud veros Dei cultores etiam ipsa bella pacata sunt, quæ non cupiditate aut crudelitate, sed pacis studio geruntur, ut mali coerceantur, et boni subleventur."

99. Ibid., *Panormia*, Lib. VIII, cap. XXXVI, 1312D: "Non persequitur nisi qui ad malum cogit. Qui vero vel factum punit vel prohibet ne fiat, non persequitur iste, sed diligit."

100. Ibid., Lib. VIII, see, for example, cap. LX, 1316C, where he begins his commentary on Augustine's claim that to fight is not a sin: "Militare non est delictum, sed propter prædam militare, peccatum est."

101. Tyerman, *God's War*, pp. 34–35.

102. Brundage provides a brief account of some of the developments in this area in *Canon Law*, 24–6. He notes especially two correspondences of Pope Alexander II from 1063, where he specifically states that those who kill Saracens are exempt from the charge of murder. For dissenting views on whether the Church did in fact confer such an indulgence, see Dominique Iogna-Prat, *Order and Exclusion: Cluny and Christendom Face Heresy, Judaism and Islam (1000–1150)*, trans. Graham Robert Edwards, Conjunctions of Religion and Power in the Medieval Past (Cornell: University Press, 2002), 328, and Marcus G. Bull, *Knightly Piety and the Lay Response to the First Crusade*, (Oxford: Clarendon Press, 1993), 112.

103. *Peregrinus* refers in the Bible to a "stranger" or "wanderer." See, for example Matt. 27:7, or Luke 24:18, where these meanings are present, also in the latter a sense of visiting. The Christian ideal of homelessness, as described by Jesus in Matt. 8:20, "Filius autem hominis non habet ubi caput reclinet" was important from the earliest times of Christianity. This homelessness and visiting quality became metaphorical for the soul's journey toward God. The pilgrimage (*peregrinatio*) in this world became a metaphor for that journey. Jerusalem became a logical destination very early on. Wandering preachers who promoted heretical ideas took this idea to its extreme.

104. Blake, "Formation," 18, drawing from the Council of Clermont, canon 2, in *Sacrorum Conciliorum Nova et Amplissima Collectio*, ed. Gian Domenico Mansi, 53 vols. (Paris and Leipzig: Welter, 1901–27) 20, 815, c. 2.

105. Cowdrey, "The Reform Papacy," 76.

106. Jean Flori views the development of Urban's crusading ideas as the culmination of a century of slowly changing attitudes, see *La Guerre sainte: La formation de l'idée de croisade dans l'Occident chrétien* (Paris: Aubier, 2001), and "Ideology and Motivations in the First Crusade," *Palgrave Advances in the Crusades*, ed. Helen Nicholson (Basingstoke: Palgrave Macmillan, 2005), 15–36. This view is not held by all scholars. In particular, Flori

has been critical of an "English" approach to crusade history.

107. See A. Gieysztor, "The Genesis of the Crusades: The Encyclical of Sergius IV (1009–12)," *Medievalia et Humanistica* 5 (1948): 3–23. Purkis discusses the issue with numerous references, in *Crusading Spirituality in the Holy Land and Iberia*, 45–57.

108. Erdmann, *Origin of the Idea of the Crusade*, 306–7. E.O. Blake discusses this and several other issues surrounding the crucial formative years before the First Crusade in "The Formation of the 'Crusade Idea,'" *Journal of Ecclesiastical History* 21 (1970): 11–31.

109. Blake "Formation," 17–18.

110. Ibid., 18.

111. Bernard McGinn, "*Iter Sancti Sepulchri*: The Piety of the First Crusaders," in *Essays on Medieval Civilization*, ed. Bede Lackner and Kenneth Philp (Austin and London: University of Texas Press, 1978), 44–46. This article gives a good treatment of the subject and an extensive discussion of the place that the city of Jerusalem held in the hearts and minds of medieval pilgrims, in both its physical and spiritual manifestations.

112. Cowdrey discusses this at length in "Pope Urban and the Idea of the Crusade," *Studi Medievali* 3rd ser. 36:2 (1995): 721–42. He is a strong advocate of Jerusalem being Urban's main goal.

113. Ibid., 724., from the Vulgate:
"1. Deus venerunt gentes in hereditatem tuam polluerunt templum sanctum tuum posuerunt Hierusalem in pomorum custodiam.
2. Posuerunt morticina servorum tuorum escas volatilibus caeli carnes sanctorum tuorum bestiis terrae.
3. Effuderunt sanguinem ipsorum tamquam aquam in circuitu Hierusalem, et non erat qui sepeliret.
4. Facti sumus obprobrium vicinis nostris subsannatio et inlusio his qui circum nos sunt." *Biblia Sacra Juxta Vulgatam Clementiam*, 520.

114. Gilchrist, "Erdmann Thesis," 41. Apocalypticism in relation to the crusades and Islam will be discussed in detail in Chapter 6.

115. Jotischky, "The Christians of Jerusalem," The article gives many examples from Byzantine and other sources about such contact, and the reported sufferings of Eastern Christians.

116. Penny Cole, *The Preaching of the Crusades to the Holy Land, 1095–1270* (Cambridge, MA: The Medieval Academy of America, 1991), 6–7.

117. Ibid., 7–8.

118. Cole provides an excellent and concise study of the various accounts of Urban's sermon, Ibid., 9–36, which covers the chronicles of the principal monastic writers, all of whom give different interpretations of his speech. These writers will also be discussed in more detail in Chapter 7, regarding their views on the concept of martyrdom.

119. See Jotischky, "The Christians of Jerusalem," at 36–38, for a discussion of how this claim may have some merit.

120. Rosalind and C.N.L. Brooke, *Popular Religion in the Middle Ages: Western Europe 1000–1300* (London: Thames and Hudson, 1984), 12. See also E.O. Blake and C. Morris, "A hermit goes to war: Peter and the origins of the First Crusade," in *Monks, Hermits, and the Ascetic Tradition*, ed. W.J. Shiels, Studies in Church History 22 (Oxford: Blackwell, 1985), 79–109.

121. Cole considers Peter's role in terms of preaching and its impact on the people, *Preaching of the Crusades*, 33–36. Accounts of Peter's rise, fall, and rise again may be found in *The First Crusade, The Chronicle of Fulcher of Chartres and other Source Materials*, ed. Edward Peters (Philadelphia: University of Pennsylvania Press, 1971), 91–114. These chronicles are from a variety of sources and authors, who will be considered in more detail in Chapter 7.

122. For a recent assessment of Peter's role, see Jay Rubenstein, "How, or How Much, to Reevaluate Peter the Hermit," in *The Medieval Crusade*, ed. Susan Janet Ridyard (Woodbridge: Boydell, 2004), pp. 53–69.

123. Purkis, "Elite and Popular Perceptions of imitatio Christi in Twelfth-Century Crusade Spirituality," in *Elite and Popular Religion*, ed. K. Cooper and J. Gregory, Studies in Church History 42 (Woodbridge: Boydell, 2006), 54–64.

124. "[...] Si quis vult post me venire, abneget semetipsum, et tollat crucem suam, et sequatur me." *Biblia Vulgata*, p. 978.

125. An excellent study of this phenomenon can be found in William J. Purkis, *Crusading Spirituality in the Holy Land and Iberia*, 22–27, and 38–42. Purkis devotes a considerable amount of work to this topic, with numerous sources and quotes cited.

126. Ibid., 51.

127. Mastnak, *Crusading Peace*, 116.

128. Ibid., and Dorothee Metlitzki, *The Matter of Araby in Medieval England* (New Haven and London: Yale University Press, 1977), 119.

129. Mastnak, *Crusading Peace*, 122, where he notes that Glaber had believed this.

130. Brundage, *Canon Law*, 29. He also makes passing reference (*f.* 104) to the similarities between this new doctrine and that of *jihad*, conceding that while sharing many characteristics, there does not appear to be a direct connection. Indeed, the *jihad*, and the Muslim and Christian concepts of martyrdom appear to be ideas that developed separately from one another. See Chapter 7.

131. Cole, *Preaching of the Crusades*, p. 3. Cowdrey is likewise suspicious of the plea for helping Eastern Christians, at least as a lure for

potential crusaders: "All things considered, historians would, I think, now be pretty generally agreed that the First crusade [...] was not, at root, caused by any pull of events in the East." "Genesis of the Crusades," 13.

132. Ibid., 25–26.

133. Tyerman, *God's War*, 50.

134. See Housely's chapter "The Intentions and Motivations of the Crusaders," in *Contesting the Crusades*, 75–98, for a good summary of some of the issues, especially at 79 and 88. See also Jonathan Riley-Smith, "The State of Mind of Crusaders to the East, 1095–1300," in *The Oxford Illustrated History of the Crusades*, ed. Riley-Smith (Oxford: Oxford University Press, 1995), 66–90.

135. Ibid., 76. See also 91 for issues surrounding pillaging by crusaders.

136. Susanna Throop, *Crusading as an Act of Vengeance*.

137. Ibid., 12–15, and 55. She notes at 15 that the chronicler Ralph of Caen suggests this, and also observes at 49 that it is the non-eyewitness chronicles that emphasize vengeance far more than those that were presumably written as the First Crusade unfolded. This suggests some degree of hindsight, and may call into question whether the participants actually saw themselves as instruments of divine vengeance.

138. Ibid., 103–07, which give a very good detailed discussion of how this came about.

139. Ibid., 107.

140. McGinn discusses the issue of the crusaders' piety in detail, "*Iter Sancti*," 46–54, with reference to the events of the First Crusade itself. See also Paul F. Crawford, "Four Myths about the Crusades," 16–19.

141. See Purkis, *Crusading Spirituality in the Holy Land and Iberia*, 12–14, for some specific references.

142. This was a constant issue of concern for Bernard and others in the twelfth century, with the rise of the Military Orders, as will be shown in Chapter 2. One finds comments such as those by the ninth-century abbot of Saint-Mihiel, Smaragdus, who drew the distinction between *milites seculi* (knights and warriors), and the *milites Christi* (here referring only to monks): "There are secular soldiers and there are soldiers of Christ; but secular soldiers bear feeble and perilous arms, while those of the soldiers of Christ are most powerful and excellent; the former fight against their enemies in such a way that they lead both themselves and those they kill into everlasting punishment; the latter fight against evil so that after death they may gain the reward of eternal life; the former fight in such a way that they descend in to Hell, the latter fight so that they may achieve glory; the former fight in such a way that after death they serve with devils in Hell, the latter so that they may possess the kingdom of heaven on eternity with angels." Alan Forey, *The Military Orders From the Twelfth to the Early Fourteenth Centuries* (Houndmills, Basingstoke: Macmillan, 1992), 10, drawn from *Commentaria in regulam sancti Benedicti*, PL 102, 696B: "Sunt enim milites sæculi infirma et lubrica arma; milites autem Christi fortissima sumunt atque præclara. Pugnant illi contra hostes, ut se et interfectos æternam perducant ad pœnam: pugnant isti contra vitia, ut post mortem æternam vitam consequi possint ad præmia: illi ut descendant ad tartara, isti ut ascendant ad gloriam; illi ut post mortem cum dæmonibus mancipentur in inferno, isti ut cum angelis in perpetuo possideant regnum; [...]"

143. Purkis, *Crusading Spirituality*, 21.

144. Norman Housley, *Contesting the Crusades*, 93.

Chapter 2

1. Malcolm Barber and Keith Bate, trans. *The Templars: Selected Sources* (Manchester: University Press, 2002), 64–5, drawing from *Papsturkunden für Templar und Johanniter*, ed. Rudolf Hiestand (Göttingen: Vandenhoeck & Ruprecht, 1972), Number 8, 215: "Milites Templi Ierusalemitani noui sub tempore gratie × Machabei abnegantes secularia desideria et propria relinquentes, tollentes crucem suam secuti sunt Christum. Ipsi sunt, × per quos Deus orientalem ecclesiam a paganorum spurcitia liberat et christiani nominis inimicos expugnat."

2. Sharan Newman, *The Real History Behind the Templars* (New York: Berkley Books, 2007), gives a good treatment of this subject. Newman's is a popular history written for a general audience, but contains a high level of scholarship and good references, with much detail in short chapters. She is particularly attentive to dismissing the many popular legends and myths surrounding the Templars, see 353–407.

3. Malcolm Barber, *The New Knighthood, A History of the Order of the Temple* (Cambridge: University Press, 1994), 310–12. This is a comprehensive account of the Templars, bringing together much of the available information. The Templar archive was kept with certain Hospitaller documents, which also seem to have been destroyed, see 312. Another excellent recent introduction is Helen Nicholson, *The Knights Templar—A New History* (Thrupp, Stroud: Sutton, 2001), a beautifully illustrated work that traces the entire history of the order. Nicholson notes that there is still much more information about the Templars waiting to be analyzed, not only from records, but also from archeological sites, at 12.

4. William of Tyre, *Chronicon*, ed. R.B.C. Huygens, CCCM, 63 (Turnhout: Brepols, 1986), 553–55. Barber is more precise in his dating: "[...] the official date of the foundation, according to information gained from the Templars themselves,

must fall between 14 January and 13 September 1120," at 9. He is reluctant to rely too heavily upon William's account, noting at 8 that William, "whose reputation for faulty chronology is well known and who was writing over a half century later," is not always accurate,.

5. Peter Partner, *The Murdered Magicians: The Templars and their Myth* (Oxford and New York: Oxford University Press, 1982), 3–4. This work is mainly concerned with the trial and downfall of the Templars, and the various accusations against them, as well as the Masonic legends which grew up long after the Order's demise.

6. Judith M. Upton-Ward, *The Rule of the Templars* (Woodbridge: Boydell, 1992), 1. This is a translation of the French-language Rule, which probably first appeared in the 1140s, and developed over the next 150 years.

7. Ibid., 2.

8. James Brundage, *Medieval Canon Law*, 12.

9. See Chapter 1.

10. Discussions of the Order's earliest years and duties can be found in Newman, *Real History*, 3–40; Nicholson, *Knights Templar*, 17–46; Upton-Ward, *Rule*; Nicholson, *Templars, Hospitallers and Teutonic Knights*, (Leicester: Leicester University Press, 1993); Alan Forey, "The Emergence of the Military Order in the Twelfth Century," *Journal of Ecclesiastical History*, 36, no. 2 (1985): 175–95; and Forey, *The Military Orders from the Twelfth to the early Fourteenth Centuries* (London: Macmillan, 1992), a good general survey. See also Marion Melville, "Les débuts de l'ordre du Temple," *Vorträge und Forschungen* 26 (1980): 23–30, and Malcolm Barber, *The New Knighthood*. These works are essential to a good understanding of the Templars, and are the principal sources of information for this chapter. Much of what is currently known about the order can be found in them. See also Barber, "The Origins of the Order of the Temple," *Studia Monastica*, 12, no. 2 (1970): 219–39. All of these accounts are excellent studies of the Templars' early years. Forey in "Emergence of the Military Order," considers some of the perplexing questions about the Templars' early years, as does Upton-Ward, who discusses some of the uncertainties about the order's founding, at 2–4. It is interesting to note the difference in each historian's approach. Barber, particularly in *The New Knighthood*, relies heavily on the sources, and chronicles, often without questioning their validity too closely (see, for example 10–11, which recall the pilgrim massacre of 1119 recorded by Albert of Aachen; Barber does not question the numbers involved). He says, for example of Fulcher: "[...] his honest and observant chronicle offers invaluable evidence of conditions in the east under the first generation of settlers," 3. He is somewhat more uncertain about William of Tyre (see note 4, above). Forey and Upton-Ward, however, are far more critical. Both approaches are certainly acceptable, yet the problem of understanding the real nature of the situation at the time is clearly revealed, hindered by the lack of detailed source material. This is undoubtedly a contributing factor to the endless speculations and fantastical stories about the Templars.

11. Barber, in "Origins of the Order" lists several examples of attacks upon those making pilgrimages to various sites in the Holy Land, 219–21.

12. Barber, *New Knighthood*, 3.

13. Barber, "Origins of the Order," 220. He notes for example, the horrific conditions of the pilgrimage of Saewulf in 1102–3 on his journey from the port of Jaffa to Jerusalem, recounted in *An Account of the Pilgrimage of Saewulf to Jerusalem and the Holy Land in the years 1102 and 1103*, trans. by W.R.B. Brownlow, P.P.T.S., IV (London: Bishop of Clifton, 1892). Barber notes: "Little provision seems to have been made along the route to supply the pilgrim with food, and above all, water, and those who survived the journey seem to have arrived at Jerusalem in a severely distressed condition. The brigands made sure that the pilgrims had no access to the natural water that was available," at 220.

14. Newman, in *Real History*, discusses at 7 the convening of a church council in Nablus on January 23, 1120, to discuss problems in the kingdom, but at which nothing is said of the new Templar order. She does note that one law absolves clerics of guilt if taking up arms in self-defense, 7–8, a rather remarkable statement. Drawn from Benjamin Kedar, "On the Origins of the Earliest Laws of Frankish Jerusalem: The Canons of the Council of Nablus, 1120," Speculum, 74, no. 2 (1999): 331–34.

15. See Helen Nicholson, note 40, which argues that prototype organizations may have existed in the Holy Land in the years immediately following the First Crusade.

16. Barber, *The New Knighthood*, 6. For individual accounts, see William of Tyr, *Chronicon*, CCCM 63, 63A, 12:7, 553–5, Walter Map, *De nugis curialium*, ed. and trans. by M.R. James, rev. C.N.L. Brooke, and R.A.B. Mynors (Oxford: Clarendon, 1983), 54–5, and Michael the Syrian, *Chronique de Michel Le Syrien, Patriarche Jacobite d'Antioche (1166–99)*, ed. and trans. by J.-B. Chabot, 3 vols. (Paris: E. Leroux, 1905), 3, 15:11, 201–3.

17. Upton-Ward, *Rule*, 2. Barber does question this number, see *The New Knighthood*, 53–54. See also Newman, *Real History*, 8, where she notes that the number nine did play a role in later Templar symbolism, and note 19 below.

18. As discussed in Chapter 1 concerning the vast numbers recorded as heeding Gregory VII's call to arms.

19. Forey believes that "William of Tyre's re-

mark that after nine years there were still only nine members can be taken as merely a play on numbers, but the chronicler was implying that during that early period there was no marked increase in membership," in "Emergence of the Military Order," at 190. In any case, the issue is that the Templar numbers were so small that very few noticed them.

20. This was also a problem with the chronicling of the Council of Clermont, where eyewitnesses discussed different key events. See Chapter 7 for some of the writers involved.

21. Barber, *The New Knighthood*, 6.

22. Barber summarizes the individual origin stories offered by the three chroniclers, Ibid., 7–8. As might be expected from his above description, Walter Map's is the most fanciful, positing a Burgundian knight named Paganus, who singlehandedly set out to defend pilgrims from attacks. When the enemy numbers became too great, he sought the support of Jerusalem and set about recruiting new knights, who were arriving as pilgrims. The choice of name is both obviously symbolic (the knight supposedly being from a small country village), and curious, given the connotation that *pagan* had been given throughout most of Christian history. One wonders if there is wordplay in the idea of Paganus, the country yokel, fighting off the "pagans."

23. Barber, "Origins of the Order," 225.

24. Ibid., 224. See specifically *f.* 32, where he considers the question of the dating of this incident, an important factor if it did indeed have an influence on the founding of the Order.

25. Barber, *The New Knighthood*, 9–10.

26. See this Chapter 1 for one exception to this.

27. Barber, *The New Knighthood*, 10.

28. Barber, "Origins," 223 and 225.

29. Barber, *The New Knighthood*, 9.

30. Ibid.

31. In fact, the main part of the population in the country was still Eastern, both Christian and Muslim, who continued to farm and live as well as possible under Frankish rule. Trying to expel every Muslim in the land, while undoubtedly a desirable goal for the Christians, would have proven to be utterly impossible. There was no choice but to let them continue living there. It was the attacks that concerned the authorities, for these were what most damaged Christian hopes of a united, peaceful kingdom. One only needs to remember that shock and horror reverberated throughout Europe when the news that the city of Edessa had fallen reached Western ears in 1145. The unthinkable had happened; the enemy had regained lands that the Christians had conquered in the name of God. This was part of an Islamic reconquest movement that had begun following the First Crusade, and such a large-scale gain for the Muslim forces had been foreshadowed by many earlier attacks on the Christian presence, including pilgrims.

32. Tyerman, *God's War*, 52.

33. Barber, "Origins of the Order," 227.

34. In contrast to the great secrecy that surrounded the order in its later years, further fueling the fires of rumor and speculation, the early order seems to have been much more open.

35. Forey holds this opinion, and stresses that the lack of patronage in the early years of the Order "is to be attributed to a lack of awareness rather than to disapproval," "Emergence of the Military Order," at 190. There is, however, no way of discerning how popular the Order would have been without special papal approval and privileges, or even if it would have survived.

36. Upton-Ward, *Rule*, 2–3, drawing from Barber, "Origins of the Order," 223. Barber includes an excellent analysis of the relation between Hugh and Hugues at 221–4, which had important implications for the justification for the Templars written by Bernard of Clairvaux. See also, Newman, *Real History*, 21–27.

37. For a recent study of how wealthy landowners contributed to that growth, see Jochen Schenk, *Templar Families: Landowning Families and the Order of the Temple in France, c.1120–1307* (Cambridge: Cambridge University Press, 2012).

38. Barber, "Origins of the Order," 225, drawing from the words of William of Tyre, *Chronicon* XII, 7, 520.

39. Nicholson, *Templars, Hospitallers and Teutonic Knights*, 2, and *Knights Templar*, 22.

40. Forey, *Military Orders*, 13–14.

41. Forey, "Emergence of the Military Order," 178. He notes that this idea was first put forth by the Spanish historian José Antonio Conde as early as 1820, and has retained popularity to this day, 177–8. See also his *Military Orders*, 8–9. For a more recent study that casts doubt on the idea, see Jörg Feuchter, "The Islamic Ribat: A Model for the Christian Military Orders? Sacred Violence, Religious Concepts and the Invention of a Cultural Transfer," in *Religion and Its Other: Secular and Sacral Concepts and Practices in Interaction*, ed. Heike Bock, Jörg Feuchter, and Michi Knecht (Frankfurt/M: Campus Verlag, 2008), 115–41.

42. See Thomas F. Glick, "Did the Islamic Ribat (military religious communities) serve as the model for the Christian Crusaders?" in *The Crusades, 1095–1291*, ed. Mark T. Abate. History and Dispute 10 (Detroit, et al: Thomson Gale, 2003), 158–160, and Thomas F. Glick, *From Muslim Fortress to Christian Castle: Social and Cultural Change in Medieval Spain* (Manchester: University Press, 1995).

43. Feuchter, "The Islamic Ribat," 116–18.

44. Forey, "Emergence of the Military Order," 178–9. Forey also dismisses the notion of influence on the Templars by the Assassins, a view which he states has been discredited. It was based largely upon supposed similarities in organization and

dress which "are based partly on questionable evidence and would in any case hardly be close enough to imply borrowing," at 177. However, the Templars were ultimately able to extort a yearly tribute out of the Assassins, Forey, *Military Orders*, 99. This suggests at least some close contact between the two organizations. The Assassins were greatly feared, intimidating even Saladin. For the Templars to have been able to exact such a tribute from them must have required complex dealings between the two organizations, the knowledge of which is now lost to us. Other possible connections between the two groups at a later time present more intriguing ideas, but are not relevant to this discussion. For a discussion of the Assassins, see Lewis Bernard, *The Assassins: A Radical Sect of Islam* (London: Weidenfeld and Nicholson, 1967). A very good study is Farhad Daftary, *The Assassin Legends—Myths of the Isma'ilis* (London: I.B. Tauris, 1994). More recently, see Marshall G.S. Hodgson. *The Secret Order of Assassins: The Struggle of the Early Nizârî Ismâ'îlîs Against the Islamic World* (Philadelphia: University of Pennsylvania Press, 2005).

45. Forey, "Emergence of the Military Order," 195.

46. Elena Lourie, "The Confraternity of Belchite, the Ribat, and the Temple," *Viator* 13 (1982): 162.

47. Ibid., 159–76.

48. Ibid., 160, *f.* 4.

49. Ibid., 164–5, where she notes: "But if as late as 1066 penance could be imposed for bloodshed in a just war [referring to the Norman conquest of England], it would seem that the presentation of war as a substitute for penance in the Crusade Indulgence was neither 'simple' nor 'inevitable.' In order for bloodshed to become the substitute for penance rather than the occasion for it, for war to be not only just but also holy, a considerable reorientation was necessary. [...] Even when Christianity had elaborated a formal, juridical notion of crusade, it is remarkable that ecclesiastical writers never discussed it in other than a fragmentary fashion. It has been suggested that this was because of a hesitation to involve the Church legally in bloodshed. Such discomfort suggests strongly that the notion was borrowed and, although successfully combined with the native concepts of pilgrimage and Just War, it was never completely at home in traditional Christian thought."

50. Ibid., 167, *f.* 35.

51. Ibid., full details are given at 166–70. Additional information about the confraternity can be found in various Spanish sources, including J. Lacarra, *Vida de Alfonso el Batallador* (Zaragoza: Publicaciones de la Caja de Ahorros y Monte, 1971), 71–74; Jose Goñi Gaztambide, *Historia de la Bula de Cruzada en España* (Vitoria: Editorial del Seminario, 1958), 75–6; A. Ubieto Arteta, "La creación de la confradía militar de Belchite," *Estudios de Edad media de la Corona de Aragón* 5 (1952): 427–434; and P. Rassow, "La confradía de Belchite," *Annuario de historia del derecho español* 3 (1926): 200–26. These sources are all cited in Lourie's article. Feuchter maintains that this still does not prove a direct link between the two, see "The Islamic Ribat," at 135–36.

52. See *La Règle du Temple*, ed. H. Parent Curzon (Paris: Librarie Renouard, 1886), which gives a version of the Latin Rule. See also Upton-Ward, *Rule*, art. 9, at 21–22: "[...] you others serving the sovereign king with horses and arms, for the salvation of your souls, for a fixed term, strive everywhere with pure desire to hear matins and the entire service according to canonical law [...]" Essentially this is saying that the temporary knights are still subject to the same conditions and ways of life as the brothers, and must obey the same rules.

53. Nicholson, *Templars, Hospitallers and Teutonic Knights*, 3. See also Newman, *Real History*, 23–27.

54. Bruno Scott James, trans., *The Letters of St. Bernard of Clairvaux* (London: Burns and Oates, 1953), 65, a portion of which reads: "If it is for God's sake that you from being a count have become a simple soldier, from being a rich man have become poor, then it is right that I should congratulate you, and glorify God in you, seeing in this a 'change of the right hand of the Most High.' But that your joyous presence which, were it possible, I would never be without, should be removed from me by an inscrutable judgement of God, this is something I find hard to bear with equanimity. How can I forget your long-standing affection and generosity to this house? [...] I am as grateful as I can be to you and keep the memory of your great goodness ever before my eyes and, if I might, I would prove my gratitude in deeds." *Epistola* XXXI, *S. Bernardi Opera*, ed. Jean Leclercq and H.M. Rochais, 8 vols. (Rome: Editiones Cistercienses, 1963) VII, 85,15 – 86,4: "Si causa Dei factus es ex comite miles et pauper ex divite, in hoc profecto tibi, ut iustum est, gratulamur, et in te Deum glorificamus, scientes quia HAEC est MUTATIO DEXTERAE EXCELSI. Ceterum, quod tua iucunda praesentia nobis ita nescio quo Dei est subtracta iudicio, ut ne interdum quidem videre te valeamus, sine quo numquam, si fieri posset, esse vellemus, hoc aequanimiter, fateor, non portamus. Quid enim? Possumusne oblivisci antiqui amoris, et beneficiorum quae domui nostrae tam largiter contulisti? [...] Nam nos, quantum in nobis est, minime prorsus ingrati, memoriam abundantiae suavitatis tuae mente retinemus et, si liceret, opere monstraremus." This is a telling commentary. Bernard is clearly acknowledging a great debt to Hugh. Was his justification of the Order an attempt to repay some of that debt?

55. This incident is reminiscent of the papal warning for crusaders not to take the cross simply to avoid inconveniences and obligations at home, see Chapter 4.
56. Pope Urban II, and later, Bernard of Clairvaux were vehement about this. See Chapter 1.
57. See Tyerman, *God's War*, 38–39, where he notes a story from Paris in 885/6, about an abbot skilled in the use of a bow against Viking invaders, and a Burgundian account from slightly earlier that suggested that St. Benedict himself had miraculously appeared on the battlefield to lend his staff to the killing of the Norsemen. See also Chapter 3 for some accounts of monastic violence at Fleury Abbey.
58. Forey, *Military Orders*, 10.
59. For a discussion of the dating of this Council, see Upton-Ward, *Rule*, 2, f. 7.
60. Ibid., 3.
61. See note 36.
62. Barber in "Origins" discusses the possible connections between the two at some length, theorizing that Hugues may have been an officer in Hugh's house, 221–4.
63. Most modern writers are of this opinion. See, for example, Barber, "Origins," at 227–40, an account of the order's meteoric rise once it had Bernard's endorsement, and Upton-Ward, *Rule*, at 3–6. This is also commented upon by Partner, *Murdered Magicians*, at 4, where he discusses how the knights were becoming disillusioned.
64. Upton-Ward, *Rule*, 3.
65. Nîmes, Benedictine Abbey of St. Giles, MS 37, f. 169ʳ-172ᵛ. The full text of the document, as well as commentary on its contents, can be found in Jean Leclercq, "Un document sur les débuts des Templiers," *Revue d'Histoire Ecclésiastique*, 52 (1957): 81–91. For questions of authorship, see 84–85.
66. Ibid., 87, 2: "Hoc idcirco dicimus, fratres, quia audiuimus quosdam uestram a quibusdam minus discretis perturbari, quasi professio uestra, qua uitam uestram ad portanda arma contra inimicos fidei et pacis pro defensione christianorum dedicastis, quasi, inquam, illa professio uel inlicita sit uel pernitiosa, id est uel peccatum uel maioris profectionis impedimentum. Hoc est quod uobis iam dixi, *quia diabolus non dormit* [my emphasis]: scit enim quia si peccatum uobis suadere uoluerit, non audietis neque consentietis."
67. Ibid., 87, 2: "[...] et quia causarum accionem corrumpere laborat intentione, suggerit odium et furorem dum occiditis, suggerit cupiditatem dum spoliatis; uos ubique insidiantem repellitis, quia occidendo non inique oditis, et spoliando non inuiste concupiscitis. Ideo enim dico: « Non inique
oditis », quia non oditis hominem, sed iniquitatem. Ideo uero dico: « Non iniuste concupiscitis », quia hoc aufertis quod pro peccatis eorum iuste tollitur, et uobis pro labore vestro iuste debetur:

Digus est enim operarius mercede sua. Si enim boui trituranti os non alligatur, homini laboranti quo pacto merces negatur?" The text from I Timothy is used here to justify the "wages" of war taken by the Templars. Leclercq explains in "Document," at 85: "Hugues la résout en insistant sur les intentions religieuses qui animent leur conduite; por justifer leur droit au butin des batailles, il applique à leur cas, de façon inatendue, le texte de S. Paul (*I Tim.*, v, 18), qui, traditionellement, était invoqué pour justifier le droit des clercs à vivre de l'autel."
68. See also Upton-Ward, *Rule*, 5.
69. Upton-Ward comments on this situation in *Rule*, at 3, as does Leclercq, "Un document," 83.
70. Upton-Ward, *Rule*, 12. Upton-Ward's is a translation of this French Rule. There are no extant versions of the original manuscripts, as these were most likely destroyed in the trials of the early fourteenth century. Other, later copies survive from the thirteenth century. The French Rule is divided into several sections, as over the decades, new laws and regulations were needed for the growing body of holy knights. The Rule proper begins with paragraph nine, the first eight comprising a prologue that details certain events and figures at the Council of Troyes. Later additions to the primitive rule can be dated approximately from 1165 (Hierarchical Statutes, Penances), the 1180s (Conventual life, the Holding of Ordinary Chapters), and ca. 1257–67 (Further Details on Penances). Upton-Ward surveys these at 13–16. While the primitive Rule was widely available, differing only moderately from the Benedictine, it was these later additions that were often difficult to obtain outside of the order's closed doors, for they contained information of value to military enemies. Indeed, such information was not even readily available to the lower-ranking members of the Templars. This ultimately led to accusations of a "secret rule" of sorcery, black magic, and devil-worship that was kept from all but the highest officials within the order, and naturally fueled the fire for more legends about what really occurred within its highest, secret levels.
71. Nicholson, *Templars, Hospitallers and Teutonic Knights*, 2.
72. Barber believes that the Hospital may have provided a model for the Templars' structure. He notes certain links between members of the Templars and the Hospitallers. See *The New Knighthood*, 8. Forey dates the transformation of the Hospital into a military order to the 1130s, given records of grants of castles such as Beit-Jibrin, given in 1136 by Fulk of Jerusalem, and a series of castles, including the famous Krak de Chevaliers, in 1144, given by Raymond of Tripoli, which survived in splendid condition through the centuries. These fortifications would not have been handed over to a purely charitable organization. Therefore, the Hospitallers must have assumed a military

function by this time, see Forey, *Military Orders*, at 18–19. For a discussion of the Hospitallers' origins, see Anthony Luttrell, "The Earliest Hospitallers," in *Montjoie*, 37–54.

73. See Chapter 3 for a discussion of his hesitancy in writing the justification. Though he would later be the Second Crusade's most vocal champion, remember that even here it was probably at least partly because of papal pressure. For a discussion of this, see James Brundage, "St Bernard and the Jurists," in *The Second Crusade and the Cistercians*, 25–33.

74. A closer examination of this aspect of his theology will follow in Chapter 6.

75. Orderic Vitalis, *Ecclesiastical History*, ed. M. Chibnall, 6 vols. (Oxford: Clarendon, 1978), 6, Book 12, chapter 29, 310–11, wherein he states of a certain knight, Fulk: "[...] ibique militibus Templi associatus aliquandiu permansit. Inde cum licencia eorum regressus tributarius illis ultro factus est; annisque singulis XXX libras Andegauensium illis largitus est. Sic uenerandis militibus quorum uita corpore et mente Deo militat, et contemptis omnibus mundanis *sese martirio cotidie preparat* [my emphasis]; nobilis heros annuum uectigal diuino instinctu erogauit, et plures alios Gallorum proceres huiusmodi exemplo ad simile opus laudabiliter incitauit." This last statement is of interest, for it suggests that the order was growing more rapidly. The subject of martyrdom will be treated in detail in Chapter 7.

76. Richard of Poitou, *Ex Richardi Pictaviensis Chronica*, ed. G Waitz, MGH *Scriptores* 26, 80: "Per haec tempora surrexit in Ierusalem novum miliciae genus [ab Hugone de Paieno viro nobili constitutum]; more monacorum viventes, castati dant operam, domi et bello disciplinam servant, cum silentio edunt; omnia illis communia; contra gentiles tantam arma summunt, et multum dilatati sunt. Sunt namque qui dicant, quod, nisi fuissent ipsi, diu est quod Franci Ierusalem et Palistinam perdidissent. Hii vocantur milites de Templo, quia in porticu Salomonis sedem suae religionis statuerunt."

77. Anselm of Havelberg, *Dialogi, Lib.* I, chapter X, PL 188, 1156B-C: "Item paulo ante hæc tempora coepit quædam nova religionis institutio in Jerusalem civitate Dei. Nempe congregati sunt ibi laici, viri religiosi, et vocant se milites de Templo, qui, relictis proprietatibus, qui vita vivunt, sub obedientia unius magistri militant, superfluitatem et pretiositatem vestium sibi absciderunt, parati ad defendendum gloriosum Domini sepulcrum contra incursus Saracenorum; [...] Horum vitam et propositum primo confirmavit papa Urbanus consilio multorum episcoporum, quos ad hoc ipsum convocaverat ad concilium, statuens ut quicunque in hanc societatem propter spem vitæ æternæ se colligerent, et in ea fideliter perseverarent, remissionem omnium haberent peccatorum, affirmans eos non esse inferioris meriti, quam vel monachos, vel communis vitæ canonicos." See also Nicholson's comments about this, note 36.

78. For a discussion of the position of Maccabees in medieval exegetical thought, see Jean Dumbadin, "The Maccabees as Exemplars in the Tenth and Eleventh Centuries," in *The Bible in the Medieval World*, ed. Katherine Walsh and Diana Wood (Oxford: Blackwell, 1985), 31–41.

79. See Chapter 1. The charter is found in *Papsturkunden*, Nr. 3, 205–10 (see especially 205–6 for references to the Old Testament and love).

80. See also Chapter 3.

81. Marie Luise Bulst-Thiele, "The Influence of St. Bernard on the Formation of the Order of the Knights Templar," in *The Second Crusade and the Cistercians*, 60. She also notes the close connection that grew up between the Orders: "The commemoration calendars of the Cistercians provide further proof of the close connection between the two orders. It was Cistercian practice to list only the names of those monasteries and communities within their own order. Out of 173 communities named in fourteen lists, only nineteen communities appear on all lists, among them the Templars," at 59.

82. Forey discusses this phenomenon in detail in "Military Orders and Secular Warfare in the Twelfth and Thirteenth Centuries," *Viator* 24 (1993): 79–100.

83. Ibid., 80.

84. Ibid., 83–4, and 90–1. There were other orders in Spain by the second half of the twelfth century, including the Calatravan Order (discussed in more detail in Chapter 4) and the Order of Santiago, and the political climate there was different than in the East.

85. However, see Ibid., 88–89, for the selective nature of this support, particularly in the thirteenth century.

Chapter 3

1. Jean Leclercq provides a summary of Bernard and his views on warfare in "Saint Bernard's Attitude toward War," in *Studies in Medieval Cistercian History* II, ed. John R. Sommerfeldt (Kalamazoo, MI: Cistercian Publications, 1976), 1–39.

2. G.R. Evans, *The Mind of St Bernard of Clairvaux* (Oxford: Clarendon Press, 1983), 25.

3. Ibid., 4.

4. See Chapter 2. Newman gives an excellent (and slightly amusing) summary of Hugh's marital and other woes in *Real History*, 23–27.

5. "Distuli sane aliquamdiu, non quod contemnenda videretur petitio, sed ne levis praecepsque culparetur assensio, si quod melius melior implere sufficeret, praesumerem imperitus, et res admodum necessaria per me minus forte commoda redderetur." Bernard, "Liber ad Milites

Templi: de laude novae militae," *Opera*, III, at 213, 10–13.

6. Aryeh Graboïs, "Militia and Malitia: The Bernardine Vision of Chivalry," in *The Second Crusade and the Cistercians*, 49–51.

7. Marie Luise Bulst-Thiele, "The Influence of St. Bernard of Clairvaux on the Formation of the Order of the Knights Templar," in *The Second Crusade and the Cistercians*, 60.

8. Conrad Greenia, trans., *In Praise of the New Knighthood*, introduction by R.J. Zwi Werblowsky, from *The Works of Bernard of Clairvaux*, vol. 7: Treatises III, *Cistercian Fathers Series* 19 (Kalamazoo, MI: Cistercian Publications, 1977), 5.10, at 143. *De laude*: "Quodque cernitur iocundius et agitur commodius, paucos admodum in tanta multitudine hominum illo confluere, nisi utique sceleratos et impios, raptores, et sacrilegos, homicidas, periuros atque adulteros, de quorum profecto profectione, sicut duplex quoddam constat provenire bonum, ita duplicatur et gaudium, quandoquidem tam suos de suo discessu laetificant, quam illos de adventu quibus subvenire festinant. Prosunt quippe utrobique, non solum utique istos tuendo, sed etiam illos iam non opprimendo." *Opera*, III, at 223, 4–11.

9. Greenia, *Praise of the New Knighthood*, 121.

10. Partner, *Murdered Magicians*, 8–9.

11. R.J. Zwi Werblowsky provides a summary of this view in his quote from Joshua Prawer, 120–1, in *Histoire de royaume latin de Jérusalem* (Paris: Éditions du Centre National de la Recherche Scientifique, 1969), 349–50: "The new knight fights for the sake of his soul and the love of his Creator. [...] The Order of the Temple is the collectivity of knights dedicated to martyrdom. This conception brought Bernard close to the idea of the crusade, and indeed of the Holy Land as well. But in the thinking of this monk, permeated by an ardent and almost ecstatic faith, the real and historical purpose of the expedition almost disappeared. It was not the end but the *means chosen for achievement* that really mattered [my emphasis]. The crusade of Bernard of Clairvaux, a crusade for the salvation of souls, sought neither revenge on Islam [see, however, the opening statements of *De laude*, which clearly reveal his opinion of the Muslims, at 101 and 104], nor a balance of power at the frontiers of the Christian and Muslim world [...] It was an expedition placed under the sign of the Cross and meant to save the souls of the faithful. As a matter of fact the faithful [...] did not need it at all. It was to the sinners [...] that a compassionate and merciful God in his boundless love offered a path to salvation commensurate to their abilities: the crusade [...]." This is not correct, for while Bernard was strongly against the idea of monks going on the crusade, he did not dismiss the idea of faithful laymen taking the cross. Further, it contradicts Prawer's previous statement and the fact that Bernard enthusiastically supported the Templars, who were most certainly the first among the faithful in his view.

12. I Corinthians. 6:19: "An nescitis quoniam membra vestra, templum sunt Spiritus sancti, qui in vobis est, quem habetis a Deo, et non estis vestri?"

13. These are found in Bernard, *Opera* V, 370–98.

14. Thomas Renna, "Bernard of Clairvaux and the Temple of Soloman," in *Law, Custom, and the Social Fabric in Medieval Europe*, ed. Bernard S. Bachrach and David Nicholas (Kalamazoo, MI: Medieval Institute Publications, 1990), 81.

15. Ibid., 81. See also Bernard, *Opera* V, *Sermo* 5, 394–96. Section 8 in particular contains a lengthy discourse on the life and holiness of the monk, ending with a reference to 1 Corinthians 6.

16. The elevation of St. Michael to the status as patron of warriors is another interesting example of this phenomenon. Indeed, in earlier times, Christian missionaries had found it expedient to use Michael, for example, to replace Odin and other war gods in pagan societies.

17. A discussion of this collection may found in Jean Leclercq, "Violence and the Devotion to St Benedict in the Middle Ages," *The Downside Review* 88 (1970): 344–360. An edition of the work is *Les Miracles de S. Benoit*, ed. by E. de Certain (Paris: Chez Mme. ve J. Renouard, 1858).

18. One can find interesting parallels between this work and the thirteenth-century collections of miracles of the Virgin Mary, such as the trouvère Gautier de Coincy's *Les Miracles de Nostre Dame*, ed. V. Frederic Koenig, 4 vols. (Geneva: Librarie Droz, 1955–70), and King Alphonso X's *Cantigas de Santa Maria*, ed. Walter Mettman, 3 vols. (Madrid: Clásicos Castalia, 1986–89). These two collections survive with music, were written in vernacular French and Gallician, and were intended for a non-monastic audience, but many of the themes remain the same. Indeed, they were intended as antidotes to the lewdness of secular song, borrowing popular melodies and setting new religious-themed texts to them, a practice known as *contrafactum*.

19. *Miracles*, IV, 9, at 185–9, and III, 7, at 147–48. See also Leclercq, "Violence," 347.

20. An extensive description is given in *Miracles* III, 5, at 138–41. Leclercq summarizes in "Violence," at 350–51.

21. Leclercq, "Violence," see especially 353–58.

22. Jane Sayers, "Violence in the Medieval Cloister," *Journal of Ecclesiastical History* 44 (1990): 533–42. She notes some extreme examples of violent acts committed against abbots and others by both monks and lay brothers, and considers the role of violence outside the monastic community (i.e., in the secular world) as an influence.

23. For a general discussion of the relation between violence and religion, see René Giraud, *Violence and the Sacred*, trans. Patrick Gregory (London: Athlone Press, 1995).

24. See, for example, his *S. Bernardi Vita Prima*, Caput Primum, PL 185: 227A-B: "Bernardus Burgundiæ partibus, Fontanis opido patris sui oriundud fuit, parentibus claris secundum dignitatem sæculi, sed dignioribus ac nobilioribus secundum christianæ religionis pietatem. Pater ejus Tecilinus, vir antiquæ et legitimæ militæ fuit, cultor Dei, justitiæ tenax. Evangelicam namque secundum instituta Præcursoris Domini militiam agens, neminem concutiebat, nemini faciebat calumniam, contentus stipendiis suis, quibus ad omne opus bonum abundabat."

25. Jean Leclercq discusses this in *Monks and Love in Twelfth-Century France — Psycho-Historical Essays* (Oxford: Clarendon, 1979), 88–98.

26. William of Saint-Thierry, *Vita*, PL 185: 257A-B, 55: "Divertit aliquando nobilium cohors militum ad Claram-Vallem, ut viderent locum, ac sanctum ejus Abbatem. Prope autem erat sacrum Quadragesimæ tempus: et illi omnes fere juvenes dediti militiæ sæculari, circumibant quærentes exsecrabiles illas nundinas, quas vulgo tornetas vocant. Coepit itaque ab eis petere, paucos illos qui ante Quaduragesimam supererant dies, ne armis interim uterentur. Quibus obstinato animo ejus acquiescere monitis renuentibus: "Confido," ait, "in Domino, quod ipse mihi dabit inducias quas negastis." Et accersito fratre, jubet eis cerevisiam propinari, benidicens eam, et dicens ut potionem biberent animarum. Biberunt ergo pariter, quidam tamen inviti præ amore sæculi, metuentes eum quem postea sunt experti divinæ virtutis effectum. Ut enim egressi sunt monasterii fores, mutuis sese coeperunt inflammare sermonibus, quia cor eorum ardens erat in eis. Inspirante igitur Deo, et currente velociter verbo ejus, eadem hora reversi et conversi a viis suis, spirituali militiæ dextras dederunt. Quorum quidam adhuc militant Deo, quidam autem cum eo jam regnant, carnis vinculis absoluti."

27. William, *Vita*, PL 185, 235C-D, 15: "Videbat ista peccator, et irascebatur, dentibus suis fremebat et tabescebat; justus autem confidens in Domino gloriose de sæculo triumphabat. Jamque eo publice et privatim prædicante, matres filios abscondebant, uxores detinebat maritos, amici amicos a vertebant; quia voci ejus Spiritus sanctus tantæ dabat vocem virtutis, ut vix aliquis aliquem teneret affectus."

28. David Carlson, "The Practical Theology of St Bernard and the Date of the *De Laude Novae Militiae*," in *Erudition at God's Service, Studies in Medieval Cistercian History*, IX, ed. John R. Sommerfeldt (Kalamazoo, MI: Cistercian Publications, 1987), 140–41. Carlson deduces that *De laude* can be dated more precisely between 1128 and 1131, though 1128 may also be incorrect if Upton-Ward's dating for the Council of Troyes is correct, see *Rule*, 3.

29. See Leclercq, *Monks*, 17–20, which includes intriguing theories about what activities Bernard might have been engaged in before his conversion, as well as allusions to such behavior in a scathing attack by Berengar, in his *Liber apologeticus*, written in defense of Abelard (PL 178, 1857–70).

30. Bernard, *Opera* VIII, Epistola CCCLV, 299, 8–12: "[...] Induerunt se armatura Dei et gladio Spiritus, quod est verbum Dei, sese accinxerunt, non ADVERSUS CARNEM ET SANGUINEM, SED CONTRA SPIRITUALIA NEQUITIAE IN CAELESTIBUS. Suscipite illos tamquam bellatores pacificos, mansuetos ad homines, violentos ad daemones. Immo Christum in eis suscipite, qui est causa peregrinationis eorum."

31. Leclercq, in *Monks and Love*, comments on some of these, 93–97.

32. Bernard, *Opera*, VI-2, *Sententiae, Series Secunda*, nos. 12–13, at 27, 5–8: "[12] Dominus noster habet proprie sagittas, quibus hostes suos vulnerat, et in brachio virtutis expugnat. Sunt autem tres sagittae, quibus hostes sauciantur: stimulus amissae pecuniae, quia valde conteritur, qui instrumenta vivendi et satellites voluptatum divitias amisisse reminiscitur."

33. Ibid., no. 26, at 31, 17–21: "Arma virtutis, quibus arma nequitiae expugnantur, sunt haec: Plena peccati cognitio, quae expellit tenebras voluptatis. Paenitentialis afflictio, contra dulcedinem carnalitatis. Humilis et vera confessio, contra venenum iniquitatis. Sufficiens et digna correptio in mutatione pristinae voluntatis. Perseverantiae plena successio, ut perfecta subrogetur custodia sanctitatis."

34. Bernard, *Opera*, I, *Sermo* I, at 3, nos. 20–4, 2: "Cum enim duo sint mala quae vel sola vel maxime militant adversus animam, vanus scilicet amor mundi, et superfluus sui, pesti utrique illi duo libri obviare noscuntur: alter saculo disciplinae prava quaeque in moribus et carnis superflua resecans, alter luce rationis in omni gloria mundi fucum vanitatis sagaciter deprehendens veraciterque distinguens a solido veritatis."

35. Bernard, *Opera*, VIII, *Epistola* CCXXI, 1, at 84, nos. 12–16: "A quo enim nisi a diabolo procedere hoc consilium dixerim, per quod fit ut incendiis incedia, homicidiis homicidia addantur, clamor denuo pauperum, et GEMITUS COMPEDITORUM, et sanguis interfectorum auribus pertonent PATRIS ORPHANORUM ET IUDICIS VIDUARUM?"

36. See Purkis, *Crusading Spirituality in the Holy Land and Iberia*, 108–11, for a more detailed examination of the texts. This topic is also discussed in Carlson, "Practical Theology," 138–40.

37. Leclercq interprets this arrangement as a clear sign of the spiritual importance of the Templars overshadowing that of their military

function: "The second part of the treatise, which is twice as long as the first, is consecrated to the prayer of the Templars who should contemplate the mysteries to which the Holy Places bear witness. There could be no clearer demonstration of the fact that war is subordinate to these higher realities; nor could one do more to spiritualize the military profession," in "Attitude," 25. He stresses that Bernard wished to emphasize the monastic aspects of the order, and whilst this is true, the brutality of the images invoked in the first five chapters cannot be ignored. Leclercq seems guilty of romanticizing the Templar's role and attitudes.

38. Greenia, *Praise*, 166–7. "Hae igitur orbis deliciae, hic thesaurus caelestis, haec fidelium hereditas populorum, vestrae sunt, carissimi, credita fidei, vestrae prudentiae et fortitudini commendata.
[...] et item NON NOBIS, DOMINE, NON NOBIS, SED NOMINI TUO DA GLORIAM, [Ps. 113:9] ut in omnibus sit ipse benedictus, qui docet manus vestras ad proelium et digitos vestros ad bellum." *Opera*, III, at 239, 9–19.

39. See also note 43.

40. Jean Leclercq provides a fine introduction to the subject in the chapter "Sacred Learning," from his *Love of Learning*, 71–88.

41. Ibid., 75–76.

42. Ibid., 76–77.

43. Ibid., 77.

44. Greenia, *Praise*, 129. "Novum militiae genus ortum nuper auditur in terris, et in illa regione, quam olim in carne praesens vistavit Oriens ex alto, ut unde tunc in fortitudine manus suae tenebrarum principes exturbavit, inde et modo ipsorum satellites, filios diffidentiae, in manu fortium suorum dissipatos exterminet [...] Novum, inquam, militiae genus, et saeculis inexpertum, qua gemino pariter conflictu atque infatigabiliter deceratur, tum adversus carnem et sanguinem, tum contra spiritualia nequitiae in caelestibus." *Opera* III, at 214, 1–10. The numerous biblical references and quotations found throughout the work are far more than can be detailed here, except as they relate to certain important points. They are excellently listed in both the *Opera*, and in the English translation by Greenia.

45. See Chapter 5.

46. In a letter to Peter the Venerable, for example, Bernard warned that to ignore the plight of Eastern Christians faced with the Muslim threat was decidedly non-Christian. In posing the possibility of ignoring their danger, he asked: "[...] ubi nostra in Deum charitas, ubi dilectio promixorum?" *Opera*, VIII, *Epistola* 364, at 318, 14.

47. Greenia, *Praise*, 129–30. *Opera*, III, at 214, 14–19: "Ceterum cum uterque homo suo quisque gladio potenter accingitur, suo cingulo nobiliter insignitur, quis hoc non aestimet omni admiratione dignissimum, quod adeo liquet esse insolitum? Impavidus profecto miles, et omni ex parte securus, qui ut corpus ferri, sic animum fidei lorica induitur. Utrisque nimirum munitus armis, nec daemonem timet, nec hominum. Nec vero mortem formidat, qui mori desiderat."

48. Greenia, *Praise*, 131. *Opera* III, at 214, 24–15, 5: "[...] in omni periculo replicantes: SIVE VIVIMUS, SIVE MORIMUR, DOMINI SUMUS [Rom.14:8]. Quam gloriosi revertuntur victores de proelio! Quam beati moriuntur martyres in proelio! [...] Vita quidem fructuosa, et victoria gloriosa; sed utrique mors sacra iure praeponitur. Nam si BEATI QUI IN DOMINO MORIUNTUR [Rev. 14:13], non multo magis qui *pro Domino moriuntur*?" [my emphasis]

49. Purkis, "Imitatio Christi," 63.

50. Greenia, *Praise*, 131, *Opera* III, at 215, 15–17: "Ex cordis nempe affectu, non belli eventu, pensatur vel periculum, vel victoria christiani. Si bona fuerit causa pugnantis, pugnae exitus malus esse non poterit [...]"

51. Greenia, *Praise*, 132, *Opera* III, at 216, 7–13: "Operitis equos sericis, et pendulos nescio quos panniculos loricis superinduitis; depingitis hastas, clypeos et sellas; frena et calcaria auro et argento gemmisque circumornatis, et cum tanta pompa pudendo furore et impudenti stupore ad mortem properatis. Militaria sunt haec insignia, an muliebria potius ornamenta? Numquid forte hostilis mucro reverebitur aurum, gemmis parcet, serica penetrare non poterit?"

52. Greenia, *Praise*, 133, *Opera*, III, at 216, 23: "Talibus certe ex causis neque occidere, neque occumbere tutum est."

53. This example is discussed by Jonathan Riley-Smith in *The Atlas of the Crusades* (London: Times Books, 1990), 24. See also the Introduction.

54. David Luscombe, "Peter Abelard's Carnal Thoughts," *Medieval Theology and the Natural Body*, ed. Peter Biller and A.J. Minnis (Woodbridge: Boydell & Brewer, in association with York Medieval Press, 1997), 35, drawn from Luscombe, *Peter Abelard's Ethics* (Oxford: Clarendon, 1971), 40: "Non enim homines de occultis, sed de manifestis iudicant, nec tam culpae reatum quam operis pensant effectum. Deus uero solus qui non tam quae fiunt, quam quo animo fiant adtendit, ueraciter in intentione nostra reatum pensat et uero iudicio culpam examinat."

55. Note how these quotes seemingly contradict the notion of the God of infinite mercy discussed by Prawer in note 11. This was just one of the inconsistencies which were faced by medieval theologians in their attempts to reconcile their beliefs with the realities of their world. The resolution came from the belief that God was just, rewarding the faithful and punishing his enemies.

56. Greenia, *Praise*, 134. *Opera* III, at 217, 4–13: "At vero Christi milites securi praeliantur praelia Domini sui, nequaquam metuentes aut de hostium caede peccatum, aut de sua nece pericu-

lum, quandoquidem mors pro Christo vel ferenda, vel inferenda, et nihil habeat criminis, et plurimum gloriae mereatur. Hinc quippe Christo, inde Christus acquiritur, qui nimirum et libentur accipit hostis mortem pro ultione, et libentius prabet seipsum militi pro consolatione. Miles, inquam, Christi securus interimit, interit securior. Sibi praestat cum interit, Christo cum interimit. NON ENIM SINE CAUSA GLADIUM PORTAT: DEI ENIM MINISTER EST [Rom. 13:4] AD VINDICTAM MALEFACTORUM, LAUDEM VERO BONORUM. Sane cum occidit malefactorem, non homicida, sed, ut ita dixerim, malicida, et plane Christi vindex in his qui male agunt, et defensor christianorum reputatur."

57. See Mastnak, *Crusading Peace*, 160–61 for a further discussion of this distinction.

58. Greenia, *Praise*, 134–5. *Opera*, III, at 217, 16–18: "In morte pagani christianus gloriatur, quia Christus glorificatur; in morte christiani, regis liberalitas aperitur, cum miles renumerandus educitur." See also Throop, *Crusading as an Act of Vengeance*, for how this passage invokes the idea of divine vengeance, 76.

59. Greenia, *Praise*, 135. *Opera*, III, at 217, 18–20: "Non quidem vel pagani necandi essent, si quo modo aliter possent a nimia infestatione seu oppressione fidelium cohiberi."

60. Greenia, *Praise*, 135. *Opera*, III, at 217, 20–22: "Nunc autem melius est ut occidantur, quam certe relinquator virga peccatorum super sortem iustorum, ne forte extendant iusti ad iniquitatem manus suas [Ps. 124:3]."

61. Lk. 3:14 "Interrogabant autem eum et milites, dicentes: Quid faciemus et nos? Et ait illis: Neminem concutiatis, neque calumniam faciatis: et contenti estote stipendiis vestris."

62. Greenia, *Praise*, 135. *Opera*, III, at 217, 23–218, 2: "Quid enim? Si percutere in gladio omnio fas non est christiano, cur ergo praeco Salvatoris contentos fore suis stipendiis militibus indixit, et non potius omnem eis militiam interdixit?"

63. Note the interesting contrast with Pauline theology, returning to 1 Cor 6:12: "Omnia mihi licent, sed non omnia expediunt: omnia mihi licent, sed ego sub nullius redigar potestate."

64. *Opera*, III, 218, 7–10. This argument bears some relation to the theology of forced conversion to Christianity, argued by Pope Gregory VII in the previous century, and discussed in Chapter 1.

65. Greenia, *Praise*, 135. *Opera*, III, at 218, 9–10: "[...] qui repositas in Ierosolymis christiani populi inaestimabiles divitias tollere gestiunt, sancta polluere, et hereditate possidere sanctuarium Dei."

66. Greenia, *Praise*, 135.

67. Ibid., 135. *Opera*, III, at 218, 11–13: "Exseratur gladius uterque fidelium in cervices inimicorum, ad destruendam omnem altitudinem extollentem se adversus scientiam Dei, quae est christianorum fides [...]"

68. Greenia, *Praise*, 136–37. *Opera*, III, at 219, 4–10: "Hoc tibi auxilium missum de sancto [Ps 19:3]. Omnio per istos tibi iam iamque illa persolvitur antiqua promissio: PONAM TE IN SUPERBIAM SAECULORUM, GAUDIUM IN GENERATIONE ET GENERATIONEM [Is. 60:15–6] [...] Videsne quam crebra veterum attestatione nova approbatur militia, et quod, SICUT AUDIVIMUS, SIC VIDEMUS IN CIVITATE DOMINI VIRTUTUM? [Ps. 47:9] [...]"

69. Greenia, *Praise*, 137. *Opera*, III, at 219, 10–14: "Dummodo sane spiritualibilis non praeindicet sensibus litteralis interpretatio, quominus scilicet speremus in aeternum, quidquid huic tempori significando ex Prophetarum vocibus usurpamus, ne perid quod cernitur evanescat quod creditur, et spei copias imminuat penuria rei, praesentium attestatio sit evacuatio futuorum."

70. Greenia, *Praise*, 137. *Opera*, III, at 219: "Alioquin terrenae civitatis temporalis gloria non destruit caelestia bona, sed astruit, si tamen istam minime dubitamus illius tenere figuram, quae in caelis est mater nostra." Werblowski comments at some length on the contrast between the heavenly and earthly Jerusalem in his introduction to Greenia's translation. See 115–7, in which he discusses the nature of medieval pilgrimage and the differing opinions regarding the act at the time.

71. *Opera* III, at 219, 19–220, 24.

72. Greenia, *Praise*, 139. *Opera*, III, at 220, 25–27: "Porro imminente bello, intus fide, foris ferro, non auro se muniunt, quatenus armati, et non ornati, hostibus metum incutiant, non provocent avaritium."

73. Greenia, *Praise*, 140. *Opera*, III, at 221, 6–15: "At vero ubi ventum fuerit ad certamen, tum demum pristina lenitate postposita, tamquam si dicerent: NONNE QUI ODERUNT TE, DOMINE, ODERAM, ET SUPER INIMICOS TUOS TABESCEBAM? [Ps.138: 21] irruunt in adversarios, hostes velut oves reputant, nequaquam, etsi paucissimi, vel saevam barbariem, vel numerosam multitudinem formidantes. Noverunt siquidem non de suis praesumere viribus, sed de virtute Domini Sabaoth sperare victoriam, cui nimirum facile esse confidunt. [...] QUIA NON IN MULTITUDINE EXERCITUS EST VICTORIA BELLI, SED DE CAELO FORTITUDO EST. [1 Mac. 3:20]"

74. Greenia, *Praise*, 140–41. *Opera*, III, at 221, 17–25: "Ita denique miro quodam ac singulari modo cernuntur et agnis mitiores, et leonibus ferociores, ut pene dubitem quid potius censeam appellandos, monachos videlicet an milites, nisi quod utrumque forsan congruentius nominarium, quibus neutrum deesse cognoscitur, nec monachi mansuetudo, nec militis fortitudo. De qua re quid dicendum, nisi quod A DOMINO FACTUM EST ISTUD, ET EST MIRABILE IN OCULIS NOSTRIS? [Ps. 117: 23] Tales sibi delegit Deus, et collegit a finibus terrae ministros ex fortissimis Israel, qui veri lectulum Salomonis sepulcrum vig-

ilanter fideliterque custodiant, omnes tenentes gladios, et ad bella doctissimi."

75. Greenia, *Praise*, 142–43. *Opera*, III, at 222, 13–19: "Plane his omnibus liquido demonstrantibus eodem pro domo Dei fervere milites zelo, quo ipse quondam militum Dux, vehementissime inflammmatus, armata illa sanctissima manu, non tamen ferro, sed flagello, quod fecerat de resticulis, introivit in templum, negotiantes expulit [...] indignissimum iudicans orationis domum huiuscemodi forensibus incestari."

76. Indeed, the *Glossa Ordinaria*, which was extensively employed by the Cistercians as well as other monastic writers, drawing from Bede, notes that the Temple was in effect a metaphor for the mind, and like the mind, must be purged of sin. The commentary on the Gospel of Mark, 11:16 reads: "*Vos autem fecistis*. Ad hoc enim in templo erant, ut vel non dantes corporaliter persequerentur, vel dantes spiritualiter necarent. Templum et domus Dei mens est et conscientia fidelium, quæ in læsione proximi perversas cogitationes profert, quasi in spelunca latrones resident, et simpliciter gradientes interficiunt: et sic mens jam non domus Dei, sed spelunca est latronum." PL 114, 222A.

77. Greenia, *Praise*, 143, Opera, III, at 222, 19–21: "Talis proinde sui Regis permotus exemplo devotus exercitus, multo sane indignius longeque intolerabilius arbitrans sancta pollui ab infidelibus quam a mercatoribus infestari [...]."

78. See chapter 1 and Purkis, *Crusading Spirituality*, 22–27.

79. Despite all of his support, Bernard apparently still preferred the purely monastic way of life; recall that when Hugh, Count of Champagne became a Temple knight, Bernard, though pleased, expressed some regret that he had not chosen instead to enter the Cistercian order. See Chapter 2. Elsewhere, however, Bernard makes it known that it is the pilgrimage of the heart that is most important, and that the "spiritual Jerusalem" of the monastery was the preferable destination. He speaks rather immodestly of Clairvaux in such terms, see Constable, *Letters*, Ep. 67, at 90–2.

80. Werblowski, introduction to *Praise*, 121.

81. See note 11.

82. Greenia, *Praise*, 144. *Opera*, III, at 223, 14–24: "Sic Christus, sic novit ulcisi in hostes suos, ut non solum de ipsis, sed per ipsos quoque frequenter soleat tanto gloriosus, quanto et potentius triumphare. [...] dum peccatoris et maligni tantis procul dubio prosit conversio, quantis et prior nocuerat conversatio."

83. Werblowski, introduction to *Praise*, 118.

84. Ibid., 118–9.

85. See James Kritzeck, *Peter the Venerable and Islam* (Princeton, NJ: Princeton University Press, 1964), 213–4 and 231. He argues that missionary work was Peter's principal concern, as was refuting the "heresy" of Islam. This has subsequently been strongly disputed, and will be discussed in detail in Chapter 5.

86. See chapter 1, Peter Damian, *Epistolae*, Liber VIII, 9, PL 144, 316B.

87. James A. Brundage, "St Bernard and the Jurists," *The Second Crusade and the Cistercians*, 27–8.

88. Ibid., Brundage lists several examples, 32. See especially Ivo of Chartres, *Decretum*, PL 161, 699–700, and 707–9.

Chapter 4

1. For a detailed survey of the beginnings of the Cistercian order, see Bede Lackner, *The Eleventh-Century Background of Cîteaux* (Washington, D.C.: Cistercian Publications, 1972). This work considers many aspects of the status of the monastic life prior to the foundation of Cîteaux, from the Carolingian period to the establishment of Molesme. A good more recent study is Constance Berman, *The Cistercian Evolution: The Invention of a Religious Order in Twelfth-Century Europe* (Philadelphia: University of Pennsylvania Press, 2000), which argues against the idea that Bernard was primarily responsible the rapid rise of the order; many other factors were involved. Berman also questions some of the traditional assumptions about the order's founding, including who the actual "founder" was, in "The Cistercian Mystery. How was the Order Formed and by Whom? Can the Anglo-Norman Sources Elucidate the Problem?" *Haskins Society Journal* 13 (1999): 1–19. An older survey of the growth of the order can be found in Archdale A. King, *Cîteaux and Her Elder Daughters* (London: Burns and Oates, 1954). For a history of the early years of the order, see Jean-Baptiste Auberger, *L'unanimité Cistercienne primitive: mythe ou réalité? Commentarii Cistercienses* III (Achel: Administration de Cîteaux, 1986), especially 67–77. This work is a most valuable collection of source documents, commentary, facsimiles of manuscripts, maps, and even geographical surveys of the earliest Cistercian houses and locations. The book also contains an extensive bibliography of related subjects.

2. Germain Morin, "Rainaud l'Ermite et Ives de Chartres: un épisode de la crise du cénobitisme au XIᵉ-XIIᵉ siècle," *Revue Bénédictine*, 40 (1928): 99–115. Lackner also employs the term, and devotes a chapter to the idea in *Background of Cîteaux*, 92–112.

3. John van Engen, "The 'Crisis of Cenobitism' Reconsidered: Benedictine Monasticism in the Years 1050–1150," *Speculum* 61 (1986): 269–304.

4. See Chapter 3 for a discussion of attacks on monastic dwellings detailed in the collection of stories from Fleury abbey, the *Miracles of Saint Benedict*.

5. Lackner, *Background of Cîteaux*, 93. See also Jean Leclerq, "La crise du monachisme aux XIe et XIIe siècles," in *Bollentino dell'Istituto St.orico Italiano per il Medio Evo e Archivio Muuratoriano*, 70 (1959), 19–41, especially *f.* 19.

6. Louis Lekai discusses aspects of this action in *The Cistercians: Ideals and Reality* (Kent, Ohio: Kent State University Press, 1977), 12. This work is a good introduction to the Cistercian order, tracing its history and the principal points of its theology from its foundation to the present day, and contains considerable bibliographical material. Lekai has also written *Les moines blancs* (Paris: Seuil, 1957), his first, though less comprehensive, survey of the order.

7. Lekai, *Cistercians*, 14–15.

8. Ibid., 17.

9. It is interesting to note that the Templars were forming in Jerusalem at almost exactly the same time, given the close associations that the two were soon to develop.

10. An older, but still useful biography of Bernard is Watkin Williams, *St. Bernard of Clairvaux* (Manchester: University Press, 1935). More recently, see Gillian R. Evans, *Bernard of Clairvaux* (Great Medieval Thinkers) (Oxford: University Press, 2000).

11. I am grateful to Tim Watkinson, MA, University of Leeds, for his assistance with the information in the above section.

12. Lekai, *Cistercians*, 35.

13. As discussed in the introduction.

14. Bernard stresses this in *De laude*, see Chapter 3.

15. Martha G. Newman, *The Boundaries of Charity: Cistercian Culture and Ecclesiastical Reform, 1098–1180* (Stanford, California: Stanford University Press, 1996), 35–6.

16. The exact dates of Isaac's life are uncertain. Hugh McCaffery, OSCO, dates him at *ca.* 1100–67 in "Isaac of Stella: A Significant Spokesman for the Sanctity of Bernard of Clairvaux," in *Cistercian Ideals and Reality*, ed. John R. Sommerfeldt (Kalamazoo, MI: Cistercian Publications, 1978), 200 and 213, *f.*, though he then confesses at 203 that the birth and death dates of Isaac are unknown. It is likely that he was English, see McCaffrey, at 204, 214, *n*. McGinn believes that he died somewhat later, dating his *Sermones in Sexagesima* from after 1167, see note 24 below. It is these sermons, and his *Tractatus de Deo* for which he is most famous. He was also an associate and friend of Thomas Becket, Benjamin Kedar, *Crusade and Mission* (Princeton, New Jersey: University Press, 1984), 106.

17. The full quote is given in note 18 below. An edition of Isaac's sermons is published in the *Sources chrétiennes* series, *Isaac de l'Etoile, Sermons (40–55)*, vol. III (Lyon: Éditions du Cerf, 1987). The PL transcription is also serviceable. Another critical edition has been prepared by G. Raciti, "Isaac de l'Etoile et son siècle: Texte et commentaire historique du sermon XLVIII," *Cîteaux: Commentarii Cistercienses* 12 (1961): 290. See also Raciti's entry "Isaac de l'Etoile," *Dictionnaire de Spiritualité*, vol. 7, 2 (Paris: Beauchesne 1971), 2011–38.

18. PL 194, 1854B-C: "Hujus simile, eademque ferme tempestate, cujusdam novæ militiæ obortum est monstrum novum, cujus, ut lepide ait quidam, Ordo de quinto Evangelio est, ut lanceis ac fustibus incredulos cogat ad fidem; et eos qui Christi nomen non habent licenter exspoliet, ac relgiose trucidet: siqui autem de eo in depopulatione talium ceciderint, Christi martyres nuncupent." There are also similarities between these words and a defense of the Templars taking booty from battle, probably written by Hugues de Payens in about 1130. This document has been discussed in greater detail in Chapter 2.

19. "[...] quia occidendo non inique oditis, et spoliando non inuiste concupiscitis." Kedar, *Crusade and Mission*, 105, *f.* 27, quoting Leclercq, "Un document sur les débuts des Templiers," 87.

20. Kedar, *Crusade and Mission*, 105–6.

21. Sermon 48 from *The Selected Works of Isaac of Stella—A Cistercian Voice from the Twelfth Century*, trans. Dániel Deme (Aldershot, Hampshire: Ashgate, 2007), 133.

22. Kedar, *Crusade and Mission*, 105. He refers to the order of Calatrava, approved in 1164 by Alexander III as "Cistercian warriors." See also Jean Leclercq, "Saint Bernard's Attitude toward War," in *Studies in Medieval Cistercian History, II*, ed. John Sommerfeldt (Kalamazoo, MI: Cistercian Publications, 1976), 1–39, especially at 27–9. Alan Forey discusses the debate in "The Military Orders and the Conversion of Muslims in the Twelfth and Thirteenth Centuries," *Journal of Medieval History* 28 (2002): 4–5.

23. A summary of the activities of the Calatravan order, and its links with the Cistercians, can be found in Joseph Francis O'Callaghan, "The Affiliation of the Oder of Calatrava with the order of Cîteaux," *Analecta Sacri ordinis Cisterciensis*, XV (1959), Fasc. 3–4, 161–193, XVI (1960), Fasc. 1–2, 3–59, Fasc. 3–4, 255–92. The order did have Cistercian approval, after an uncertain beginning dating back to the year 1158, see XV, at 178–91. Nevertheless, as O'Callaghan writes at 188, that in 1164: "In a letter addressed to 'venerable brother García, master, and all the brethren of Calatrava,' Abbot Gilbert of Cîteaux and his fellow abbots expressed their gratification concerning the conversion of the knights from the *militia mundi* to the *militia Dei* [note the Bernardine language], and received them into full communion in the benefits of the order of Cîteaux, not as *familiares*, but as true brethren." "Quod autem humiliter postulastis suscipi vos videlicet in communionem beneficiorum Ordinis nostri, non ut familiares sed ut vere fratres, gratanter anuimus." Drawn from

Bullarium Ordinis Militiae de Calatrava (Madrid: A. Marin, 1761), 3–4. There is still some doubt about 1164 being the date of this letter, however, owing to the short time between the supposed date of the letter (September 14, 1164) and the subsequent issuance of the official papal bull sanctioning the Calatravan order and granting it the protection of the Holy See (September 26, 1164). 1163 has thus been proposed as a possibility. See O'Callaghan, 188–9, *f.* 3, regarding this.

24. Bernard McGinn has shown in "Isaac of Stella on the Divine Nature," *Analecta Cisterciensia*, 29 (1973), at 3–4, for example, that his Sexagesima sermons, though numbered from 18–24 in the PL listing, in fact date from only a few short years before his death, probably 1167. The numberings seem to be arbitrary, and largely based on manuscript cataloging, which was not always chronological.

25. Kedar notes in *Crusade and Mission*, 105: "[...] Isaac's attitude is clear: Forcing unbelievers into the faith at the point of the lance, plundering and murdering them, are activities that do not conform to the true teachings of Christianity."

26. Ibid., 203.

27. Another supporter of the theory that Isaac was denouncing the Calatravan order is Raciti, "Isaac," *Cîteaux* 13 (1962): 20–1. Kedar disagrees, *Crusade and Mission*, 105, *f.* It seems the matter will be unresolved for the time being.

28. Leclercq, "Saint Bernard's Attitude," 28.

29. Ibid. See also McCaffrey, "Isaac of Stella: A Significant Spokesman," 199–219.

30. Ibid., 201–2.

31. Ibid., 202. Caroline Walker Bynum explores this theme in *Jesus as Mother: Studies in the Spirituality of the High Middle Ages* (Berkeley: University of California Press, 1982): "The males who popularized maternal and feminine imagery were those who had renounced the family and the company of women; the 'society' out of which their language comes is a substitute for (and implicitly a critique of) the world. This is what Bernard means when he describes his monks as mountebanks, walking on their hands: their life and their images invert the values of the world. To call monks women, as Bernard does, is to use the feminine as something positive (humility) but also to imply that such is *not* the opinion of society. The wisdom of the world is not the wisdom of God," 144. See Bernard's *Sermo* XII, *Opera* I, at 66, par. 9. One can see a connection here with the general prohibition on monks going on crusade except in special circumstances, just as women were discouraged or forbidden, even when wanting to accompany their husbands, though this tended to be more because of a belief that women were a "distraction" to the holy mission of the crusade. Bynum also notes his letter to the parents of one Geoffrey of Péronne, a noble youth who joined the monastery. He writes: "[...] Have comfort, do not worry, I shall look after him like a father and he will be to me a son [...] I will be for him both a mother and a father, both a brother and a sister. I will make the crooked path straight for him and the rough places smooth. I will temper and arrange all things that his soul may advance and his body not suffer." Bruno Scott James, *The Letters of St. Bernard of Clairvaux*, (London: Burns and Oates, 1953), Letter 112, at 169.

32. Isaac of Stella, *Sermo* 15 , PL 194, 1740A: "Ideo, fratres, quotiescunque tentatio vos apprehendit, sive infirmitatis, sive paupertatis, sive durioris disciplinæ, aut prolongatioris incolatus, tædii etiam tam remotæ solitudinis, et profundi silentii, sive cujuscunque generis, quæ prorsus innumerabilia sunt, legendo, meditando, orando, excitemus nobis Christum dormientem. In exemplum crucis et passionis ipsius pro nobis intendamus, tanquam morsi a serpente repente deorsum contemplemur serpentem pendentem sursum." (*Num* XXI), and *Sermo* 27, 1780 C-D: "Abbas noster pater sit animarum, tortor corporum. Pater fit Filii Dei in nobis et nutritor, pædagogus et tutor, quanto tempore parvulus est, qui hæres futurus est, et qui in domo mansurus est in æternum; filii autem hominis sit flagellator, proditor, seductor, exspoliator, ac tandem crucifixor et sepultor. Quod si ipse fuerit nobis negligens, nos sumus nobis abbates, filii hominis homicidæ, et Filii Dei nutrirores, ut crescat, et fiat magnus valde,sicut de Isaac legitur, et sicut ait Apostolus: *Donec formetur Christus in nobis, et occurramus in virum perfectum, in mensuram ætatis plenitudinis Christi* (*Gal* IV) [...]" The difference in their approach is also revealed in Isaac's second sermon for the Assumption of Mary, which, as McCaffery notes in "Isaac of Stella," "contains express reference to Saint Bernard's sanctity and to his sermons on the *Song of Songs* and not a word about his devotion to Mary!" 200–01.

33. Ibid., 202. These words are in fact reminiscent of the language of the crusaders: that they were, through the act of self-sacrifice and mortification, "taking up their own crosses" and following Christ to Jerusalem, in their case the real Jerusalem as opposed to the monastic spiritual Jerusalem.

34. McCaffrey comments upon this in "Isaac," at 202.

35. An example of his dominance even in modern scholarship may be found in *The Second Crusade and the Cistercians*. The majority of the articles collected within are devoted to Bernardine teachings and theology concerning the Second Crusade. What Bernard had to say was usually what the order also wanted to say.

36. For a fuller description of the situation, see Giles Constable, "The Second Crusade as Seen by Contemporaries," *Traditio* 9 (1953): 276–78. This detailed and impressive study contains extensive bibliographical material and thoroughly discusses

the issue of how those at the time viewed their own crusading practices.

37. Bernard, *Opera*, VIII, Ep. CCCLXII, 311–17.

38. Throop, *Crusading as an Act of Vengeance*, 83.

39. Constable., "Second Crusade," 253. The full text of *Quantum predecessores* can be found in Eugenii, *Epistolæ et Privilegia*, PL 180, 1064–66. Two short surveys of the events leading to the Second Crusade are John G. Rowe, "The Origins of the Second Crusade: Pope Eugenius III, Bernard of Clairvaux and Louis VII of France," and George Ferzoco, "The Origins of the Second Crusade," both in *The Second Crusade and the Cistercians*, at 79–90, and 91–100 respectively. The book also contains an excellent bibliography of primary and secondary source materials concerning the crusades and the Second Crusade in particular, as well as twelfth-century French political and religious life. Purkis argues, in *Crusading Spirituality*, at 86, that Eugenius "may well not have been the first pope to issue a general letter for a crusade to the East," drawing on research from Jonathan Riley-Smith (see *f.* 3).

40. Constable, "Second Crusade," 249, which is a translation of Valmar Cramer, "Kreuzpredigt un Kreuzzugsgedanke von Bernard von Clairvaux bis Humbert von Romans," in *Das Heilige Land in Vergangenheit und Gegenwart, Palästinahefte des deutschen Vereins vom heiligen Lande*, 17–20, ed. Cramer and G. Meinertz (Köln: Bachem, 1939), 48.

41. See Constable, "Second Crusade," 249–50, for a discussion of the effects of sin, and *f.*189 especially for additional references to the novelty or lack thereof of Eugenius' proclamation. It is likely that the bull was a synthesis of many ideas, set down in one document for the first time.

42. Purkis, *Crusading Spirituality*, 86.

43. See Purkis, "Imitatio Christi," at 57–58. See also 59–60, for a discussion of difference between "elite" and "popular" understandings of what the *imitatio Christi* meant.

44. Ibid., 82–117. Purkis devotes considerable time and detail to making the convincing argument for this view.

45. We shall return to this in more detail in Chapter 6.

46. Constable, "Second Crusade," 252. See also Chapter 2, note 62.

47. See Purkis, *Crusading Spirituality*, 96, for a discussion of how the Spanish and Baltic crusades were probably reactions to existing circumstances, rather than being conceived in the papal curia as part of a grander vision. However, they did present a convenient opportunity to expand the theater of holy war.

48. Constable, "Second Crusade," 265.

49. A recent and comprehensive study of the entire crusade is Jonathan Philips, *The Second Crusade: Extending the Frontiers of Christendom* (Yale: Yale University Press, 2010), which according to the author, is the first book in 140 years devoted exclusively to this crusade. See 269–79 for a discussion of the aftermath of the crusade and its ramifications. See also Graham Loud, "Some Reflections on the Failure of the Second Crusade," *Crusades* 4 (2005): 1–14.

50. Philips, *The Second Crusade: Extending the Frontiers*, 272 and 278.

51. Brenda Bolton, "The Cistercians and the Aftermath of the Second Crusade," *The Second Crusade and the Cistercians*, 131. Eugenius expressed his concern in a letter to Abbot Suger: "Immensum pietatis opus, quod carissimo filio nostro Ludovico, illustri Francorum Regi, divina misericordia inspiravit, nos plurimùm anxios reddit. Gravem namque christiani nominis jacturam, quam nostris temporibus ecclesia Dei sustinuit, et recentem adhuc effusionem sanguinis tantorum virorum ad memoriam revocantes, grandi timore concutimur, et mœror inconsolabilis renovatur." Eugenius, *Epistolæ*, LXV ad Sugerium. RHGF, XV, 457. More recently, *The Second Crusade: Scope and Consequences*, ed. Jonathan Philips, and Martin Hoch (Manchester: Manchester University Press, 2001), discusses various aspects of preparations for the crusade, and the fallout from its failure. See also Constable, "The Crusading Project of 1150," in *Montjoie*, 67–75.

52. Bernard himself wrote a lengthy and apologetic letter to Hugh, abbot of Prémontré, in an attempt to reestablish harmony between the two orders. Bernard, *Opera*, VIII, Ep. 253, 149–55.

53. Bolton, "Cistercians and the Aftermath," 133.

54. Ibid., 132.

55. Virginia Berry, "Peter the Venerable and the Crusades," in *Petrus Venerabilis, St.udies and Texts Commemorating the Eighth Centenary of His Death*, ed. Giles Constable and James Kritzeck (Rome: Pontificium Instituum S. Anselmi, 1956), 162. The pope wrote to Abbot Suger: "[...] "Inde est quòd petitioni tuæ et aliorum qui nobis super causa ipsa scripserunt (quamvis gravissimum nobis fuerit propter imbecilitatem personæ [refering here to Bernard] in qua omnium vota, Domino favente, concurrunt) assensum tamen denegare nequaquam potuimus. Monemus itaque dilectionem tuam quatinus, in tanto et tam præclaro opere, tamquam vir discretus et prudens, opem et studium diligenter exhibeas." *Ep.* LXXII, RHGF, 459. Eugenius was, in fact, one of Bernard's protégés, and when he was elected pope, Bernard sent him rather strict advice on the responsibilities that lay before him. See *Bernard of Clairvaux, Five Books of Consideration: Advice to a Pope*, Cistercian Fathers 13, trans. John D. Anderson & Elizabeth T. Keenan (Kalamazoo: Cistercian Publications, 1976).

56. Cistercian monks were, of course, in any

event prohibited from going on crusade, as was the usual case with monastic communities. The General Chapter of 1157 says as much. See Constable, "Second Crusade," 269, and *f.* 290.

57. Bruno Scott James, trans. *The Letters of Bernard of Clairvaux*, 471–2. *Ep.* XCV *Ad EUGENIUM III*, RHGF, vol. XV, 615–16: "Tu ergo, amice Sponsi, amicum te in necessitate probato. Si triplici illo amore de quo tuus interrogatus est prædecessor, tu quoeque toto corde, totâ animâ, totâ virtute Christum diligis, ut oportet; nihil reservabis, nihil dissimulabis in tanto periculo sponsæ ejus; sed quidquid habes virium, quidquid zeli, quidquid sollicitudinis, quidquid auctoritatis, quidquid potestates impendes. Singulare periculum singularem exigit operam. [...] De cætero, verbum illud quod jam, nî fallor, audisits: quomodo videlicet in Carnotensi conuentu (quoniam judicio satis miror) me quasi in ducem et principem militiæ elegerunt, certum sit vobis nec consilii mei nec voluntatis meæ fuisse vel esse, sed nec possibilitatis meæ (quantùm metior vires meas) pervenire usque illuc. Quis sum ego, ut disponam castrorum acies, ut egrediar ante faciem armatorum? aut quid tam remotum à professione mea, etiam si vires suppeterent, etiam si peritia non de esset?" Also in Bernard, *Opera*, VII, CCLVI, 163–5.

58. Philips, *The Second Crusade: Extending the Frontiers*, 273, referring to Giles Constable, "A Report on a Lost Sermon by St Bernard on the Failure of the Second Crusade," in *Studies in Medieval Cistercian History Presented to Jeremiah O'-Sullivan* (Spencer, MA: Cistercian Publications, 1971), 49–54.

59. See Constable, "Second Crusade," at 267–68, for a fuller discussion.

60. Ibid., translated from the *Annales Herbipolenses A. 1145–1147*, MGH *Scriptores* 16 (Hanover: Hahn, 1859) , 3: "Etenim perrexerunt quidam pseudoprophete, filii Belial, testes antichristi, qui inanibus verbis christianos seducerent, et pro Iherosolimorum liberatione omne genus hominum contra Sarracenos ire vana predicatione compellerent."

61. Constable provides additional commentary in "Second Crusade," 268–69.

62. Suger wrote to Peter: "Orientalis aecclesiae calamitatem, et dominicae crucis et regis Iherosolimitani ac fratrum Templi et aliorum fidelium in urbe Antiochena obsessionem, ex litteris quae a partibus illis nuper delatae sunt, cognouimus, et ad aures uestras peruenisse non ambigimus. Inde est quod Archiepiscopi et episcopi, quin etiam dominus rex, et regni optimates et nos super hoc Lauduni conuenimus et usque adeo res processit, quod.. XV. dies post octuas paschae Carnoti generaliter conuentum celebrare super hac causa, et multarum prouinciarum archiepiscopos, episcopos, abbates conuocare, et *pro domo* dei *murum* nos opponere, tantoque dolori pene inconsolabili consulte prouidere, et ne fides ab illis sacratissimis locis exterminetur, a quibus ad nos deportata est, dei misericordia praecaedente et subsequente, omnimodam operam adhibere disposuimus. [...]." Giles Constable, ed. *The Letters of Peter the Venerable*, two vols. (Cambridge, MA: Harvard University Press, 1967), I, 398–9.

Bernard wrote: "[...] Nam et patres nostri, episcopi Franciae, una cum domino rege et principibus, tertia dominica post pascha apud Carnotum uenturi sunt, et de uerbo hoc tractaturi, ubi utinam mereamur habere prasentiam uestram. Quia enim magnis omnino magnorum uirorum consiliis, hoc uerbum constat egere, gratum profecto obsequium praestabitis deo, si negotium eius a uobis non duxeritis alienum, sed caritatis uestrae zelum probaueritis, in oportunitatibus, in tribulatione. Nostis enim pater amantissime, nostis, quoniam amicus in necessitate probatur. Confidimus autem, quod magnum huic uerbo prouentum praesentia uestra praestabit, tum pro auctoritate sanctae Cluniacensis aecclesiae, cui deo disponente praeestis, tum maxime pro sapientia et gratia quam uobis ipse donauit, ad utilitatem utique proximorum, et suum ipsius honorem. [...]." Constable, *Letters*, 396.

Part of Peter's response to Bernard: "[...] Apparet inde maxime, uerum esse quod dico, quod cum in ultimo occidente, immo in ipso pene occidui oceani littore positus sitis, tot interiectis terrarum spaciis, laboranti in oriente Christiano nomini, summo quantoque potestis studio succurrere festinatis. Inde est quod apud Carnotum cum domino rege et aliis patribus aecclesiae, ac regni maioribus, die indicta conuenire decreuistis, meque sacro illi conuentui interesse rogastis. Fateor quod uerum est, quia et excusare aduentum meum erubesco, et tamen omnio uenire non possum." Constable, *Ep.* 164, 397–8.

63. James Kritzeck is the most notable supporter of this idea, *Peter the Venerable and Islam* (Princeton, NJ: Princeton University Press, 1964). However, Berry effectively counters this thesis, see Chapter 5. Various other writers over the years have also disagreed with him, and convincingly argued that his hypothesis is flawed.

64. Bolton, "The Cistercians and the Aftermath," 134, drawn from Peter the Venerable, *Sel. Ltrs*, letter 164, 89–91. "Doleo, et supra dicere possum doleo, quia sacro conuentui uestro quem apud Carnotum dominus rex consilio sapientiae uestrae et aliorum sapientum indixit, interesse non ualeo. Credite intim amico, credite uera dicenti, quia uera uolo, sed non ualeo, et quia non ualeo, doleo. Quis enim non doleat se non interesse tam sancto collegio, ubi nullus proprium lucrum, ubi nullus *quae sua sunt quaeret*, sed quae Ihsu Christ?" Constable, "Letters," *Ep.* 166, I, 399.

65. The question of Peter's support, for the crusading movement (which seems to have been genuine and strong) will be discussed more in Chapter 5.

66. Berry, "Peter the Venerable," 160–1.
67. Additional commentary on the whole affair can be found in Constable, "The Crusading Project of 1150," *Montjoie*, 67–76, and Philips, *The Second Crusade: Extending the Frontiers*, 272.
68. Ibid., 161.
69. Ibid.
70. See Mastnak, *Crusading Peace*, at 168, for a discussion of Bernard's *De Consideratione* to the pope, wherein he stresses that emphasis on conversion or a return to the faith is a papal duty.
71. Documentary sources for the Christian practice of enslaving Muslims are scarce before the thirteenth century. Though beyond the boundaries of this study, a good discussion of Muslim slavery from the thirteenth to the fifteenth centuries is Charles Verlinden, "Les esclaves musulmans du Midi de la France," in *Islam et chrétiens du Midi (XII*ᵉ*-XIV*ᵉ *s.)*, *Cahiers de Fanjeaux*, 18 (Fanjeaux: Centre National de la Recherche Scientific, 1983), 215–34. Verlinden's monumental studies of medieval slavery, *L'esclavage dans l'Europe médiévale*, I (Brugge: De Tempel, 1955), and II (Gent: Rijksuniversiteit, 1977), are surprisingly silent on the issue of monastic slave holding, particularly among the Cistercians, with the exception of a few references noted below. Nevertheless, given the number of Cistercian statutes issued over the years, it must have been a relatively widespread practice, especially in Mediterranean countries. For an introduction to the Church's positions on slavery in general throughout its history, see John Francis Maxwell, *Slavery and the Catholic Church* (Chichester and London: Barry Rose, 1975), especially at 30–43. For a recent study of medieval slavery in Spain and its transition to feudalism, see Pierre Bonnassie, *From Slavery to Feudalism in South-Western Europe*, trans. Jean Birrell (Cambridge: Cambridge University Press, 2009).
72. Kedar, *Crusade and Mission*, 48. The guideline regarding the discouraging of engaging in Muslim slave-trading states: "De Saracenis antiqua sententia teneatur, scilicet ut nec emantur, nec baptizari prohibeantur." *St.atua Capitulorum Generalium Ordinis Cisterciensis, 1116–1786*, ed. J.M. Canivez, 8 vols. (Louvain: Revue d'histoire ecclésiastique, 1933–41), vol. 1, 49. For an excellent survey of the slave trade of both Muslim and Christian slaves in medieval Iberia, see Olivia Remie Constable, "Muslim Spain and Mediterranean slavery: the medieval slave trade as an aspect of Muslim-Christian relations," in *Christendom and its Discontents*, ed. Scott L. Waugh and Peter D. Diehl (Cambridge: University Press, 1996), 264–84.
73. Kedar, *Crusade and Mission*, 46. This was an address to Bernard de Sédirac, archbishop-elect of Toledo, which had been recently taken from the Moors. See also D. Mansilla, ed., *La documentación pontifica hasta Inocencio III (965–1216), Monumenta Hispaniae Vaticana*, registros 1 (Rome: Instituto Español de Estudios Eclesiasticos, 1955), doc. 27, at 44.
74. In many places, slavery seems to have simply "died out" such as in England, where Anglo-Saxon practices of slavery were replaced by Anglo-Norman feudalism. One might argue that such a difference is merely a question of rewording, yet the systems were noticeably different, a topic beyond the boundaries of the current discussion. See, for example, David A.E. Pelteret, *Slavery in Anglo-Saxon England* (Woodbridge: Boydell, 1995).
75. Examples may be found in Gal. 3:26–28, I Cor. 12:13, and Col. 3:11 and 3:22–4:1. Summaries are also given in Maxwell, *Slavery and the Catholic Church*, 28–29, and a fuller summary of teachings and writings during the medieval period up to 1200 can be found at 30–43.
76. Ibid., 34, in a discussion on the views of Pope Gregory I.
77. Augustine, *Enarratio in Ps.*, XCIX, 7, PL 37, 1275: "Simul es et servus et liber: servus, quia factus es; liber, quia amaris a Deo a quo factus es: imo etiam inde liber, quia amas cum a quo factus es. Noli servire cum murmure; non enim id agunt murmura tua, ut non servias, sed ut malus servus servias. Servus es Domini, libertus es Domini; non te sic quæras manumitti, ut recedas de domo manumissoris tui."
78. Maxwell, in *Slavery and the Catholic Church*, 30. He translates: "If anyone, on the pretext of religion, teaches another man's slave to despise his master, and to withdraw from his service, and not to serve his master with good will and all respect, let him be anathema." This is recorded by Gratian, *Decreti Secunda Pars*, Causa XVII, Quest. IV, Cap. 37, 825–26: "*Religionis occasione dominum suum non audeat seruus contempnere*. Si quis seruum alienum occasione religionis docet dominum suum contempnere, et eius ministerium destituere, ac non pocius docuerit eum suo domino bona fide et cum omni honorificentia deseruire, anathema sit."
79. Maxwell, *Slavery and the Catholic Church*, 36. Isadore, *Sententiarum*, Lib. III, Cap. 47, PL 83, 717A-B.
80. Maxwell, *Slavery and the Catholic Church*, 37.
81. Ibid., 32. Guibert makes note of this in a lengthy passage in *De vita sua*, Lib. III, Cap. 10, PL 156, 932D — 933A-B. I Peter 12:18 is also invoked in support.
82. R.W. Carlyle and A.J. Carlyle, *A History of Medieval Political Thought in the West*, 6 vols. (Edinburgh and London: William Blackwood, 1903–1936, 1909), vol. 2, at 39, quoting at length in *f.* 2 from Azo, *Summa Institutionem*, I, 3, 16. Larger selections from Azo's commentaries on slavery can be found in F.W. Maitland, ed., *Select Passages from the Works of Bracton and Azo*, Selden Society, vol. 8 (London: Quartich, 1895), 42–52.
83. There are such vague statements that the

Jews "ought not to be killed," but rather spared as witnesses to the end of time, when they would be converted. This belief dated to the time of Augustine, who commented upon the status of the Jews in Christian society. See, for example, *De Civitate Dei*, Book XVIII, 46, wherin he states: "Demonstravit ergo Deus ecclesiae in eius inimicis Iudaeis gratiam misericordiae suae, quoniam, sicut dicit apostolus, *delictum illorum salus gentibus*; et ideo non eos occidit, id est non in eis perdidit quod sunt Iudaei, quamvis a Romanis fuerint devicti et oppressi, ne obliti legem Dei ad hoc, de quo agimus, testimonium nihil valerent. Ideo parum fuit, ut diceret: *Ne occideris eos, ne quando obliviscantur legem tuam*, nisi adderet etiam: *Disperge eos*; quoniam si cum isto testimonio scripturarum in sua tantummodo terra, non ubique essent, profecto ecclesia, quae ubique est, eos prophetiarum quae de Christo praemissae sunt testes in omnibus gentibus habere non posset." William Chase Green, trans., *The City of God Against the Pagans*, 7 vols., with parallel Latin and English texts (Cambridge, MA: Harvard University Press, 1960), VI, 50. In Augustinian thought, therefore, the Jews, however blind, evil, and sinful they might be, were in a sense instrumental in the process of Christianity's self-definition. A similar attitude eventually developed about Islam. Often, however, there was no real condemnation of the practice of Jewish persecution, though Bernard is known to have made attempts to defend the Jews against the dreadful pogroms that always came with crusading movements. He held that God alone would "settle the accounts" with the Jews. See Mastnak, *Crusading Peace*, 167.

84. Kedar further notes: "In 1246 the Cistercians were prohibited from buying Saracen concubines for their Saracen slaves, as three southern French abbots had done, evidently for breeding purposes." *Crusade and Mission*, 48, f. 18, quoting from *Statua Capitulorum*, 1:490; 2:303, 308. That this practice continued for so long shows how unwilling or unable the Cistercians were to address the issue, and probably how widespread the practice was, at least in Spain.

85. This would, of course, depend upon the actual number of Muslim slaves held by any particular house, its overall size and membership, etc.

86. Olivia Constable, "Muslim Spain," 264.

87. Ibid., 265.

88. See, however Forey, "The Military Orders and the Conversion of Muslims," at 9, and f. 45, for some exceptions.

89. Ibid.

90. Kedar, *Crusade and Mission*, 53, though this was not always the case. He notes at 53 that a Saracen slave girl who had been baptized was bought by a Cistercian monk from Poblet, Catalonia, for example, also recorded in Verlinden, *Esclavage*, II, 456. This rather astonishing situation brings up many questions about ethics, morals, perhaps even race. See also Verlinden at II, 300, where he states: "Les esclaves baptisés, avec ou sans autorisation du maître, ne sont pas affranchis par le baptême, mais on ne peut les vendre à des juifs ou des Sarrasins. Toutefois, seuls les esclaves chrétiens peuvent être affranchis. Le baptême est donc une condition préalable, non une cause d'affranchissement." Further, he adds, at 303: "Dans la pratique, comme dans la théorie juridique, le baptême affranchit l'esclave d'un juif, mais non celui d'un chrétien." Therefore, it was possible for Christians to continue to hold slaves converted to Christianity from Judaism and Islam, but not for Jews to do the same.

91. Forey, in "The Military Orders and the Conversion of Muslims," discusses this extensively, looking at twelfth through early fourteenth-century records.

92. Ibid., 6.

93. Ibid., 8.

94. See note 91 above.

95. Lawrence J. McCrank, "The Frontier of the Spanish Reconquest and the Land Acquisitions of the Cistercians of Poblet, 1150–1276," *Analecta Cisterciensia* 29 (1973): 60.

96. Ibid., 61.

Chapter 5

1. This chapter is a greatly expanded version of an article by the author that first appeared under the title "Peter the Venerable and the Toledan Collection," *Medieval Life* 6 (Spring 1997): 15–18.

2. Mastnak, *Crusading Peace*, 113.

3. R.W. Southern, *Western Views of Islam in the Middle Ages* (Cambridge, MA: Harvard University Press, 1962), 37.

4. Several studies of Peter's works and relationship to Islam have emerged over the years. The most recent is the excellent work by Dominique Iogna-Prat: *Order and Exclusion: Cluny and Christendom Face Heresy, Judaism and Islam (1000–1150)*, trans. Graham Robert Edwards, Conjunctions of Religion and Power in the Medieval Past (Cornell: Cornell University Press, 2002). This book takes a broader survey of the age, also reviewing Peter's writings against the Jews and the heretic Petrobrusians, but one section is particularly useful: "The Creation of a Christian Armory against Islam," at 338–57, which specifically looks at Peter's writing of the *Liber contra sectam haeresim Saracenorum* (it is part of a larger chapter, "Islam and the Antichrist," 323–57). This portion is also available in an edited form in *Medieval Religion: New Approaches*, ed. Constance Berman (New York: Routledge, 2005), 325–46. The best-known of the earlier works is the previously cited James Kritzeck, *Peter the Venerable and Islam*. His work is an analysis of the texts obtained by Peter through his translators. Kritzeck refers to them as

the Toledan Collection, owing to the city of origin, though they are also commonly known as the Cluniac Corpus. He includes a modern text edition of Peter's refutation, along with several other works. The book is most useful for bringing together the collected facts of the translation project, but suffers from Kritzeck's insistence that Peter's primary concern was the conversion of Muslims by peaceful means, which is categorically not the case. Indeed, his position seems quite naïve in light of more recent critical studies. An excellent and comprehensive critique of the weaknesses of Kritzeck's work appears in Iogna-Prat's work, as well as in the review article by Allan Cutler, "Peter the Venerable and Islam," *Journal of the American Oriental Society*, 86 (1966): 184–98. Kritzeck has also commented on the edition of the Qur'an produced for the translation project in "Robert of Ketton's Translation of the Qur'an," *Islamic Quarterly*, 2 (1955): 309–12, including a survey of the work done by M.T. d'Alverny, "Deux traductions latines du Coran au Moyen Âge," *Archives d'histoire doctrinale et litteraire du moyen âge*, 16 (1948): 69–131. Other studies of Peter include Jean Leclercq, *Pierre le Vénérable* (S. Wandrille: Éditions de Fontenelle, 1946), an assessment of Peter and his times that should be read with some caution given Leclercq's own biases, see also note 78 below. Also cited is the noteworthy Constable and Kritzeck, eds., *Petrus Venerabilis, Studies and Texts Commemorating the Eighth Centenary of his Death*, (Rome: Pontificium Institutum S. Anselmi, 1956), a *festschrift* consisting of a variety of studies, including an opposing opinion to Kritzeck's by Virginia Berry on Peter's view of the Second Crusade (see note 81 below), and aspects of the Cistercian/Cluniac controversy. A modern edition of Peter's letters has been prepared by Giles Constable, *The Letters of Peter the Venerable* (see Chapter 2). Aspects of the role that Cluny played in the formulation of the crusading idea in the eleventh century, given that Urban II was a former Cluniac monk, are to be found in *Cluniac Monasticism in the Central Middle Ages*, ed. Noreen Hunt (Hamden, CT: Archon Books, 1971). Maria Teresa Brolis considers Peter's view of warfare in "La crociata per Pietro il Venerabile: guerra di armi o guerra di idee," *Aevum*, 61, no. 2 (1987): 327–54. Jean-Pierre Torrell discusses Peter's polemical method in the light of medieval prophecy in "La notion de prophétie et la méthode apologétique dans le *Contra Saracenos* de Pierre le Vénérable," *Studia Monastica* 17, no. 2 (1975): 257–82.

5. Kritzeck, *Peter the Venerable*, 3.

6. Ibid.

7. Adriaan Bredero, "The Controversy between Peter the Venerable and Bernard of Clairvaux," in *Petrus Venerabilis*, at 53, is a fine summary which enters into much more detail than is necessary to give here, and provides good bibliographical references for further study. Letter 28 from Constable, *The Letters of Peter the Venerable*, contains the longest and fullest description of the controversy in Peter's own words; it lays out the charges against the Cluniacs, and Peter's responses, I, at 52–101. Constable provides commentary in II, 270–4.

8. David Knowles, "The Reforming Decrees of Peter the Venerable," *Petrus Venerabilis*, 4, drawn from Peter's *Epistola* IV, 17, PL 189, 321–44. This is a lengthy letter that seeks reconciliation between the orders, though by this time, many of the suggestions for improvement were already being enacted by Peter. The tone is summarized by Knowles: "We both follow the Rule: you with zeal for its purity and we with charity for the weaker brethren. Why should we quarrel? Why not admit the excellence of both ways? Why not each abound in his own sense?" at 4. PL 189, 329–31 especially is devoted to the Rule and its observance.

9. Bredero, "Controversy between Peter the Venerable," 70.

10. Alfonso, like most Spanish kings, was active in the *reconquista* efforts to drive back the Moors and retake territory for Christianity, but he also extended protections to the Muslims who lived in his realms. This kind of contradictory behavior was displayed by many Spanish monarchs during the Middle Ages. For a recent study of his life and reign, see Bernard F. Reilly, *The Kingdom of León-Castilla under King Alfonso VII*, 1126–1157, (Philadelphia: University of Pennsylvania Press, 1998), especially 90–134.

11. Kritzeck, *Peter the Venerable and Islam*, 10–13, and Charles Julian Bishko, "Peter the Venerable's Journey to Spain," in *Petrus Venerabilis*, 163–6. Bishko presents an interesting and detailed account of the journey, and draws the conclusion that Peter probably only decided on the project after meeting the translators, at 164. There is no evidence that he set out for Spain primarily for that purpose. Bishko writes, "[...] pending more precise dating of Peter's anti-Islamic interests in connection with his whole scheme of combating heretical Christian, Jewish and Muslim doctrine, this motive must remain uncertain." 163.

12. Ibid., 171–2.

13. However, see note 40 regarding his birth date.

14. Tolan, *Petrus Alfonsi and His Medieval Readers* (Gainesville, Florida: University Press of Florida, 1993), 10–11. See also his commentary at 213–14, *f.* 17, which casts doubts on the truth of this claim.

15. Petrus Alphonsi, *Dialogi contra Iudaeos*, *Præfatio*, PL 157, 537C-38C: "[...] et baptizatus in sede Oscensis civitatis [...] Hoc autem factum est anno a nativitate Domini millesimo centesimo sexto [...]

mense, Julio, die natalis apostolorum Petri et Pauli. Unde mihi ob venerationem et memoriam ejusdem apostoli, nomen quod est Petrus, imposui. Fuit autem pater meus spiritualis ALFUNSUS, gloriosus Hispaniæ imperator, qui me de sacro fonte suscepit, quare nomen ejus præfato nomini meo apponens, Petrus Alfunsi mihi nomen imposui. [...] rationibus vero adversarii confutandis, nomen quod ante baptismum habueram, id est Moysen." See especially chapter 2, 12–41.

16. The full text is to be found in PL 157, 535–672. For a recent English translation, see *Petrus Alfonsi: Dialogue Against the Jews* (Fathers of the Church: Mediaeval Continuation), trans. Irven Resnick (Washington, D.C.: Catholic University of America Press, 2006).

17. An excellent summary of Alfonsi's life and times, and the effect of his works can be found in John Tolan, *Petrus Alfonsi and His Medieval Readers*. See especially chapter 2, 12–41.

18. Ibid., 28. A comparison of Qur'anic citations found in the writings of Petrus Alfonsi and Peter the Venerable's chosen translator of the Qur'an, Rober of Ketton, reveals few similarities. See Guy Monnot, "Les citations coraniques dans le 'Dialogus' de Pierre Alfonse," in *Islam et chrétiens du Midi (XIIe–XIVe s.)*, Cahiers de Fanjeaux 18, 272–73. Monnot feels that Alfonsi's citations are superior, even though they draw indirectly from al-Kindi: "Deux conclusions sautent aux yeux. D'une part, les deux versions sont tout à fait différentes. D'autre part, celle de Pierre Alfonse est presque toujours plus simple, plus claire et plus précise," 274.

19. A detailed listing of the beliefs and practices of Islam can be found in PL 157, 597–98, perhaps most importantly from the *Dialogi, Titulus* V, 597D: "Hoc facto, publica voce præconatur, unum confitentes Deum, qui nullum vel similem habaet vel æqualem, ejusque Mahometh esse prophetam."

20. A study of some of these inaccuracies can be found in Bernard Septimus, "Petrus Alfonsi on the Cult at Mecca," *Speculum* 56:3 (1981): 517–33, which analyzes the Jewish commentary tradition in detail.

21. See chapter 1 for a discussion of the etymology of "Saracen," and beliefs about Arab lineage.

22. Septimus, "Petrus Alfonsi on the Cult at Mecca," 520.

23. Ibid. This discrepancy is discussed at 521–22.

24. Ibid., 525. *Dialogi* V, PL 157, 602D: "Duo filii Lot Amon et Moab, hanc domum honorabant, et duo idola ab eisdem ibi colebantur, alterum ex albo, alterum ex nigro lapide paratum, Nomen quidem illius quod ex niro erat lapide. Mercurius, nomen vero alterius Chamos, Alterum quod ex nigro lapide est, in honore Saturni, alterum quod ex albo in honore Martis ædificatum est." The commentary continues into column 603B, explaining the relationship between this situation and the arrival of Muhammad.

25. Septimus, "Petrus Alfonsi on the Cult at Mecca," 530 and 532. The Satanic Verses were an apparent Qur'anic revelation to Muhammad authorizing the Muslims to recognize the so-called "daughters of Allah," three goddesses of importance in pagan Arabia. These verses were later removed and replaced by verses affirming Islam's monotheism. They were thereafter seen as a trick of Satan, not genuine revelation, hence their name.

26. PL 157, 598A: "Semel autem per singulos annos propter solam recognitionem præcipiuntur omnes ire ad Dei domum, quæ est in Mecha videndam, et ibi adorare eamque inconsutilibus tegumentis induti circuire, et lapides prout lex præcepit, per media scilicet femora jacere retro pro lapidando diabolo." See also 602A-B, for references to the Venus cult.

27. Tolan, *Petrus Alfonsi and His Medieval Readers*, 29–31. The entire polemic can be found in PL 157, 602–05.

28. There is also the possibility that Alfonsi was the author of another treatise, in Arabic, which extolled the virtues of Christianity. Entitled *Tathlīth al-waḥdānīyah*, it is a short work that attempts to demonstrate that reason proves the Trinity. It argues that power, knowledge, and will are all necessary to create, and that these are other names for the Father, Son, and Holy Spirit. It survives in an Islamic polemic which seeks to refute it, known as "Information about the Corruption and Delusions of the Christians, and Presentation of the Merits of the Religion of Islam, and Affirmation of Prophethood of Our Prophet Muhammad," by a Muslim author known only as al-Imām al-Qurṭubī (the Imam of Cordoba), *al-Iʿlām bi-mā fī dīn al-naṣárá min al-fasād wa-awhām wa-iẓhār maḥasīn dīn al-islām wa-ithbāt nubuwwat nabīnā Muḥammad ʿalayhi al-ṣalāt wa-al-salām*, ed. Aḥmad Hijāzī al-Saqqā (Cairo: Maktabat al-Kullīyāt al-Azharīyah, 1980). A summary of its contents can be found in Thomas Burman, *Religious Polemic and the Intellectual History of the Mozarabs* (Leiden, New York, Köln: E.J. Brill, 1994), 70–80. The possibility of authorship by Alfonsi is discussed at 76–77. It contains Latin methods of apologetic and reasoning, drawn from the works of Augustine, and more significantly, Abelard. Therefore, its author must have known Latin as well as Arabic, and been familiar with these writings, see 78. It is likely, according to the Islamic tract, that the author was a *converso* Jew. Further, there are similarities in style between the *Tathlīth al-waḥdānīyah*, and Alfonsi's *Dialogi*, see 77. This does not, of course, prove Alfonsi's authorship, but it is likely that if it was not Alfonsi, the author must have known of his work.

29. Burman, *Religious Polemic*, 95.
30. Ibid.
31. Ibid., 241, *f.* 55.
32. Dijon, Bibliothèque municipale MS 228,

Tolan gives a complete listing of all known manuscripts and their current locations at 100–01, and Appendix 2, 182–98.

33. Douai, Bibliothèque municipale MS 199. A modern edition of this work is *Adversus Iudeorum inveteratam duritiem*, ed. by Yvonne Friedman, CCCM, 58, 1985.

34. Tolan analyzes these in *Petrus Alfonsi and His Medieval Readers*, 116–17. Peter had none of the tolerance for the Jews that Bernard did. For Peter, Jews are the *humani generis feces* (Tolan, 242, *f.* 59), and as Tolan remarks: "Jews oppose Christian truth, *ergo*, for Peter, they are irrational beasts," 117.

35. Iogna-Prat, *Order and Exclusion*, 323.

36. Several manuscripts of Alfonsi's *Dialogi* also contain Peter's own attack on Islam. Clearly, medieval readers felt that the two belonged together. See Tolan, *Petrus Alfonsi and His Medieval Readers*, 108.

37. For a discussion of medieval Toledo's importance in the field of translation, see Charles Burnett, "The Coherence of the Arabic-Latin Translation Program in Toledo in the Twelfth Century," *Science in Context* 14 (2001): 249–288.

38. Ketton's work and the translation are excellently surveyed in detail by Marie-Thérèse d'Alverny, "Deux traductions latines du Corans au moyen âge," in *Archives d'histoire doctrinale et littéraire du moyen âge*, 16 (Paris: Librarie Vrin, 1948), 69–131. She also considers the later work of Mark of Toledo. See her "Quelques manuscrits de la 'Collection Toletana,'" in *Petrus Venerablilis*, 202–18. Many of d'Alverny's works on Christian perceptions of Islam, including the two above, have been collected and republished by Variorum under the title *La connaissance de l'Islam dans l'Occident médiéval*, ed. Charles Burnett (Aldershot, Hampshire: Variorum, Ashgate, 1994). A good, short biography of Robert can also be found in Dorothee Metlitzki, *The Matter of Araby in Medieval England* (New Haven and London: Yale University Press, 1977), 30–35. Metlitzki offers a reasonable, if rather amusing explanation for Robert's viciousness in addressing Islam, which he referred to as a "stagnant swamp" (31, see also 32 and 34, where she notes that Robert dated the completion of the project in 1143, apparently with great relief). She writes that his feelings, "are no doubt an echo of Peter's, but it is probably also an expression of his suppressed anger at having to spend his time on religious doctrine and theology instead of on what really concerned him — astronomical and mathematical science," 31. This is a rather unusual attitude for an archdeacon to take, yet one can amusingly imagine him, compelled by duty and Peter's pleas, working on the Qur'an and annoyed about his task, because it is distracting him from more important matters. A more recent study of Robert is Thomas Burman, "Tafsir and Translation: Traditional Arabic Qur'an Exegesis and the Latin Qur'ans of Robert of Ketton and Mark of Toledo," *Speculum* 73 (1998): 703–32.

39. Kritzeck, *Peter the Venerable*, 57–8. Kritzeck's remains the definitive study of this topic, and is the prime source of information for this section. Bishko notes in "Peter the Venerable's Journey," 167, how Peter of Toledo was far more fluent in Arabic than in Latin, a situation common among Mozarabic scholars for centuries. Indeed, it had been one of Alvarus' great laments in the ninth century at the height of the Martyr's Movement, see Chapter 7. Bishko writes at167 that "Peter of Poitiers was assigned to polish to literary standards the 'rough Latin' of Peter of Toledo."

40. Cutler, "Peter the Venerable," 190–91. He points to doubts about Alfonsi's age. It is generally argued that Alfonsi was born in 1062, which would have put him in his 80s by the time Peter the Venerable was in Toledo. However, Cutler notes that it is possible that Alfonsi's birth year was considerably later, owing to a corrupted reading in printed versions of his *Dialogi*. He points to the early work of C. Nedelcou, "Sur la date de la naissance de Pierre Alphonsi," *Romania* 35 (1906): 462–63. The issue has been in debate for some time.

41. Kritzeck argues convincingly in *Peter the Venerable*, 57–58, that Peter of Toledo was the annotator of the Arsenal MS 1162. If he was indeed Alfonsi, it would explain the accuracy of the annotations in relation to actual facts about Islam. See also Cutler's comments in "Peter the Venerable," 190.

42. Kritzeck, *Peter the Venerable*, 69.

43. Iogna-Prat discusses many of the translating errors that were made, *Order and Exclusion*, 342–43.

44. Ibid., 338.

45. Kritzeck gives a good detailed summary of each at 73–112. See also his "Peter the Venerable and the Toledan Collection" from *Petrus Venerabilis*, 176–201. In the latter, Kritzeck takes the opposite view of Bishko: "I am persuaded that this project was not a chance notion on Peter's part, but was intimately related to singularities of his education and temperament, to his other apologetical and polemical endeavors, and to his dissatisfaction, in some degree, with the direction taken by the Crusade movement in his time, most notably in its omission of the aim of converting the Moslems to Christianity," 177. He bases his argument on the supposition that Peter's intent was conversion of Muslims. There are problems with this theory, see notes 80 and 81. He uses as evidence a selection from the *Prologus* of the *Contra Sectam*: "Unde concaluit cor meum intra me, et in meditatione mea exarsit ignis, indignatus sum causam tantæ perditionis Latinos ignorare, et ipsa ignorantia nullum ad resistendum posse animari; nam non erat qui responderet, quia non erat qui agnosceret." PL 189, 671B-C. However,

this does not provide conclusive proof, as it appears in the actual work refuting Islam, not prior to the project commencing. Peter does not say exactly when the "flame" of the idea arose.

46. Kritzeck, *Peter the Venerable*, 102.
47. Ibid., 103, where he writes that the lengthy Christian letter "leaves the desired impression that [Al-Hashimi] got the worst of the argument."
48. Ibid., 75.
49. Ibid., and *f.* 12.
50. Ibid., 84.
51. Ibid., 90–1. See also M-T d'Alverny, "Pierre le Vénérable et la légende de Mahomet," in *A Cluny, Congrès scientifique, Fêtes et cérémonies liturgiques en l'honneur des saints Abbés Odon et Odilon, 9–11 juillet 1949* (Dijon: Société des Amis de Cluny avec le CNRS, 1950), 161–70, also included in the Variorum reprint.
52. Regarding Qur'an 2:179, for example, he exclaims: "Nota quam stulte et quotiens repetit istud." Drawn from Paris, Bibliothèque de l'Arsenal, MS lat. 1162, fol. 30ra, rm, c. ll. 5–8, transcribed by Thomas E. Burman in *Religious Polemic*, 85. See 87–89 for a discussion on the identity of the Annotator. Concurring with d'Alverny's view ("Deux traductions," 103), Burman concludes that it was in fact a team effort, probably consisting of Peter of Poitiers (who had no knowledge of Arabic), Robert of Ketton and Peter of Toledo.
53. Annotator, fol. 28vb, lm, c. ii. 1–14, v. 2:125ff, transcribed Burman, *Religious Polemic*, 86.
54. Ibid., 87. See also Burman, "Tafsir and Translation."
55. Mastnak, *Crusading Peace*, 180.
56. Throop, *Crusading as an Act of Vengeance*, 94.
57. Ibid., 173.
58. See Chapter 6 regarding apocalypticism in relation to Islam for a fuller discussion of this.
59. Iogna-Prat, *Order and Exclusion*, 342.
60. "Pierre le Vénérable s'en rendit compte, surtout en ce qui concerne le dialogue d'Abdia [the fictitious Jew engaging Muhammad in discussion], qualifié avec peu de discernement par les rubricateurs: Doctrine de Mahomet, d'une grande autorité auprès des Sarrasins, et il stigmatise les 'deliramenta' ridicules et insensés contenus dans ces récits. Il estime qu'aucun mortel n'aurait été capable de les imaginer par lui-même et que c'est Satan qui les a suggérés pour détourner le genre humain du vrai Dieu." d'Alverny, "Legende," 167. See also 168–9 for a discussion of Islam as a Christian heresy.
61. Mastnak, *Crusading Peace*, 177–78. See also Chapter 6 for Peter's comments on this.
62. Ibid., 178.
63. G.R. Evans, *The Mind of St. Bernard of Clairvaux* (Oxford: Clarendon Press, 1983), and Southern *Western Views of Islam*, 39.
64. Kritzeck, *Peter the Venerable*, 213, and PL 189, 651B-52A: "Nec tamen ut mihi uidetur opus istud etiam tempore ociosum uocare debeo, quoniam iuxta apostolum, uestrum est et omnium doctorum uirorum, omnem scientiam extollentem se aduersus altitudinem Dei, omni studio uerbo et scripto impugnare, destruere, conculcare." There are few full translations of Peter's texts. Where adequate translations of texts are available, I include them in the chapter. Otherwise the original texts suffice.
65. Kritzeck, *Peter the Venerable*, 213–14, and PL, 189, 652A. "Quod si hinc errantes converti non possunt, saltem infirmis Ecclesiæ, qui scandalizari et occulte moveri levibus etiam ex causis solent, consulere et providere doctus, vel doctior, si zelum habet justitiae, non debet negligere."
66. Iogna-Prat argues this throughout her chapter on Peter, see, for example, *Order and Exclusion*, 357.
67. Kritzeck, "Toledan Collection," 186, *f.* See note 73 below, however, for one problem regarding this theory.
68. Evans, *Mind of St. Bernard*, 31–2.
69. See note 4. Peter's writings against this heresy stand as a trilogy with his works against the Jews and Muslims.
70. Ibid., which raises the question of how serious their rivalry was, if they were able to set aside differences for this affair. Why then, would they not do the same for the refutation of Islam, if Kritzeck is to be believed? It is likely that Bernard felt he was doing his part in preaching the Second Crusade.
71. Bernard, *Epistola Ad Archiepiscopos Orientalis Franciae*, 363, 5, *Opera*, VIII, pp. 316–17: "Si Iudaei oenitus atteruntur, unde iam sperabitur eorum in fine promissa salus, in fine futura conversio? Plane et gentiles, si essent similiter in fine futura subiugati, in eo quidem iudicio essent similiter expectandi quam gladiis appetendi. Nunc autem cum in nos esse coeperint violenti, oportet vim vi repellere eos, qui non sine causa gladium portant." See also Benjamin Kedar, *Crusade and Mission*, 60–61.
72. Cutler, "Peter the Venerable," 189.
73. Letter 111 in Constable, *Letters*, I, 274–99, contains Peter's plea to Bernard to take up the struggle in word against Islam. There has been considerable debate as to whether this letter was written first, or whether Peter wrote the *Summa totius haeresis Saracenorum* first, and based this letter upon it, as it contains large sections of text from the *Summa*. D'Alverny and Kritzeck have argued the former, Constable the latter. He bases his conclusions on the language and style, as well as several internal clues which support his thesis. See 276–8 for a full description. Peter's letter describes his frustration at having to undertake the task himself: "Quod quia, pro dolor, iam pene toto huiusmodi studiorum sanctorum ubique in ecclesia tepefacto feruore, non est qui faciat, ex-

pectaui enim diu, et non fuit qui aperiret os, et zelo sancte christianitatis moueret penam et ganniret, ego ipse saltem si magne occupationes me permiserint, quandoque id aggredi, Domino adiuuante, proposui." PL 189, 658A.

74. The complete work is found in Kritzeck, *Peter the Venerable*, 220–91, and in PL 189, 659–719.

75. The text is in Kritzeck, *Peter the Venerable*, 204–11.

76. "Poterit inquam quod scriptum fuerit in eorum linguam transferri [...]," Kritzeck, *Peter the Venerable*, 225, and PL 189, 672A.

77. Kritzeck, *Peter the Venerable*, 231, and PL 189, 673B-C: "Aggredior, inquam, vos, non, ut nostri sæpe faciunt, armis, sed verbis, non vi, sed ratione, non odio, sed amore; amore tamen tali, qualis inter Christicolas et a Christo aversos esse debet; [...]."

78. Kritzeck, *Peter the Venerable*, 20–3. See also the earlier work of Jean Leclercq in "L'invitation au salut," in *Pierre le Vénérable*, 233–52. He speaks of *la croisade intellectuelle*, and argues for the position that Peter primarily wanted to attack Islam verbally, drawing from Peter's own words. Leclercq writes approvingly: "Le sens universel de Pierre le Vénérable incline son âme à se soucier de la foi des fidèles et du salut des infidèles." p. 233. "[...] Toute misère spirituelle émeut Pierre le Vénérable: il veut y remédier. A son amour des musulmans nous devons un dossier de documents humains dont les pièces jalonnent les quinze dernières années de sa vie. Il n'est que de les présenter pour faire apprécier la grandeur de son âme: les textes parleront d'eux-mêmes." p. 241. This discussion of Peter's great love is overstated, being based only on the opening address in which Peter invites Muslims to salvation. Like Kritzeck, he has read the conciliatory passages out of context, and ignored Peter's strong invective in other sources. In many of his writings, Leclercq seems unwilling to fully accept that his medieval co-religionists were capable of harboring unpleasant or war-like attitudes.

79. Ibid., 20, *f.*

80. See note 65, drawing from his letter to Bernard of Clairvaux, PL 189, 651–2. However, it must also be stressed that that Peter may have already considered the Muslims a lost cause. See Benjamin Kedar, *Crusade and Mission*, at 102, where he notes: "Indeed, in a letter urging Bernard of Clairvaux to undertake such a refutation, Peter voices the opinion that such a work will be of no use to 'those lost ones,' namely, the Saracens, but may be helpful to weak Christians who are apt to be seduced by evil."

81. Berry has asserted her convincing case in "Peter the Venerable and the Crusades," *Petrus Venerabilis*, 141–62. Her thesis is that Peter was in fact a supporter of the Second Crusade, and the idea of crusading in general, though she does tend to emphasize that Peter's support probably came from his view that the crusade was a defensive war, i.e., in defense of Christendom (Kedar takes issue with this at 101). She points to his *De laude Dominici Sepulchri* (PL 189, 973–92), and various correspondences, among them his address to Ebrardus, Master of the Templars in *Ep.* XXVI, 434–6, Constable, I, 172, at 407–9. Note his description of their duties: "At uos ut dictum est, et fortem armatum eisdem eorum artibus superatis, et contra illa eius quae aperte aduersus Christum producit infernalia castra, Sarracenorum dico agmina, pugnando assidue non cessatis. Estis monachi uirtutibus, milites actibus, illud spiritualiter implendo, istud corporaliter exercendo," 408. There is none of his conciliatory tone toward the Muslims in these words. He clearly supports the Templars and their mission. There is also a letter to Louis VII of France in 1146 in support of the crusade, *Ep.* XXXVI, 366–8, Constable, *Letters*, I, 130, at 327–30, and a letter to Jerusalem, wherein concerning the Kingdom's non-Christian neighbors, he states: "[...] inimicos autem crucis Christi et nominis Christiani, Turcos dico et Sarracenos, Persas et Arabes, seu quoslibet barbaros, humanæ immo suae saluti aduersantes [...] Ad quod uiriliter exsequendum quia armis non possumus, animis prosequimur, quia gladio non ualemus precibus ut possumus bellicos sudores uestros iuuare satagimus. Date ergo illi qui uos glorificauit gloriam, ut sicut Christus in sacerdotibus suis cotidie de diabolo eiusque angelis triumphat, [...]" *Ep.* XLVI, 269–70. (269), Constable, I, 82, at 219. There is no talk here of attacking the Muslims with words rather than arms. In a late letter to Bernard, dated April 1150, he discusses the crusade (the pilgrimage) as a means to salvation, despite the recent failure in the East, and how all should be moved by the injustices there: "Quem non moueat, ne forte terra illa sancta, a iugo impiorum tantis patrum laboribus, tanto Christicolarum sanguine, ante non multum temporis eruta, rursum impiis et blasphemiis subdatur? Quem non moueat, si tam salubris peccatorum paenitentium uia, quae ut dignum est credere innumera peregrinantium milia, a quinquagesima iam annis, infernis abstulit, caelo restituit, nequam Sarracenorum obice obstante claudatur?" Constable, Letter 167, 397.

82. Iogna-Prat, *Order and Exclusion*, 338–357. Her whole argument in these pages is that Peter had no interest in rational debate or conversion. She is highly critical of Peter in several instances, but her arguments are well justified.

83. Kedar, *Crusade and Mission*, 100–1, *f.* Peter's support for future Christian expeditions to the east can be found in his letters 162, 164, 166, Constable, *Letters*, I, 394–400. An earlier portion of letter 162, addressed to the King of Sicily, reads: "Nam cum multa sicut frequenter audiuimus, augmenta aecclesiae dei, bellica uirtute uestra de terris

inimicorum dei, hoc est, Sarracenorum proueniat, longe ut credimus maiora prouenirent, si firma pax et concordia uos et regem supra dictum unirent," 394–5.

84. Berry, "Peter the Venerable," 156. Constable, *Letters*, I, 162, 395: "Est et aliud quod longe magis accendit animos nostros, et animos pene omnium Gallorum nostrorum, ad amandam et quaerendam pacem uestram, illa scilicet pessima, inaudita et lamentabilis Graecorum et nequam regis eorum de peregrinis nostris, hoc est exercitu dei uiuentis, facta proditio. Vt enim iuxta quod in mente mea uideo loquar, si necesse esset quantam ad monachum pertinere potest, non recusarem mori, si mortem tantorum, tam nobilium, immo pene totius Galliae et Germaniae miserabili fraude extinctum florem, iustitia dei per aliquem suorum dignaretur ulcisi."

85. For a discussion of the "Greek problem" following the crusade's failure, see Jonathan Philips, *The Second Crusade*, 274–76. See also Chapter 4. This proposed venture was a massive undertaking in and of itself, and was the chief issue of the Council of Chartres in 1150. Peter's inability to attend that council has, as discussed, been taken as evidence for his disinterest in the project, though Berry shows that this was not the case, and gives extensive details about the affair, which could have resulted in another all-out assault on the East by Western Christian forces. It became apparent, however, that such an action would not have been wise politically, and many of Europe's secular rulers did not support it. See Berry, "Peter the Venerable," 157–62.

86. See Berry's comments and evidence in note 81 above, as well as Kedar's in note 80. Peter had no love for Muslims at all, and the only "evidence" for it is in the formulaic address inviting them to convert, a salutation they would never hear.

87. Kedar, *Crusade and Mission*, 102.

88. Peter's attitude can probably be linked with the role that Cluny played in the formulation of crusading ideas during the eleventh century. A detailed examination of this is out of the boundaries of this chapter, but the topic bears some relevance to this discussion. It has been traditionally held that Cluny was important, even instrumental, in the development of papal crusading policies as part of the Gregorian Reform, but some writers have challenged this notion, due to a lack of evidence. E. Delaruelle, in "The Crusading Idea in Cluniac Literature of the Eleventh Century," in *Cluniac Monasticism in the Central Middle Ages*, 195–210, discusses the persistent silence of eleventh-century texts in connecting Cluny with any aspect of crusading, whether in papal letters or Spanish correspondence, two principal sources. Indeed, Delaruelle writes that "[...] the mystique of the holy war then developing was foreign to the spirit of Cluny," at 201. Cluniacs sought flight from the world, not immersion in it.

They saw themselves as performing a different duty than those in the secular world, a duty of prayer and contemplation. Nevertheless, they did not necessarily condemn the actions of the secular world (see, for example, 202). Cowdrey generally concurs, in "Cluny and the First Crusade," in *Revue Bénédictine* 83 (1973): 285–311. However, he argues that Cluny indirectly (and perhaps unintentionally) endorsed the crusading ideal through its support of the general peace declared at the Council of Clermont (1095), and its encouragement of rival factions to set aside their differences, 295–6. In addition, Cluny was particularly supportive of the idea of pilgrimage. The result was to condition people to respond favorably to such calls from authority. He notes: "[Cluny's] propaganda was widespread in those regions of France from which the First Crusade largely drew its strength — Burgundy, Provence, and Aquitaine, and, by the 1090s, in northern France and Flanders as well. Here, it prepared the ground for a widespread response to the Crusade by its unceasing insistence that men should be vigilant to undertake good works, and especially to enter upon ways of personal commitment like monastic vows or pilgrimage, in order to secure the remission of their sins. It thereby conditioned them to respond to fresh calls to commitment when these were issued by due authority [...] the summons of the Crusade gained so widespread a response in large measure because of such propaganda as that of the Cluniacs [...]" 293. Promoted as a pilgrimage, the idea of the crusade gained acceptance over time in the Cluniac Order, certainly by Peter's time and the advent of the Second Crusade. Peter, as Abbot of Cluny, would have been influenced by this attitude.

89. See note 82 above, and also *Ep*. XLIV, 266, PL 189, for Peter's view of the First Crusade, and *Ep*. XXXIX, 260–2.

90. See note 82 above, Constable, *Letters*, I, 172, at 407–9, *Ep*. XXVI, 434–6, PL 189. A full translation of his letter to Everard of Les Barres, Master of the Temple, dated *ca*. 1150, can be found in Malcolm Barber and Keith Bate, trans. *The Templars: Selected Sources*, 227–30, and shows clearly his enthusiasm for the Templars.

91. Kedar, *Crusade and Mission*, 101–2.

92. See Cutler, "Peter the Venerable," 196, and Kritzeck, *Peter the Venerable*, 195–96. Cutler notes: "Much more likely, this defect in the work [i.e., the lack of Christian doctrine] shows that it was directed primarily at Christians."

93. Mastnak, *Crusading Peace*, 179.

94. Cutler, "Peter the Venerable," 192, drawing from Kritzeck's edition in *Peter the Venerable*, 229–30.

95. Mastnak, *Crusading Peace*, 183.

96. Hugh of Saint Victor, *Epistolæ*, III, PL 176, 1014–18. Though neither Jews nor Muslims are specifically mentioned in the letter, it is likely that

the Muslims are the subject of his plea, for the Jews are usually not mentioned in such contexts. For a discussion of the relation between the Victorines and the Jews of Northern France, see Beryl Smalley, *The Study of the Bible in the Middle Ages* (Oxford: Blackwell, 1952). See also note 98, below, for a curious reference by Hugh to his subjects as having the Holy Spirit, something the Jews would never claim.

97. Hugh, PL 176, 1014D: "Quomodo ergo salutem habere putas, si confessionem non habes? Christum negas et dicis te Spiritum sanctum habere?" The reference to the Holy Spirit here likely refers to the Islamic belief in Muhammad as the "holy spirit," the paraclete whom Jesus said would come after him. Muslims interpret this to mean the Prophet, while Christians associate it with Pentecost and an actual descending of the Holy Spirit into the apostles. Thus, Muslims could claim to "have the Holy Spirit" in the form of the Prophet and the Qur'an, but not in a Christian Trinitarian sense.

98. Ibid., 1014D-1015A: "Si dicis anathema Jesu, Spiritum Christi quomodo habes. Si vero non habes Spiritum Christi, non es Christi [...] Sed dicis bene: Qui pro erubescentia Christum negat, juste damnatur, juste a Christo non cognoscitur."

99. James M. Powell, "The Papacy and the Muslim Frontier," in *Muslims under Latin Rule, 1100–1300*, ed. Powell (Princeton: University Press, 1990), 186. See also Kedar, *Crusade and Mission*, 145–54.

100. Perhaps also being the inspiration, in the form of the "flame" that he mentions, for the translation project.

101. The twelfth-century accounts are excellently surveyed in Burman, *Religious Polemic*, 33–94. The second half of his book (215–385) is an edition of the longest of these works, the early twelfth-century *Liber Denudationis Siue Ostensionis Aut Patefaciens*, a work translated from Arabic into Latin, for which the Arabic original is lost and the only surviving edition dates from the sixteenth century. Despite these deficiencies, it contains a fascinating glimpse into the minds and thought processes of Mozarabic Christians, asserting their identity as a subject people to a foreign religion.

102. Burman, *Religious Polemic*, 157–189. See also note 28.

103. A fuller treatment of the subject is found in Ibid., 177–81.

104. Iogna-Prat, *Order and Exclusion*, 357.

105. Mastnak, *Crusading Peace*, 173.

Chapter 6

1. Sabina Flanagan, "Twelfth-Century Apocalyptic Imaginations and the Coming of the Antichrist," *Journal of Religious History* 24, no. 1 (2000): 60. This article is a good introduction to medieval apocalyptic ideas, particularly as expressed through four twelfth-century individuals, including Bernard of Clairvaux.

2. Flanagan, "Twelfth-Century Apocalyptic Imaginations," 59, where she discusses this at more length and notes Bernard McGinn's contribution to the topic, f. 5.

3. Ibid., 60–61.

4. Bernard McGinn, *The Calabrian Abbot: Joachim of Fiore in the History of Western Thought* (New York: Macmillan, 1985), 26.

5. The author will survey this topic in great detail in a forthcoming McFarland book, which will look at the development of anticlerical and antifraternal attitudes from a variety of sources (including universities, theologians, heretical movements, literature, and music in medieval France and England).

6. Bernard McGinn, *Visions of the End—Apocalyptic Traditions in the Middle Ages* (New York: Columbia University Press, 1979), 25. This is a fine introduction to the subject. It is also a useful anthology, and provides many fine examples and text translations of the development of Western apocalyptic thought from the early Church to the beginning of the sixteenth century. McGinn is one of the principal scholars writing on the subject of medieval apocalypticism. Several works of his are of importance to this study, and include: "Apocalypticism and Church Reform, 1100–1500," in *The Continuum History of Apocalypticism*, John J. Collins, Stephen Stein, and Bernard McGinn, eds. (New York: Continuum, 2003), 273–298; *Antichrist* (New York: Columbia University Press, 2000); *Apocalypticism in the Western Tradition* (Collected Studies, Cs 430) (Farnham, Surrey: Ashgate Variorum, 1994); *The Apocalypse in the Middle Ages*, ed. by Richard K. Emmerson and Bernard McGinn (Ithaca, New York: Cornell University Press, 1993). Older useful works of his include: "Portraying Antichrist in the Middle Ages," in *The Use and Abuse of Eschatology in the Middle Ages*, Werner Verbeke, Daniel Verhelst, and Andries Welkenhuysen, eds. (Leuven: University Press, 1988), 1–48; "Awaiting the End: Research in Medieval Apocalypticism, 1974–81," *Medievalia et Humanistica*, NS 11 (1982): 263–89; *Apocalyptic Spirituality* (New York: Paulist Press, 1979); "Apocalypticism in the Middle Ages: An Historiographical Sketch," *Mediaeval Studies* 37 (1975): 155–73; and "St Bernard and Eschatology" in *Bernard of Clairvaux, Studies Presented to Dom Jean Leclercq* (Washington D.C.: Cistercian Publications, 1973), 163–85.

7. McGinn, *Visions of the End*, 27, drawing from Auguste Luneau, *L'Histoire du salut chez les pères de l'église: La doctrine des âges du monde*, Théologie Historique, vol. 2 (Paris: Beauchesne, 1964), 12–14.

8. McGinn's *Visions of the End* provides a comprehensive introduction, and is recommended for further reading. This and his later works contain extensive bibliographies of original and secondary sources.
9. McGinn, *Visions of the End*, 88.
10. See, for example, Henri Focillon, *The Year 1000* (New York: Harper and Row, 1971).
11. Bear in mind McGinn's argument in *Visions of the End*, 88 and see note 13 below. A new form of apocalypticism may have been a part of the developing theology in the reformed Church when Urban II preached the crusade, and as we have seen, Guibert and Ekkehard thought it important to include such references in their writings. See note 19.
12. Kahl, "Crusade Eschatology," 39.
13. McGinn, *Visions of the End*, 91, translated by McGinn from RHC 4, *Gesta Dei per Francos*, IV, at 138G-39B: "Et est vobis prætera summa deliberatione pensandum, si ipsam matrem ecclesiarum ecclesiam, vobis elaborantibus, ad Christianitatis cultum reflorere, Deo per vos agente, contigerit, ne forte contra propinqua Antichristi tempora ad fidem partes Orientis aliquas restitui velit. Perspicuum namque est, Antichristum, non contra Judæos, non contra gentiles bella facturum; sed juxta etymologiam sui nominis, Christianos pervasurum. Et, si Antichristus Ibidem Christianorum neminem, sicuti hodie vix aliquis habetur, inveniat, non erit qui sibi refragetur, [...] Si ergo piorum præliorum exercitio studeatis, ut sicut ab Iherosolimis Dei notitiæ seminarium accepistis, ita propagetur, quod Antichristi Antichristianorumque perfidiæ refragetur [...]."
14. Michael Camille, *The Gothic Idol* (Cambridge: University Press, 1989, rep. 1992), 143–45, the original text being found in Auctore Radulfo Cadomensi, *Gesta Tancredi in Expeditione Hierosolymitana*, ch. 129, RHC 3, pp. 695E-96A:

"Stabat in excelso simulacrum fusile throno,
Scilicet argentum grave, cui vix sena ferendo
Dextera sufficiat fortis, vi dena levando.
Hoc ubi Tancredus prospectat : 'Proh pudor! inquit.
'Quid sibi vult præsens, quæ stat sublimis, imago?
'Quid sibi vult hæc effiges? quid gemma? quid aurum?
'Quid sibi vult ostrum?» Nam gemmis totus etostro
Mahummet redimitus erat, radiabat et auro.
'Forsitan hoc Martis vel Appollinis est simulacrum:
'Numquid enim Christus? non hic insignia Christi,
'Non crux, non serttum, non clavi, non latus haustum.
'Ergo neque hic Christus: quin pristinus Antichristus,
'Mahummet pravus, Mahummet perniciosus.
'O si hujus socius nunc afforet, ille futurus!
'Jam meus hic ambos pes supprimat Antichristos.
'Proh pudor! arce Dei potitur conviva baratri;
'Vernaque Plutonis Deus est operi Salomonis!
'Corruat ergo citus, jam dudm corruat iste!
'Statne superbus adhuc quasi non quoque sorpserit ipse?' [...]"

The account then records how such a vile object could be made precious again by simply melting it down. Apparently the taint of sin was washed away. Modern observers might comment that this was a convenient exercise for crusaders desiring booty; the medieval mind would probably merely have seen it as a blessing from God. There remains the problem of the very unlikely situation of what an idol would have been doing in a mosque, a highly improbable object to be found there. It was possibly a piece of antique Roman statuary found elsewhere (as Camille suggests at 144), or perhaps the story was a fabrication of the chronicler, eager to support the popular notion of Muslims as idol worshippers. Lucy-Anne Hunt comments in "Excommunicata Generatione," at 82–3: [descriptions of the presence of idols in a mosque] "surely draw on the memory of the defeat of Jerusalem's pagan past, read afresh to reassert Christianity's symbols in the face of the 'pagan idol.' [...] In adopting this rhetoric of the overthrow of pagan idols Ralph would not be referring directly to a real statue, as these had been removed in the fourth century and in any case would not be permitted within the Islamic enclosure of the mosque. Instead he brings his own description up to date. [...] Ralph of Caen satisfies his audience's expectations by appealing to what his readers already knew."

15. For a discussion of the crusaders' belief in Muslims as idol worshippers, see John Tolan, "Muslims as Pagan Idolaters in Chronicles of the First Crusade," in *Western Views of Islam in Medieval and Early Modern Europe: Perception of Other*, Michael, Frassetto and David R. Blanks, eds. (New York: St. Martin's Press, 1999), 99–117.

16. There certainly were theologians who wrote in support of such ideas. McGinn, in *Visions*, includes a translation of a selection by Guibert of Nogent, 91–2, from his *Gesta Dei per Francos* (RHC 4, 138–9), a work whose very title shows the political and religious beliefs prevailing at the time. Guibert's argument centers around the notion that the retaking of Jerusalem is indeed a prelude to the end time, as Antichrist will come to wage war against Christians in the Holy Land, a condition that until recently had not been met.

17. McGinn, *Visions of the End*, 89, and in his *The Crusades* (Morristown, NJ: General Learning Press, 1973).

18. McGinn, *Visions of the End*, 89.

19. Ibid. McGinn argues against this point on the basis of questionable evidence, despite the testimony of Guibert of Nogent and Ekkehard of Aura to the contrary. Ekkehard, whilst not speaking specifically in apocalyptic tones, nevertheless uses the imagery of various "signs" in the sky and on earth, a popular theme in apocalyptic writings. In chapter ten of his *Hierosolymita*, he writes: "Præterea signum in sole, quod præscriptum est, visum, multaque quæ tam in aere, quam in terris portenta apparuerunt, ad hujusmodi exercitia non paucos antea torpidos excitaverunt, e quibus aliqua hic interseri duximus utilissimum, cuncta vero longissimum." RHC 5, at 18B-C. He goes on to describe comets, stars changing position in the sky, blood-red clouds arising and rushing toward each other, and fires and sparks in the night sky, as well as signs of the cross appearing on bodies and clothes, 18–19. Guibert's comments on the Antichrist are detailed in McGinn, *Visions*, 143, and *f.* 21. McGinn points out that both wrote after the event, when it would have been easy to read such ideals into the movement. A more recent survey by Hans-Dietrich Kahl argues the opposite point, see note 21.

20. Hans-Dietrich Kahl, "Crusade Eschatology as Seen by St. Bernard in the Years 1146 to 1148," in *The Second Crusade and the Cistercians*, 39.

21. Ibid. Kahl is more inclined to trust the writings of Ekkhard than McGinn, and gives an extensive reference at 46, *f.* 22, of an extraordinary event in 1117 at the cathedral of Liège during the vigil of Ascension Day. Ekkehard relates how an amazing thunderstorm broke out, and all assembled believed that it was a clear sign that the end had come. Apparently three people died of excitement. When the storm subsided, the error in judgement became clear. *Ekkehardi Chronica*, ed. and trans. Franz-Josef Scmalle and Irene Schmale-Ott (Darmstadt: Wissenschaftliche Buchgesellschaft, 1972), Rescensio IV. Such miscalculations did little to stem the speculation of the seemingly eternally watchful and determined apocalypticists.

22. Jay Rubenstein, *Armies of Heaven*. He notes, for example, at xiii: "Despite the abundance of evidence, the apocalyptic crusade has not received its due, in part because historians mistrust our best and most abundant evidence for it: a collection of chronicles written by churchmen in France and Germany starting around the year 1107. Apocalyptic language permeates these books, but among all the available evidence, they have usually held a position of secondary importance." Housley is not as convinced that apocalyptic fears played such a significant role initially, see *Contesting the Crusades*, 12.

23. Ibid., xvi.

24. Rubenstein, "How Much to Reevaluate Peter the Hermit," 61, noting that Guibert of Nogent makes insulting reference to this, the inference being that he was not much of a true ascetic: "Lanea tunica ad purpum, cucullo super, birro desuper utebatur, brachis minime, nudipes autem; pane vix aut numquam, vino alebatur ac pisce." Guibert, *Gesta Dei per Francos,* RHC 4, 113–263 (1879), 121.

25. Rubenstein, *Armies of Heaven*, 12–15. See also, Rubenstein, "How Much to Reevaluate Peter the Hermit," 54–55, drawing from Albert's account, who credits Peter with essentially initiating the crusade, see Albert of Aachen, *Historia Hierosolymitana*. RHC 4, 265–713, (1879).

26. Rubenstein, *Armies of Heaven*, 159.

27. Ibid., 264–66, where he also discusses the problems associated with the "last emperor," who must relinquish his power, something these crusaders seemed unlikely to do.

28. Ibid., 28.

29. Rubenstein, "How Much to Reevaluate Peter the Hermit," 62–63, drawing from Guibert: "[...] et iuxta eundem prophetam tres reges, Egypti videlicet, Africae ac Ethiopiae, haud dubium quin pro christiana fide, primos interficiat. Quod quidem nullatenus fieri poterit, nisi ubi nunc paganismus est Christianitas fiat." Guibert, *Gesta*, 114.

30. Ibid., 45–47. See also Rubenstein, "How Much to Reevaluate Peter the Hermit," 60–61, where he discusses how Guibert sneered sarcastically at many of these so-called miracles. There was clearly room for healthy skepticism even in those times.

31. Rubenstein mentions, however, that crusader Raymond of Aguilers was still using apocalyptic imagery in describing the post-crusade battle of Ascalon, which allowed the Frankish forces to beat back the Egyptian Fatimids and consolidate their power. He described it in very final terms, and made use of many classic apocalyptic tropes: earthquakes, a comet, new suns appearing to either side of the existing sun, etc. See *Armies of Heaven*, 310–11.

32. Norman Housley, drawing on the work of Jean Flori, suggests that it may have been the main viewpoint of at least certain groups on the First Crusade, see *Fighting for the Cross: Crusading to the Holy Land* (New Haven: Yale University Press, 2008), 197–98. For those who followed preachers such as Peter the Hermit, this was certainly true.

33. Ibid., 198.

34. McGinn, *Visions*, 88.

35. The phrase "Sibylline Prophecy" derives from the concept of the Sibylline Oracles, a class of female seers originating in Asia Minor, whose responses to questions came in the form of riddles. The name likely derives from the Greek ὑ Θεοβύλη, signifying "one who announces the counsels or plans of the gods," E. Des Places, "Sibylline Oracles," *New Catholic Encyclopedia*, 15 vols. (Washington D.C.: Catholic University, 1967), vol. 13, 190. Popular in Greece, particularly at Del-

phi, a form of prophecy also developed within the Judeo-Christian tradition, as early as the Maccabeean period (second century BCE). It was this tradition that came to be used by medieval theologians in apocalyptic exegesis. Des Places notes, for example: "The author of the great medieval sequence, the Dies irae, will place the Sibyl beside David (Teste David cum Sibylla), and she will be honored, [...] for having foretold not only the Last Judgement, but also the coming of our Savior," 190. The tradition seems to have been taken up by the Christians in the second century. See McGinn, *Visions*, 19–21, who also provides translations of selections of the Tiburtine Sibyl, 43–50.

36. Rubesntein in "How Much to Reevaluate Peter the Hermit," 63, suggests that Guibert either did not know about the Sibylline prophecies, or otherwise had no use for them.

37. Kenneth Baxter Wolf, "Muammad as Antichrist in Ninth-Century Córdoba," in *Christians, Muslims, and Jews in Medieval and Early Modern Spain: Interaction and Cultural Change*, ed. Mark D. Meyerson and Edward English (Notre Dame, IN: University of Notre Dame Press, 2000), 6.

38. PL 121, 535C-36B. A good account of this event is by Kenneth Baxter-Wolf, *Christian Martyrs in Muslim Spain* (Cambridge and New York: Cambridge University Press, 1988), which examines Eulogius' life and motivations. See also his article in its entirety, cited in note 37 above. Other studies include Ann Christys, *Christians in Al-Andalus, 711–1000* (Richmond, Surrey: Curzon Press, 2002); Dominique Millet-Gérard, *Chrétiens mozarabes et culture islamique dans l'Espagne des VIIIe— IXe siècles* (Paris: Études augustiniennes, 1984); and Roger Collins, *Early Medieval Spain: Unity in Diversity, 400–1000* (London: Macmillan, 1983). Alvarus' writings are contained in PL 121, 387–566, and Eulogius' in PL 115, 703–940. See also Chapter 7.

39. New Living Translation of the Bible. "Et sermones contra Excelsum loquetur, et sanctos Altissimi conteret [which, to Alvaro, the Muslims had most certainly done] [...] et tradentur in manu eius usque ad tempus, et tempora, et dimidium temporis." Daniel 7:25, *Biblia Vulgata*, 862. See Bernard McGinn, *Antichrist*, 86–87, for additional biblical references.

40. R.W. Southern, *Western Views*, 24.

41. "Quæ omnia historice, et proprie Porfirius in Antiocho posnit. Nostri vero in Antioco typice, et verius in Antichristo, et rectius specialiter posuere. Nos tamen in hunc nostri temporis damnati hominis præcursorem ex parte dicimus convenire. Nam in undenario numero surgens, qui Scriptoris sanctis semper infaustus est, tria regna perdomuit, dum Græcorum, Francorum, quæ sub nomine Romanorum vigebant, provincias occupavit, et Gothorum Occidentalium cola vitriciplanta calcavit: vel dum decalogum, hoc est, universalem religionem, et numerum, qui plerumque pro toto inseritur, dissipare conavit, et contra fidem Trinitatis, spe, fide, charitate munitam, superbire tentavit. Contra Deum excelsum sermones petulanti contumacia fabricans, grandia trutinans, et fumosa illa contexens, quæ vere Antichristo sunt prævia, et humili religioni nostræ satis adversa. [...] Jam vero tempus, tempora, et dimidium temporis, capiti ejus specialietr injungendum est Antichristo: et requirendum cur non aperte tres annos et medium dixerit, sed obscure vocabulo sermo hujus fuerit divinus, quo solitum est diversum sensum in corda parturire doctorum." *Indiculus Luminosis*, PL 121, 535C-36B.

42. Wolf, "Muḥammad as Antichrist," 14–17. Alan Cutler takes an opposing view in "The Ninth-Century Spanish Martyr's Movement and the Origins of Western Christian Missions to the Muslims." *Muslim World* 55 (1965): 321–29.

43. Southern, *Western Views*, 25.

44. McGinn provides a fine summary of some of the key points in *Visions of the End*, 70–76, and his notes to the section are particularly useful, 301–3.

45. Ibid., 72.

46. Richard Kenneth Emmerson, *Antichrist in the Middle Ages* (Manchester: Manchester University Press, 1981), 76.

47. Ibid., 84–5, from McGinn's translation of Adso's *Letter on the Antichrist*. His source is D. Verhelst, ed. *Adso Dervensis: De Ortu et Tempore Antichristi*, CCCM 45 (Turnhout: Brepols, 1976), 22–23. This was a popular and ancient theme among theologians, and may have had its origins within Judaism itself.

48. Emmerson, *Antichrist in the Middle Ages*, 77.

49. McGinn, in *Visions of the End*, includes some useful summary material of their works, at 95–107. Gerhoh was later to condemn the Second Crusade and its outcome as a deception by the devil.

50. James Kritzeck, *Peter the Venerable and Islam*, 145, drawing from the *Summa Totius Hæresis Saracenorum*, his own transcription, 204–10: "Summa uero huius heresis intentio est, ut Christus Dominus neque Deus, neque Dei filius esse credatur, sed licet magnus Deoque dilectus, homo tamen purus, et uir quidem sapiens, et propheta maximus. Quae quidem olim diaboli machinatione concepta, primo per Arrium seminata, deinde per istum Sathanan scilicet Mahumet, prouecta, per Antichristum uero, ex toto secundum diabolicam intentionem complebitur. [...] merito impiissimus Mahumeth inter utrumque medius a diabolo prouisus ac preparatus esse uidetur, qui et Arrii quodammodo supplementum, et Antichristi peiora dicturi, apud infidelium mentes maximum fieret nutrimentum," 208–9.

51. Ibid., translation at121–3, original text at 204–5.

52. Ibid., 123. Original text at 204–5: "Sic enim docuit eos miserrimus atque impiissimus Mahumet, qui omnia sacramenta Christianae pietatis, quibus maxime homines sauantur, abnegans, iam pene terciam humani generis partem, nescimus quo Dei iudicio, inauditis fabularum deliramentis, diabolo et morti aeternae contradidit."

53. Ibid., 149, text at 210: "Quod quare illi permissum sit, ille solus nouit cui nemo potest dicere, 'Cur ita facis?' et qui 'de multis etiam uocatis, paucos electos esse' dixit. Vnde ego magis eligens contresmiscere, quam disputare, itsta breuiter prenotaui [...]"

54. Ibid., 265: "Vt sicut dicere caeperam cogitetis et recogitetis non solum illos quos praemisi paganos, non solum Iudaeos, non solum Christianos hereticos, sed etiam uos potuisse falli, potuisse decepi, potuisse tenebras pro luce, falsum pro uero, seductorem pro propheta, et ut Iudaei circa mundi finem facturi sunt, Antichristum pro Christo suscipere."

55. Cutler, "Peter the Venerable and Islam," 193.

56. See, for example, his *Epistolae*, nos. 124–27, 336, and 338, *Opera* VIII.

57. McGinn, *Visions of the End*, 109. See also Flanagan, "Twelfth-Century Apocalyptic Imaginations," at 61–62.

58. Kahl, "Crusade Eschatology," 36, and f. 7, at 45: [Pseudo-] Alcuin, in Adso, *De ortu*, 125: "Sicut ex sibyllinis libris habemus, tempore predicti regis, cuius nomen erit C. rex Romanorum totius imperii [...]"

59. Kahl, "Crusade Eschatology," 36.

60. Ibid., 38. Kahl further notes that Bernard resisted placing an absolute time on the approaching end (much like the Church Fathers), and did not necessarily feel that it was imminent.

61. McGinn, "St Bernard and Eschatology," 169–70. See also Flanagan, "Twelfth-Century Apocalyptic Imaginations," 57–58, where she discusses Bernard's apparent disagreement with St. Norbert (founder of the Premonstratensian order) about whether the Antichrist was already alive in the world. Norbert believed this, but Bernard seemed to disagree, though, as Flanagan points out, his response is ambiguous.

62. Ibid., 184.

63. Rubenstein, *Armies of Heaven*, pp. 323–24.

64. Ibid., 318.

Chapter 7

1. See Chapter 3.

2. Norman Daniel, *Islam and the West* (Edinburgh: University Press, 1960, rep. 1980), 315

3. Housley, *Contesting the Crusades*, 16. See also his comments in *Fighting for the Cross*, 188–89, where he notes that the idea was "a grass-roots phenomenon," at 189.

4. Riley-Smith, *The First Crusade and the Idea of Crusading* (London: Athlone Press, 1986, revised 2009), 72–74.

5. The early twelfth-century vernacular poem, *Song of Roland* is an example of such use. Though not concerned with crusading, it features Moors as villains, and refers at one point to those who die at the hands of the Saracens dying the deaths of martyrs, in Archbishop Turpin's address to the barons (LXXXIX, 1133–35):

"I will absolve you to save your souls,
If you die, you'll be holy martyrs,
You'll have seats in highest Paradise"
"A soldrai vos pur vos anmes guarir,
Se vos murez, esterez seinz martirs,
Sieges avrez el greignor pareïs"

Gerard J. Brault, *The Song of Roland, An Analytical Edition*, 2 vols. (University Park and London: Pennsylvania State University Press, 1978), 2, 73.

6. H.E.J. Cowdrey, "Martyrdom and the First Crusade," in *Crusade and Settlement*, ed. Peter W. Edbury (Cardiff: University College Cardiff Press, 1985), 46–56.

7. Ibid., 53.

8. Bernard's numerous comments on the Templars, for example, in Chapter 3.

9. A good work on this topic is Jessica A. Coope, *The Martyrs of Córdoba, Community and Family Conflict in an Age of Mass Conversion* (Lincoln and London: University of Nebraska Press, 1995), a fine short summary of the whole affair that analyzes the social backgrounds of the Christian and Muslim communities, culture, race, and religious beliefs. Other recent accounts and studies of this event have been cited in Chapter 6, note 38.

10. Cutler believes that the account had an influence on Peter's anti-Islamic writings, particularly in their apocalyptic content. See "Peter the Venerable," 193. He also argues for the movement's influence on later medieval Christian missionary efforts to Islam in "The Ninth-Century Spanish Martyrs' Movement and the Origins of Western Christian Missions to the Muslims," *Muslim World* 55 (1965): 321–39.

11. Daniel, *Islam and the West*, 5–6. See also 181 of this chapter.

12. Eulogius claimed to have found the Life in a monastery of Leyre near Pamplona in Navarre, see his *Liber Apologeticus Martyrum*, cap. 15, PL 115, 859B. Though it was based on similar writings from Byzantine sources, it was given Western characteristics as well, as Southern notes: "It was clearly a Spanish product because its symbolism depends on the use of the chronological era of Spain, which was 38 years in advance of the normal reckoning." *Western Views*, 24.

13. Written by a monk of Saint Germain-des-Prés, see Cutler, "Martyrs' Movement," p. 334, citing B. de Gaiffer, "Les notices hispaniques dans le Martyrologe d'Usuard," *Analecta Bollandiana* 55 (1937): 268–83.

14. Cutler, "Martyr's Movement," 334.

15. Ibid.

16. Ibid., 335. For instance, Cutler notes that both Eulogius and Hugh record that Muhammad was led astray and deceived by the Devil, who spoke with a "golden mouth" (*os aureum*). Eulogius, *Liber Apologeticus Martyrum*, PL 115, 859D, and Hugh, *Chronicon*, I, MGH Scriptores 8, p. 323, 36. Apparently, no other writer between the two used this description, allowing for the probability that Hugh knew of Eulogius' works.

17. Norman Daniel, *The Arabs and Medieval Europe* (London and Beirut: Longman, 1975), 23. He devotes an entire chapter to this affair, which is a good survey of events, 23–48. Cutler also provides an excellent historical and social background in "Martyr's Movement," 321–24.

18. A detailed account of the status of the Peoples of the Book under Islamic rule is given in Bat Ye'or, *The Dhimmi: Jews and Christians under Islam* (Rutherford: Fairleigh Dickinson University Press, London: Associated University Presses, 1985). It discusses the many restrictions and conditions that Muslims placed on protected religious minorities over the centuries. Indeed, there were many occasions where they considered Christians and Jews as little more than slaves.

19. Qur'an 9:29: "Fight against such of those who have been given the Scripture as believe not in Allah nor the Last Day, and forbid not that which Allah hath forbidden by his Messenger, and follow not the religion of truth, until they pay the tribute readily, being brought low." *The Meaning of the Glorious Qur'an*, trans. M.M. Pickthall (London: Ta-Ha Publishers, 1930), 147–8.

20. Roger Collins, *Early Medieval Spain* (London: Macmillan, 1983), 214.

21. John, however, was not executed, but rather imprisoned. Baxter Wolf, *Christian Martyrs*, 12, and recorded by Eulogius in his *Memoriale Sanctorum*, 1:9, PL 115, 746C.

22. Baxter Wolf, *Christian Martyrs*, 23–5.

23. Ibid., 25.

24. See also note 9 above, and Chapter 6, note 38, for references.

25. Roger Collins, *Early Medieval Spain*, 216.

26. Joseph F. O'Callaghan, *A History of Medieval Spain* (Ithaca, New York: Cornell University Press, 1975), 110, where he points out, "The council redacted an ambiguous decree forbidding the faithful to court martyrdom, but it did not censure those who had already been executed."

27. This council, the first recorded Church council in Spain, occurred in the first decade of the fourth century, and was characterized by its strict regulations governing the practices of Christians and their relations with non-Christians.

28. Baxter Wolf, *Christian Martyrs*, 72. Eulogius and Alvarus certainly thought this was the case, Coope, *Martyrs*, 25.

29. Baxter Wolf "Earliest Spanish Christian Views," 291 and 293.

30. Daniel, *Arabs and Medieval Europe*, 34–5. It would be inappropriate here to make psychological generalizations, but it is interesting to note such sentiments and to see possible relations to the later crusading ideologies. If martyrdom in this instance was an aggression, a kind of defiant last stand against the perceived enemy, than such motivations probably existed among some crusaders as well.

31. Though this account is relayed by most historians of the movement, Coope provides a good detailed summary of the events surrounding Eulogius' protection of the Christian apostate, *Martyrs*, at 29–30.

32. Collins, *Early Medieval Spain*, 218.

33. Baxter Wolf "Earliest Spanish Christian Views," 291–92.

34. Southern gives a concise summary of this in *Western Views of Islam*, 23–4. A notable section of important text can be found in Chapter 6, note 41.

35. Southern, *Western Views*, 24.

36. Daniel, *Arabs and Medieval Europe*, 39.

37. Benjamin Kedar, *Crusade and Mission*, 9.

38. Ibid., 9–10, quoting from R. Jiménez Pedrajas, "San Eulogio de Córdoba, autor de la Pasión francesca de los mártires mozárabes cordobese Jorge, Aurelio, y Natalia," *Anthologica Annua* 17 (1970): 567–68. The text states: "Ipsos enim solum vident saraceni interimendos, qui relicta eorum secta, vertunt se ad Xpistianam fidem; vel qui blasphemias garriunt adversus legislatorem suum."

39. Ibid.

40. Kedar, *Crusade and Mission*, 10–12. See also Cutler, "Monk of France," regarding possible Cluniac missionary activity to Muslim Spain in the eleventh century.

41. See James Brundage, *Medieval Canon Law and the Crusader* (Madison, Milwuakee, and London: University of Wisconsin Press, 1969), 22. The text of the letter reads: "Omni timore ac terrore deposito contra inimicos sanctæ fidei et adversarios omnium regionum viriliter agere studete. Item. Ubi usque nunc parentes vestri publicum moverunt procinctum semper victores extiterunt, nullaque eos multitudo populi superare potuit. Non enim audivimus, ut aliquando sine fama victoriæ reversi fuissent. Item. Omnium vestrum nosse volumus karitatem, quoniam quisquis (quod non optantes dicimus) in hoc belli certamine fideliter mortuus fuerit, regna illi cælestia minime negabuntur. Novit enim omnipotens, si quislibet vestrum morietur, quod pro veritate fidei et salvatione animæ ac defensione patriæ christianorum

mortuus est, ideo ab eo pretitulatum premium consequetur." *Epistolae selectae Leonis IV*, no. 28 (853), MGH *Epistolarum*, V, 601.

42. Brundage, *Medieval Canon Law*, 22.

43. The full text of the letter reads: "Quia veneranda fraternitas vestra modesta interrogatione sciscitans quæsivit, utrum hi, qui pro defensione sanctæ Dei ecclesiæ, et pro statu Christiane religionis ac rei publicæ in bello nuper ceciderunt aut de reliquo pro eadem re casuri sunt, indulgentiam possint consequi delictorum, audenter Chrisi Dei nostri piætate respondemus, quoniam illi, qui cum pietate catholicæ religionis in belli certamine cadunt, requies eos æternæ vitæ suscipiet contra paganos atque infideles strenue dimicantes, eo quod Dominus per prophetam piet contra paganos atque infideles strenue dimicantes, eo quod Dominus per prophetam dignatus est dicere: "Peccator quacumque hora conversus fuerit, omnium iniquitatum illius non recordabor amplius," et venerabilis ille latro in una confessionis voce de cruce meruit paradysum; Manasses quoque impurissimus quondam rex captus carcerique artissimo religatus ibi penitentiam agens cum perfectione indulgentiæ etiam regni pristini propter Domini misericordiam, quia inmensa est circa genus humanum, adeptus est solium. Nostra prefatos mediocritate, intercessione beati Petri apostloi, cuius potestas ligandi atque solvendi est in cælo et in terra, quantum fas est, absolvimus præcibusque illos Domino commendamus. Optamus fraternitatem vestram in Christo bene valere." Iohannes VIII *Epistolae*, no. 150, 878, MGH *Epistolarum*, VII, 26–7.

44. See Mastnak, *Crusading Peace*, 108–11, where he gives a detailed account of John's very emphatic objections.

45. Brundage, *Medieval Canon Law*, 23.

46. Kedar, *Crusade and Mission*, 15, drawing from the *Vita Argentee et comitum eius martyrum*, ed. A. Fabréga Grau, in *Pasionário hispánico* (*siglos VII-IX*), 2 vols. (Madrid and Barcelona, 1953–55), 2, 382–87. Kedar points out that the account does not specifically say that Vulfra attacked Islam, but the reaction of the Muslim officials in giving him a choice between conversion to Islam or death, make it clear that he must have done so. Indeed, there would have been no other reason for him to journey to Córdoba if he was truly desirous of martyrdom.

47. A. Gieysztor, "The Genesis of the Crusades: The Encyclical of Sergius IV (1009–12)," *Medievalia et Humanistica* 5 (1948): 3–23, and 6 (1950): 3–34, which contains the text of the document.

48. See Cowdrey "Pope Gregory VII and the Bearing of Arms," 34, and *f.* 51.

49. Cowdrey, "Pope Gregory VII and Martyrdom," in *Dei gesta per Francos: Crusade Studies in Honour of Jean Richard*. Ed. M. Balard, Bemjamin Kedar, and Jonathan Riley-Smith (Aldershot: Ashgate, 2001), 4–5. See 5–7 for some specific examples, including the case of Bishop Cyriacus in Carthage, who suffered at the hands of the emir, but did not die. Gregory commended him, but stressed that his suffering would have had even more merit if he had been martyred.

50. Cowdrey gives an excellent summary of the events surrounding this campaign, as well as an edition of the text in "The Mahdia Campaign of 1087," *English Historical Review* 92 (1977): 1–29.

51. Ibid., 6–7.

52. Recall that Gregory had appealed to her for help in his proposed campaign against the Seljuk Turks in 1074, see Chapter 1.

53. *Carmen*, v. 34d: "nam videbat signum sui cum scarsellis populum." Cowdrey, "Mahdia Campaign," 26.

54. Ibid., 22.

55. Ibid., 22–3.

56. *Carmen*, v. 42–46:

42. Hic evenit tibi Pisa magnum infortunium, nam hic perdis capud urbis et coronam iuvenum; cadit Ugo vicecomes omnium pulcherrimus; dolor magnus Pisanorum et planctus miserrimus.

43. Nam cum omnes Saraceni erupissent subito, sustinet hic mille viros cum asta et clippeo; cum nescit cessare loco et recusat fugere, mille cesis Saracenis cadit ante iuvenes.

44. Hic inponunt illum scuto et ad naves deferunt; plangunt omnes super illum quasi unigenitum; O decus et dolor magnus Pisanorum omnium! O confusio triumphi et magnum incommodum!

45. O dux noster atque princeps cum corde fortissimo! similatus rex Grecorum regi nobilissimo, qui sic fecit ut audivit responsum Apollinis; nam ut sui triumpharent sponte mortem subiit.

46. Sic infernus spoliatur et Sathan destruitur, cum Ihesus redemptor mundi sponte sua moritur; pro cuius amore care et cuius servitio, *martyr pulcherrutilabis venturo iudicio*." [my emphasis], Cowdrey, "Mahdia Campaign," 27.

57. *Carmen*, v. 32, 52:

"32. Et excelsi Agareni invocant Machumata, quod conturbavit orbem terre de sua perfidia; inimicus trinitatis atque sancte fidei, negat Ihesum Nazarenum verbum Dei fieri.

52. Alii petunt meschitam pretiosam scemate; mille truncant sacerdotes qui erant Machumate, qui fuit heresiarcha pontentior Arrio, cuius error iam permansit longo mundi spatio."

58. *Carmen*, v. 5ab: "Hic Timinus presidebat saracenus impius, similatus Antichristo draco crudelissimus;"

v. 12b: "[...] suscitatum pro Timini infamimartirio;"

v. 13cd: "cum forte et astuta potenti astutia est confusa, maledicti Timini versutia."

59. Penny J. Cole, *The Preaching of the Crusades to the Holy Land*, 27–30. These pages provide a fine summary of the essence of Hrabanus' conclu-

sions. She also draws some interesting parallels between the martyrs of the early Church and apocalyptic sentiments at 30–32.

60. W.H.C. Frend, *Martyrdom and Persecution in the Early Church: A Study of a Conflict from the Maccabees to Donatus* (Oxford: University Press, 1965), 43.

61. Hrabanus Maurus, *Commentaria in libros Machabaeorum*, PL 109: 1125–1256.

62. The *Legenda Aurea* of Jocobus de Voragine, ed. Th. Graesse (Breslau: Koebner, 1895), which was written in the early thirteenth century, collected a large number of these popular stories of saints' lives and passions together. Sherry Reames notes at 162 of *The Legenda Aurea: A Reexamination of Its Paradoxical History* (Madison: University of Wisonsin Press, 1958), "A number of martyrs are so eager for torture and death that they present themselves before the persecutors instead of waiting to be arrested; at least one of them, Saint Apollonia, actually commits suicide, leaping into the fire that her tormentors have kindled to frighten her." Note the similarity to the eagerness to die in the Martyrs' Movement.

63. Cowdrey, "Martyrdom and the First Crusade," 46–56. This is the central argument of his article, that the idea of martyrdom in connection with fighting the infidel did not actually have much effect in implementing the First Crusade, but rather served as a dramatic form of religious inspiration to those who would read and hear of the deeds of the crusaders later on.

64. Cutler believes that there may have been some direct influence, see "Martyrs' Movement," 338–39.

65. In addition to the sources below, excerpts from these and other authors' writings can be found in translation in *Chronicles of the Crusades*, ed. Elizabeth Hallam (New York: Weidenfeld and Nicolson, 1989). This work provides excerpts from chronicles from the eleventh to the fifteenth centuries. An excellent selection of writings in English translation can be found in Edward Peters, ed., *The First Crusade: The Chronicle of Fulcher of Chartres and Other Source Materials* (Philadelphia: University of Pennsylvania Press, 1971), which includes the various versions of Urban's Clermont speech, and excerpts from the many chronicles of the First Crusade.

66. One may invoke the cliché "absence of evidence is not evidence of absence." In other words, we cannot assume, because of a lack of something (in this case extensive references to martyrs on crusade), that it must not have existed. The references to martyrdom are often in a matter-of-fact manner, as if already accepted, and do not seem to imply something particularly novel. Given that martyrdom had long been important as an ideal in the Church, any such references would have been written with this in mind.

67. Louise and Jonathan Riley-Smith, *The Crusades, Idea and Reality*, 1095–1274 (London: Edward Arnold, 1981), 45. This is an excellent introductory survey, which provides useful translations of many key texts relating to crusade chronicles.

68. Cowdrey, "Martyrdom," 50. Several references are to be found in Guibert's *Gesta Dei per Francos*:

"Tempus huic operæ breve, prospera cuncta fuere,
Quum Deus esset in his: probat optimus omnia finis.
Obtigerit cui mors cum martyre, gloria fit sors.
Quisquis eget taxat, quia crimina poena relaxat." RHC 4, III, p. 158, J-K.

Guibert gives more detail later on:
"Septem hebdomadis tribusque diebus hac sunt obsidione detenti; et ex nostris multi munus Ibidem recepere martyrii. De quibus indubie sententia proferetur; quod qui mortis exitio sese pro fidei objecere justitia, inter eos profecto apud Deum censeantur, qui sanguine in pretium dato præmia meruere coelestia. Nec eos illis impares dixerim qui famis occubuere miseria: hoc enim ibi modo pertiit multitudo perplurima. Si namque juxta Prophetam, quod historialiter dicere liceat, *melius fuit occisis gladio quam interfectis fame*, qui procul dubio cruciatu diuturniore sunt moriendo torti, non erunt, ut credi fas est, absque corona nobiliore martyrii." RHC 4, 159, F-G.

The preface to Book VII invokes the theme again:
"Fidei nostræ incentivum non minimum præbet quod Occidentalium labore fidelium Orientalis restauratur Ecclesia. Videmus prælia , solius intentione Dei piisima, quorum tota efferbuit martyrii amore militia: sine rege, sine principe, sola eis extitit suæ ipsorum salutis devotio prævia. [...]

"[...] Hic, inquam, libet Deum pensare mirabilem: ut qui quondam ad tromenta ferenda animos martyrum, pro invisibilium dilectione, firmaverit, ipse nostris temporibus, quod a nemine sperari poterat et dictum pro ridiculo habebatur [...]" RHC 4, 221A, C.

69. Riley-Smith, *The First Crusade and the Idea of Crusading* (London: Athlone Press, 1993), 46, drawing from Guibert, *Gesta*: "Indebita hactenus bella gessistis; in mutuas cædes vesana aliquotiens tela, solius cupiditatis ac superbiæ causa, torsistis: ex quo perpetuos interitus et certa damnationis exitia meruistis. Nunc vobis bella proponimus quæ in se habent gloriosum martyrii munus, quibus restat præsentis et æternæ laudis titulus." RHC 4, p. 138E. The complete speech is given at 137–40.

70. Riley-Smith, *The First Crusade and the Idea of Crusading*, 152.

71. Ibid., 151–52. Section XVIII, the last of Book Four of Guibert's *Gesta* is devoted to this story, which is too lengthy to be included in its

entirety here. After proclaiming him to be a martyr, and describing at length his last words in which he refused apostasy, Guibert concludes: "His dictis, gladio imminenti subjectum protendit jugulum, et, cæso capite, transmittitur ad eum cujus similitudini mortis inhiaverat, Deum. Is vocabatur Matthæus: vere, juxta interpretationem sui nominis, non alii quam Deo donatus." RHC 4, 184C.

72. Riley-Smith, *First Crusade*, 152.

73. Cowdrey, "Martyrdom and the First Crusade," 50. Robert devotes a short chapter to this theme in his *Historia Iheroslimitana*: "Tandem princeps illorum, Rainaldus, cum Turcis furtivum iniit foedus, malens temporalem vitam retinere, quam pro Christo mortem in tali martyrio subire. Dispositis itaque agminibus suis, simulavit cum adversariis inire congressionem; sed mox, ut exiit, fecit ad illos cum multis aliis digressionem. Heu! heu! meticulosis miles, non ab Austro, sed ab Aquilone progressus, quam enerviter et effeminate pro coelesti et rege et regno dimicavit, qui necdum vel levistipula tactis, martyrium subire perhorruit, et fidei Christianæ professionem, sanus, eques et armatus, abdicavit. Jure igitur apud Deum evanescentis gratiæ jacturam promeruit, et in sortem illius qui sedem suam elegit ad Aquilonem devenit. Qui vero remanserunt, nec Christianæ fidei titulum mutare voluerunt, mortis exterminum subierunt." RHC 3, cap. IX, 721–882, and 734A-C.

74. Hallam, *Chronicles of the Crusades*, p. 90. For a recent translation of the account, see Carol Sweetenham, *Robert the Monk's History of the First Crusade, Historia Iheroslimitana* (Aldershot: Ashgate), 2005.

75. Riley-Smith, *The First Crusade and the Idea of Crusading*, 42.

76. Ibid., 49.

77. Ibid., 52, drawing from the *Historia Jerosolimitana*: "Pulchrum sit vobis mori in illa civitate pro Christo, in qua Christus pro vobis mortuus est. Ceterum si vos citra mori contigerit, id ipsum autumate mori in via, si tamen in sua Christus vos invenerit militia." RHC 4, 1, 15B.

78. Cowdrey, "Martyrdom and the First Crusade," 50.

79. See, for example, chapter XXIV of his *Historia Hierosolimitana*, where at the close he states: "[...] adeo ut, sicut hi pro vero affirmant qui præsentes vix evaserunt, exstinctis et occisis corporibus et sanguine tota planities Belegravæ occuparentur, et pauci ab hoc martyrio liberarentur." RHC 4, 291E. Chapter 33 states at its close: "Hac itaque adinventione aptata, dixerit nuncios ad præfatos principes, in circuitu Gibel jam per ebdomadam residentes, quatenus sibi festinato ad auxilium Archas properarent, alioquin se et confratres, qui secum erant, a facie Gentilium non posse mortis evadere periculum, eosque dehinc simile sperare posse martyrium." 453G. More information, and a good bibliography concerning Albert, can be found in Peter Koch, *Studien zu Albert von Aachen Der erste Kreuzzug in der Deutschen Chronistik* (Stuttgart: Ernst Klett Verlag, 1966).

80. Riley-Smith, *The First Crusade and the Idea of Crusading*, 114–15.

81. Ibid., 67.

82. Ibid., 117.

83. Rubenstein devotes considerable attention to Peter, his visions, and the Holy Lance, with a suitably skeptical eye, as many of the crusaders then also had. See *Armies of Heaven*, 156–58, 216–18, and 257–62.

84. Ibid., 117–18. A particularly notable account of this is given by Ralph of Caen, who, unlike the others mentioned here journeyed to the Holy Land after the crusade. He writes in his *Gesta Tancredi in Expeditione Hierosolymitana* of the words delivered by the ghost: "Hi sunt Hierosolimipetæ, qui viam Dei, in quam adhuc et tu laboras, ab initio aggressi, rebus humanis excesserunt et meruerunt habere coronas perpetuas: tu quoque in proximo, ne forte invideas, ad nos conscendes: bonum enim certamen certavisti, et cursum consumasti." RHC 3, Cap. CLI, 681C-D. The account leaves no doubt as to his fate: "illuc corpus reportant cum lacrymis unde modo gaudentes exierant: spiritus ad beatitudinem ascendit promissam." 681F. Raymond of Aguilers records a similar story, a good English translation of which is John Hugh Hill and Laurita L. Hill, trans., *Raymond D'Aguilers, Historia Francorum Qui Ceperunt Iherusalem* (Philadelphia: American Philosophical Society, 1968). The full accounts are given in his *Liber*, RHC 3, Cap. XIII, 261–66, and XVII, 279–82.

85. Riley-Smith, *The First Crusade and the Idea of Crusading*, 118.

86. Rubenstein, *Armies of Heaven*, 313–14, drawing from RHC Oc. 5, 307–08.

87. Rubenstein, *Armies of Heaven*, 255–62.

88. Ibid., 211–12.

89. *Praise of the New Knighthood*, 130, *De laude*, 215: "Ceterum in bello tanto profecto pretiosior, quanto et gloriosior."

90. "Sed quia non est consilium nec prudentia contra Deum [Prov. 21:30], elegerunt viam per Graeciam morituri." Odo of Deuil, *De profectione Ludovici VII in orientem*, ed. and trans. Virginia Berry (New York: Columbia University Press, 1948), 14–15.

91. Ibid., xiv, f. 7.

92. Ibid., 118–19. "Sed mori dominos ut servi viverent esset lugendum commercium nisi tale dedisset exemplum Dominus omnium. Marcescunt flores Franciae antequam frunstum faciant in Damasco. Quo relatu suffundor lacrimis, et de visceribus intimis ingemisco. De hoc tamen potest mens sobria tali remedio consolari, quod haec eorum probitas et anterior mundo convivet et finis, correptis erratibus fide fervida, martyrio

meruit coronari." See also Purkis, *Crusading Spirituality*, 81.

93. Previously used to denote a "dark" period of time due to a lack of written records, this is now considered an anachronistic phrase in current scholarship, owing to the different levels of advancement to be found throughout Europe from the fall of Rome to the time of Charlemagne, and our increased understanding of the times.

94. A scan of the pages of *Praise of the New Knighthood* or *De laude* will reveal the numerous examples of scripture-citing that Bernard used. He cites many passages that seem to make points that the modern reader might think have little to do with the original biblical quotation. An example would be a quote from Chapter 1 of *De laude*, wherein Bernard states: "Nam si BEATI QUI IN DOMINO MORIUNTUR, non multo magis qui pro Domino moriuntur?" at 215. The capitalized quote is drawn from Revelation 14:13. Since medieval theologians believed that the events described in Revelation were yet to occur, this is a statement for the future, not for Bernard's time. In fact, this phrase has nothing to do with war, *per se*. However, if Bernard was envisioning the Christian/Muslim conflict in terms of apocalyptic confrontation, this might perhaps be a valid reference. His words do not indicate at this point that he is doing so, but it seems likely. He uses a quote from Psalm 115 a few lines later, in a similar manner. This style of interpretation is found in Gregory VII's interpretation of *compelle intrare*, discussed in Chapter 1. See also the discussion on medieval biblical interpretation in Chapter 3.

95. See Chapter 3. Purkis, *Crusading Spirituality*, 107–08 discusses the use of John 15:13 in relation to the Templar *imitatio Christi*.

96. There is, of course the reference in II Timothy 2:5, which states: "Nam et qui certat in agone, non coronatur nisi legitime certaverit," used by Hrabanus and others. The notion of a legitimate battle or competition is at the heart of the justification of crusading. The passage can, of course, be translated as either a military or athletic reference, a curious double meaning that was also employed by the Spanish martyrs in the ninth century. They were "athletes" for the cause of God.

Bibliography

Select Manuscripts

Anonymous Works

Carmen in victoram Pisanorum. Brussels: Bibliothèque royale Albert Ier, MS 3879–919, f. 3^r-65^v.

Christi militibus in Templo Iehrosolimitano. Nîmes: Benedictine Abbey of St Giles, MS 37, f. 169^v-172^v. Also contains *De laude* and the Templar Rule.

Attributed Works

Petrus Alfonsi. *Dialogi.* Dijon: Bibliothèque municipale, MS 228.

———. *Dialogi.* Douai: Bibliothèque municipale, MS 199.

Peter the Venerable. *Adversus Iudeorum inveteratam duritiem.* Douai: Bibliothèque municipale, MS 199.

Robert of Ketton, and the Annotator. *Liber legis Saracenorum quem Alcoran vocant.* Paris: Bibliothèque de l'Arsenal, MS lat. 1162. Part of the *Corpus toledanum*.

Primary Sources

An Account of the Pilgrimage of Saewulf to Jerusalem and the Holy Land in the Years 1102 and 1103. Translated by W.R.B. Brownlow. London: Bishop of Clifton, 1892.

Adso Dervensis. *De Ortu et Tempore Antichristi.* Edited by D. Verhelst. CCCM 45. Turnhout: Brepols, 1976.

Albert of Aachen. *Historia Hierosolymitana.* RHC 4, 265–713, 1879.

———. *Historia Hierosolymitana.* Edited and translated by Susan B. Edgington. Oxford: Oxford University Press, 2007.

Alfonso X, El Sabio. *Cantigas de Santa Maria.* Edited by Walter Mettman. 3 vols. Madrid: Clásicos Castalia, 1986–89.

Annales Herbipolenses A. 1145–1147. MGH, *Scriptores*. 1–12. Hannover: Hahn, 1859.

Anselm of Havelberg. *Dialogi. Lib.* I. PL 188, 1139–1248.

Anselm of Lucca. *Collectio Canonica.* PL 149, 486–536.

Augustine of Hippo. *Augustine: The City of God Against the Pagans.* Translated by Demetrius B. Zenna, SJ, and Gerard Walsh, SJ. 7 vols. *Fathers of the Church.* Washington D.C.: Catholic University of America Press, Consortium Books, 1951.

———. *Augustine: Commentary on the Sermon on the Mount, Fathers of the Church.* Translated by Denis J. Kavanagh, OSA. Washington, D.C.: Catholic University of America Press, Consortium Books, 1951.

———. *The City of God Against the Pagans.* 7 vols. Translated by William Chase Green, parallel Latin and English texts. Cambridge, Massachusetts: Harvard University Press, 1960.

———. *De Civitate Dei.* PL 41, 13–804.

———. *Enarratio in Ps.* PL 37, 1055–1968.

———. *Quaestiones in Heptateuchum.* CCSL 33, 1–377. Turnhout: Brepols, 1958.

———. *De sermone Domini* I. Edited by Almut Mutzenbecher. CCSL 35. Turnhout: Brepols, 1967.

Baldric of Bourgueil. *Historia Jeroslimitana.* RHC Oc. 4, 1–111, 1879.

Bernard of Clairvaux. *Five Books of Consideration: Advice to a Pope,* Cistercian Fathers 13. Translated by John D. Anderson and Elizabeth T. Keenan. Kalamazoo: Cistercian Publications, 1976.

———. *The Letters of Bernard of Clairvaux.* Translated by Bruno Scott James. London: Burns and Oates,1953.

———. *Opera.* PL 182–85 (bis).

———. *Opera Omnia.* Edited by J. Leclercq, Ch.

Talbot, and H.M. Rochais. 8 vols. Rome: Editiones Cistercienses, 1957–77.

———. *In Praise of the New Knighthood*. Translated by Conrad Greenia; intro. R.J. Zwi Werblowski. *The Works of Bernard of Clairvaux*. Vol. 7: Treatises III. Cistercian Fathers Series 19B. Kalamzoo, MI: Cistercian Publications, 1977, revised 2000.

Berengar. *Apologia pro Petro Abælardo*. PL 178, 1857–70.

Biblia Sacra Juxta Vulgatam Clementiam. Edited by Alberto Colunga and Laurentio Turrado, 7th ed. Madrid: Biblioteca de Autores Cristianos, 1985.

Bullarium Ordinis Militae de Calatrava. Madrid: A. Marin, 1761.

Cartulaire général de l'Ordre du Temple. Edited by Marquis d'Albon, 2 vols. Paris: E. Champion, 1913

Chronicles of the Crusades. Edited by Elizabeth Hallam. New York: Weidenfeld and Nicholson, 1989.

Corpus scriptorum muzarabicorum. Edited by Juan Gil, 2 vols. Madrid: Instituto "Antonio de Nebrija," 1973.

La documentación pontífica hasta Inocencio III (965–1216). Edited by D. Mansilla. *Monumenta Hispaniae Vaticana*, registros 1, Rome: Instituto Español de Estudios Eclesiasticos 1955.

Ekkehard. *Ekkehardi Chronica. Frutolfs und Ekkehards Chroniken und die anonyme Kaiserchronik*, 267–334. Edited and translated by Franz-Josef Schmale and Iren Schmale-Ott. Ausgewählte Quellen zur deutschen Geschichte des Mittelalters, 15. Darmstadt: Wissenschaftliche Buchgesellschaft, 1972.

———. *Hierosolymitana: De oppressione, liberatione, ac restauratione Jerosolymitanae Ecclesiae*, RHC 5, 1–40, 1895.

Eugenius III. *Epistolæ*. Edited by Michel-Jean-Joseph Brial. RHGF. 21 vols., 15, 426–483. Paris:

Victor Palmé, 1878.

———. *Epistolæ et Privilegia*. PL 180, 1013–1648.

Eulogius. *S. Documentum martyriale*, PL 115, 819–842.

———. *Memoriale Sanctorum*, PL 115, 731–818.

———. *Eulogii vita*. PL115, 705–732.

Fulcher of Chartres. *The First Crusade: The Chronicle of Fulcher of Chartres and Other Source Materials*. Edited by Edward Peters. Philadelphia: University of Pennsylvania Press, 1971, 2d ed., 1998.

———. *Historia Hierosolymitana (1095–1127)*. Edited by Heinrich Hagenmeyer Heidleberg: Carl Winters Universitätsbuchhandlung, 1913.

———. *A History of the Expedition to Jerusalem, 1095–1127*. Translated by Frances Rita Ryan. Edited and introduction by Harold S. Fink. Knoxville: University of Tennessee Press, 1969.

Gautier de Coincy. *Les Miracles de Nostre Dame*. Edited by V. Frederic Koenig, 4 vols. Geneva: Librarie Droz, 1955–70.

Gerhoh of Reichersberg. *L'Oeuvre littéraire de Géroch de Reichersberg*. Edited by Damien-van den Eynde. Rome: Athenaeum Antonianum, 1957.

Gesta Francorum: The Deeds of the Franks and the Other Pilgrims to Jerusalem. Edited by Rosalind Hill. London: Thomas Nelson and Sons, 1962, reprinted Oxford University Press, 2003.

Gilo of Paris, and anon. *Historia vie Hierosolimitane*. Edited and translated by C.W. Grocock and Elizabeth Siberry. Oxford: Clarendon, 1997.

Glossa Ordinaria. PL 114, 9–752.

Gratian. *Decretum. Corpus Iuris Canonici*. 2 vols. Edited by A. Friedberg. Leipzig: Tauchnitz, 1929, I.

———. PL 187.

Gregory I. *Homiliæ in Evangelia*. PL 76, 1075–1312.

Gregory VII. *The Correspondence of Gregory VII*. Edited and translated by Ephraim Emerton. New York: Columbia University Press, 1932.

———. *Epistolae*. PL 148, 643–750.

———. *Epistolae Selectae. Das Register Gregors VII*. Edited by Erich Casparr. MGH, *Epistolae Selectae* 2. Berlin: Weidmannsche Buchhandlung, 1920.

———. *The Epistolae Vagantes of Pope Gregory VII*. Edited and tranlsated by H.E.J. Cowdrey. Oxford: Clarendon Press, 1972.

Guibert of Nogent. *Dei gesta per Francos*. RHC 4, 113–263, 1879.

———. *Dei gesta per Francos et cinq autres textes*. Edited by R. B. C. Huygens. Turnhout: Brepols, 1996.

———. *De vita sua*. PL 156, 837–962.

Hrabanus Maurus. *Commentaria in libros Machabaeorum*. PL 109, 1127–1256.

Hugh of Fleury, *Chronicon*. Edited by Georg H. Pertz. MGH Scriptores 8, 280–503. Hannover: Hahn, 1858.

Hugh of St Victor. *Epistolae*. PL 176, 1011–18.

al-Imām al-Qurṭubī (the Imam of Cordoba). *al-I'lām bi-mā fī dīn al-naṣārá min al-fasād wa-awhām wa-iẓhār maḥasin dīn al-islām wa-ithbāt nubuwwat nabīnā Muḥammad 'alayhi al-ṣalāt wa-al-salām*. Edited by Aḥmad Hijāzī al-Saqqā. Cairo: Maktabat al-Kullīyāt al-Azharīyah, 1980.

Isaac of Stella. *Sermones*. PL 194, 1689–1876.

———. *The Selected Works of Isaac of Stella: A Cistercian Voice from the Twelfth Century*.

Translated by Dániel Deme. Aldershot: Ashgate, 2007.
Isadore of Seville. *Sententiarum.* PL 83, 537–738.
Ivo of Chartres. *Decretum. Panormia.* PL 161.
Jacobis de Voragine. *The Golden Legend, Readings on the Saints.* Translated by William Granger Ryan, 2 vols. Princeton, NJ: Princeton University Press, 1993.
―――. *Legenda Aurea.* Edited by Dr. Th. Graesse. Breslau: Koebner, 1895.
John VIII. *Epistolae.* MGH *Epistolarum*, VII, 313–29. Edited by E. Caspar. Berlin: Weidmann, 1928.
John of Damascus. *John Damascene: Écrits sur l'Islam.* Translated by Raymond Le Coz. Paris: Cerf, 1992.
Lambertus Hersfeldensis. *Annales.* PL 146, 1053–1248.
Leo IV. *Epistolae selectae.* MGH *Epistolarum* 5, 585–612. Berlin: Weidmann, 1899.
Magister Rolandus. *Summa magistri Rolandi.* Edited by Friedrich Thaner. Innsbruck: Wagner'schen Universitæts-Buchhandlung, 1874.
The Meaning of the Glorious Qur'an. Translated by Mohammed Marmaduke Pickthall. London: Ta-Ha Publishers, 1930.
Michael the Syrian. *Chronique de Michel Le Syrien, Patriarche Jacobite d'Antioche (1166–99).* Edited and translated by J.-B. Chabot., 3 vols. Paris: E. Leroux, 1905.
Les Miracles de S. Benoit. Edited by E. de Certain. Paris: Chez Mme. ve J. Renouard, 1858.
Monk of Neider-Altaich. *Annales Altahenses maiores.* Edited by E.L.B. von Oefele. MGH Scriptores rerum Germanicarum 4, 1–86. Hannover: Hahn, 1891.
Oderic Vitalis. *Ecclesiastical History.* Edited by M. Chibnall, 6 vols. Oxford: Clarendon, 1978.
Odilo. *Vita B. Maili abbatis.* PL 142, 943–62.
Odo of Deuil. *De profectione Ludovici VII in Orientem, of Odo de Deuil.* Translated by Virginia Berry. New York: Columbia University Press, 1948.
Papsturkunden für Templar und Johanniter. Edited by Rudolf Hiestand. Göttingen: Vandenhoeck and Ruprecht, 1972.
Paul Alvarus. "Life of Eulogius." Translated by C. M. Sage. *Medieval Iberia: Readings from Christian, Muslim, and Jewish Sources.* Edited by Olivia Remie Constable. Philadelphia: University of Pennsylvania Press, 1997.
Paulus Alvarus. *Indiculus Luminosis.* PL 121, 513–556.
Peter Damian. *Epistolae.* PL 144, 205–498.
Peter of Poitiers. *Sententarium libri quinque.* PL 211, 783–1286.
Peter the Venerable. *Adversus Iudeorum inveteratam duritiem.* Edited by Yvonne Friedman. CCCM 58. Turnhout: Brepols, 1985.
―――. *Opera.* PL 189, 9–1076.
―――. *The Letters of Peter the Venerable.* Edited by Giles Constable, 2 vols. Cambridge, Massachusetts: Harvard University Press, 1967.
―――. *Summa totius haeresis Sarracenorum.* Edited by Reinhold Glei. *Petrus Venerabilis Schriften zum Islam.* Corpus Islamico-Christianum, series Latina I. Altenberge: CIS Verlag, 1985, pp. 2–22.
Petrus Alfonsi. *Disciplina Clericalis. Dialogi contra Iudaeos.* PL 157, 671–706.
―――. *The Disciplina Clericalis of Petrus Alfonsi.* Edited and translated by Eberhard Hermes. Translated into English P.R. Quarrie. Berkeley and Los Angeles: University of California Press, 1977.
―――. *Petrus Alfonsi: Dialogue Against the Jews* (Fathers of the Church: Mediaeval Continuation). Translated by Irven Resnick. Washington D.C.: Catholic University of America Press, 2006.
Ralph Glaber. *Rodulfi Glabri—Historium Libri Quinque.* Edited by John France. Oxford: Clarendon Press, 1989.
Ralph of Caen. *Gesta Tancredi in Expiditione Hierosolymitania*, RHC 3, 587–716, 1866.
Raymond of Aguilers. *Liber Historia Francorum qui Ceperunt Iherusalem.* RHC 3, 311–485, 1866.
―――. *Historia Francorum Qui Ceperunt Iherusalem.* Translated by John H. and Laurita L. Hill. Philadelphia: American Philosophical Society, 1968.
La Règle du Temple. Edited by Henri de Curzon. Paris: Librarie Renouard, 1886.
Richard of Poitou. *Ex Richardi Pictaviensis Chronica.* Edited by G. Waitz, MGH Scriptores 26, 74–82. Hannover: Hahn, 1882.
Robert the Monk. *Historia Iherosolimitana.* RHC 3, 717–882, 1866.
Robert the Monk's History of the First Crusade, Historia Iherosolimitana. Translated by Carol Sweetenham. Aldershot: Ashgate, 2005.
The Rule of St. Benedict. Edited and translated by Justin McCann. London: Sheed and Ward, 1972.
The Rule of the Templars: The French Text of the Rule of the Knights Templar. Translated by Judith Upton-Ward. Woodbridge: Boydell, 1992.
Sacrorum Conciliorum Nova et Amplissima Collectio. Edited by Gian Domenico Mansi. 53 vols., 20. Paris and Leipzig: Welter, 1901–27.
Select Passages from the Works of Bracton and Azo. Edited by F.W. Maitland. Selden Society. Vol. 8. London: Quartich, 1895.

Smaragdus. *Commentaria in regulam sancti Benedicti.* PL 102, 689–932.
The Song of Roland, An Analytical Edition. Edited by Gerard J. Brault. 2 vols. University Park and London: Pennsylvania State University Press, 1978.
Statua Capitulorum Generalium Ordinis Cisterciensis, 1116–1786. Edited by J.M. Canivez, 8 vols. Louvain: Revue d'histoire ecclesiastique, 1933–41.
Suger. *Epistolae.* PL 186, 1347–1440.
Syrus. *Vita Maioli.* PL 137, 763–68.
The Templars: Selected Sources. Translated by Malcolm Barber, and Keith Bate. Manchester: Manchester University Press, 2002.
Vita Argentee et comitum eius martyrum. Edited by A. Fabréga Grau, *Pasionário hispánico (siglos VII–IX).* 2 vols. 2, 382–87. Madrid and Barcelona: Instituo P. Enrique Florez, C.S.I.C., 1953–55.
Walter Map. *De nugis curialium.* Edited and translated by M.R. James, C.N.L. Brooke, and R.A.B. Mynors. Oxford: Clarendon Press, 1983.
William of Saint-Thierry. *S. Bernardi Vita Prima. Bernardi Opera*, PL 185, 225–642.
William of Tyre. *Chronicon.* Edited by R.B.C. Huygens, CCCM, 63. Turnhout: Brepols, 1986.
———. *A History of Deeds Done Beyond the Sea*, 2 vols. Translated by E. A. Babcock and A. C. Krey. New York: Columbia University Press, 1943.

Secondary Sources

Adolph, Helen. "Christendom and Islam in the Middle Ages: New Light on 'Grail Stone' and 'Hidden Host.'" *Speculum* 32 (1957): 103–15.
D'Alverny, M.T. *La connaisance de Islam dans l'Occident médiéval.* Edited by C. Burnett. Aldershot: Ashgate, 1994.
———. "Deux traductions latines du Coran au Moyen Age." *Archives d'histoire doctrinale etlitteraire du Moyen Age* 16 (1948): 69–131.
———. "Pierre le Vénérable et la légende de Mahomet." In *A Cluny, Congrès scientifique, Fêtes et cérémonies liturgiques en l'honneur des saints Abbés Odon et Odillon, 9–11juillet 1949*, 161–70. Dijon: Société des Amis de Cluny avec le CNRS, 1950.
———. "Quelques manuscrits de la 'Collection Toletana.'" In *Petrus Venerabilis, Studies and Texts Commemorating the Eighth Centenary of His Death*, edited by Giles Constable and James Kritzeck, 202–18. Rome: Pontificium Institutum S. Anselmi, 1956.
Arquillière, H. -X. "Origines de la théorie des deux glaives." *Studi Gregoriani* 1 (1947): 501–21.
———. *Saint Gregoire VII.* Paris: Librarie Philosophique J. Vrin, 1934.
Arteta, A. Ubieto. "La creación de la confradía militar de Belchite." *Estudios de Edad media de la Corona de Aragón* 5 (1952): 427–34.
Asbridge, Thomas. *The First Crusade: A New History.* Oxford: Oxford University Press, 2004.
Auberger, Jean-Baptiste. *L'unanimité cistercienne primitive: mythe ou realité?* Cîteaux studia et documenta, *Commentarii Cistercienses*, vol. 3. Achel: Administration de Cîteaux, 1986.
Ayoub, Mahmond M. "Roots of Muslim-Christian Conflict." *Muslim World* 79 (1989): 25–45.
Bachrach, Bernard S. "Papal War Aims in 1096: The Option Not Chosen." In *In Laudem Hierosolymitani: Studies in Crusades and Medieval Culture in Honour of Benjamin Z. Kedar*, edited by Iris Shagrir, Roni Ellenblum, and Jonathan Riley-Smith, 319–43. Aldershot: Ashgate, 2007.
———. and David Nicholas, eds. *Law, Custom, and the Social Fabric of Medieval Europe.* Kalamazoo, Michigan: Medieval Institute Publications, 1990.
Baker, Derek. "Crossroads and Crises in the Religious Life of the Later Eleventh Century with reference to Cluny and Cîteaux." *Studies in Church History* 16 (1979): 137–48.
———, ed. *Relations Between East and West in the Middle Ages.* Edinburgh: Edinburgh University Press, 1973.
Barber, Malcolm. *The Crusader States.* New Haven: Yale Univerist Press, 2012.
———. *The New Knighthood: A History of the Order of the Temple* Cambridge: University Press, 1994.
———. "The Origins of the Order of the Temple." *Studia Monastica* 12, no. 2 (1970): 219–39.
———. "The Social Context of the Templars." *Transactions of the Royal Historical Society.* Fifth series, 34 (1984): 27–46.
Bell, David N. *The Image and the Likeness: The Augustinian Spirituality of William of St. Thierry.* Kalamazoo, MI: Cistercian Publications, 1984.
Bennet, Matthew. "The First Crusaders' Images of Muslims: The Influence of Vernacular Poetry?" *Forum for Modern Language Studies* 22 (1986): 101–22.
Benson, Robert L., and Giles Constable, eds. *Renaissance and Renewal in the Twelfth Century.* Oxford: Clarendon Press, 1982.

Berman, Constance Hoffman. *The Cistercian Evolution: The Invention of a Religious Order in Twelfth-Century Europe*, Middle Ages Series. Philadelphia: University of Pennsylvania Press, 2000.

———. "The Cistercian Mystery. How was the Order Formed and by Whom? Can the Anglo-Norman Sources Elucidate the Problem?" *Haskins Society Journal* 13 (1999): 1–19.

Bernard, Lewis. *The Assassins: A Radical Sect of Islam*. London: Weidenfeld and Nicolson, 1967.

Berry, Virginia. "Peter the Venerable and the Crusades." In *Petrus Venerabilis, Studies and Texts Commemorating the Eighth Centenary of His Death*, edited by Giles Constable and James Kritzeck, 141–62. Rome: Pontificium Institutum S. Anselmi, 1956.

Bishko, Charles Julian. "Peter the Venerable's Journey to Spain." In *Petrus Venerabilis, Studies and Texts Commemorating the Eighth Centenary of His Death*, edited by Giles Constable and James Kritzeck, 163–75. Rome: Pontificium Institutum S. Anselmi, 1956.

Blake, E.O. "The Formation of the 'Crusade Idea.'" *Journal of Ecclesiastical History* 21 (1970): 11–31.

———, and Colin Morris. "A Hermit Goes to War: Peter and the Origins of the First Crusade." In *Monks, Hermits, and the Ascetic Tradition*, edited by W.J. Shiels, 70–109. Studies in Church History 22. Oxford: Blackwell, 1985.

Bliese, John R.E. "The Just War as Concept and Motive in the Central Middle Ages." *Medievalia et Humanistica* 17 (1991): 1–26.

Blumenthal, Uta-Renate. "The Papacy and Canon Law in the Eleventh-Century Reform." *Catholic Historical Review* 84 (1998): 201–218.

Bobzin, Hartmut. "Latin Translations of the Qur'an: A Short Overview." *Der Islam* 70 (1993): 193–206.

Bolton, Brenda. "The Cistercians and the Aftermath of the Second Crusade." In *The Second Crusade and the Cistercians*, edited by Michael Gervers, 131–140. New York: St. Martin's Press, 1992.

Bonnassie, Pierre. *From Slavery to Feudalism in South-Western Europe*. Translated by Jean Birrell. Cambridge: Cambridge University Press, 2009.

Bouchard, Constance Brittain. *Holy Entrepreneurs: Cistercians, Knights, and Economic Exchange in Twelfth-Century Burgundy*. Ithaca and London: Cornell University Press, 1991.

———. "Merovingian and Cluniac Monasticism." *Journal of Ecclesiastical History* 41 (1990): 365–88.

———. *Sword, Miter and Cloister: Nobility and the Church in Burgundy, 980–1198*. Ithaca and London: Cornell University Press, 1987.

Bredero, Adriaan H. *Bernard of Clairvaux: Between Cult and History*. Translated by Reinder Bruinsma. Grand Rapids, Michigan: Eerdmans, 1996.

———. *Cluny et Cîteaux au douziéme siècle*. Amsterdam and Maarssen: APA, HollandUniversity Press, 1985.

———. "The Controversy between Peter the Venerable and Bernard of Clairvaux." In *Petrus Venerabilis, Studies and Texts Commemorating the Eighth Centenary of His Death*, edited by Giles Constable and James Kritzeck, 53–71. Rome: Pontificium Institutum S. Anselmi, 1956.

Bresc-Bautier, Geneviève. *La Cartulaire du chapitre du Saint-Sépulcre de Jérusalem*. Paris: P. Geuthner, 1984.

Brolis, Maria Teresa. "La crociata per Pietro il Venerabile: guerra di armi o guerra di idee." *Aevum* 61 (1987): 327–54.

Brooke, C. *Europe in the Central Middle Ages, 962–1154*. London and New York: Longman, 1987.

Brooke, Rosalind, and C.N.L. Brooke. *Popular Religion in the Middle Ages: Western Europe 1000–1300*. London: Thames and Hudson, 1984.

Bruce, Scott G. "An Abbot Between Two Cultures: Maiolus of Cluny Considers the Muslims of La Garde-Freinet." *Early Medieval Europe* 15, no. 4 (2007), 426–440.

Brundage, James A. *The Crusades: A Documentary Survey*. Milwaukee, WI: Marquette University Press, 1962.

———. *The Crusades, Holy War and Canon Law*. Aldershot: Ashgate Variorum, 1991.

———. "The Hierarchy of Violence in Twelfth and Thirteenth-Century Canonists." *The International History Review* 17 (1995): 670–92.

———. "Holy War and the Medieval Lawyers." In *Holy War*, edited by T.P. Murphy, 117–128. Columbus: Ohio State University Press, 1976.

———. *Medieval Canon Law and the Crusader*. Madison, Milwaukee and London: University of Wisconsin Press, 1969.

———. "St. Bernard and the Jurists." In *The Second Crusade and the Cistercians*, edited by Michael Gervers, 25–33. New York: St. Martin's Press, 1992.

———. "A Transformed Angel: The Problem of the Crusading Monk." In *Studies in Medieval Cistercian History Presented to Jeremiah F. O'Sullivan*, 55–62. Cistercian Studies Series 13. Spencer, MA: Cistercian Publications, 1971.

Buc, Phillipe. "La Vengeance de Dieu: De

l'Exégèse Patristique à la Réforme Ecclésiastique et à la Première Croisade." In *La Vengeance 400–1200*, edited by Dominique Barthelemy, Francois Bougard, and Regine Le Jan, 451–486. Rome: École française de Rome, 2006.

Bull, Marcus G. *Knightly Piety and the Lay Response to the First Crusade*. Oxford: Clarendon Press, 1993.

———. "Views of Muslims and of Jerusalem in Miracle Stories, c.1000–c.1200: Reflections on the Study of First Crusaders' Motivations," in *The Experience of Crusading*, vol. 1. *Western Approaches*, edited by Marcus Bull and Norman Housley, 13–39. Cambridge: Cambrudge University Press, 2003.

———, and Norman Housley, eds. *The Experience of Crusading*, Vol. 1: *Western Approaches*. Cambridge: Cambridge University Press, 2003.

Bulst-Thiele. "The Influence of St. Bernard on the Formation of the Order of the Knights Templar." In *The Second Crusade and the Cistercians*, edited by Michael Gervers, 57–65. New York: St. Martin's Press, 1992.

Burman, Thomas. *Reading the Qur'_n in Latin Christendom, 1140–1560*. Philadelphia: University of Pennsylvania Press, 2007.

———. *Religious Polemic and the Intellectual History of the Mozarabs, c. 1050–1200*. Leiden, New York, Köln: Brill, 1994.

———. "Tafsir and Translation: Traditional Arabic Qur'an Exegesis in the Latin Qur'ans of Robert of Ketton and Mark of Toledo." *Speculum* 73 (1998): 703–32.

———. "The 'Tathlîth al-wahdânîyah' and the Twelfth-Century Andalusian Approach to Islam." In *Medieval Christian Perceptions of Islam: A Book of Essays*, edited by John Tolan, 109–30. Garland Medieval Casebooks, vol. 10. New York and London: Garland, 1996.

Burnett, Charles. "The Coherence of the Arabic-Latin Translation Program in Toledo in the Twelfth Century." *Science in Context* 14 (2001): 249–288.

Burns, Robert Ignatius. *Moors and Crusaders in Mediterranean Spain*. London: Variorum, 1978.

Burton, Janet. "Reform or Revolution?" *Medieval History* 1 (1991): 23–36.

Bynum, Caroline Walker. *Jesus as Mother—Studies in the Spirituality of the High Middle Ages*. Berkeley: University of California Press, 1982.

Cahen, Claude. *Turcobyzantia et Oriens Christianus*. London: Variorum Reprints, 1974.

Cambridge Medieval History. 8 vols., 4. General editor J.B. Bury. Edited by H.M. Gwatkin and J.P. Whitney. Cambridge: University Press, 1923.

Camille, Michael, *The Gothic Idol*. Cambridge: University Press, 1989.

Carlson, David. "The Practical Theology of St. Bernard and the Date of the *De Laude Novae Militae*." In *Erudition at God's Service*. Studies in Medieval Cistercian History 9, 133–48. Kalamazoo, MI: Cistercian Publications, 1987.

Carlyle, R.W., and A.J. Carlyle. *A History of Political Thought in the West*. 6 vols., no. 2. Edinburgh and London: William Blackwood, 1903–36.

Carrière, V. "Les Débuts de l'Ordre du Temple en France." *Le Moyen Age* 18 (1914): 308–35.

Chareyon, Nicole, *Pilgrims to Jerusalem in the Middle Ages*. New York: Columbia University Press, 2005.

Chatillon, Jean. "The Spiritual Renaissance of the End of the Eleventh and the Beginning of the Twelfth Centuries." *American Benedictine Review* 36 (1985): 292–317.

Chazan, Robert. *European Jewry and the First Crusade*. Berkeley, California: University of California Berkeley Press, 1987.

Chenu, M.D. *Nature, Man, and Society in the Twelfth Century*. Translated by Jerome Taylor and Lester K. Little. Chicago and London: University of Chicago Press, 1968.

Chevedden, Paul. "Canon 2 of the Council of Clermont (1095) and the Goal of the Eastern Crusade: 'To liberate Jerusalem' or 'To liberate the Church of God.'" *Annuarium historiae conciliorum* 37:1 (2005): 57–108.

Chowdrow, Stanley A. "Ecclesiastical Politics and the Ending of the Investiture Contest: The Papal Election of 1119 and the Negotiations of Mouzon." *Speculum* 46 (1971): 613–40.

Christys, Ann. *Christians in Al-Andalus, 711–1000*. Richmond, Surrey: Curzon Press, 2002.

Clagett, Marshall, Gaines Post, and Robert Reynolds, eds. *Twelfth Century Europe and the Foundations of Western Society*. Madison: University of Wisconsin Press, 1961.

Claster, Jill N. *Sacred Violence: The European Crusades to the Middle East, 1095–1396*. Toronto: University of Toronto Press, 2009.

Cohen, Mark R. *Under Crescent and Cross: The Jews in the Middle Ages*. Princeton, NJ: Princeton University Press, 1994.

Colbert, Edward P. *The Martyrs of Córdoba (850–859): A Study of the Sources*. Dissertation at the Catholic University of America. Washington, D.C.: Catholic University of America Press, 1962.

Cole, Penny J. "Christians, Muslims, and the 'Liberation' of the Holy Land." *Catholic Historical Review*, 54 (1998): 1–10.

———. "John of Abbeville and a Theology of War." *Toronto Journal of Theology*, 6, no. 1 (1990): 56–62.

———. "'O God, the Heathen have come into your Inheritance'(Ps. 78.1): The Theme of Religious Pollution in Crusade Documents, 1095–1188." In *Crusaders and Muslims in Twelfth-Century Syria*, edited by M. Schatzmiller, 84–111. Medieval Mediterranean, no. 1. Leiden: Brill, 1993.

———. *The Preaching of the Crusades to the Holy Land, 1095–1270*, Medieval Academy Books no. 98. Cambridge, Massachusetts: The Medieval Academy of America, 1991.

Collins, Roger. *Early Medieval Spain: Unity in Diversity*, 400–1000. London: Macmillan, 1983.

Constable, Giles. *Cluny from the Tenth to the Twelfth Centuries*. Aldershot: Ashgate, 2000.

———. *Crusaders and Crusading in the Twelfth Century*. Aldershot: Ashgate, 2008.

———. "The Crusading Project of 1150." In *Montjoie: Studies in Crusade History in Honor of Hans Eberhard Mayer*, edited by Benjamin Kedar, Jonathan Riley-Smith, and Rudolph Hiestand, 67–75. Aldershot: Variorum, 1997.

———. *Medieval Monasticism: A Select Bibliography*. Toronto: University of Toronto Press, 1976.

———. *The Reformation of the Twelfth Century*. Cambridge: Cambridge University Press, 1998.

———. "A Report on a Lost Sermon by St Bernard on the Failure of the Second Crusade." In *Studies in Medieval Cistercian History Presented to Jeremiah O'Sullivan*. Spencer, MA: Cistercian Publications, 1971.

———. "The Second Crusade as seen by Contemporaries:" *Traditio* 128 (1953): 213–79.

———, and James Kritzeck, eds., *Petrus Venerabilis: Studies and Texts Commemorating the Eighth Centenary of his Death*. Rome: Pontificium Institutum S. Anselmi, 1956.

Constable, Olivia Remie. "Muslim Spain and Mediterranean Slavery: The Medieval Slave Trade as an Aspect of Muslim-Christian Relations." In *Christendom and its Discontents*, edited by Scott L. Waugh and Peter D. Diehl, 264–84. Cambridge: Cambridge University Press, 1996.

Coupe, Jessica A. *The Martyrs of Córdoba: Community and Family in an Age of Mass Conversion*. Lincoln and London: University of Nebraska Press, 1995.

Cousin, P. "Les débuts de l'Ordre des Templiers et saint Bernard." *Mélange saint Bernard*, 41–52. Dijon: Trouve, 1953.

Cowdrey, H.E.J. "Christianity and the Morality of Warfare during the First Century of Crusading." In *The Experience of Crusading, Volume I: Western Approaches*, edited by Marcus Bull and Norman Housley, 175–92. Cambridge: Cambridge University Press, 2003.

———. *The Cluniacs and the Gregorian Reform*. Oxford: Clarendon Press, 1970.

———. "Cluny and the First Crusade." *Revue Bénédictine* 83 (1973): 285–311.

———. *The Crusades and Latin Monasticism, 11th–12th Centuries*. Variorum Collected Studies Series, Cs 662. Aldershot: Ashgate Variorum, 1999 (collected essays in one volume).

———. "The Eleventh Century Peace and Truce of God." *Past and Present* 46, (1970): 42–67.

———. "The Genesis of the Crusades: The Springs of Western Ideas of Holy War." In *The Holy War*, edited by Thomas Patrick Murphy, 9–32. Columbus: Ohio State University Press, 1976.

———. "The Mahdia Campaign of 1087." *English Historical Review* 92 (1977): 1–29.

———. "Martyrdom and the First Crusade." In *Crusade and Settlement*, edited by Peter Edbury, 46–56. Cardiff: University College Cardiff Press, 1985.

———. "*The Papacy and the Origins of Crusading*." Medieval History 1 (1991): 48–60.

———. "Pope Gregory VII and Martyrdom," In *Dei gesta per Francos: Crusade Studies in Honour of Jean Richard*, edited by M. Balard, Bemjamin Kedar, and Jonathan Riley-Smith, 3–11. Aldershot: Ashgate, 2001.

———. "Pope Gregory VII and the Bearing of Arms." In *Montjoie — Studies in Crusade History in Honor of Hans Eberhard Mayer*, edited by Benjamin Kedar, Jonathan Riley-Smith, and Rudolf Hiestand, 21–36. Aldershot: Variorum, 1997.

———. *Pope Gregory VII, 1073–1085*. Oxford: Oxford University Press, 1998.

———. "Pope Gregory's 'Crusading' Plans of 1074." In *Outremer: Studies in the History of the Crusading Kingom of Jerusalem Presented to Joshua Prawer*, edited by Benjamin Kedar, H.E. Mayer, amd R.C. Smail, 30–37. Jerusalem: Yad Izhak Ben-Zvi Institute, 1982.

———. "Pope Urban and the Idea of the Crusade," *Studi Medievali* 3rd ser. 36, no. 2 (1995): 721–42.

———. *Popes and Church Reform in the 11th Century*. Aldershot: Ashgate, 2000.

———. *Popes, Monks, and Crusaders*. London: Hambledon Press, 1984, reprinted 2003.

———. "The Reform Papacy and Origin of the Crusades." In *Le concile de Clermont de 1095 et l'appel à la Croisade*, 65–83. Rome: École française de Rome, 1997.

———. *The Register of Pope Gregory VII, 1073–1085: An English Translation*. New York: Oxford University Press, 2002.

Cramer, Valmar. "Kreuzpredigt un Kreuzzugsgedanke von Bernard von Clairvaux bis Humbert von Romans." In *Das Heilige Land in Vergangenheit und Gegenwart, Palästinahefte des deutschen Vereins vom heiligen Lande*, edited by Cramer and G. Meinertz, 17–20. Köln: Bachem, 1939.

Crawford, Paul F. "Four Myths About the Crusades." *The Intercollegiate Review* 46, no.1 (2011): 13–22.

Cushing, Kathleen G. *Reform and the Papacy in the Eleventh Century: Spirituality and Social Change*. Manchester: University of Manchester Press, 2005.

Cutler, Allan. "The Ninth-Century Spanish Martyr's Movement and the Origins of Western Christian Missions to the Muslims." *Muslim World* 55 (1965): 321–29

———. "Peter the Venerable and Islam." *Journal of the American Oriental Society* 86 (1966): 184–98.

———. "Who was the 'Monk of France' and When Did he Write?" *Al-Andalus* 28 (1963): 249–69.

———, and Helen Cutler. *The Jew As Ally of the Muslim: Medieval Roots of Anti-Semitism*. Notre Dame: University of Notre Dame Press, 1986.

Daftary, Farhad. *The Assassin Legends: Myths of the Isma'ilis*. London: I.B. Tauris, 1994.

Daillez, Laurent, ed. *Règle et Status de L'Ordre du Temple*. Paris: Éditions Dervy, 1972.

Daniel, Norman. *The Arabs and Medieval Europe*. London: Longman, 1975.

———. *Islam and the West*. Edinburgh: University Press, 1960, revised 2009.

———. "Spanish Christian Sources of Information about Islam." *Al-Qantara* 15, no. 2 (1994), 365–84.

De Poorter, A., "Le texte original de la Règle du Templiers." *Annual de la Societé d'Emulation de Bruges* 62 (1912): 193–8.

Delaruelle, E. "The Crusading Idea in Cluniac Literature of the Eleventh Century." In *Cluniac Monasticism in the Central Middle Ages*, edited by Noreen Hunt, 191–216. Hamden, Connecticut: Archon Books, 1971.

Des Places, E. "Sibylline Oracles." *New Catholic Encyclopedia*, 15 vols., 13, 190. Washington, D.C.: Catholic University of America, 1967.

Dessubré, Marguerite. *Bibliographie de l'ordre des Templiers*. Paris: É. Nourry, 1928.

Dunbabin, Jean. "The Maccabees as Exemplars in the Tenth and Eleventh Centuries." In *The Bible in the Medieval World*, edited by Katherine Walsh and Diana Wood, 31–41. Oxford: Blackwell, 1985.

Dupront, Alphonse. *La chrétienté ei l'idée de croisade*. 2 vols. Paris: Éditions Albin Michel, 1954 and 59.

———. *Du sacré: croisades et plerinages, images et langages*. Paris: Gallimard, 1987.

———. "Guerre sainte, et chrétienté." In *Cahiers de Fanjeaux* 4, 17–50. Fanjeaux: Centre National de la Recherche Scientifique, 1969.

Edbury, Peter W, and Rowe, J. G. *William of Tyre, Historian of the Latin East*. Cambridge: Cambridge University Press, reprinted 1991.

———, ed. *Crusade and Settlement*. Cardiff: University College Cardiff Press, 1985.

Elder, E. Rozanne, ed. *Noble Piety and Reformed Monasticism*. Cistercian Studies no. 65. Kalamazoo: Cistercian Publications, 1981.

Emmerson, Richard Kenneth. *Antichrist in the Middle Ages*. Manchester: Manchester University Press, 1981.

———, and Bernard McGinn, eds. *The Apocalypse in the Middle Ages*. Ithaca: Cornell University Press, 1993.

Engen, John van. "The 'Crisis of Cenobitism' Reconsidered: Benedictine Monasticism in the Years 1050–1150." *Speculum* 61 (1986): 269–304.

Erdman, Carl. *Die Entstehung des Kreuzzugsgedankens*. Stuttgart: Kohlhammer, 1935.

———. *The Origin of the Idea of the Crusade*. Translated by Marshall W. Baldwin and Walter Goffart. Princeton, New Jersey: Princeton University Press, 1977.

Evans, Gillian R. *Bernard of Clairvaux (Great Medieval Thinkers)*. Oxford: University Press, 2000.

———. *The Mind of St. Bernard of Clairvaux*. Oxford: Clarendon Press, 1983.

Evans, Joan. *Monastic Life at Cluny, 910–1157*. London: Humphrey Milford, Oxford University Press, 1931.

Ferreiro, Alberto. "Simon Magus, Nicolas of Antioch, and Muhammad." *Church History* 72, no. 1 (2003): 53–70.

Ferzoco, George. "The Origins of the Second Crusade." In *The Second Crusade and the Cistercians*, edited by Michael Gervers, 91–100. New York: St. Martin's Press, 1992.

Feuchter, Jörg. "The Islamic Ribāt: A Model for the Christian Military Orders? Sacred Violence, Religious Concepts and the Invention of a Cultural Transfer" in *Religion and Its Other: Secular and Sacral Concepts and Practices in Interaction*, edited by Heike Bock, Jörg Feuchter, and Michi Knecht, 115–41. Frankfurt/M: Campus Verlag, 2008.

Flanagan, Sabina. "Twelfth-Century Apocalyptic Imaginations and the Coming of the Antichrist." *Journal of Religious History* 24, no. 1 (2000): 57–69.

Fletcher, Richard. *The Cross and The Crescent*. London: Penguin, 2003.

Flori, Jean. *La Guerre sainte: La formation de l'idée de croisade dans l'Occident chrétien.* Paris: Aubier, 2001.

———. "Ideology and Motivations in the First Crusade," In *Palgrave Advances in the Crusades*, edited by Helen Nicholson, 15–36. Basingstoke: Palgrave Macmillan, 2005.

———. *L'islam et la Fin des Temps. L'interprétation prophétique des invasions musulmanes dans la chrétienté medieval.* Paris: Seuil, 2007.

———. "Mort et martyre des guerriers vers 1100. L'exemple de la première croisade." *Cahiers de Civilisation Médiévale* 34, no. 134 (1991): 121–139.

———. *Pierre l'Ermite et la première croisade,* Paris: Fayard, 1999.

———. "Une ou plusieurs 'premiere croisade'?" *Revue Historique* 285 (1991): 3–27.

Focillon, Henri. *The Year 1000.* New York: Harper and Row, 1971.

Forey, Alan. "The Emergence of the Military Order in the Twelfth Century." *Journal of Ecclesiastical History* 36 (1985): 175–95.

———. "The Failure of the Siege of Damascus in 1148." *Journal of Medieval History* 10 (1984): 13–23.

———. *Military Orders and Crusades.* Aldershot: Ashgate Variorum, 1994.

———. "The Military Orders and the Conversion of Muslims in the Twelfth and Thirteenth Centuries." *Journal of Medieval History* 28 (2002): 1–22.

———. "The Military Orders and the Ransoming of Captives from Islam, Twelfth to Early Fourteenth Centuries." *Studia Monastica* 33 (1991): 259–79.

———. "Military Orders and Secular Warfare in the Twelfth and Thirteenth Centuries." *Viator* 24 (1993): 79–100.

———. *The Military Orders from the Twelfth to the Early Fourteenth Centuries.* London: Macmillan, 1992.

———. "Novitiate and Instruction in the Military Orders during the Twelfth and Thirteenth Centuries." *Speculum* 61 (1986): 1–17.

———. "Recruitment to the Military Orders, Twelfth to the Fourteenth Centuries." *Viator* 17 (1986): 141–71.

France, John. *The Crusades and the Expansion of Catholic Christendom, 1000–1714.* London and New York: Routledge, 2005.

———. "The Destruction of Jerusalem and the First Crusade." *Journal of Ecclesiastical History* 47 (1996): 1–17.

———. "Glaber and French Politics in the Early Eleventh Century." *Francia* 16 (1989): 101–12.

———. "Glaber as Reformer." *Studia Monastica* 34 (1992): 41–50.

———. "Patronage and the Appeal of the First Crusade." In *The First Crusade: Origins and Impact*, edited by Jonathan Phillips, 5–20. Manchester and New York: Manchester University Press, St. Martin's Press, 1997.

———. "Two Types of Vision on the First Crusade: Stephen of Valence and Peter Bartholomew." *Crusades* 5 (2006): 1–20.

———. "War and Christendom in the Thought of Rodulfus Glaber." *Studia Monastica* 30 (1988): 105–20.

Frassetto, Michael. "Heretics, Antichrists, and the Year 1000: Apocalyptic Expectations in the Writings of Ademar of Chabannes." In *The Year 1000: Religious and Social Response to the Turning of the First Millennium*, edited by Michael Frassetto, 73–84. New York: Palgrave Macmillan, 2002.

———. "The Image of the Saracen as Heretic in the Sermons of Ademar of Chabannes." In *Western Views of Islam in Medieval and Early Modern Europe: Perception of Other*, edited by David R. Blanks and Michael Frassetto, 83–96. New York: St. Martin's Press, 1999.

———, and David R. Blanks, eds. *Western Views of Islam in Medieval and Early Modern Europe: Perception of Other.* New York: St. Martin's Press, 1999.

Fregosi, Paul. *Jihad.* New York: Prometheus Books, 1998.

Freidenreich, David M. "Muslims in Western Canon Law, 1000–1500." In *Christian-Muslim Relations. A Bibliographical History, Volume 3 (1050–1200)*, editd by David Thomas and Alex Mallett, 41–68. Leiden: Brill, 2011.

Frend, W.H.C. *Martyrdom and Persecution in the Early Church: A Study of Conflict from the Maccabees to Donatus.* Oxford: Oxford University Press, 1965.

Gabrieli, Francesco. *Arab Historians of the Crusades.* Trans E.J. Costello. London, Melbourne, and Henley: Routledge & Kegan Paul, 1969.

Gaiffier, B de. "Les notices hispaniques dans le Martyrologe d'Usuard." *Analecta Bollandiana* 55 (1937): 268–83.

Gaztambide, Jose Goñi. *Historia de la Bula de Cruzada en España.* Vitoria: Editorial del Seminario, 1958.

Gervers, Michael, ed. *Conversion and Continuity.* Papers in Medieval Studies 9. Toronto: Pontifical Institute of Mediaeval Studies, 1990.

———, ed. *The Second Crusade and the Cistercians.* New York: St. Martin's Press, 1992.

Gieysztor, A. "The Genesis of the Crusades: The Encyclical of Sergius IV (1009–12)." *Medievalia et Humanistica* 5 (1948): 3–23.

Gilchrist, John. "The Erdmann Thesis and Canon Law, 1083–1141." In *Crusade and Settlement*, edited by Peter W. Edbury, 37–45. Cardiff: University Press, 1985.

———. "The Papacy and the War Against the Saracens, 795–1216." *International History Review* 10 (1988): 174–97.

Giraud, René. *Violence and the Sacred*. Translated by Patrick Gregory. London: Athlone Press, 1995.

Glick, Thomas F. "Did the Islamic Ribat (Military Religious Communities) Serve as the Model for the Christian Crusaders?" In *The Crusades, 1095–1291*, edited by Mark T. Abate, 158–160. History and Dispute 10. Detroit: Thomson Gale, 2003.

———. *From Muslim Fortress to Christian Castle: Social and Cultural Change in Medieval Spain*. Manchester: University Press, 1995.

Goddard, Hugh. *A History of Muslim-Christian Relations*. Edinburgh: Edinburgh University Press, 2000.

Golb, Norman. *The Jews in Medieval History*. Cambridge: Cambridge University Press, 1998.

Goodich, Michael, Sophia Menarche, and Sylvia Schein, eds. *Cross Cultural Convergences in the Crusader Period—Essays Presented to Aryeh Graboïs on his Sixty-Fifth Birthday*. New York: Peter Lang, 1995.

Goss, Vladimir P., ed. *The Meeting of Two Worlds*. Kalamazoo, MI: Medieval Institute Publications, 1986.

Graboïs, Aryeh. "Militia and Malitia: The Bernardine Vision of Chivalry." In *The Second Crusade and the Cistercians*, edited by Michael Gervers, 49–56. New York: St. Martin's Press, 1992.

Grier, James. "Hoax, History, and Hagiography in Adémar de Chabannes' Texts for the Divine Office." In *Representing History, 900–1300: Art, Music, History*, edited by Robert A. Maxwell, 67–72. University Park: Pennsylvania State University Press, 2010.

Haddad, Wadi.' "Crusaders through Muslim Eyes." *Muslim World* 73 (1983): 234–52.

Hamilton, Bernard. *The Latin Church in the Crusader States*. London: Variorum, 1980.

———, ed. *Monastic Reform, Catharism, and the Crusades*. London: Variorum Reprints, 1979.

Hamilton, Sarah. "Penance in the Age of Gregorian Reform." In *Repentance, Retribution and Reconciliation*, edited by J. Gregory, K. Cooper, 47–73. Studies in Church History 40. Woodbridge: Boydell, 2004.

Harper-Bill, Christopher, ed. *Studies in Medieval History Presented to R. Allen Brown*. Woodbridge: Boydell, 1989.

Hillenbrand, Carole. *The Crusades: Islamic Perspectives*. Edinburgh: Edinburgh University Press, 1998.

———. "The First Crusade: the Muslim Perspective." In *The First Crusade: Origins and Impact*, edited by Jonathan Phillips, 130–41. Manchester and New York: Manchester University Press, St. Martin's Press, 1997.

Hitti, Philip K. *Islam and the West, A Historical Cultural Survey*. New York: Robert E. Krieger, 1962.

Hodgson, Marshall G.S. *The Secret Order of Assassins: The Struggle of the Early Nizârî Ismâ_îlîs Against the Islamic World*. Philadelphia, PA: University of Pennsylvania Press, 2005.

Hollier, Robert. "Bernard de Clairvaux et les Templiers, ou l'unitie de l'Europe dans sa diversité." *Atlantis* 52 (1979): 222–6.

Holt, Peter Malcom, ed. *The Eastern Mediterranean Lands in the Period of the Crusades*. Warminster: Aris and Philips, 1977.

Hourani, Albert. *Europe and the Middle East*. London and Basingstoke: Macmillan, 1980.

Housley Norman. *Contesting the Crusades*. Contesting the Past. Malden, MA, and Oxford: Wiley-Blackwell, 2006.

———. "The Crusades and Islam." *Medieval Encounters* 13, 189–208. Leiden: Brill, 2007.

———. *Fighting for the Cross: Crusading to the Holy Land*. New Haven: Yale University Press, 2008.

———, ed. *Knighthoods of Christ: Essays on the History of the Crusades and the Knights Templar Presented to Malcolm Barber*. Aldershot: Ashgate, 2007.

Hunt, Lucy-Anne. "'Excommunicata Generatione': Christian Imagery and Conversion of the Muslim Other between the First Crusade and the Early Fourteenth Century." *Al-Masaq* 8 (1995): 79–153.

Hunt, Noreen, ed. *Cluniac Monasticism in the Central Middle Ages*. Hamden, CT: Archon Books, 1971.

———, ed. *Cluny Under St. Hugh, 1049–1109*. London: E. Arnold, 1967.

Iogna-Prat, Dominique. "The Creation of a Christian Armory Against Islam." In *Medieval Religion: New Approaches*, edited by Constance Berman, 325–46. New York: Routledge, 2005.

———. *Order and Exclusion: Cluny and Christendom Face Heresy, Judaism and Islam (1000–1150)*. Translated by Graham Robert Edwards. Conjunctions of Religion and Power in the Medieval Past. Ithaca, NY: Cornell University Press, 2002.

Jacoby, David. "Bishop Gunther of Bamberg, Byzantium and Christian Pilgrimage to the Holy Land in the Eleventh Century." In *Zwischen Polis, Provinz Und Peripherie: Beitrage Zur Byzantinischen Geschichte Und Kultur*, edited by Lars M. Hoffmann, 267–285. Wiesbaden: Harrassowitz, 2005.

Johnson, James Turner. *The Holy War Idea in*

Western and Islamic Tradition. University Park: Pennsylvania State University Press, 1997.
Joranson, Einar. "The Great German Pilgrimage of 1064–1065." In *The Crusades and Other Historical Essays*, edited by Louis J. Paetow, 3–43. New York: F.S. Crofts, 1928.
Jotischky, Andrew. "The Christians of Jerusalem, the Holy Sepulchre and the Origins of the First Crusade." *Crusades* 7 (2008): 35–57.
Kahl, Hans-Dietrich. "Crusade Eschatology as Seen by St. Bernard in the Years 1146 to 1148." In *The Second Crusade and the Cistercians*, edited by Michael Gervers, 35–47. New York: St. Martin's Press, 1992.
Kassis, Hanna. "Muslim Revival in Spain in the Fifth (Eleventh) Century — Causes and Ramifications." *Der Islam* 67 (1990): 78–110.
Katzir, Yael. "The Second Crusade and the Redefinition of Ecclesia, Christianitas, and Papal Coercive Power." In *The Second Crusade and the Cistercians*, edited by Michael Gervers, 3–11. New York: St. Martin's Press, 1992.
Kedar, Benjamin. *Crusade and Mission: European Approaches toward the Muslims*. Princeton: Princeton University Press, 1984.
_____. "The Jerusalem Massacre of July 1099 in the Western Historiography of the Crusades." *Crusades* 3 (2004): 15–75.
_____."On the Origins of the Earliest Laws of Frankish Jerusalem: The Canons of the Council of Nablus, 1120." *Speculum*, 74, no. 2 (1999): 331–34.
_____, ed. *The Horns of Hattin*. Aldershot: Ashgate Variorum, 1992.
Kedar, Benjamin, H.E. Mayer, and R.C. Smail, eds. *Outremer: Studies in the History of the Crusading Kingdom of Jerusalem Presented to Joshua Prawer*. Jerusalem: Yad Izhak Ben-Zvi Institute, 1982.
King, Archdale Arthur. *Cîteaux and Her Elder Daughters*. London: Burns and Oates, 1954.
Knight, Gillian. *The Correspondence Between Peter the Venerable and Bernard of Clairvaux:A Semantic and Structural Analysis*. Aldershot: Ashgate, 2002.
Knowles, David. "The Reforming Decrees of Peter the Venerable." In *Petrus Venerabilis, Studies and Texts Commemorating the Eighth Centenary of His Death*, edited by Giles Constable and James Kritzeck, 1–20. Rome: Pontificium Institutum S. Anselmi, 1956.
_____. "The Rise and Decline of Cluny." *Concilium*, n. ser. 7–8, no. 10 (1974–5): 20–9.
Kostick, Conor. *The Social Structure of the First Crusade (The Medieval Mediterranean)*. Leiden: Brill, 2008.
Kritzeck, James. *Peter the Venerable and Islam*. Princeton, NJ: Princeton University Press, 1964.
_____. "Robert of Ketton's Translation of the Qur'an." *Islamic Quarterly* 2 (1955), 309–12.
Labande, Edmond René. *Études de civilisation médiévale (IXe-XIIe siècles)*. Poitiers: C.È.S.C.M., 1974.
Lacarra, J. *Vida de Alfonso el Batallador*. Zaragoza: Publicaciones de la Caja de Ahorros y Monte, 1971.
Lacey, Robert, and Danny Danziger. *The Year 1000*. London: Abacus, 2000.
Lackner, Bede K. *The Eleventh-Century Background of Cîteaux*. Washington: Cistercian Publications, 1972.
_____, and Kenneth Roy Philp, eds. *Essays on Medieval Civilization*, Austin and London: University of Texas Press, 1980.
Landes, Richard. "The Fear of an Apocalyptic Year 1000: Augustinian Historiography, Medieval and Modern." *Speculum* 75 (2000): 97–145.
_____. *Relics, Apocalypse, and the Deceits of History: Ademar of Chabannes, 989–1034*. Cambridge, MA: Harvard University Press, 1995.
_____, Andrew Gow, and David Van Meter, eds. *The Apocalyptic Year 1000: Religious Expectaton and Social Change, 950–1050*. Oxford: Oxford University Press, 2003.
Lawrence, C.H. *Medieval Monasticism*. London and New York: Longman, 1989.
Leclercq, Jean. "L'attitude spirituelle de Saint Bernard devant la guerre." *Collectanea Cisterciensia* 36 (1974): 195–225.
_____. "La crise du monachisme aux XIe et XIIe siècles." *Bollentino dell'Instituto Storico Italiano per il Medio Evo e Archivo Muuratoriano* 70 (1959): 19–41.
_____. "Christian Monasticism: Encounters with other Traditions." *Monastic Studies* 18 (1988): 64–78.
_____. "Un document sur les débuts des Templiers." *Revue d'Histoire Ecclésiastique* 52 (1957): 81–91.
_____. "L'encyclique de Saint Bernard en faveur de la croisade." *Revue Bénédictine* 81, no. 3–4, (1971): 282–308.
_____. *The Love of Learning and the Desire for God: A Study of Monastic Culture*. Translated by Catherine Misrahi. New York: Fordham University Press, 1982.
_____. *Monks and Love in Twelfth-Century France: Psycho-Historical Essays*. Oxford: Clarendon, 1979.
_____. "Naming the Theologians of the Early Twelfth Century." *Medieval Studies* 53 (1991): 327–36.
_____. *Pierre le Vénérable*. Abbaye S. Wandrille: Éditions de Fontenelle, 1946.

———. "A propos de l'encyclique de Saint Bernard sur la croisade." *Revue Bénédictine* 82 (1972): 312.

———. "Saint Bernard's Attitude toward War." In *Studies in Medieval Cistercian History*, edited by John R. Sommerfeldt, 1–39. Kalamazoo, MI: Cistercian Publications, 1976.

———. "St Bernard et les débuts de l'Ordre Cistercien." *Studia Monastica*, 34 (1992): 63–78.

———. "Violence and the Devotion to St. Benedict in the Middle Ages." *The Downside Review* 88 (1970): 344–60.

Lehtonen, Tuomas M.S., and Kurt Villads Jensen, with Janne Malkki and Katja Ritari, eds. *Medieval History Writing and Crusading Ideology*. Studia Fennica, Historica 9. Helsinki: Finnish Literature Society, 2005.

Lekai, Louis. *The Cistercians: Ideals and Reality*. Kent, Ohio: Kent State University Press, 1977.

———. *Les moines blancs*. Paris: Seuil, 1957.

Léonard, M. *Introduction au Cartulaire manuscrit del'Ordre du Temple*. Paris: E. Champion, 1930.

Leroy, Thierry. *Hughes de Payns, Chevalier, Champenois, Fondateur de L'Ordre des Templiers*. Troyes: La Maison de Boulanger, 2001.

License, Tom. "The Military Orders as Monastic Orders." *Crusades* 5 (2006): 39–53.

Linehan, Peter, and Janet L. Nelson, eds. *The Medieval World*. New York and London: Routledge, 2001.

Loades, David, ed. *The End of Strife*. Edinburgh: T. and T. Clark, 1984.

Loud, Graham. "Some Reflections on the Failure of the Second Crusade," *Crusades* 4 (2005): 1–14.

Lourie, Elena. "The Confraternity of Belchite, the Ribat, and the Temple." *Viator* 13 (1982): 159–76.

Loutchitskaja, Svetlana. "L'Image des musulmans dans les chroniques des croisades." *Le Moyen Age* 105 (1999): 717–35.

Luddy, Ailbe J. *The Life and Teaching of Saint Bernard*. Dublin: Gill, 1950.

Luneau, Auguste. *L'Histoire du salut chez les pères de l'église: La doctrine des âges du monde*. Théologie Historique, vol. 2. Paris: Beauchesne, 1964.

Luscombe, David. "Peter Abelard's Carnal Thoughts." In *Medieval Theology and the Natural Body*, edited by Peter Biller and A.J. Minnis, 31–42. Woodbridge: Boydell and Brewer, in association with York Medieval Press, 1997.

———. *Peter Abelard's Ethics*. Oxford: Clarendon, 1971.

Luttrell, Anthony. "The Earliest Hospitallers." In *Montjoie: Studies in Crusade History in Honor of Hans Eberhard Mayer*, edited by Benjamin Kedar, Jonathan Riley-Smith, and Rudolph Hiestand, 37–54. Aldershot: Variorum, 1997.

Lynch, Joseph H. *The Medieval Church: A Brief History*. London and New York: Longman, 1992.

Mabillon, John, ed. *The Life and Works of St. Bernard*. Translated by Samuel J. Eales, 2 vols. London: Burns and Oates, n.d.

Markus, R.A. "Saint Augustine's Views on the 'Just War.'" In *The Church and War*, edited by W. J. Shiels, 1–14. Studies in Church History 20. Oxford: Blackwell, 1983.

Mastnak, Tomaž. *Crusading Peace: Christendom, the Muslim World, and Western Political Order*. Berkeley: University of California Press, 2002.

Maxwell, John Francis. *Slavery and the Catholic Church*. Chichester and London: Barry Rose, 1975.

McCaffery, Hugh. "Isaac of Stella: A Significant Spokesman for the Sanctity of Bernard of Clairvaux." In *Cistercian Ideals and Reality*, edited by John R. Sommerfeldt, 199–219. Kalamazoo, MI: Cistercian Publications, 1978.

McCrank, Lawrence J. "The Frontier of the Spanish Reconquest and the Land Acquisitions of the Cistercians of Poblet, 1150–1276." *Analecta Cisterciensia* 29 (1973): 57–78.

McGinn, Bernard. *Antichrist*. New York: Columbia University Press, 2000.

———. *Apocalyptic Spirituality*. New York: Paulist Press, 1979.

———. "Apocalypticism and Church Reform, 1100–1500." In *The Continuum History of Apocalypticism*, edited by John J. Collins, Stephen Stein, and Bernard McGinn, 273–298. New York: Continuum, 2003.

———. "Apocalypticism in the Middle Ages: An Historiographical Sketch." *Medieaval Studies* 37 (1975): 155–73.

———. *Apocalypticism in the Western Tradition*. Collected Studies, Cs 430. Farnham, Surrey: Ashgate Variorum, 1994.

———. "Awaiting the End: Research in Medieval Apocalypticism, 1974–81." *Medievalia et Humanistica* NS 11 (1982): 563–89.

———. *The Calabrian Abbot: Joachim of Fiore in the History of Western Thought*. New York: Macmillan, 1985.

———. *The Crusades*. Morristown, NJ: General Learning Press, 1973.

———. "*Iter Sancti Sepuchri*: The Piety of the First Crusaders." In *Essays on Medieval Civilization*, edited by Bede Lackner and Kenneth Philp, 33–71. Austin and London: University of Texas Press, 1978.

———. "Portraying Antichrist in the Middle Ages." In *The Use and Abuse of Eschatology in the Middle Ages*, edited by Werner Verbeke, Daniel Verhelst, and Andries Welkenhuysen, 1–48. Leuven: Leuven University Press, 1988.

———. "St. Bernard and Eschatology." In *Bernard of Clairvaux: Studies Presented to Dom Jean Leclercq*, 163–85. Washington D.C.: Cistercian Publications, 1973.

———. *Visions of the End: Apocalyptic Traditions in the Middle Ages*. Manchester: Manchester University Press, 1981, revised 1998.

———, John Meyendorff, and Jean Leclercq, eds. *Christian Spirituality I: Origins to the Twelfth Century*. London: SCM Press, 1989.

Melville, Marion. "Les débuts de l'ordre du Temple." *Vorträge und Forschungen* 26 (1980): 23–30.

Metlitzki, Dorothee. *The Matter of Araby in Medieval England*. New Haven and London: Yale University Press, 1977.

Millet-Gérard, Dominique. *Chrétiens, mozarabes et culture islamique dans l'Espagne de VIIe–IXe siècles*. Paris: Études augustiniennes, 1984.

Monnot, Guy. "Les citations coraniques dans le 'Dialogus' de Pierre Alfonse." *Islam et chrétiens du Midi (XIIe–XIVe s.)*. *Cahiers de Fanjeaux* 18, nos. 261–77. Fanjeaux: Centre National de la Recherche Scientifique, ca. 1983.

Moore, R.I. *The Formation of a Persecuting Society*. Oxford: Blackwell, 1987, updated 2007.

———. "Heresy, Repression, and Social Change in the Age of the Gregorian Reform." In *Christendom and its Discontents*, edited by Scott L. Waugh and Peter D. Diehl, 19–46. Cambridge: University Press, 1996.

Morin, Germain "Rainaud l'Ermite et Ives de Chartres: un épisode de la crise du cénobitisme au XIe–XIIe siècle." *Revue Bénédictine* 40 (1928): 99–115.

Morris, Colin. "The Aims and spirituality of the First Crusade, as Seen Through the Eyes of Albert of Aix." *Reading Medieval Studies* 16 (1990): 99–117.

———. "Martyrs on the Field of Battle Before and During the First Crusade." In *Martyrs and Martyrologies*, edited by D. Wood, 93–105. Studies in Church History 30. Oxford: Ecclesiastical History Society, 1993.

———. *The Papal Monarchy: The Western Church from 1050 to 1250*, Oxford History of the Christian Church. New York: Oxford University Press, 1991.

———. "Peter the Hermit and the Chroniclers." In *The First Crusade: Origins and Impact*, edited by Jonathan Phillips, 21–34. Manchester and New York: Manchester University Press, St. Martin's Press, 1997.

———. "Propaganda for War: the Dissemination of the Crusading Ideal in the Twelfth Century." *Studies in Church History* 20 (1983): 79–101.

Morrison, Karl F. "The Gregorian Reform," in *Christian Spirituality: Origins to the Twelfth Century*, edited by Bernard McGinn, John Myendorf, and Jean Leclercq, 177–93. London: SCM, 1989.

———. "Hermeneutics and Enigma: Bernard's *De Consideratione*." *Viator* 19 (1988): 129–51.

———. *Tradition and Authority in the Western Church, 300–1140*. Princeton: Princeton University Press, 1969.

Munro, Dana Carleton. "The Western Attitude Toward Islam During the Period of the Crusades." *Speculum* 6 (1931): 329–43.

Murphy, Thomas Patrick, ed. *The Holy War*. Columbus: Ohio State University Press, 1976.

Murray, Alan, ed. *From Clermont to Jerusalem. The Crusades and Crusader Societies 1095–1500*. Turnhout: Brepols, 1998.

Nedelcou, C. "Sur la date de la naissance de Pierre Alphonsi." *Romania* 35 (1906): 462–63.

Newman, Martha G. *The Boundaries of Charity: Cistercian Culture and Ecclesiastical Reform, 1098–1180*. Stanford: Stanford University Press, 1996.

———. "Stephen Harding and the Creation of the Cistercian Community." *Revue Bénédictine* 107 (1997): 307–329.

Newman, Sharan. *The Real History Behind the Templars*. New York: Berkley Books, 2007.

Nicholson, Helen. "Crusade Q&A." Accessed September 17, 2112. http://freespace.virgin.net/nigel.nicholson/SSCLE/Crusade Faqs/f-babies.html.

———. *The Knights Templar: A New History*. Thrupp: Sutton Publishing, 2001.

———. *Templars, Hospitallers, and Teutonic Knights: Images of the Military Orders, 1128–1291*. Leicester: Leicester University Press, 1993.

Nicol, Donald M. *The Crusades and the Unity of Christendom*. Friends of Dr. William's Library, Lecture 40. London: Dr. William's Trust, 1986.

O'Callaghan, Joseph Francis. "The Affiliation of the Order of Calatrava with the Order of Cîteaux." *Analecta Sacri ordinis Cisterciensis*, 15 (1959), Fasc. 3–4, 161–93, 16 (1960), Fasc. 1–2, 3–59, Fasc. 3–4, 255–92.

———. *A History of Medieval Spain*. Ithaca, NY: Cornell University Press, 1975.

———. *Reconquest and Crusade in Medieval Spain*. Philadelphia: University of Pennsylvania Press, 2004.

Oldenbourg, Zoé. *The Crusades*. London: Weidenfeld and Nicholson, 1998.
Pacaut, Marcel. *Louis VII et son Royaume*. Paris: S.E.V.P.E.N., 1964.
Paetow, Louis J., ed. *The Crusades and Other Historical Essays, Presented to Dana C. Munro by His Former Students*. New York: F.S. Crofts, 1928.
Partner, Peter. *The Murdered Magicians: The Templars and Their Myth*. Oxford and New York: Oxford University Press, 1982.
Paulsell, William O. "St. Bernard on the Duties of the Christian Prince." In *Erudition at God's Service*, 63–74. Studies in Medieval Cistercian History 11. Kalamazoo, MI: Cistercian Publications, 1987.
Pedrajas, R. Jiménez. "San Eulogio de Córdoba, autor de la Pasión francesca de los mártires mozárabes cordobese Jorge, Aurelio, y Natalia." *Anthologica Annua* 17 (1970): 567–68.
Pelteret, David A.E. *Slavery in Anglo-Saxon England*. Woodbridge: Boydell, 1995.
Pensoye, P. "Saint Bernard et la règle du Temple." *Études Traditionelles* 364 (1961): 81–88.
Pernoud, Regine. *The Templars: Knights of Christ*. Translated by Henry Taylor. San Francisco: Ignatius Press, 2009.
Philips, Jonathan. *Defenders of the Holy Land: Relations Between the Latin East and the West, 1119–1187*. Oxford: Clarendon, 1996.
_____, ed. *The First Crusade: Origins and Impact*. Manchester and New York: Manchester University Press, St. Martin's Press, 1997.
_____. *The Second Crusade: Extending the Frontiers of Christendom*. Yale: Yale University Press, 2010.
_____, and Martin Hoch, eds. *The Second Crusade: Scope and Consequences*. Manchester: Manchester University Press, 2001.
Powell, James M., "The Papacy and the Muslim Frontier." In *Muslims under Latin Rule, 1100 1300*, edited by James M. Powell, 175–204. Princeton, NJ: Princeton University Press, 1990.
Prawer, Joshua. *Histoire de royaume latin de Jérusalem*. Paris: Éditions du Centre National de la recherche scientifique, 1969.
_____. *The World of the Crusaders*. London: Weidenfeld and Nicholson, 1972.
Purkis, William J. *Crusading Spirituality in the Holy Land and Iberia, c.1095–c.1187*. Woodbridge: Boydell, 2008.
_____. "Elite and Popular Perceptions of *imitatio Christi* in Twelfth-Century Crusade Spirituality." In *Elite and Popular Religion*, edited by K. Cooper and J. Gregory, 54–64. Studies in Church History 42. Woodbridge: Boydell and Brewer, 2006.
Quesnay, Jeremy du. "The Patriotism of Abbot Suger." *Proceedings of the Annual Meeting of the Western Society for French History* 15 (1988): 19–29.
Raciti, G. "Isaac de l'Etoile et son siècle: Texte et commentaire historique du sermon XLVIII." *Cîteaux: Commentarii Cistercienses* 12 (1961): 290.
Ranft, Patricia. "The Maintenance and Transformation of Society through Eschatology: Cluniac Monasticism." *Journal of Religious History* 14 (1987): 246–55.
Rassow, P. "La confradía de Belchite." *Annuario de historia del derecho español* 3 (1926): 200–26.
Rayborn, Tim. "Peter the Venerable and the Toledan Collection." *Medieval Life* 6 (Spring 1997): 15–18.
Reilly, Bernard F. *The Kingdom of León-Castilla under King Alfonso VII, 1126–1157*. Philadelphia: University of Pennsylvania Press, 1998.
Renna, Thomas. "Bernard of Clairvaux and the Temple of Solomon." In *Law, Custom, and the Social Fabric in Medieval Europe*, edited by Bernard S. Bachrach and David Nichols, 73–88. Kalamazoo, MI: Medieval Institute Publications, 1990.
_____. "Early Cistercian Attitudes toward War in Historical Perspective." *Cîteaux*, 31 (1980): 119–29.
Riley-Smith, Jonathan, ed. *The Atlas of the Crusades*. London: Times Books, 1991.
_____. *The Crusades, Christianity, and Islam*. New York: Columbia University Press, 2008.
_____. "Crusading as an Act of Love." *History*, 65, no. 214 (1980): 177–92.
_____. *The First Crusade and the Idea of Crusading*. London: Athlone Press, 1986, revised 2009.
_____. *The First Crusaders, 1095–1131*. Cambridge: University Press, 1997.
_____. "The State of Mind of Crusaders to the East, 1095–1300." In *The Oxford Illustrated History of the Crusades*, edited by Jonathan Riley-Smith, 66–90. Oxford: Oxford University Press, 1995.
_____. *Templars and Hospitallers as Professed Religious in the Holy Land*. Notre Dame: University of Notre Dame, 2009.
_____. *What Were the Crusades?* London: Macmillan, 1992.
_____, ed. *The Oxford Illustrated History of the Crusades*. Oxford: Oxford University Press, 1995.
Riley-Smith, Louise, and Jonathan Riley-Smith. *The Crusades, Idea and Reality,1095–1274*. London: Edward Arnold, 1981.
Rissanen, Seppo. *Theological Encounter of Oriental Christians with Islam during Early Abbasid Rule*. Åbo: Åbo Akademis förlag, 1993.

Roberts, Michael. *Essays Presented to Michael Roberts*. Belfast: Blackstaff Press, 1976.
Robinson, I.S. "Gregory VII and the Soldiers of Christ." *History* 58 (1973): 169–92.
———. *The Papacy 1073–1198: Continuity and Innovation*. Cambridge: Cambridge University Press, 1990.
———. *The Papal Reform of the Eleventh Century: Lives of Pope Leo IX and Pope Gregory VII*. Manchester Medieval Sources. Manchester University Press, 2004.
Roper, G.J. *Index Islamicus*. London: Mansell, 1991.
Rowe, John G. "The Origins of the Second Crusade: Pope Eugenius III, Bernard of Clairvaux and Louis VII of France." In *The Second Crusade and the Cistercians*, edited by Michael Gervers, 79–90. New York: St Martin's Press, 1992.
Rubenstein, Jay. *Armies of Heaven: The First Crusade and the Quest for Apocalypse*. Philadelphia: Basic Books, 2011.
———. "Cannibals and Crusaders." *French Historical Studies* 31, no. 4 (2008): 525–52.
———. "How, or How Much, to Reevaluate Peter the Hermit." In *The Medieval Crusade*, edited by Susan Janet Ridyard, 53–69. Woodbridge: Boydell, 2004.
Runciman, Steven. *A History of the Crusades*, vol. 2: *The Kingdom of Jerusalem and the Frankish East, 1100–1187*. Cambridge: Cambridge University Press, 1952.
Russell, F.H. *The Just War in the Middle Ages*. Cambridge: University Press, 1975.
Saget, Hubert. "St. Bernard et son temps." *Revue universitaire des marches de l'est* 2 (1980): 5–14.
Sargent-Baur, Barbara N., ed. *Journeys Toward God: Pilgrimage and Crusade*. Kalamazoo, MI: Medieval Institute Publications, 1992.
Sayers, Jane. "Violence in the Medieval Cloister." *Journal of Ecclesiastical History* 41 (1994): 533–42.
Schenk, Jochen. *Templar Families: Landowning Families and the Order of the Temple in France, c.1120–1307*. Cambridge: Cambridge University Press, 2012.
Schindele, M. Pia. "Monastic Life According to the Teaching of St. Bernard." *Tjurunga* 38 (1990): 22–50; and 40 (1991): 41–62.
Sclafert, C. "Lettre inédite de Hugues de Saint-Victor aux Chevaliers du Temple." *Revue d' ascétique et de mystique* 34 (1958): 275–99.
Schwinges, Rainer Christoph. "William of Tyre, the Muslim Enemy, and the Problem of Tolerance." In *Tolerance and Intolerance: Social Conflict in the Age of the Crusades*, edited by M. Gervers and J. M. Powell, 124–32. Syracuse: Syracuse University Press, 2001.
Septimus, Bernard. "Petrus Alfonsi on the Cult at Mecca." *Speculum* 56 (1981): 517–33.
Setton, Kenneth M., ed. *A History of the Crusades*, 6 vols. Madison: University of Wisconsin Press, 1955–1989.
Shafer, Grant R. "Hell, Martyrdom, and War: Violence in Early Christianity." In *The Destructive Power of Religion: Violence in Judaism, Christianity, and Islam*, vol. 3, *Models and Cases of Violence in Religion*, edited by J. Harold Ellens, 193–246. Westport, CT: Praeger, 2004.
Shatzmiller, Maya. "The Crusades and Islamic Warfare: A Re-evaluation." *Der Islam* 69 (1992): 246–88).
———. ed. *Crusaders and Muslims in Twelfth-Century Syria*. Leiden: Brill, 1993.
Sheils, W.J., ed. *The Church and War*. The Ecclesiastical History Society. Oxford: Blackwell, 1983.
Siberry, Elizabeth. *Criticism of Crusading, 1095–1274*. Oxford: Clarendon Press, 1985.
———. "Missionaries and Crusaders, 1095–1274: Opponents or Allies?" *Studies in Church History* 20 (1983): 103–10.
Smalley, Beryl. "Ecclesiastical Attitudes to Novelty c. 1100–1250." *Studies in Church History* 12 (1975): 113–31.
———. *The Spiritual Teachings of St. Bernard*, Cistercian Fathers Series no. 125. Kalamazoo: Cistercian Publications, 1991.
———. *The Study of the Bible in the Middle Ages*. Oxford: Blackwell, 1952.
Sommerfeldt, John R. "The Bernardine Reform and the Crusading Spirit." *The Catholic Historical Review* 86, no. 4 (2000), 567–78.
———, ed. *Cistercian Ideals and Reality*. Kalamazoo: Cistercian Publications, 1978.
———, ed. *Erudition at God's Service, Cistercian Studies Series no. 98*. Kalamazoo: Cistercian Publications, 1987.
———, ed. *Studies in Medieval Cistercian History* 2. Kalamazoo, Michigan: Cistercian Publications, 1976.
Southern, R.W. *Western Society and the Church in the Middle Ages*. London, UK: Pelican Books, 1970; reprinted 1990.
———. *Western Views of Islam in the Middle Ages*. Cambridge, MA: Harvard University Press, 1962.
Straw, Carole. *Gregory the Great, Perfection and Imperfection*. Berkeley: University of California Press, 1988.
Strickland, Debra Higgs. *Saracens, Demons, and Jews: Making Monsters in Medieval Art*. Princeton, NJ: Princeton University Press, 2003.
Stroll, Mary. *The Jewish Pope: Ideology and Politics in the Papal Schism of 1130*. Leiden: E.J. Brill, 1987.
Sumberg, L. A. M. "The 'Tafurs' and the First Crusade." *Mediaeval Studies* 21 (1959), 224–46.

Sweetman, James Windrow. *Islam and Christian Theology: A Study of the Interpretation of Theological Ideas in the Two Religions*. Vol. 2, Medieval Scholastic Developments. London: Lutterworth Press, 1967.

Thomas, David, and Alex Mallett, eds. *Christian-Muslim Relations. A Bibliographical History*, Volume 3 *(1050–1200)*. Leiden: Brill, 2011.

Throop, Palmer Allan. *Criticism of the Crusade: A Study of Public Opinion and Crusade Propaganda*. Philadelphia: Porcupine Press, 1975.

Throop, Susanna A. *Crusading as an Act of Vengeance, 1095–1216*. Aldershot: Ashgate, 2011.

Tolan, John. "Anti-Hagiography: Embrico of Mainz's *Vita Mahumeti*." *Journal of Medieval History* 22 (1996): 25–41.

——. *Medieval Christian Perceptions of Islam: A Collection of Essays*. New York: Garland, 1996.

——. "Peter the Venerable on the 'Diabolical Heresy of the Saracens.'" In *The Devil, Heresy, and Witchcraft in the Middle Ages: Essays in Honor of Jeffrey B. Russell*, edited by Alberto Ferreiro, 345–67. Leiden: Brill, 1998.

——. *Petrus Alfonsi and His Medieval Readers*. Gainesville: University Press of Florida, 1993.

——. *Saracens: Islam in the Medieval European Imagination*. New York: Columbia University Press, 2002.

——. *Sons of Ishmael: Muslims through European Eyes in the Middle Ages*. Gainesville: University Press of Florida, 2008.

Torrell, Jean-Pierre. "L'eglise dans l'oeuvre et la vie de Pierre le Vénérable." *Revue Thomiste* 77 (1977): 357–92, 558–91.

——. "La notion de prophétie et la méthode apologétique dans le *Contra Saracenos* de Pierre le Vénérable." *Studia Monastica* 17 (1975): 257–82.

Tyerman, Christopher. *God's War: A New History of the Crusades*. Cambridge, MA: Harvard University Press, 2006.

——. *The Invention of the Crusades*. Basingstoke: Macmillan, 1998.

Ullmann, W. *A Short History of the Papacy in the Middle Ages*. London: Methuen, 1972.

Vandecasteele, M. "Étude comparative de deux versions latines médiévales d'une apologie arabo-chrétienne: Pierre le Vénérable et le rapport grégorien." *Mededelingen van de Koninklijke Academie voor Wetenschappen, Letteren en Schone Kunsten van België, klasse Letteren* 53 (1991), 81–134.

Vauchez, Andre. *The Laity In the Middle Ages: Religious Beliefs and Devotional Practices*. Ed. D. E. Bornstein. Notre Dame, IN: University of Notre Dame Press, 1996.

Verlinden, Charles. *L'esclavage dans l'Europe médiévale*, I. Brugge: De Tempel, 1955.

——. *L'esclavage dans l'Europe médiévale*, II. Gent: Rijksuniversitiet, 1977.

——. "Les esclaves musulmans du Midi de la France." *Islam et chrétiens du Midi (XIIe–XIVe s.)*, Cahiers de Fanjeaux, 18, 215–34. Fanjeaux: Centre National de la Recherche Scientifique, ca. 1983.

Viola, Coloman Etienne, ed. *Mediaevalia Christiana XIe–XIIIe siècles*. Tournai: De Boeck Universite, 1989.

Waltz, James. "The Significance of the Voluntary Martyrs in Ninth-Century Córdoba." *Muslim World* 60 (1970): 143–159, 226–236.

Weiler, Anton Gerard, "Christianity and the Rest: The Medieval Theory of a Just and Holy War." *Concilium* 200 (1988): 109–19.

Wilkinson, John. *Jerusalem Pilgrims Before the Crusades*. Warminster: Aris and Phillips, 1997.

Williams, David H. *The Cistercians in the Early Middle Ages: Written to Commemorate the Nine Hundredth Anniversary of Foundation of the Order of Cîteaux in 1098*. Leominster: Gracewing, 1998.

Williams, E. "Cîteaux et la seconde croisade." *Revue d'histoire ecclésiastique* 49 (1954): 116–51.

Williams, Watkin. *St. Bernard of Clairvaux*. Manchester: University Press, 1935.

Wolf, Kenneth Baxter. *Christian Martyrs in Muslim Spain*. Cambridge and New York: Cambridge University Press, 1988.

——. "Christian Views of Islam in Early Medieval Spain." In *Medieval Christian Perceptions of Islam: A Book of Essays*, edited by John Victor Tolan, 85–108. Garland Medieval Casebooks, vol. 10. New York and London: Garland Publishing, 1996.

——. "The Earliest Latin Lives of Muhammad," In *Conversion and Continuity: Indigenous Christian Communities in Islamic Lands, Eighth to Eighteenth Centuries*, edited by Michael Gervers and Ramzi Jibran Bikhazi, 89–101. Toronto: Pontifical Institute of Mediaeval Studies, 1990.

——. "The Earliest Spanish Christian Views of Islam," *Church History* 55 (1986): 281–293.

——. "Muḥammad as Antichrist in Ninth-Century Córdoba." In *Christians, Muslims, and Jews in Medieval and Early Modern Spain: Interaction and Cultural Change*, edited by Mark D. Meyerson and Edward D. English, 3–19. Notre Dame, IN: University of Notre Dame Press, 2000.

Ye'or, Bat. *The Dhimmi: Jews and Christians under Islam*. Rutherford: Fairleigh Dickinson University Press, London: Associated University Presses, 1985.

Index

Abd ar-Rahman II, Emir of Córdoba 122, 134
Abelard 68–69, 83, 100, 105, 109, 113, 125, 187; the *Ethics*, 68–69; the *Theologia "summi boni"* 109
Abraham 7, 16, 28, 100–01, 134; and Hagar 16; and Sarah 16
Adémar of Chabannes 21
Adhémar of Le Puy 146
Adso of Montier-en-Der 112–13, 122; the *De ortu et tempore Antichristi* 112; the *Libellus de Antichristo* 122–23
Ælred of Rievaulx 79
Aghlabid dynasty 19, 162n26
Ahmad al-Muqtadir, ruler of Saragossa 27
Alberic, Abbot of Cîteaux 78
Albert of Aachen (Albert of Aix) 46, 118, 142–43, 145
Alexander III, Pope 9
Alexandria 6
Alexios I Komnenos 34–37, 39
Alfonso I, King of Aragon 51
Alfonso IV, King of Aragon 97
Alfonso VI, King of León and Castile 99
Alfonso VII, King of León and Castile 51, 99
Almohads 102, 132
Alp Arslan, Seljuk Sultan 29
Amanus March, Syria 56
An-Nasir ibn Alnas, Hammadid ruler of Maghreb 27–28
Analectus II, Antipope 125
Angels 61
Angoulême 21
Annales Herbipolenses 89
Anselm, Bishop of Havelburg 55
Anselm of Baggio, Bishop of Lucca 32, 34
Anselm of Ribemont 146
Antichrist 13, 27, 104, 112, 114–16, 118–19, 122–27, 136, 141, 193n16, 196n61; Islamic *see* al-Masih ad-Dajjal; mendicant orders as precursors 114

antichrists 112–13, 116, 122
Antioch 45, 118, 146–48
apocalypse 4, 21, 85, 112, 119, 122, 128
apocalypticism 4, 12–13, 36, 54, 111–28, 134, 136, 153–54, 194n22, 194n31
Al-Aqsa mosque 116
al-Ashraf Khalil 155
assassins 171–72n44
Atsiz ibn-Abaq 29, 165n74
Augustine of Hippo 7, 20, 24–25, 33–34, 91, 114, 118, 150, 163n45, 164n54, 187n28; the *City of God* 33, 185n83; *see also* compelle intrare
Augustinian Order 44
Azo of Bologna 92

Baghdad 7, 15, 47
Baldric of Bourgueil 10, 36, 142, 144; the *Historia Jerosolimitana* 145
Baldwin II, King of Jerusalem 44, 46, 53, 119
bandits and outlaws 22, 29, 47–48, 61–62, 170n13
baptism 91, 93–95, 104
Benedictine Order 10, 18, 24, 42, 74, 77, 96, 153, 191n88
Benedictine Rule 17, 54, 77, 83, 96, 98, 173n70
Bernard de Sédirac 97
Bernard of Clairvaux 9, 11–12, 17–18, 28, 32–35, 42, 44, 52–55, 58–59, 61–76, 78–85, 87–91, 93, 96–101, 105–07, 109, 113, 123, 125–27, 129–30, 142, 147–49, 152–54, 175n11, 179n79, 179n1, 185n3, 201n94; appeal 53, 57, 63, 79–80, 84, 127, 149, 181n35; desire to convert criminals 59–60, 72–73; frailty 58–59, 83, 88, 106; Second Crusade and 84–85, 87–88, 90, 120, 125–26; the *Sententiae* 64; sermons 61, 64, 88, 127; use of military imagery 62–64, 66–72, 74, 80, 84, 135; the *Vita sancti Malachiae* 126–27; *see also*

219

Cistercian Order; *De laude novae miltiae*; knights; Knights Templar
Bible, Old Testament 6, 9–10, 40, 55, 70, 112, 119, 151; New Testament 9, 66
Bonaventure 109
Burchard of Worms 26
Burgundy 42, 173n57, 191n88
Byzantium 7, 20, 27, 31–32, 35, 39, 56, 107, 122, 136, 153, 162n30

Calatrava (military order) 82, 180n22, 180–81n23
Calixtus II, Pope 16, 78, 142
cannibalism 5
canon law 8–9, 14, 24–25, 35, 52–53, 74, 159n11, 162n13
Carmen in victoriam Pisanorum 140–41
Carolingians 15, 17, 128
Celestine II, Pope 43, 55
cenobitic monasticism 76–77
chansons de geste 14
Charlemagne 15–16, 148, 201n93; Abul-Abbas the elephant 16
Chartres 87–89
Christ 3–6, 10, 12, 19, 21–22, 24, 26, 30–31, 35–36, 38, 40–41, 43, 52, 55, 60, 64, 67, 69, 72–74, 80–81, 83, 85, 88–89, 104, 109, 112, 117–18, 122–25, 141, 145–46, 148–51, 181n3
Christianitas 17
Christians, Eastern 6–7, 20, 31, 36, 43, 56, 109, 132, 166n82, 171n31, 177n46; Armenians 7, 56; Nestorians 7
Christians, Mozarabic 13, 27, 96, 105, 108–10, 131, 188n39, 192n101
Chronica Byzantia-Arabica 160n3
Chronicle of Fredegar 16
chroniclers 3, 9–11, 21, 37, 41, 44–46, 48, 80, 119, 142, 147, 149, 153, 169n137, 170–71n19, 171n22, 193n14
Church councils *see* listings under council name
Church fathers 6–7, 28, 33, 91, 114
Cistercian Order 11–12, 17–18, 42, 52, 54–55, 63, 75–96, 98, 105, 110, 153–54, 161n15, 174n81, 179n76, 179n79, 179n1, 184n71, 185n84
Cîteaux 42, 78, 80, 101
Ciurana (Spanish Moorish settlement) 95
Clairvaux 53, 79–80, 87, 179n79
clergy 3, 6, 17, 23, 37, 41, 52, 62, 79, 84, 108, 113, 116, 135, 140, 144
Cluniac Order 42, 55, 89, 97–99, 112, 191n88
Cluny 17, 20, 42, 89, 96–99, 105, 127, 131, 191n88
Collectio toledana 103–04
compelle intrare 24–25, 164n53, 201n94; *see also* Augustine; Gregory VII

Concordat of Worms 123
Confraternity of Belchite 49, 51–52, 57
Conrad III, King of Germany 86, 125–26
Constantine and the Edict of Milan 6
Constantinople 30–31, 37, 155, 162n30
conversion, to Christianity 6, 15, 24–25, 27, 29, 33, 59–60, 63, 73–74, 76, 81–82, 84, 91–96, 106, 108, 110, 157, 163n44, 164n46, 173n29, 180n23, 186n4; to Islam 132, 145, 198n46
Córdoba 7, 13, 109, 121–22, 128–29, 131, 133–37, 139, 143, 149, 153, 187n28, 198n46
Corpus toledanum 103–04
Council of Chartres 88–89, 191n85
Council of Clermont 25, 34, 37, 39, 117, 119, 143–44, 191n88
Council of Clovesho 36
Council of Elvira 135, 197n27
Council of Gangra 91–2
Council of Piacenza 34
Council of Rheims 16
Council of Troyes 53–54, 173n70, 176n28
crusade chronicles 1, 4–5, 11, 14, 48, 50, 62, 117, 120, 143, 168n118, 169n137, 194n22
crusades: First 3–4, 7–8, 10, 13, 20, 25, 34–42, 44–45, 47–49, 55, 65, 80, 85, 97, 99, 115–20, 128, 130–31, 138, 140–47, 149, 191n88; Second 9, 11–12, 39, 42, 54, 59, 63, 75, 81, 84–90, 107, 111, 113, 115, 120, 125, 127, 142, 147–49, 152–53, 155, 181n35, 182n39; Third 90, 113

Damascus 47, 56, 86, 148
Daniel, Book of 13, 112, 119, 121–22, 136
Daniel, Russian abbot 45
De laude novae miltiae 12, 54–55, 57–61, 63–75, 98, 147, 149
Decretum of Gratian 8
Diego Gelmirez, Archbishop of Compostella 47
Doctrina Mahumet 103–04
Dome of the Rock 44
Donatists 25

Ecclesia 17, 41–42
Edessa 5, 45, 85, 90, 98, 115, 126, 152, 171n31
Egypt 10, 22, 29, 76, 119, 194n31
Ekkehard of Aura 193n11, 194n19, 194n21
Eleanor of Aquitaine 14
Embrico of Mainz 27; the *Vita Mahumeti* 27
Enguerrand of St. Pol (ghost) 146
Eugenius III, Pope 11, 80, 84–85, 87–88, 90, 153, 182n39, 182n55; the *Immensu-mpietatis opus* 87; *see also* Quantum predecessors
Eulogius, titular Bishop of Seville 109, 121,

125, 131, 134–40, 143, 149, 196n12, 197n16; the *Apologeticus Martyrum* 134, 196n12; the *Memorialis Sanctorum* 134
exegesis, biblical 9, 11, 36, 65–66, 111, 121, 125, 136–37, 141, 148–50, 156, 163n44, 195n35

Fabulae Saracenorum 103–04
Fatimids 19, 22–23, 29, 162n26, 194n31
feudalism 9, 77, 79, 91, 160n17, 184n71, 184n74
filioque controversy 31, 166n82
First Lateran Council 17, 51, 123
Fleury 61–62
Fontfroide 95
Francis of Assisi 107
Franciscan Order 114, 143, 161n15
Franks 11, 55–56, 84, 136, 138–39, 144, 155, 159n5
Fulcher of Chartres 45, 47, 170n10
Fulk V, Count of Anjou and King of Jerusalem 48, 173n72

Galdemar Carpenel 146
Gerhoh of Reichersberg 123, 195n49
Germanic tribes 6, 8, 16, 38, 164n61
Gesta Francorum 143
God, will of 8–10, 12, 19, 23, 30, 32–33, 38, 42–43, 48, 56, 61, 65–66, 69–70, 72–73, 85, 90, 92, 107–08, 112–13, 116–17, 124, 130, 133, 141, 144–48, 156–57, 160n25, 175n11, 177n55, 185n83
Godfrey of Bouillon, Duke of Lower Lorraine 119
Godfrey of St. Omer 44
Gregorian Reform *see* Reform movement
Gregory I, Pope 24, 151
Gregory VII, Pope 11–12, 16–17, 24–28, 30–32, 39–40, 57, 74, 120, 140, 152, 161n10, 161n13, 164n46, 165n80, 198n49; the *Dictatus papae* 161n13
Guibert of Nogent 10–11, 92, 116, 118–119, 142–44, 193n16, 194n30, 195n36
Gunther, Bishop of Bamberg 21–23, 29, 117, 163n37

hadith 109, 154
Hajj 100–01
Al-Hakim bi-Amr Allah 19, 21, 35–36, 162n24, n28
Harun ar-Rashid 16
Henry I, King of England 99
Henry II, King of England 48
Henry IV, Holy Roman Emperor 30–3; *see also* Investiture Contest
heresy 26, 84, 105, 113; Islam as a Christian heresy 7, 21, 26–29, 98, 101, 104–05, 107–08, 123–25, 127, 132, 136, 186n11

heretics 4, 7, 25, 27–29, 32, 40, 66, 92–93, 101, 104, 112, 127, 152, 163n45, 164n61, 167n103; Arians 26, 105, 136; Donatists 25; Manichaeans 33, 92; Peter of Bruys and the Petrobrusians 105, 185n4; *see also* Simon Magus
Herman of Dalmatia 102–03
Holy City *see* Jerusalem
Holy Lance 146
Holy Land 4, 12, 14, 16, 21, 24, 28–30, 44–45, 47, 55–56, 60, 66, 69, 72–74, 76, 84–88, 105, 111, 117, 120, 126, 142, 145, 147, 150, 152, 155
Holy Roman Emperor 4, 16, 30–32, 123, 127
Holy Sepulcher 19–21, 29, 35, 44, 47, 64, 118
holy war 1, 5, 8–9, 12–13, 15, 24, 32, 38, 40, 70, 74–75, 84–85, 116, 138–39, 151, 160n17, 164n54, 182n47; *see also* just war
Hrabanus Maurus 141
Hugh, Count of Champagne 49, 51–53, 59, 179n79; marital problems 51–52
Hugh de Die, Archbishop of Lyon 78, 146
Hugh of Cluny 27, 32
Hugh of Fleury 131
Hugh of St. Victor 53, 108–09; the *Epistola ad Johannem Hispalensem Archiepiscopum* 108–09
Hugh the Insane 147
Hugues de Payens 44, 46, 49, 51, 53–54, 59–60, 173n60

Ibn Tumart 102
idols 38, 101, 193n14
al-Imām al-Qurṭubī (the Imam of Cordoba) 187n28
Imitatio Christi 4, 38–39, 40–41, 64, 85, 122
Innocent II, Pope 55, 125
Investiture Contest 32, 39, 116, 120
Isaac, Abbot of l'Etoile (Stella) 54–55, 75, 81–84, 152, 180n16, 181n32
Isaac, son of Abraham 100, 134
Ishmael, son of Abraham 16, 19, 100–01
Isidore of Seville 92, 134; the *Etymologiae* 134
Islam 1, 3, 7, 8, 11–16, 18–21, 24, 26, 28–29, 34, 38, 40, 42, 48–52, 66, 74, 76, 79, 84, 91–93, 95–111, 113–16, 119, 121–25, 127–38, 140–43, 145, 148–51, 153–56, 159n9, 162n24, 165n72, 187n25, 192n97, 193n14; Five Pillars of 108; Shi'a 29, 155, 162n24; *see also* heresy; Muslims
Israel 9–10, 55, 72, 90
Italy 15–16, 21, 93, 140
itinerant preachers 36, 113, 166n103
Ivo of Chartres 34, 52, 55, the *Decretum* 34; the *Panormia* 34

Jerome 114, 122
Jerusalem, city 3–6, 9–10, 20, 22, 27, 29, 31–32, 34–39, 42, 45, 46–48, 51–52, 55–56, 61, 65, 70–73, 80, 85, 89–90, 115–20, 125, 144–46, 148, 152–53, 155, 168n111, 171n22, 181n33, 193n14; Latin Kingdom 44–45, 55
Jews 7, 9–10, 13, 19–21, 28, 37, 40, 90, 92–93, 100–02, 104, 106–07, 109, 114, 116, 120, 122, 124, 132, 155, 163n28, 184–85n83, 185n90, 188n34, 191–92n96, 197n18; Sephardim 13, 96, 99–100
jihad 49, 154–55, 159n9, 168n30
Joachim of Fiore 13, 113–14, 156
John, Gospel of 67, 149
John VIII, Pope 138–39
John the Baptist 70, 134
just war 8–9, 24–25, 34–38, 143, 172n49; *see also* holy war

Ka'ba 100–01
Knights Hospitaller (Order of St. John) 14, 50, 52, 54, 173n72
knights, secular 9, 12, 18, 24, 30–31, 37, 39–40, 46, 49, 55, 77, 118, 145, 169n142; Bernard's condemnation of 12, 59, 63–64, 67–68, 71, 74–75, 147
Knights Templar 11–12, 14, 18, 32–33, 35, 42–75, 81–83, 94–95, 98, 105–07, 125–26, 130, 142, 149, 152–55, 169n3, 170n10, 171–72n44; dual nature 48, 50, 52–54, 57–61, 64–67, 69–75; as martyrs 67, 69, 130, 142, 147, 149, 153, 175n11; motto 65; protecting pilgrims 23; Rule of 51, 54–55, 58, 71, 170n6, 173n70

laity 4–5, 14, 16–17, 36–37, 39, 41–42, 48, 53, 62, 77, 84, 91, 95, 121, 134, 142, 144–45, 149, 157, 160n35, 175n11, 175n22
Lambert 21–23
Laodicea (Turkey) 148
Last World Emperor 120, 125
Legenda Aurea 199n62
Leo IV, Pope 138, 141
Leo IX, Pope 16, 21, 31
Liber Generationis Mahumet 103–04
Liber Ordinum (Mozarabic martyrology) 131
Lisbon 86
Louis VII, King of France 64, 86–87, 148

Maccabees, compared to crusaders 10, 43, 55, 141
Magister Rolandus *see* Alexander III, Pope
Mahdia campaign 140–41
Mahomet I, Emir of Córdoba 122
Mamelukes 155
Al-Ma'mun, Caliph 103
al-Mansur 15

Martin Luther 113
martyrdom 10, 13, 66–67, 121, 128–150, 153, 168n130, 175n11, 197n30, 198n46, 198n49, 199n63, 199n66
Martyrology of Usuard 131
martyrs, crusaders as 5, 10, 13, 38, 128–30, 139–50, 153, 197n30, 199n66; *see also* martyrs of Córdoba; Matthew
Martyrs' Movement 15, 121–22, 129–39, 201n96
martyrs of Córdoba: Aurelius 137; George 137; Ishaq (Isaac) 133–34; Nathalia 137; Perfectus (al-Kamil) 133; Servus Dei (Abdallah) 133; Vulfra 139, 198n46
al-Masih ad-Dajjal (Islamic antichrist) 124
Matilda, Countess of Tuscany 31, 140
Mattathias and Antiochus *see* Maccabees
Matthew (knight and friend of Guibert of Nogent) 143–44, 199–200n71
Matthew, Gospel 19, 38, 124
Mayol, abbot of Cluny 19–20
Mecca 100
Michael, Archangel 175
Michael the Syrian, Patriarch of Antioch 45–46
militia Christi 24, 40
militia secularis 24
millenarianism 118; *see also* apocalypticsim
Molesme 77–78, 80
monasteries: security of 61–62, 77–78, 94–95; *see also* Angoulême; Cîteaux; Clairvaux; Cluny; Fleury; Fontfroide; Molesme; Poblet; St. Martial; San Pedro de Cardeña
monks 11, 20, 24, 29, 36, 41, 52, 54, 57–59, 61–63, 70, 72, 77–83, 85, 88, 91–92, 95, 97, 107, 127, 137–38, 145, 151, 153, 157, 169n142, 175n11, 175n22, 181n31, 182–83n56
Moors 16, 18, 51, 86, 91, 94–95, 97, 99, 186n10, 196n5
Muhammad (Toledo translator) 103
Muhammad, Prophet of Islam 13, 19, 27, 38, 100–04, 114, 116, 121–25, 127, 131, 133–34, 136, 141, 154, 160n3, 187n25, 187n28, 192n97, 197n16
Mujahid ibn 'Abdullah 20
Muslims 3, 5, 7, 11–14, 16, 19–22, 26–30, 33–36, 38, 40, 42, 44–48, 50–52, 56–57, 61, 64, 66, 69–70, 72, 74, 76, 84, 91–97, 99–110, 113, 116, 119, 121, 124, 130–41, 145, 149, 152, 154, 162n24, 162n28, 165n74, 171n31, 184n71, 186n4, 186n10, 187n25, 190n80, 191–92n96; 192n97, 193n14, 197n18; *see also* Islam

Nicholas II, Pope 44
Normans 21, 31, 116, 172n49, 184n74
Nur ad-Din 155

Odilard of St. Germain-des-Prés 137
Odilo 19
Odo of Deuil, 147–49; the *De Profectione Ludovici VII in orientem* 147–48
Odo of Lagery 40; *see also* Urban II
Orderic Vitalis 55
Origen 6
Otto of Freising 123

pagans 7, 16, 22–23, 26–30, 32, 38, 43, 52, 64, 66, 69, 72, 74, 85, 93–94, 100–01, 104, 112, 116, 120, 133, 136, 164n61, 171n22, 175n16, 187n25, 193n14
Paganus, Burgundian knight 171n22
Palestine 22, 156
papacy 4, 12–13, 16–18, 24, 28, 32, 39–40, 42, 44, 47, 53, 56–57, 74, 80, 84, 86, 90, 116, 121, 123, 140–42, 152, 161n13, 182n47, 184n70
Paschal II, Pope 78
Patriarch of Jerusalem 37, 46–49, 57, 118; *see also* Warmund
Paul Alvarus 109, 121–22, 125, 134–37, 143, 149, 188n39; the *Indiculus luminosis* 121–22, 134–36
Pauline writings 61, 91, 114
Peace of God 18–19
penitence 5, 15, 27, 41, 85, 129
Persian Empire 7
Peter Bartholomew 146
Peter Damian 24, 74, 152
Peter of Poitiers 102, 188n39, 189n52
Peter of Toledo 103, 188n39, 188n41; *see also* Petrus Alfonsi
Peter of Troyes 86
Peter the Hermit (Peter of Amiens) 36–37, 118–19, 144, 194n30
Peter the Venerable 11–13, 28–29, 39, 42, 66, 74, 89, 93, 96–99, 101–11, 123–25, 127, 131, 138, 153–54, 185–86n4, 186n11, 188n34, 188n45, 190n78, 190n81, 191n86, 191n88; the *Adversus Iudeorum* 102; the *Epistola de translatione sua* 103; the *Liber contra sectam haeresim Saracenorum* 106, 110, 124; the *Summa totius haeresis Saracenorum* 106, 123, 189n73; *see also Collectio toledana*; *Corpus toledanum*
Petrus Alfonsi 13, 96, 99–102, 106, 108–10, 131, 153, 187n28, 188n40; the *Dialogi contra Iudaeos* 99–102, 188n40; the *Tathlīth al-waḥdānīyah* 109, 187n28
Philip I, King of France 30, 165n80
pilgrimage 21–23, 29–31, 34, 47–48, 51, 99, 117, 139–40, 167n103, 170n13, 179n79, 191n88; armed 11–12, 17, 32, 34–35, 60, 90, 120, 129, 141, 190n81
pilgrims 4, 12, 14, 18–23, 29, 34, 42–49, 52, 54, 56–57, 84, 107, 117, 130, 140–41, 146, 165n74, 168n111, 170n13, 171n22, 171n31
Pippin the Short 15
Poblet 95–96, 185n90
Premonstratensian Order 63, 87, 196n61
prophecy 5, 10–11, 71, 111, 114, 116, 119, 120–23, 125–28, 144, 153, 194–95n35
prophets 7, 10, 19, 28, 102–04, 113, 123; false 89, 10, 133
Pseudo-Methodius 122

qadis (Islamic judges) 133, 136
Quantum predecessores 84–86
Qur'an 12, 96–98, 100–04, 109, 124, 132, 136, 187, 192n97; *Lex sarracenorum* 103

Radulphus, Archbishop of Rheims 92
Ralph of Caen 169n137, 193n14, 200n84
Rama (Palestinian town) 22
Ramadan 100, 133
Ramón Berenguer, Count 95
Ramon Llull 143
Raymond of Aguilers 3, 6, 142, 194n31
Reccafred, Bishop of Seville 134–35
reconquista 12, 34, 94, 102, 186n10
Reform movement 8, 11–12, 16–18, 24, 26, 32, 36, 41–42, 50, 52, 55, 58, 61, 74–80, 97, 113, 115, 123, 139–40, 150, 152, 154, 157, 161n10, 161n13, 164n46, 192n88
Revelation, Book of 13, 112, 114, 118, 125, 201n94
Ribāt 49–50
Richard of Poitou 55
Richard the Lionheart, King of England 90, 113
Risālah (Apology) of al-Kindi 100, 103, 108
Robert de Champagne 77
Robert Guiscard 31, 166n85
Robert of Ketton 98, 102–04, 188n38, 189n52
Robert the Monk (Robert of Rheims) 10, 142–144
Rodulfus Glaber 18–21, 26, 28, 97; the *Historium Libri Quinque* 18–20
Roger, King of Sicily 107
Rome 22, 31–32, 138, 140
Rupert of Deutz 123

Saewulf 170n13
St. Benedict, miracles at Fleury Abbey 61–62, 173n57
St. Martial (monastery) 21
St. Martial (saint) 21
Saladin 90, 113–14, 155, 172n99
Sancho the Great 20
San Pedro de Cardeña 99
Santiago de Compostela 22, 99
Saracens 13, 16, 19, 22, 28, 38, 40, 47–48,

59, 61, 66, 89, 91, 93, 102–03, 106–07, 110, 123–24, 128, 138–39, 145, 165n80, 167n102, 185n84, 185n90, 190n80, 196n5; *see also* Muslims
Satan, the devil 24, 28, 32, 53, 61, 64, 86–87, 89, 101, 104, 112, 118, 123–24, 128, 157, 173n70, 187n25, 195n49, 197n16
Satanic Verses 101, 187n25
Saxons 16, 38
Sergius IV, Pope 35, 140
Sermon on the Mount 6, 22, 33, 151
sermons 4, 14, 36–37, 39, 55, 61, 64, 81–84, 88, 115, 127, 144, 181n32
Sibylline oracles 120–23, 125, 127, 194–95n35, 195n36
signs and omens 111–12, 115, 119, 123–25, 136, 194n19, 194n21
Simon Magus 26–27
sin, remission of 9, 18, 22, 30, 34, 37–38, 40, 51–52, 58, 69, 73, 86, 139, 144, 153, 191n88, 193n14
slavery 16, 91–96, 153; Anglo-Saxon 184n74; biblical justification 91; Christians 91, 93– 95, 185n90, 197n18; conversion to Christianity discouraged 91, 93–94; economics 91–94; manumission 91–94; Muslims 12, 76, 91–96, 184n71, 185n84, 185n90; pagan 93
Smaragdus, Abbot of Saint-Mihiel 169n142
Song of Roland 14, 196n5
Spain 8, 11–13, 15–16, 18, 20, 34, 39, 51, 56–57, 82, 85, 91–111, 121, 125, 131–37, 139, 174n84, 186n11, 196n12, 197n27
Stephen I, King of Hungary 23
Stephen Harding, Abbot of Cîteaux 78–79
Suger, Abbot of St. Denis 87, 89–90, 107
Synod of Charroux 18–19, 44
Syria 5, 29, 56, 156
Syrus 19

tafsir (Qur'anic commentary) 104
Tancred 116, 118
Temple of Solomon, Jerusalem 61, 72, 179n76
tempus gratiae 9
tempus legis 9
Tescelin le Sor, father of Bernard of Clairvaux 63
Thomas Aquinas 109

Toledo School of Translators 102; *see also Collectio toledana*; *Doctrina Mahumet*; *Fabulae Saracenorum*; Herman of Dalmatia; *Liber Generationis Mahumet*; Muhammad; Peter of Poitiers; Peter of Toledo; Peter the Venerable; Robert of Ketton
Tunisia 19, 140
Turks, Ottoman 44, 155–56, 162n30; Seljuk 21–22, 28–31, 34, 37, 39, 42, 47, 118, 140, 144, 147–48, 152, 155, 165
"two swords" doctrine in *De laude* 66–67, 70

unbelievers 4–8, 15, 29, 60, 76, 81, 84, 86, 90, 95, 103, 113, 123, 138, 157, 181n25
Urban II, Pope 3, 12, 34–41, 55, 72, 84–85, 91, 115, 117–19, 130, 141, 143–45, 149, 152; *see also* Council of Clermont
Usuard of St. Germain-des-Prés 137

vengeance, divine, in relation to the crusade 4, 19, 40, 73, 84, 149, 169n137, 175n11
Vikings 52, 128, 173n57
violence 3, 6, 9, 11, 23, 38, 59, 62–63, 80–81, 132–133, 137, 160n17, 177n22; Augustine and 7, 24–25, 33–34; Christians must reject 6, 22, 24, 74, 81, 84, 151–52, 166n90; as a morally neutral act 7, 68–70; religious justifications for 8–9, 11, 18, 22–23, 25, 29–30, 32–34, 38, 41, 50, 54, 57, 61–62, 67– 72, 73, 80, 107, 126, 141, 151, 154, 156, 163n44, 163n45, 167n91; *see also compelle intrare*
Visigothic Spain 134

Walter Map, Archdeacon of Oxford 45–46, 171n22
Warmund, Patriarch of Jerusalem 46–48
William, Count of Poitou 30
William of Saint-Thierry 63
William of Tyre 44–46, 169–70n4, 170–71n19
William the Carpenter 118
William the Conqueror 18, 172n49; *see also* Normans
William IX, Duke of Aquitaine 165–66n80

Zangi, Imad al-Din 86, 90

www.ingramcontent.com/pod-product-compliance
Ingram Content Group UK Ltd.
Pitfield, Milton Keynes, MK11 3LW, UK
UKHW041952140426
5217IPUK00015B/760